On that day deaf men shall hear
when a book is read,
and the eyes of the blind shall see
out of impenetrable darkness.

—*Isaiah 29:18*

I'VE SEEN THE DAY

BY

GEORGE M. DOCHERTY

WILLIAM B. EERDMANS PUBLISHING COMPANY
GRAND RAPIDS, MICHIGAN

Dedicated, in gratitude,
to
the Church,
Mother of us all,
And in particular to the congregations at
Ruchill, Glasgow
King's Park, Glasgow
Sandyhills, Glasgow
The Barony of Glasgow
The North Kirk, Aberdeen
New York Avenue Presbyterian, Washington, D.C.

Copyright © 1984 by Wm. B. Eerdmans Publishing Co.
255 Jefferson Ave. S.E., Grand Rapids, Mich. 49503
All rights reserved
Printed in the United States of America

Library of Congress Cataloging in Publication Data

Docherty, George M., 1911-
I've seen the day.

Includes index.
1. Docherty, George M., 1911-   . 2. Presbyterian
Church — Washington (D.C.) — Clergy — Biography.
3. Washington (D.C.) — Biography. 4. Church of Scotland —
Clergy — Biography. I. Title.
BX9225.D58A34   1983   285'.23 [B]   83-25439
ISBN 0-8028-3591-0

Contents

None of us at this moment could give anything like a full account of his own life for the last twenty-four hours. . . . Most of the experiences in "the past as it really was" were instantly forgotten by the subject himself. Of the small percentage which he remembered (and never remembered with perfect accuracy) a smaller percentage was ever communicated even to his closest intimates; of this, a smaller percentage still was recorded; of the recorded fraction, only another fraction has ever reached posterity.

—C. S. Lewis, "Historicism"

Preface

I RECALL READING somewhere that on completing his manuscript of *David Copperfield*, Charles Dickens went out into his garden and wept; it was as if he had said a final goodbye to a dear friend. After six struggling years writing this account of my life, I feel more like Atlas might have felt had he been suddenly disencumbered of the burden of the globe. Writing this book has been like attending a psychiatrist over a prolonged period, with myself both patient and doctor. The process of delving into the past, stirring up the still, almost forgotten waters of memory — the sights, sounds, smells of places, the voices and faces out of long ago, and not least the emerging vividness of myself as child, lad, young man, and preacher, with all my ambivalences, frailties, blunderings, and, in their time, the ecstacies — has been a deeply emotional experience, bordering at times on the traumatic.

Yet I now let go of this manuscript only with the utmost reluctance: the finished product falls so very far short of what I had hoped it would be! But I send it forth nonetheless to the William B. Eerdmans Publishing Company, into the understanding and capable hands of my editors, Chuck Van Hof and Tim Straayer, granting them an indulgence for cutting the book down to size.

I had believed that after more than forty years of the weekly discipline of typing out in full my Sunday sermons, all that would be required to write a biography would be to sit still at my desk, remember, and set down the images in words as they returned "to bless or burn." Dr. Richard Dabney disabused me of this naive notion early on. Not only did he point up the difference between the word written to be read and the word written to be preached, but he assailed my Scottish reticence in holding back feelings and thoughts that he believed my autobiography demands, however intimate they might be. As Dick put it to me, "That guy outside the church in Main Street wants to know what makes a Holy Joe tick."

Dick I had known since back in the fifties. He was an outstanding young man among an alert group of young adults at New York Avenue Presbyterian Church. It took this brilliant, compassionate lad a little time to settle into his obviously foreordained literary career. He majored in English and became a Professor of English Literature at the American

University in Washington, D.C., before forsaking the seductive sinecure of academia for the hazardous but more exciting venture of freelance journalism. His name became known to an ever-widening appreciative audience through his essays in the *Washington Magazine* and the *Washington Post*, although he undertook that writing only to keep food on the table while he pursued his more serious work as a novelist and biographer.

Happily, my publisher assigned Dick to work with me on this volume. He was a gentle mentor, if at times a caustic (but not insensitive) critic. In November 1981, when I was visiting the States, Dick and I spent two glorious days together over large mugfuls of strong coffee, talking about life and writing, while he methodically pruned many of my splendid purple passages.

"Why do you suddenly leave the reader wondering what you felt or thought by floating away into a cloud of poetic fancy," he demanded. Forty-eight hours later he was dead of a heart attack.

Even yet it is a shock to recall delivering the eulogy at his funeral service in the church we both loved, before a large congregation that included the academic and literary lights of the nation, all of us trying to bring a fragment of comfort to his young wife, Donna, and their two bright, beautiful children.

Dick saw only half the manuscript, but if there is any incisive writing in the completed work, much of the credit must go to him.

Over the six years of writing, the manuscript has been typed out at odd times and in even odder places, on both sides of the Atlantic—motels, bedrooms of friends, manse studies, and at my own desk here in St. Andrews. I have to thank Willie Williams of the First Presbyterian Church of Huntingdon, Tennessee, for the use of his chapel over many weeks of writing there. I record my appreciation to President Frederick Binder and the Trustees of Juniata College in Huntingdon, Pennsylvania, for the hospitality they extended to me and my wife and our baby Julie during the academic year 1979–80, when I was the Omar J. Good Visiting Professor of Evangelical Christianity, and for the secretarial assistance of Denise Kemp. My friend Barry Wright, President of Temporaries Incorporated of Washington, D.C., gave invaluable help in typing and copying. And I thank Kim Noble and my former secretary Mary Jane Young for generously typing some of the chapters. Herb Ruckmick and Dave Jones seemed always at hand with their cameras.

And let me record my loving thanks to Sue: for her patience with me, especially during those seasons when I seemed to be an absentee member of the family, lost in my world of remembering; for her encouragement when I was tempted to throw in the towel and call it quits; and for her love that has sustained me in this and so many other adventures we have shared together.

St. Andrews, Scotland Harvesttide 1983   G. M. D.

Introduction

Home is the sailor, home from sea.
                                    — Robert Louis Stevenson

When the present has latched its postern behind my tremulous stay,
And the May month flaps its glad green leaves like wings,
Delicate-filmed as new spun silk, will the neighbors say,
"He was a man who used to notice such things"?
                                    — Thomas Hardy, "Afterwards"

OUTSIDE MY STUDY WINDOW in this medieval city of St. Andrews, a fierce autumnal gale is blowing, bending low the slim cherry tree that will brighten our gray Scottish winter with its precocious blossoms. Above the moan of the wind, I catch the sound of a minor-key honking chorus of three skeins of Brent geese from Norway high overhead against the blue morning sky, beating their way southward in rough formation.

The yearly homing instinct of these migratory birds resonates to a pattern that has evolved in my own life. After twenty-six years in the United States we have returned to Scotland, where I spent the first thirty-eight years of my life and where, now, long or short, I plan to end my days. While we lived in America, most of our summer vacations were spent in Scotland, where we were drawn by sentiment and real friendships. Now we visit the United States at least once a year. In St. Andrews, Washington, D.C., seems like a fond dream from the distant past.

If Robert Frost is right, and "Home is the place where, when you have to go there, / They have to take you in," then we are rich in homes. Across Scotland, in city, glen, and by the sea, at my unexpected knock doors are opened wide in welcome; and I like to believe that in almost every state in the Union, there are doors that would not be locked against us.

Sometimes, when I am golfing the Old Course at St. Andrews or perhaps while reading a book in these long Scottish winter forenights, a sudden gulp of homesickness comes over me to be back again in Washington, D.C. As I have done a thousand times, I see from the plane bearing me home the spread of the contours of the city, the dark Potomac water seemingly rising to meet me as we race over Alexandria; and then the gentle bumps of the undercarriage on the runway as we touch down at National Airport. I feel again the warm night air as I cross the tarmac, climb the airport stairs to the parking lot, and make my way to my car, which may have been standing there for days. As I pull away, I look admiringly once more at the uncharacteristic American skyline of the city, pierced by the floodlit gleaming sandstone needle of the Washington Monument and dominated by the Wrenish dome of the Capitol buildings. My car joins the rush of traffic over the broad Fourteenth Street bridge, past the classical Federal Triangle, and northward on Twelfth Street, until before my eyes as I turn onto H Street on a triangular island stands the spire of a noble red brick colonial building that even today I find it difficult not to call my church.

I feel at home in two continents, though I'd rather be in Scotland longing for America than be in America homesick for Scotland, under whose soil, sooner or later, I shall be buried.

If I am uncertain about my home, I know who I am and the vocation in which I have happily spent my life. I am a preacher; not a very good one, yet an unrepentant preacher. Malcolm Muggeridge confesses in his splendid autobiography, *Chronicles of Wasted Time*, that his life has seemed like a "part looking for play. Feeling at times like an actor stumbling, falling over familiar scenery, I make my way on stage and look for guidance of the prompter . . . and I realize of course that his script is different from mine." In contrast, I know my part, rather obscure, I realize, like that of an obsequious butler, on stage only to utter "Dinner is served." But what a script! And a play that will go on long after I have made my quietus. It tells

> Of man's first disobedience and the fruit
> Of that forbidden tree, whose mortal taste
> Brought death into the world, and all our woe,
> With loss of Eden, till one greater Man
> Restore us, and regain the blissful seat.

Thus has Milton summed up the meaning of the gospel. Some of us who have witnessed death, known grief, and found no satisfactory human solution for the world's suffering and woe might, with Edwin Muir, daringly claim that,

> One foot in Eden, still I stand
> And look across the other land. . . .
> Yet strange these fields that we have planted
> So long with crops of love and hate.

And if I know who I am, and what my part has been, the stage on which I have played it has been the Church. Here I encountered the Christ. Christian conversion came to me not as an existential crisis, born of fear of a final judgment that might cast me into everlasting torment, nor in the terror of nature, as the thunderstorm seemed for Luther the voice of God. Nor was mine the rake's progress and that ultimate scunner at himself that drives a man to his knees crying, "God be merciful to me, a sinner." My struggles with the demons came after my ordination. In my youth, Christ came to me as imperceptible as the opening of the day and as natural as light. The fellowship of the Church nurtured me until that hour when I became aware that there could be no other life for me than that of the preacher.

Indeed, when I recall my adolescent years, I realize how my whole being was focused in the life of the Church. She was my other mother. In those impressionable years, the Church was sharing in a joyous companionship that both challenged my stretching horizon and stamped upon me forever afterward a quality of life that I can only call Christian. I cannot now conceive what life must be like for those young people who have had the misfortune never to have known from within the fellowship and adventure of the Church.

A friend who read most of the manuscript of this book astounded me by declaring that he saw no evidence in the first six chapters that I believed in God. Perhaps I was the uncommunicative Scot, too reticent about the inner experiences of the heart. Yet on further reflection, I believe that since God is the God of the living (as well as the religious!), the life of Ruchill Church, Glasgow, in the days of my youth was a profoundly religious experience, though I was hardly aware of its dimension at the time. The banter of healthy youth, the debates, and the Sunday morning services, when I sat in the side balcony, head bowed and supported by my right hand — all these were no less than an encounter with God.

This nurture within the Church did not lead me to regard myself as a special favorite in the eyes of the Lord, nor do I believe I was the smug Pharisee unaware of his own spiritual blindness. When I became a minister, I was not called to those congregations I would have loved to serve and for which I prayed. I can number at least five churches in the Church of Scotland that I dreamed of serving as preacher, imagining myself of a Sunday morning, seated in the well-appointed vestry, surrounded by richly framed portraits of stern-looking Victorian and Edwardian giants of the pulpit, smugly aware I was marching in their revered footsteps, preaching to great congregations my masterpiece sermons, and knowing that one day my portrait would hang alongside theirs. The realization came only slowly that the good Lord, in his gracious wisdom, was leading me *away* from the sentimental ideals of my self-centered, prideful daydreaming.

This book is a poor attempt to tell something of my encounters with many folk I've known down the years, and reflections on my life and God's Providence. Why did so many of them go out of their way to help me? Some, almost complete strangers, stopped to whisper, "Lower your voice, George. People will mistake your lack of self-confidence for conceit." I hear them still, voices of encouragement when as student and pastor I needed them badly, words of caution when I got wound up and forgot that I must be servant of my people as well as my Lord. Three stand high, like King Saul, head and shoulders above the rest: Archibald Allan Bowman, who introduced me to the wonder that is philosophy; Arthur John Gossip, who incarnated the glory that is preaching; and George MacLeod, through whose vision I glimpsed the prophetic light of a New Heaven and a New Earth.

And of course my parents, my stepfather, my brother Jack, and my bairns five. And two gifts of God to me, one arriving in the springtime of my life, the other bringing a second springtime to the autumn of my days.

1

The Wee Room and Kitchen

As we age, the mystery of Time more and more dominates the mind. We live less in the present, which no longer has the solidity it had in youth; less in the future, for the future every day narrows its span. The abiding things lie in the past.
— John Buchan, *Memory Hold the Door*

Fancy living in one of those streets, never seeing anything beautiful, never eating anything savoury — *never saying anything clever*!
— Winston Churchill, to a friend as they entered a particularly drab street in Manchester, 1906

MY EARLIEST RECOLLECTION goes back to 1914, the year the Great War began. I was three years old. Quite vividly I recall the day we flitted. Watching wide-eyed, I gripped my brother Jack's hand — he was seven years my senior — as my father and some neighbors sweated and groaned under the load of furniture, easing it gingerly down the tenement stairwell from the third floor of 28 Hathaway Street, Maryhill, Glasgow. They packed the load onto the grimy horse-drawn coal lorry rented from Mr. Macdonald — not very spacious at that, but large enough to accommodate the simple gear my parents had garnered through the years: some odd kitchen chairs, two tables, a parlor suite, carpets, worn linoleum, wicker baskets jammed with clothes, a few framed pictures, and some orange crates filled with bric-a-brac, wrapped in newspapers.

"Dinna drop that basket now, Tom; it's got my best china!" My mother bustled around delivering orders, cries of fear, and dire warnings like a cloaking hen. When the last stick of furniture had been balanced precariously and secured with a stout tarred rope, my father scrambled atop the load with two bird cages, one containing Peggy, our yellow canary, and the other Barney, a sparrow-like creature. With a click from the back of his throat, Mr. Macdonald coaxed on Bessie, a knowing nag who rattled her harness with impatience as if protesting against the unseemly load. Jackie and I set off together to walk the two miles to Shawpark Street, pushing our way through the crowd of youngsters who had gathered boisterously around the close mouth and watched by curious neighbors gossiping behind their white-lace-curtained windows.

1

That was an unforgettable day for all of us, but especially for my mother, for whom it represented emancipation from an outmoded room-and-kitchen flat with a stairhead lavatory shared by the other two families on the landing. We were on our way to the more adequate room and kitchen, third floor, 32 Shawpark Street, Maryhill, with its pleasant mottled marble stairs, wooden bannisters (with little brass nobs to keep you from sliding down), walley tiled close, and cold-water closet indoors.

Subtle distinctions exist within what are called the "working classes" that only those who have been reared in Glasgow's ashlar tenements can appreciate. Residents of our side of the street looked down with a rather superior if sympathetic view on those folk who lived opposite us. They reached their homes through dismal, ill-ventilated closes, the paint on the walls peeling and disfigured with chalked graffiti ("J. W. loves M. S."), up a worn stone turnpike stair, past ominously dark doorways illumined by gulping naked gas jets, past odiferous communal toilets with lockless open doors revealing stained toilet bowls and a crumple of sodden newspapers on the wet concrete floor. Below the street level were the "dunnies," single-room homes looking out upon a dreary, macadamized back court strewn with litter and rubbish.

On the other hand, the view from our kitchen window across the back court — kitchens always faced the back court — looked on to Craigmont Drive, the title itself carrying overtones of middle-class status. Craigmont Drive residents reached their homes from a walley close, through a painted-glass storm door that opened into a wide, square hallway. The flats consisted of kitchen, parlor, bedroom, and bathroom with hot and cold water. Mother would one day reach such social heights, but that would be years after the Great War was ended.

In our new home, three up and on the right, I recall liturgies of the dusk shared with my mother. Seated in my child's chair, an heirloom from Grannie's childhood, perched on the kitchen sink, I watched with her in the gathering gloom as the lights went on one by one in the tenements in Craigmont Drive, Mother all the while peeling potatoes for dinner in an enamel basin in the sink under a brightly polished brass cold-water tap. These daily chats must have taken place before the German zeppelins flew overhead terrorizing the land. After that, the windows were blacked out, and if one chink of light lanced the darkness, there would arise from the street below the shrill of a bobby's whistle.

"Mamma! There's another!" I would cry out, as another firefly glowed in the gloom. "When are we going to put our light on?"

"In a wee whiley, Georgie," she would answer.

My mother was then over forty. Her dark eyes shone like a gypsy's beneath heavy eyebrows; she had dark hair and the cheekbones of the Celt. A buxom five feet, she walked all her life with a poker-straight back, and she lived until she was ninety-one. My uncle George told me she had often been the belle of the ball at the barn dances in the Banffshire days of their youth. She remained to the last a country lass transplanted to live the life of a city wife, shopping in Gairbraid Street, her netbag full of groceries, joshing with the neighbors she encountered in this daily promenade, her infectious laugh carrying above the clang of streetcar bells and the clop of horse-drawn lorries in the causey stone street. She never completely integrated herself into the warm-hearted community life of Glasgow and never quite caught on to its bawdy but innocent humor. Home was always in the North, where she longed to feel again in her face the bracing nor'easters of the Moray Firth.

My mother was a Macpherson, related to the Macphersons of Ballindalloch Castle. There were stories — as there are in most Highland families — about an illegal litigation that prevented me from inheriting the spacious lands of Ballindalloch. In times of personal crisis, my mother would always admonish me, "Remember, Georgie! You are a Macpherson!" — the name rolling reverently from her tongue.

She was what was known in Glasgow as a "room-and-kitchen Tory" having little patience with the burgeoning Labour Movement, calling all Socialists "tinks" and "dirt." On occasion she would expostulate: "And who dae they think they are, these tinks, going ahead about doing away with the Royal Family when they get into power" — as indeed some of the early Socialists were promising to do.

"Mamma!" I'd cry out as another firefly pierced the gathering darkness. "There's another light on!"

We talked about all sorts of things during these twilight conversations, especially tall tales about the old days in the North. And I would probe such ultimate questions about life as Paul Tillich believed every child asks.

"Mamma, where did I come from?"

"The Shaws."

"Tell me again how you got me, Mamma."

"Well, it was like this. Daddy and I were out walking along Pollokshaws Road and we saw across the street a little boy sitting on a doorstep crying. . . ."

"Was that me, Mamma?"

"Dinna interrupt me! Well, your Daddy and I just walked across the street and the wee boy looked up at us pathetically and stopped crying and I lifted the dear lamb up and put him in my bosey and wrapped my shawl around him because he was cauld and took him hame and gave him his tea and washed him and put him to bed. And that was that. And now I think we'll light the gas."

Drying her hands on her apron, she would select a wax taper from the vase on the stone mantelpiece over the iron grate (Carron Ironworks, Falkirk) built into the kitchen wall, and insert it into the glowing coal fire. Turning on the gas with her left hand, she applied the flame to the swiveling brass bracket; there was a hiss of gas and a gulp as the incandescent mantle filled the twelve-by-twelve kitchen-sitting room with so bright a flare of light that I blinked. That gas-lit room where I lived until I was fifteen is etched in my mind more permanently than any other room I can remember.

Perched over the glowing coals on the brightly polished grate stood a brown enamel kettle, a black dent on its side, always on the boil for the inevitable cup of tea. The clothes pulley was suspended from the ceiling over the grate, always loaded with yesterday's washing, casting weird shadows on the opposite wall. Above the mantelpiece hung a large framed print depicting a spacious Adams drawing room in which a broad-shouldered young man stood in front of a massive stone fireplace reciting to an audience of bewigged gentlemen and crinolined ladies. In front of the speaker, standing apart, was a pantalooned boy, a look of wonder in his face. Years later I learned the title of the print: "Robert Burns in Edinburgh, 1787; reading a poem 'A Winter's Night' to a literary gathering at the Duchess of Gordons before the boy Walter Scott."

Opposite our kitchen grate stood a wooden dresser, divided into two sections, one a press for pots and pans, on which stood the white enamel bread box, and the other the coal bunker into which the faithful Mr. Macdonald unloaded a hundred-weight bag of coal every Saturday morning. When mother heard his voice filling the street like a towncrier — "Yeaoll! Yeaoll!" — she laid out on the dresser the two-shilling piece and opened the door. Soon the clomp of his tackety boots grew louder as he laboriously climbed the six flights of stairs until suddenly his huge black bulk materialized in the kitchen doorway, panting somewhat, a bulky burlap bag perched on the leather cowl spread over his broad shoulders. He dumped his load into the open bunker amidst a rumbling volcano of dust that seemed to permeate every corner of the kitchen. Straightening his back with a grumbling comment on his lumbago, he would pick up the silver coin with his squat, blackened fingers, count out three halfpence he extracted from the leather bag around his neck, fold the grimy bag under his arm, glance out the window with a remark on the weather prospects, and be off on his rounds again, his whistle fading away downstairs.

Along the entire length of the wall opposite the grate ran a shelf displaying mother's pride and joy — her dishes: a willow-patterned tureen and soup plates, a large delft wash basin with jug to match, and near the kitchen door a large copper jelly pan on its end, in which I could see the reflection of my face. The delicate set of china dishware (through which you could see the shadow of your fingers when you lifted it up to the light) was used only for visitors, and four crystal wine decanters used only on Hogmanay, that mystical pagan and peculiarly Scottish festival, more celebrated in my childhood than Christmas.

4

The Wee Room and Kitchen

The celebration of Hogmanay took place on New Year's Eve. On the stroke of midnight, my father would open the windows, ostensibly (and I believed him) to let out the Old and to let in the New Year. Carried in the snell wind from the street below came the soulful singing of inebriated revelers, and in the distance we could hear the booming of the great bell of the University and the hooting of factory whistles. At that mystic moment, my dad would charge his glass with whiskey (it was the only time I ever saw him take hard liquor) and with the natural gravity and grace of the Celt, he would repeat his ritual toast, looking at my mother with serious eyes; "I wonder, Jeannie, will we all be here together this time next year?"

When I grew older, I went out "first footing," the custom of being first in the New Year to cross the doorsteps of your friends' homes. I was greatly in demand in those days for my hair was dark; fair or red-haired first footers, for some reason I could never understand, brought ill luck to the house. Armed with a bottle of ginger wine, a lump of coal symbolizing warmth and comfort throughout the New Year, Seville oranges, and Newton Pippin apples, I would venture forth into the dark with my bosom cronies, visiting until the wee sma' hours.

Ben the room was our parlor, larger than the kitchen, with a spacious oriel window, its three lights looking out to the front street. In the center was a well-worn carpet, surrounded by a broad linoleum border designed like oak parquet. A three-branched gasolier hung from a molded cornice in the center of the ceiling. In front of the cast-iron fireplace, flanked with green tiles, was a fender of polished brass with matching brass poker and tongs, used only for display. Filling the wall above the mantelpiece hung a dark oak overmantel, its large center mirror flanked by little brackets on which stood various oddments: demitasse cups and colored china ornaments bearing the coats of arms of towns mother and dad had visited when they were young; a framed photograph of my American cousin Nettie, in Highland dress, right foot gracefully poised, her bosom covered with silver medals she had won for piping and dancing in Chicago; in the center, a chiming clock, which my father wound up religiously every Saturday night.

In the bed recess in the wall stood a "bun-in-bed" shared by my brother and me, hidden behind a heavy maroon velvet curtain during the day or when we had visitors. A wardrobe with a full-length beveled mirror, two easy chairs, a small setee, and an oak table with legs covered by dark purple velveteen cloth completed the inventory of furniture in the "best room."

Never a piano! But in a corner, on a shaky, bamboo-leg table stood a cabinet gramophone. Stored on the shelf under the table were the few records we possessed, most featuring the red label with the spotted dog listening for "His Master's Voice." "The Sinking of the Titanic" struck

5

both terror and mystification as I lay on the floor, head cupped in my hands, listening to the crunching of the bow of the great unsinkable liner against the fateful iceberg, the howl of the Atlantic winds, the wash of mighty breakers, voices crying in distress, and above the cacophony a brass band playing "Nearer My God to Thee" with dignified measure until at last they too were muted in a terrifying gurgling of waters, giving place to the gentler swish of the sea and the dying moan of the wind.

I recall a night when we had company in the best room, a wild night it was, the wind whining down the chimney, outside the sound of slates and broken chimney pots crashing on the street below. Suddenly, the main light of the oriel window blew in with a thunderous crash, the lace curtains and my father's large aspidestra plant saving us all from serious injury. My father and our guests rushed to stem the storm as it howled through the gaping hole. The gasolier swirled dangerously. My mother panicked. I cowered under the table in silent fear. To this day I have an irrational dread of high winds howling in the night.

Unlike other districts of Glasgow such as Townhead or Parkhead, we residents of Maryhill grew up on the periphery of a city with easy access to green fields and moors. I have seen a sentinel deer sniffing the air like Landseer's "Monarch of the Glen" not more than ten miles away from Maryhill on the moors around Milngavie. I could see the Campsie Falls and the nub of Dungoyne covered in snow from our parlor window. Our tenement was an island between two leveled dumps with a few brave trees, euphemistically called "The Wee Park" and "The Big Park." Whatever else they were, they provided splendid open space where we played soccer all year round, cricket (with three stumps), and a form of golf with my father's walking stick and gutta percha balls we called "gutties."

At the top of Shawpark Street stood Shaw Ironworks Ltd., whose smelting furnaces, "a pillar of fire by night," glowed in misty winter skies. Every morning around five minutes to eight, the "clingkimclang" of Shaw's tinny bell drew a slow procession of silent, sleepy workers in hodden grey suits, cloth caps, and tackety boots past our window. At stopping time, half past five, when the same wee bell peeled out, our street was transformed into a Spanish town during a fiesta as those same workers dashed as if chased by wild bulls to catch the streetcars that passed by the bottom of our street. Similar scenes can be seen to this day at every public works gate in the city. Indeed, Glasgow is one of the few cities in the world where you may be in serious danger of being run over by a pedestrian!

Behind Shaw's Ironworks flowed the Forth and Clyde Canal, along whose banks we played—and where some fell in and drowned—during the long sunny summer holidays. When we caught sight of the flat-bottomed iron pleasure steamer *Fairy Queen*, we ran alongside, cheering the laughing Glaswegians on a pleasant day's sail from Monkland's Wharf in

6

downtown Glasgow, through the lush farmlands, to the terminal at the market town of Kirkintilloch, some twenty miles away. We trotted alongside, keeping time to the strains of a Strauss waltz played by the ship's piano and string ensemble, shouting, with cupped hands, "Gie us a penny! Fling us a penny!" Not a few of the passengers lining the deck responded to the invitation and laughed, as we groaned, when an errant coin fell short into the churning waters.

And there was a public park ten minutes' walk from home along the River Kelvin where we played on long summer days and where I carved my name on a tree. Today the carving is a mere blur, as I noticed recently on a return visit.

Once while wading in the Kelvin, I slipped and flopped in the water, polluted by paperworks sewage. Terrified what mother might say or do — for she advocated, unlike my father, Proverbs' "spare the rod and spoil the child" — I tried to dry off my sodden garments among the bushes, hanging them up on a tree and remaining out of sight the long afternoon. Finally, shivering, miserable, and hungry, I braved the prospect of my mother's wrath and wearily set off home. As I approached Maryhill Railway Station, I caught sight of her hurrying toward me at full speed, coatless, apron flying in the wind, her sleeves pulled up. I stopped, with half a mind to make a bolt for it. She approached me at a run, and gathering me up into her arms, pressed her tear-stained cheeks against mine, sobbing out, "Oh! Georgie, my wee dearie! my ain wee dearie!"

Not until the following day did I learn that a child had been drowned in the canal, the body still unrecovered. A search among the neighborhood children had revealed all present, except Georgie Docherty.

Until I left school at the age of fifteen, Shawpark Street was my world, greatly beloved, unchanging except by death, knit together in the intimate pattern only the tenement dweller fully understands; doors were ever open for the exchange of gossip over tea, where sorrows were grieved over and injury, sickness, and unemployment shared as if we were one family. Of course there were quarrels, sometimes even stairhead brawls, though these seldom cut deeply.

Some strange folk would come occasionally to stay a while in our street. There was the secretive woman who lived in the close first on the right, a single-end apartment, and was particularly niggardly when we ran errands for her. She disappeared. After a time, we were astounded to read in the *Evening Times* that she had murdered a newsboy, stolen his few coppers, bundled his body in a perambulator, and upended it into the River Clyde. She was hanged in Duke Street Prison.

I recall the ubiquitous Nurse Gates, whom my mother told me (changing somewhat the account of my origin) had brought me home in her little black leather bag to Hathaway Street. A little lady, somewhat buxom, she wore an Eton celluloid collar, a pale blue uniform with a belt around a surprisingly narrow waist, and a Florence Nightingale cap.

"I'm Georgie Docherty, Nurse Gates," I said to her one day in the street. "My mother said you brung me."

"Why, of course I did, Georgie," she replied with a twinkle in her eye, enjoying a joke that was eluding me, and handing me a pan drop from a wee paper bag from under her thick woolen cape. With a pat on my head, she was off again on her rounds. I followed her from a distance until she arrived at another close into which she disappeared with her wee black leather bag, no doubt to deliver yet another war baby.

Our closest friends in the stair were Madgie and Jimmy McCormick who lived next door in the single-end, where they reared three children. A dustman employed by the Cleansing Department, Jimmy spent his workdays shouldering wicket baskets full of evil-smelling refuse from the moldering lean-to brick middens beside the washhouse—coal cinders and clinkers that stank in wet weather, decayed vegetation mixed with dogs' piddle and excreta. Every Saturday, a Sabbath of rest and recreation, Jimmy would wash away his ennui and noxious coal dust in one of the many public houses that seemed to support every street corner along Gairbraid Street. Gleefully we would await the weekly pantomime of Jimmy's triumphant journey homeward, his worries drowned, his surprisingly good tenor voice bawling out unsteadily a beloved Irish chorus. Staggering from side to side on the sidewalk, he would occasionally stop and support himself with the ornate cast-iron railings that fenced off the grubby little front gardens. Bleary-eyed, he would catch sight of us and, letting go, come loping toward us, arms outstretched.

"Come here, my wee Georgie, into your auld Jimmy's airms! Come on, son! Dinna be afraid."

And struggling into his trouser pocket, he would extract a penny.

"Here's a penny, son. Tak' it! It'll no' bite ye! And dinna spend it all in the one shop!"

With unerring homing instinct he would locate our close—last on the righthand side of the street—and pad up the six flights of stairs, supported by the wooden bannister rail, the whole close echoing with "When Irish Eyes Are Smiling." On one occasion Madgie, driven to distraction, dared to close the door on him; Jimmy put his fair-haired bullet head through its upper panel, leaving an ineradicable reminder: *memento mori*. Everybody loved Jimmy—"a good man," as the neighbors said, "and a pity that he was a wee bit foolish with the drink."

Despite her own chores, Madgie often helped my mother on wash days, a day-long undertaking. Each neighbor was allocated her turn in the wash house in the back court, a concrete-floored brick structure with a large coal-fired boiler. First thing in the morning, these two elemental women would pad down the six flights of stairs carrying two large wicker baskets full of clothes, a cast-iron hand wringer, a pail of coal, and sticks and newspaper to kindle the fire, to boil the water, to wash the clothes. When it rained, as it did all too frequently, they hauled the wet wash, smelling of ammonia, back upstairs to be hung up on the pulley in the kitchen and on the brass rail across the mantelpiece over the red glow of the kitchen fire.

Madgie was a devout Roman Catholic, faithfully in her place at eight o'clock mass every Sunday. Her devotion to me is perhaps best to be measured by her attendance at my ordination to the ministry, at a time when her church held it to be a mortal sin for Catholics to attend any Protestant place of worship.

It must have been some thirty years after those daunting days we shared with Jimmy and Madgie that I met them again, for the last time. They now lived in a new three-bedroom public housing home; their children had grown up, married, and were making their own way in the world. I was on my way back from a vacation in Europe. Madgie opened the door to my knock. She had changed little, though the golden hair was now quite white. The reticent smile was still there. When I bussed her, she blushed like a maiden kissed for the first time. The years had etched Jimmy's face. He was on his deathbed. Over a cup of tea we talked of the old days in Shawpark Street; when I recalled Jimmy's roistering Saturday nights, he laughed aloud until he coughed.

In Rome I had purchased a rosary specially for Madgie near Bernini's Piazza. I had gathered with the multitude of pilgrims in St. Peter's Square to catch a glimpse of the Pope at the distant window of his remote Vatican residence. When his voice boomed over the loudspeaker "In nomine Patri et Filii et Spiritu sancti," I raised aloft the rosary.

"Madgie, my dear, I've brought you a rosary. Got it in Rome. It has been blessed by the Pope himself, right there in St. Peter's Square. He made the sign of the cross over it."

She silently looked down at the little gift, turning it over gently, caressing the glossy black beads between her fingers, as if she were saying her rosary. "Auch, Georgie! Ye mean to tell me it has been blessed by the Holy Father himself? Now, you wouldn't be kidding me now, would you?"

I sat down on the edge of Jimmy's bed and gently held his calloused hands, now quite soft. I offered a wee prayer, a prayer of thanksgiving. I bent down and kissed his stubbly cheek. He smiled self-consciously and his eyes lighted up for a moment. He returned a long, steady, silent look.

Jack and I were knit closer in love and admiration than most brothers; yet the wanderlust that seems to have held sway in our destinies kept us apart most of our lives. I stood three inches taller than Jack, but always called him my big brother. At the age of fourteen, Jack flew the coop when he got a job as resident page boy at the prestigious Western Club in

Glasgow. The wages were beggarly, but he lived in and thrived on tips, and the perquisites from the kitchen were always welcome.

On one occasion at the club, he assisted to his rooms a Scottish member of the House of Lords after a night out with friends. As Jack helped the staggering Lord to undress, the man's pocketbook fell out of his evening dress coat, scattering on the floor a sheaf of crisp white ten-pound Bank of England notes.

"I was greatly tempted to take one, mother," Jack confessed later. And she, who never in her whole life had handled one crisp white ten-pound Bank of England note, replied, "Aye! Aye! You were quite right not to take one. That would have been stealing, son! And, you know, that's a sin."

Later the sea beckoned, as it beckons every lad who lives in a great seaport like Glasgow, where daily he may wander around the docks and see ships with such magical names on their stern as Ceylon, Sydney, Singapore, Hong King. Jack became a steward on the Anchor Liner *California*, a 17,000-ton twin-screw ship, its majestic black funnel towering over a sparkling white hull. It sailed every three weeks from Kelvinhaugh Wharf to New York harbor. Later, he became a certified cook on tramp steamers, the oil tanker *War Sudra* being his favorite ship; it took him around the globe several times. He married an English lass, Lilly, and settled down to a career ashore in England as a landscape architect, laying out playing and recreational fields all over Britain. By the time he had returned to Glasgow, I was away on my own sojourn across the Atlantic. Thereafter we met only on my vacations back to Scotland.

The memories of our childhood years together are both precious and vivid, some almost too vivid in the recalling. There was one exploit we never dared share with our parents until we were grown men. It happened during a walk to the Bardowie Loch where we used to go to watch the swans nesting and to catch minnows. At the railroad crossing, we saw a freight train approaching. Jack, as always fooling, said, "Let's pretend we are tied down to the rails, as they do in the pictures; then we'll jump away just in time, when the train comes nearer."

"No! No!" I screamed, struggling and terrified.

"Come on, son! It's just for fun!"

In the ensuing struggle, my boot became wedged between the sleepers and the rail. My foot refused to budge, despite Jack's frantic efforts to pull it free. He fumbled at the book laces, but they were in a fankle. The hiss of steam of the oncoming train grew louder; its whistle was screaming; already we could hear the whine of grinding steel as the driver applied the steam brakes. In a final desperate effort, Jack managed to wrench me free and threw me with all his force toward the green railway enbankment, while he himself jumped to safety on the other side of the track. I landed in a terrified heap, aware only of hissing steam as the train lumbered past, gathering up speed again, and a lump of coal hurled at me by the cursing driver just missing my head.

At school I wrote about the incident in an essay, "My Greatest Adventure." I got a zero on the grounds that I had invented the whole tale!

My father was a Scot, born in Gourock, a delightful little holiday resort town nestling at the "Tail of the Bank" of the Firth of Clyde, beloved by generations of Glaswegians. His parents were Irish, born in Buncrana, whence they emigrated sometime in the nineteenth century during one of the perennial potato famines, the scourge of that troubled land. I thus have both Irish and Highland blood in my veins—a contentious combination! Although I have no evidence of the fact from the family tree, I guess my paternal grandparents probably were Roman Catholics who changed their faith on arriving in Scotland to escape the invidious discrimination against Catholics that was still too much in evidence in the southwest of Scotland. Like his father before him, my father was apprenticed as a gardener on one of the great estates of the Victorians, whose red sandstone castles stand half hidden in the woody hills overlooking the Firth of Clyde.

My father was a natural artist and poet. His walk was graceful, and when called upon, his inborn Irish oratory flowed to the amusement and admiration of his listeners. At our wedding he gave, without previous notice, a speech declared by Dr. Craig, who officiated, to be the finest natural oratory he had ever listened to. He was forever declaiming his own poetry in the meter of Robert Burns. One fragment only I now recall:

> I wandered sadly down yon lonely glen
> Where curlews sleep.

In those early years during and after the Great War, ours was not a church-going family, though later my parents joined the Ruchill Church, Glasgow, when I myself became a member there. Yet our home was a religious one, where the Bible was revered. Going to church on Sunday meant dressing up. Church people seemed to us to be of the Craigmont Drive type, epitomized in the Sabbath journey of Mr. Brown in his bowler hat, a small man with a large Bible under his arm, a faithful elder of Ruchill Church, always smartly dressed, so clean-cut. Nevertheless, mother saw to it that I attended Sunday School every Sunday afternoon, walking the three miles to the Old Parish Church of Maryhill, out near the Garscube Estate of the Campbells, where in a huddle of boys on wooden benches around a teacher, I was introduced to tales from the Old Testament and the stories of Jesus. Here I learned those hymns that have stayed with me throughout a lifetime, especially on winter days the closing praise, "Now the day is over; / Night is drawing nigh; / Shadows of the evening / Steal across the sky."

At home the black Bible with the gold leaf edges was always at hand. If my parents said their prayers, it was a private matter, too private for even us children to know about.

My father, laboring among his beloved plants, was a pantheist, though I doubt that he would have understood the term. My mother was without a doubt a Calvinist, though she had never even heard of *The Institutes of the Christian Religion.* Life for her was a dubious balance between good and evil forces, almost always tipped in favor of evil. Joy and sorrow, pleasure and pain, justice and injustice were meted out to mankind in fatefully equal measures. I recall that when at breakfast on summer holiday mornings, with no dread of school to frighten, the sunshine blessing our little kitchen with new radiance, as I supped my porridge, suddenly for no apparent reason, as every child so frequently does, I'd burst out into laughter at nothing at all, my mother would turn and scold me.

"Wheesht, Georgie! Stop your laughing! You'll be greeting afore the day's out!"

No blasphemy was ever uttered in our home. If we were not "kirk-fond," the church was respected and never criticized. Ministers were given the respect of their profession. They were godly men.

In my mother's childhood, she attended the Macpherson's little country parish church of Rathven in Banffshire. Mr. Donald, the minister, entered from the back of the pulpit through a heavy maroon velvet curtain; the service concluded, he would part the curtain and disappear until the following Sunday. My mother was sure that Mr. Donald came each Sunday morning straight from heaven, to which he returned again until the following Sunday. Heaven was indeed the manse, beautifully set in the midst of the glebe at the end of a winding road of stolid Scots beach trees, hidden away from the world save for the smoke rising from the study chimney — incense certainly.

Sunday morning worship came to us when the Salvation Army, heralded by a brass band playing "Onward Christian Soldiers," gathered around in a circle in our street. As he preached, the major held in his outstretched hand a dark blue military cap with a red band and the words *Salvation Army* in gold. Under his dark blue tunic we could glimpse a crimson sweater emblazoned with the Army's motto, *Blood and Fire.* He proclaimed the gospel from within the circle formed by his fellow salvationists, Bible in his other hand, his fine voice echoing up and down the natural amphitheater of the street as he warmed to his message. When the collection was solicited from the congregation watching from windows above, pennies cascaded to the street (mother always gave) to be gathered by a pretty black-straw-bonneted girl, who placed them in her tambourine, which tintinnabulated as she darted about searching the gutters for elusive coins, calling out the while in an English accent, "Thank you, dear friends, and God bless you."

With the passing of many years a realization of the horror of four years of trench warfare on the western front of the Great War has grown on me. As a child living in innocent bliss, I thought the war was a great game, shooting with my father's walking stick from behind stone ramparts at every German in sight and laughing with adults at the "Wee Willie" cartoons of the Crown Prince of Germany and his exaggerated hooked nose. The Kaiser with his full black moustache was a "bad yin."

Quite early in 1915, my father volunteered for the navy, as would be expected of one who had been reared on the Firth of Clyde. He was posted as a stoker on the coal-burning minesweeper H.M.S. *Glen Usk*, a converted pleasure paddle steamer out of Bristol.

His homecoming on leave created great excitement, especially since we were never warned that he would be arriving. Mother, of course, recognized his footfall on the stairs and the magisterial erat-a-tata-tat on the door. Though not tall (about five feet eight), he seemed to fill the doorway, his beguiling Irish smile and large kit bag slung over his shoulder. Rushing toward his outstretched arms, I would try on his white-covered sailor's cap while diving into the open kit bag out of which poured a remarkable assortment of knicknackery: a large roll of tobacco like a small torpedo, wrapped around by a pungent, tarry rope; a blouse for mother; toys for Jackie and me, always ships; once a captured German sailor's cap; a pillow case tied in the middle full of tea and sugar (our sugar had tea leaves in it for weeks); a colored tin of tobacco, the gift of King George V, whose portrait in the uniform of an admiral adorned it, and which mother would use for years as a tea caddy; and a year's supply of cocoa in large, hard, bitter bars.

Before going to bed, I would sit on his knee, engrossed in tales of his exploits in the North Sea and his explanation of the sailors' strange uniform. Bell-bottoms made swabbing decks easier, since they could be rolled up. The broad collar over his shoulder went back to the days when sailors wore greasy pigtails. The three white lines around its edge symbolized Lord Nelson's three naval victories — Cape Vincent, the Nile, and the greatest (which had cost him his life), Trafalgar. The black silk cravat was worn in perpetual mourning for Britain's greatest admiral.

"Tell me more about the war, daddy. How do you beat the Germans?"

"Well, son, it's like this. The *Glen Usk* sails ahead of the Grand Fleet with her sister ship, joined by a long strong wire rope, just like a skipping rope. We steam steadily ahead. Suddenly there is a jolt all over the ship and we know that our wire has tangled with the chain that anchors the mine to the bottom of the sea. We sail on, cutting the chain of the mine with our wire. The mine bobs to the surface of the water like a football and starts to float around. Now we have to be very careful lest one of these spikes touch our ship; that would blow us up. We man the gun at the stern of the ship and blow the mine up; and when that happens, a great black column of smoke rises straight up into the air."

At this point, he produced a picture postcard showing a mine destroyed in the North Sea, just as he had described it.

"Daddy, what would happen if your ship did touch a mine?"

"Auch, son, don't ask such silly questions. Off to your bed with you!"

The disruption of those grim days was to me nothing but the normal course of events. Food rationing had become a way of life. The news that Madgie's young brother had died in the Dardanelles I took for granted. I recall the gathering gloom of one spring evening and a newsboy's glottal-stop voice echoing up our street: "Speshull! Speshull! *Lusitania* sunk! *Lusitania* sunk! Speshull!"

Indeed, the war brought to our door was only another pageant in the playground of my childhood. At the foot of our street stood the Maryhill Barracks on a hundred or more acres, surrounded by a twenty-foot rough-cast stone wall. Here was fun indeed as we hung around the wrought-iron gate and the sentry with his glengarry bonnet, khaki tunic, and MacKenzie tartan, eyes gazing forward, oblivious to the rumble of traffic or the children playing around him. When the skirl of the pipes and the beat of drums carried to us from deep within the barracks, the sentry with a metallic click of heels presented arms, his rifle poised before his eyes, where it would stay until a contingent of the Glasgow Battalion of the Highland Light Infantry marched through the gate, led gloriously by the pipe band, and turned right in unison up the incline of Gairbraid Street toward the Maryhill Railway Station . . . *left, right, left, right,* the kilts swinging in unison, *erub-i-de-dub* from the leopard-skinned big drummer, the lads singing lustily to the martial tune of "The Grenadier Guards" — "Ma barra broke at ten o'clock / And I lost my hurl on the barra" — each with his glengarry roguishly cocked, rifle over left shoulder, *left, right, left, right,* metal-heeled boots reverberating on the causey stones. Huddled beneath brooding grey skies, a solemn group had gathered, mostly women and a few old men, the young women with drab grey paisley shawls wrapped around their sullen, stooping shoulders. Some appeared to be sobbing, and all of them seemed to miss the fun of it all as we strode, arms swinging, alongside the soldiers.

At the entrance to the red sandstone station a sergeant major bawled out some incoherent command; the soldiers drew up smartly to a halt; the pipes subsided into sudden silence, like a throttled hen. They shuffled into a column two deep and, at another bawl from the sergeant major, marched into the station entrance hall. As they passed out of sight, some of the lads looked round and with brave smiles and defiant shakes of the fist, were gone, bound for some distant land to earn costly glory.

It was at this same station that I once saw "Old Bill," the British prototype of the modern tank, a camouflaged caterpillar-tread monster. Its imprint on the macadamized road remained for years afterwards.

One morning a special quiet hung over our street. A large gathering of neighbors crowded round the close where Willie Ferguson lived. Willie's father had been killed in Flanders. From a vantage point up a tree in the Wee Park we watched the pageant of a military pipe band marching up the street to the strangely awesome beat of a single kettledrum, followed by a contingent of Black Watch Highlanders around a gun carriage caisson drawn by six black horses. The procession halted outside the close, and six soldiers preceded by an army chaplain emerged from the close bearing high on their shoulders a coffin covered with the Union Jack, their cheeks pressed against their burden as they advanced until they reverently laid it on the caisson. The soldier on the lead horse spurred his mount forward with a rattle of harness and the creak of gun carriage wheels. The pipe band wailed the poignant pibroch "The Land o' the Leal":

> I'm wearing awa', Jean,
> Like snaw when it's thaw, Jean;
> I'm wearing awa'
> To the land o' the leal.
> . . . .
> Now fare ye weel, my ain Jean,
> This warld's care is vain, Jean;
> We'll meet and aye be fain
> In the land o' the leal.

The cortege wound its way to the Western Necropolis, where Grannie was buried and where on Sunday afternoons Jack and I would make a pilgrimage, wandering among the tombstones without any sense of life's finitude, listening to the blackbirds in the rhododendron bush and the lark singing in the sky.

Armistice Day, November 11, 1918. Our teacher announced there would be no school after ten o'clock. Mother and Madgie awaited me at the school gate, and we joined the thin line of self-conscious folk in Gairbraid Street. At precisely eleven o'clock, the thunder of distant gunfire came rolling from the direction of the barracks. The people raised a cheer, though their hearts were obviously not in it, the pipe band drew near, the kilted soldiers singing *con brio*, "Ma barra broke at ten o'clock. . . ." I waved a little Union Jack mother had brought.

"This war's over, Jean," commented Madgie with a sigh, thinking of the return of Jimmy from France, "but mine is just starting up again."

It was another year before my father returned home. The H.M.S. *Glen Usk* remained on duty mopping up German mines in the North Sea. They brought him home in an ambulance, and he remained at home, an invalid, for over two years. I was never able to learn what really was wrong with my father. Mother always put off my questions with the

15

response "Daddy's jist no' weel." It was some form of pleurisy, no doubt brought on by his work as a stoker, bared to the waist shoveling coal, then coming aloft to cool off in the teeth of cutting North Sea winds. The only confirmation I ever had was in a letter intended for his doctor that my father brought home after undergoing a test at the hospital. Mother's curiosity got the better of her; she steamed open the official-looking envelope over the kettle. The enclosed form contained only one handwritten word, "Negative." Of course none of us knew what "negative" meant; perhaps it had something to do with photography? After his return to work, he gradually recovered his full and virile strength, greatly helped, I am certain, by his occupation as a gardener in the Glasgow Botanical Gardens and the outdoor life in the invigorating Scottish air.

Many years later, as we would walk together round these same Botanical Gardens, he would point out to me the flower beds he cut out in the greensward — they are still to be seen. When we entered the Kibble Palace out of the snell winds, he was able to discuss the varieties of tropical and desert plants. Hardly a plant he could not name and give its Latin origin, so vivid was his memory.

During the war years, until I was twelve, I attended Eastpark Public School, a wearisome experience that even the joys of childhood could not erase. A class photograph from those days shows me with wrinkled brow, a much-too-solemn visage for a seven-year-old. Promptly at nine o'clock the clang of the school bell summoned us to our classes. My classroom was on the first floor, rather pleasantly lit, with a terraced floor. The window sills were lined with bulb pots from which, as the dreary winter days passed into the light of springtime, brave tulips and hyacinths emerged. During dark winter days the room was lit by an eight-jet gasolier that hung from the ceiling. Boys and girls sat segregated at wooden desks, two at a desk, each desk defaced with ink stains and the initials of former pupils, including my own — "G. D. sat here." On one wall hung a large colored map of the world, a quarter of it dominated by large splashes of red indicating the territories of the British Empire, upon which the sun was never to set. Africa, in particular, had a wide swath of red that stretched from Cairo to Capetown.

During the war years meals were served in the school hall, a provision made for needy children and for those whose fathers were at the war. At breakfast the school hall was a bedlam of shouting children, steaming hot water radiators loaded with sodden coats, the humid air smelling of sweaty clothes, burnt porridge, and stewed urn tea. For some reason unknown to me (I now suspect malnutrition as the cause) I was singled out along with several other pale, skinny lads for a dose of Scott's Emulsion of Cod Liver Oil after every meal. I stayed at school nearly every day for lunch, which usually consisted of harricot bean soup, steak mince and potatoes, and milk pudding. After school at three o'clock there was cocoa served in an enamel mug, with bread and margarine. I then adjourned to the library, a part of the dining room set off by a portable screen. There I was introduced to the mythical world of Aesop, the Brothers Grimm, and Hans Christian Anderson; there too I read stumblingly through the South Sea adventures of R. M. Ballantyne. I'd return home, running always, in time to meet mother who worked in those days as a cleaner at Kelvinside Academy, a school for the privileged sons of Kelvinside toffs, scrubbing the cold stone stairs and rough wooden floors.

Extra afternoon class sessions were required to improve my poor reading skills. The printed page always appeared as an indecipherable amalgam of letters, staggering around as if inebriated; in time I was to recognize these symptoms as a mild form of visual agnosis. To sober the letters was the specific task of a specialist, Miss Beaton, a middle-aged lady, invariably dressed in cashmere suits. Blinking through thick lenses, she set about her task with skill and infinite patience, seeking to instill through the ear the sounds of the words and through the eye their shape, domesticating them and making their pattern familiar. Her method consisted of little else than rote repetition — still, I believe, the best method of dealing with dyslexia.

"Once more, and altogether," she would bawl out like a not-unkindly sergeant major, marching up and down the aisle and stopping to point out to me the place in the soft yellow leather textbook. "Come on, GEORGE DOCHERTY! You are holding up the class! Yes, it's page thirteen, silly boy! Are we all ready? Siege! Siege! S.I.E.G.E. — Siege!"

Sometimes she would creep up behind and prod me in the back as I stood shouting out some quite unintelligible sound, although always in unison with the rest of the class, after the mode of a Gregorian chant.

I now bless in my heart the memory of this fine woman, who worked so tirelessly to correct an impediment in reading that is with me still, though to a lesser degree, since I have spent so much of my life with books. My inability to type without reversing the letters is something more than lack of skill in typing. It also explains my ponderously slow reading, which drives me away from speed-reading courses as one would flee a plague. Though I live until I am a hundred, I shall never be able to read through the complete corpus of Sir Walter Scott, whose lovely blue leather-bound volumes have lined my bookshelf for the past fifty years.

December in Scotland is a dark, forbidding month. In Glasgow the day was further shortened by the enveloping yellow fog; shop windows were alight by three in the afternoon. It seldom snowed. When it did, our snow was mostly slush. Only twice do I recall downtown Glasgow streets piled deep in radiant white snow. Yet we contrived to enjoy ourselves, tobogganing in the Wee Park on the kitchen shovel, climbing back uphill again, our breath like steam coming from under our woolen balaclavas.

The memory of one Christmas Eve—I was eight at the time—remains particularly vivid. A yellow fog carried on a damp wind enveloped the late shoppers thronging Gairbraid Street, among whom my pals and I had been playing hide-and-seek. I made my way home earlier than usual, full of Christmas Eve anticipation. But at the head of our stair, instead of an open and inviting doorway, the door was shut. I beat my fists upon it until they hurt. Through the brass letterslot I could see Bunty, our cat, in the lobby looking up at me, meowing and obviously as lonely as I was. I trudged slowly downstairs into the inhospitable cold night, wandering past the brightly lit shops, jostled by the holiday crowd. I pressed my nose against the cold plate glass window of Wyndford Post Office, gazing at the rows of books for sale—*The Mill on the Floss*, *Nicholas Nickleby*—determined that one day I would read through a big adult book. The window of Jimmy the fruiter was stacked high with apples, oranges, pomegranates, and boxes of dates with exotic pictures of palm trees sprouting from desert oases. Gibson the grocer's window was frosted over, except for two transparent circles the lighted candles had melted, through which I looked at the ends of hams in a row side by side, Ayrshire, Belfast, and Danish. I crossed over to the barracks gate where the ever-present sentry stood, a statue in khaki. I jumped on the cars, a favorite if dangerous pastime, leaping onto a moving streetcar and alighting nimbly at the sound of the conductor's footsteps racing down the stairs from the top deck to catch me; but it was no fun without the other boys. I returned mournfully up our street, kicking a wayward tin can en route, and climbed again the long flights of stairs to the locked door of an echoing, empty house. Seated on the cold marble stairs, I wept away the leaden, shivering minutes, until I finally heard the familiar footfall below. Downstairs I ran into engulfing arms, burying my cheek into my mother's bosom.

"I thought . . . I thought . . . you . . . were . . . lost, mama," I managed through huge, gulping sobs.

"But," she replied, "it's only five o'clock, son, and the shops were very busy."

In the warm kitchen, she poked the half-burnt clinker in the grate into a spluttering, splendid flame and put the kettle on the gas ring for tea, pouring out some of the water into an enamel basin on the floor in front of me. To the water she added a pickle of Coleman's mustard, and I immersed my chilled feet in the concoction. Bunty, rolled up in a ball beside me, purred with similar contentment.

After supper, mother helped me into a warm bed ben the room and tucked me in under the quilt, a hot water bottle at my feet. She kissed me, patted my head, reached up to the gasolier and turned off the light, leaving me alone in blessed comfort and assurance, watching the yellow light of the street lamps playing on the ceiling.

Intimations of this timeless moment of the consummate peace of childhood return at fleeting moments. I have felt it after the turn of the year, when the days lengthen perceptibly and the first caress of gentle winds heralds spring after the snell blasts of winter. I feel it sometimes on long Sabbath afternoons anywhere across the world, as if God and I were at rest, and his peace that passes all understanding were mine. Dylan Thomas recognizes in "Fern Hill" such childhood moments

> . . . that time allows
> In all his tuneful turning so few and such morning songs
> Before the children green and golden
> Follow him out of grace. . . .

Childhood is gone and life can never be quite so innocent again.

Was it a happy childhood? Every childhood is a quick succession of childish joys and childish sorrows. Mine was a happy childhood. Certainly a rather ordinary childhood. I suffered no personal grief; my father and mother lived on into my maturity. If there were worries, they were shared; you cannot keep secrets in a room and kitchen. A favorite saying of my mother was "Aye, it's the Lord's will," and God's will was manifested in a universe of moral order. Among the absolutes of that order was the certainty that it was morally wrong to lie or steal. I would never dare tell my mother of the unjust punishments I believed had been meted out to me at school; she would have paddled me again for telling tales!

It seems only the other day that I returned to the haunts of my childhood and found the old familiar places gone or transformed. The Forth and Clyde Canal, which once the radiant, stately *Fairy Queen* plied on summery days, her engines throbbing to the rhythm of Strauss, is now a scummy stretch of stagnant water, almost entirely choked by ugly watergrasses. The old Caledonian Railway is gone, its tracks lifted, now the receptacle for all sorts of junk, broken bathtubs from a nearby plumber's shop, and sodden cardboard cartons. The Wee Park and the Big Park have been replaced by unimaginative, depressing concrete-and-brick public housing with derelict gardens.

The Barracks is no more, but on its hundred acres stands a splendid housing development showing signs of a creative architect as well as a good builder. To my astonishment, the wee red sandstone railways station whence left the boys for "Blighty" in the Great War has vanished along with its marshalling yards. In its place stands the enormous red-brick Maryhill Super Market, surrounded by a parking lot of at least two acres.

I visited Shawpark Street. At that very moment the powerful steel fangs of a huge bulldozer were methodically uprooting the remnants of the foot-thick concrete foundations of our old tenement. The uncommunicative driver, perched high on his seat, no doubt thinking of his tea break, could not realize he was erasing forever more than a crumbling Victorian ashlar tenement. I was a spectator to the end of the world of my childhood in that wee room and kitchen three up on the right at 32 Shawpark Street.

2

No Mean City

I am a Jew, a Tarsian of Cilicia, a citizen of no mean city.
— St. Paul, Acts 21:39

I belong to Glesca,
Dear auld Glesca toon.
— Popular Song

IN THE GLASGOW of my youth, a class-conscious educational system contributed in no small measure to the hard-shell structure of society in which working-class youth were from earliest childhood made aware of "their place." At the age of twelve, a lad from the tenements might attend one of two classes of school. The Supplementary School provided him with a practical comprehensive education: a smattering of elementary French, a course in basic English, mechanical drawing, woodwork, and a good grounding in mathematics — sufficient to prepare him at the age of fourteen to leave school and be apprenticed to a trade.

On the other hand, he might try for High School, provided he passed the qualifying examination. There he would be exposed to a classical education: French certainly, and a second language, German or Latin, in his second year; and for those who were thinking about the Christian ministry, classical Greek. In addition there were Shakespeare and Euclid, and science from Archimedes to Newton. The history of the British Empire was really a course in world history and geography. Woodwork, art, and sports completed a curriculum that enabled the student to sit, at the age of seventeen or eighteen, for the Preliminary Examination to one of the four Scottish universities. Or he could earn a Lower Dayschool Certificate at the age of fifteen, and then be absorbed into the offices of commerce, insurance, banking, stockbroking, or shipping in the city, joining the ranks of white-collar workers who might be seen any morning at their "elevenses" in Miss Cranston's tearoom in Renfield Street, sipping *cafe au lait*, bowler hats still perched on their heads, chatting idly (as Dylan Thomas might have expressed it) about the "criminal sloth" of the miners and railwaymen.

Looming above these schools were such historic fee-paying schools as the High School of Glasgow, whose standard of education was second to none in Britain. About two out of five applicants were accepted; it was accounted unto you for righteousness if your father (better, your grandfather) had attended the school. Their students hailed from the city and its far-flung environs. Of course bursary students were welcomed—they raised the educational standards—but it soon became apparent who *were* the bursary students, a formative factor many such spent the rest of their lives trying to forget.

The headmaster of Aberdeen Grammar School once confided to me that there were really only two Scottish public schools; the rest were attempts to emulate Winchester or Rugby, staffed too often with masters from south of the border. These Oxbridge masters contributed in no small measure to what Professor Ian Henderson has described as the "disloyalty syndrome," when students assimilated the accent of their English masters. In Glasgow it has produced a jaundiced accent called "Kelvinside" (*crash* is pronounced as in *crèche*).

Such were the mores when, sixty years ago, I graduated from Eastpark School and entered at the age of twelve the heady environment of North Kelvinside Secondary School, having passed the guillotine qualifying examination by a narrow margin. My brother, a product of Shakespeare Supplementary School, had been able to get the approval of my Tory-minded mother, though she needed little persuasion. She wanted to see her Georgie "getting oan" in the world. It was to be a watershed in my life.

North Kelvinside School (non-fee-paying), an imposing five-story red sandstone structure, stands out against the hill of Oban Drive. I loved every moment of those days. I was blessed with exceptionally gifted teachers including Miss Margaret Kennedy, the author of a standard French grammar that was published during my first year.

My new friends settled their disagreements by argument rather than by fisticuffs after the school bell as we did at Eastpark School. Eagerly each morning I marched the three miles to school dressed in a new, specially bought grey suit, schoolbooks in a wooden case inscribed with the initials "G. D.," and school cap with a crest depicting a three-turreted castle keep, with the Latin tag *Vires, Acquirit, Eundo* (from the fourth book of Vergil's *Aeneid*, which years later I learned—"strength she [Gossip] gathers in going on"—now appropriated to describe the pursuit of knowledge).

Until now "shoes were for Sunday." When I entered High School, all I owned was a pair of tackety boots. Since the other fellows wore shoes, my mother let me wear her flat-heeled brogues. I was mortified when one of the fellows giggled, very Kelvinside, "Oh, I do say, George! I do declare! Wearing a pair of woman's shoes!"

I soon found myself caught up in the social milieu of boys who lived

22

in streets with such class-conscious designations as "Crescent," "Circle," and "Quadrant." In their speech and dress they were a contrast to my rough-spoken pals in Shawpark Street, most of whom now attended Shakespeare Supplementary School. In no time (*culpa mea*) I found myself studiously avoiding the Glaswegian glottal-stop vowels and paying lip service to final labial consonants in my conversation. The neighbors, much to mother's delight noting the transformation, commented on how "proper" Georgie was now speaking!

But I was also discovering the beauty of the English language, caressing the words, savoring their assonance, alliteration, and rhyme. Like Dylan Thomas answering the question why he became a poet, I too could say, "I fell in love with words. What the words stood for or symbolized or meant was of secondary importance; what mattered was the sound of them."

This new love of words was almost nipped in the bud in my first year by a rather unimaginative teacher who believed English poetry is best taught by mechanically memorizing two poems every week. I am sure he had some admirable qualities that have since escaped me, but at the time he was a minor nightmare to me, this paunchy, round-faced man with oily black hair featuring an unruly curl he would caress as he spoke in his pseudo-English accent, peering at me through rimless steel spectacles.

My dyslexia (if that is what I had) made a jumble of the words of the poem. With the perennial logic of the schoolboy, because it was difficult, I did nothing about it. Second period Tuesday afternoons rapidly became a charade the class anticipated with some glee. The experienced oracle, interpreting my indolence as defiance, would enter the classroom and, before the door swung closed behind him, reach instinctively for the strap, a two-tongued strip of hardened brown leather. Without even looking up, he would mutter in half-amused, saccharine tones, "Well, Docherty? Have we done our homework this week? No? A pity! Come OUT! Hold out your hand!" Bam! Bam! Bam!

I cannot recall that I ever winced. My anger seemed to cauterize the pain; besides, I did not wish to give him the satisfaction of knowing that it hurt or that I could be cowed by him. I merely returned to my seat at the back of the class in a moody silence, nursing my throbbing left hand under my right armpit—fully aware of the sympathetic looks from the girls. I hoped Margaret would notice my stoic reaction.

This spartan regimen finally drove me to attempt to get into my unresponsive head the verses to be memorized. Came a certain Tuesday, second period; the teacher entered, reaching already for his strap. But before he bawled out my name, I had answered his question: "Yes, sir!"

"Really, Docherty? Well! I believe that the poem this week is Christina Rossetti's 'Up-Hill.' "

"Yes, sir! 'Does the road wind up-hill all the way? / Yes, to the very end.' " Confidence was returning with every word. " 'Will the day's journey take the whole long day? / From morn to night, my friend.' " Then darkness descended. I seemed to remember it had something to do with beds ("Will there be beds for me and all who seek?"); I ventured, "Will there be enough beds for me. . . ."

"Not when I'm finished with you, Docherty! Come OUT to the floor!"

Charlotte Fleming rescued me from this educational treadmill. First she won over my confidence with her warm smile and alert eyes; realizing memory work might be more difficult for me than for others, she simply asked me to read the poems. She knew I was not stupid; I stood third in the class exams. When the words seemed to whirl around my head like a carousel, she just smiled patiently. "Now, George, why do you pucker your brows as if you were bearing the burdens of the whole world? Don't try too hard. Let us read the poem, even if you cannot memorize it. It's the sound and the meaning that really matter."

And I would read to her a poem whose words meant absolutely nothing to me, though I loved the sound of them.

> Quinquereme of Nineveh, from distant Ophir,
> Rowing home to haven in sunny Palestine,
> With a cargo of ivory,
> And apes and peacocks,
> Sandalwood, cedarwood, and sweet white wine.

Many years afterwards I would preach a sermon — "Peacocks for Beauty and Apes for Laughter," from the biblical passage on which John Masefield based his poem (1 Kings 10:22) — and remember gratefully dear Charlotte Fleming, the wavy brunette hair, the smile.

My initiation into the music and magic of words coincided with my falling in love with Margaret. While Moses Miller instructed us in Euclid, Book 1, I would sit sighing, looking over at her as she shook her brown bobbed hair, hoping I would catch her eye. She had a slight lisp, delightful I thought, and her thumb bent backwards as she wrote. Every day at four o'clock I would be awaiting her at the school gate, eager to carry her books home.

Through Margaret I was introduced to her music teacher, Miss Isabel Marshall. Miss Marshall opened up to me the ineffable world of music. She was a plump, middle-aged woman with thick rimless spectacles, yet it seemed that her sensitivity to music and literature had brought out an inner serenity and joy. Though not a great soloist, despite a Gaund French violin, she was a teacher of infinite patience. From her I took violin lessons for six years, paid for out of my milk route earnings, though she seemed not to need our pennies and never wrote out her bills. Her sufficient reward was to hear us play, especially our string ensemble. Every Friday night about a dozen of us would gather in the parlor of her semi-detached villa — six first violins, four seconds, one viola (which she played), one cello, a double bass played by Mr. Kelly, who drove a streetcar, and a piano. Those adolescent years were filled with music in all its moods — courants by Corelli and Tartini, the haunting Elizabethan music of William Byrd, Bach (*Suite in D. for Strings*), Handel (*Watermusic*), Haydn (the delightful *Toy Symphony*), and, happiest of all, Mozart's *Eine Kleine Nachtmusik* — "music of heaven" as Karl Barth has described it. For me, Heaven will always be playing second fiddle in Mozart and Beethoven string quartets.

Miss Marshall believed it brought out our confidence to compete at the various musical festivals held annually around the country at Lanark, Greenock, Edinburgh, Glasgow, and once as far south as Blackpool, where I played first fiddle in Schubert's *Trout Quintet*. It was a disaster; midway through the *allegro*, my fingers slipped off the fingerboard when negotiating a seventh position on the E string. Once I competed in the senior violin solo class at the Glasgow Musical Festival held in the great St. Andrews Hall. The competition was in two parts. In the morning session, competitors played a violin arrangement of the Chorale from Bach's Cantata 156, "Ich steh mit einem Fuss im Grave." The title reflected my state of mind, though I played this *adagio expressivo* well enough to be chosen as one of the three finalists to play at the afternoon session an *allegretto* by Locatelli demanding delicate *spicatto* bowing; mastery of the bow is the great challenge for all violinists. The other two finalists played the piece *andante*, the notes and bowing exactly right, but the running happy mood of the piece destroyed. I marched onto the platform exactly as I had seen the great Fritz Kreisler walk on this same platform, my violin dangling by my side, held delicately by the scroll in my left hand, bow poised in my right, ready for action. My instrument duly tuned, I nodded to my accompanist, gave a furtive look toward Miss Marshall in the third row, anxiety written all over her gentle face, and attacked the piece *molto vivace*. As every beginner knows, paradoxically we play faster and faster when we do not know a piece well. I finished with a flourish of my bow that brought ringing applause just short of a standing ovation in contrast to the cool hand clapping awarded the other two performers.

The adjudicator, a Miss Knocker, strode onto the platform in a tweed costume with tie and cashmere stockings, her heels echoing in the sparsely filled hall. "Now we come to competitor number three," she announced in a deep contralto voice, removing her pince-nez and doodling them at the end of a black silk cord, her exasperation obvious to all. "Let me put it this way, ladies and gentlemen: I have been adjudicating at musical festivals for nigh some twenty-five years all around the country. Never before have I witnessed as I have seen this afternoon such a musical fraud perpetrated upon an unwitting public. This young man strides onto the platform like a maestro, plays Locatelli at twice the speed of a normal *allegretto*, his fingers often on one string, his bow on the other, and finishes the piece with a sweep of the bow that would have done credit to Paganini, much to the apparent appreciation and delight of this bemused and victimized audience. I give him seventy-two marks for his courage in not stopping."

After school hours I was a soap boy for Mr. Sarolli, the barber, an immaculate Italian with a Rudolph Valentino face. His shop stood on Maryhill Road at Queens Cross, beside the strangely haunting yet paganistic architecture of a Rennie Mackintosh church. I also worked on Saturday mornings, a busy time, when conversation scintillated (no radio blared in our shop) and Jimmy the Scot kept up a running patter as he and Frank the Italian moved with the grace of ballet dancers from chair to chair, scything away the mountains of foam I had piled up on the faces of the customers.

"It's no' good for your health, sitting in that barber's all day on Saturday," mother would say. While I sat on my hands on the hard wooden bench in the shop awaiting the next batch of customers, my friends were enjoying themselves dribbling down the wings of some soccer pitch or punting lozenge-shaped ruggerballs between high H uprights. Delivering milk in the mornings was much healthier and took up less time. Before long I got a job at the Co-operative Dairy on Maryhill Road. Up every morning at five, Sundays included, I would race through the Big Park to book my place in the line of boys awaiting their cans. Armed with my first delivery of six quart cans and three pint cans (and a half pint can for Mrs. Campbell's cream), I would stagger down a deserted Maryhill Road, dark from October until March, silent except for the occasional rumbling streetcar, swaying and crowded with workmen, and the clang of the driver's bell to frighten away a furtive cat picking its way slowly and delicately through rain puddles in the causey stone street. On occasion, I excitedly would wave to my father when I caught sight of him, smoking his pipe, smiling back at me and waving happily, seated in the open rear deck, bound for the south side of the river, where he would be working on a new suburban garden.

I plodded with heavy milk cans up worn stone spiral tenement stairways reeking of stale humanity, past the bubbling gas-mantled stairhead lights, my tackety boots sending up echoes around me, rousing a paper-curled sleepy housewife in spacious flannel nightgown, the inevitable stray cat at her feet as she poured the contents of my can into a white enamel jug. My delivery over, it was runningly back to the dairy, the empty cans reverberating in the awakening streets like symbols in a Wagnerian overture.

For two years, this was the routine seven days a week, summer mornings with a burnished sun blinking between the lums on the rooftops of the tenements, dreich winter mornings with the rain stotting off my fisherman's oilskin cap and cape supplied by the Co-op. After a breakfast of porridge, with milk in a separate bowl, and dressed in fresh clothes and crested school cap, hair brilliantined, brogues polished, I would be on my way, head high and whistling, eager for that smile from Margaret as I entered the classroom and made my way to the back seat.

Margaret was my sweetheart for three years — from a distance. We never kissed, save on one occasion, a Hallowe'en party at Miss Marshall's, when we played Post Office. My lips touched her cheek just under the left ear. Our first and only date was to be a picnic. She would bring the sandwiches, I would buy the lemonade, and we would tramp along the canal bank, thence out to Killermont and Hillfoot, where we would sit and picnic under a tree near the foundations of the Roman Antonine Wall, which severs Scotland from Clyde to Forth. I had gone over the exact ground the previous day, but on the appointed morning — sun-kissed it was — I waited for two hours, my heart pounding, beside the locks of the canal, watching the waters gush between the sluices of the ancient lock gates. She never turned up. Two days later, a postcard, our only love letter, explained how a certain cousin from Ireland had arrived unexpectedly.

In June of 1926, at the confident age of fifteen, I joyfully and irrevocably parted company from school and everything associated with classrooms — noisy corridors thronged with bantering students, period bells like fire engine alarms, the smell of the chemistry lab, the gnawing anxiety about homework. I came out fourth in the class in the Lower Dayschool Certificate Examination. The headmaster suggested that I stay on at school, take my Highers, and enter the University; but not even my fertile imagination could stretch that far.

Brimming with brash confidence on that last unforgettable day, I bounded into the room where Madgie had been specially invited, over tea, to witness this epochal event in our family. "I'm finished with school, forever! I'm going out to get a job and I'm going to make lots of money and you'll never again have to worry about making ends meet. And that is true for you too, Madgie. I'm going to become famous and make enough money to keep you both for the rest of your lives."

Of course there had to be one last fling during that memorable summer of 1926. In the Wee Park, I pretended to be Bobby Jones (who had won the Open that year) with my father's walking stick and gutta-percha balls. And there was cricket. That year (or was it in 1928?) a fair-haired young cricketer with the Australian team, Don Bradman, had with effortless glances, drives, cuts, and an occasional six over the boundary shredded the English bowling.

Every morning I rose late, mother having been given specific instructions that I would "lie in." There were outings alone or with my pal Bert

Scott, trekking the bottle-green moors around Milngavie under the shadows of Dungoyne, the nub at the end of the Campsie Fells.

At summer's end, when the first touch of frost gleamed on the grass and my friends studying for the university resumed their trek to school, I bestirred myself to conquer the world. Unhurriedly I sauntered the two miles to the Maryhill Public Library Reading Room, spacious and square, bright from the sun streaming through the central glass dome and smelling of rubber doormats and printer's ink, and stood in a row of melancholy silent men in drab grey suits and cloth caps, their eyes roving the newspapers fixed in racks along the oak-paneled walls, part of the lengthening line of unemployed, though I did not seem to number myself with them. I soon found what I was looking for: "Office Boy; smart; shipping office. Lower Dayschool Certificate essential; Box number. . . ." From a book borrowed from the library, *How to Apply For a Job*, I copied out in my fine cursive handwriting: "Having seen by your advertisement in today's *Glasgow Herald* for a smart boy, I beg. . . ."

With this masterpiece in my pocket, I walked the three miles downtown to Buchanan Street, deposited it in the brass "Answers to Advertisements" receptacle in the *Glasgow Herald* building, and then spent an idle day sauntering around Kelvingrove Park. Back home, I awaited the reply that would most assuredly arrive within three days. Two weeks passed before I convinced myself that the letter must somehow have gone astray.

For the next four months, I made the same weary pilgrimage six days a week to the Maryhill Public Library, joining the lengthening line of the unemployed, and then trudged downtown to the *Glasgow Herald* office, in my pocket sometimes as many as ten letters replying to advertisements: "Having seen by your advertisement . . . ," vainly, eagerly, awaiting news from the big world. After delivering my letters to the *Herald* office, I would visit on foot literally scores of offices, especially shipping offices: Paddy Henderson, The Clan Line, The Anchor Line, Furness Withy, Chris Salveson. I visited wholesale businesses, located at the top of dark, stale stairs down by the Broomielaw Piers. The ritual was always the same: when I did manage to get beyond the youth of my own age, obviously the office boy, and had an opportunity to speak with a senior clerk, I noted he would scrutinize my school tie before replying that he "greatly regreted. . . ." (All the other clerks were wearing Academy, High School, or Kelvinside Academy ties.)

On December 15 there arrived through our letterbox a neatly typed envelope from a firm of lawyers, Fyfe, MacLean, and Co., 21 West George Street. A Mr. Kerr wished to interview me for the position of office boy. Excitedly I pressed my Sunday suit, smearing the inside of the trousers with Lifebuoy soap to enhance the crease, brushed my school cap, tucked a handkerchief into the upper pocket of my jacket, and, with shoes sparkling, arrived exactly on the dot of the appointed time, having gone over the ground the previous day to be quite sure of the distance. Mr. Kerr, a courtly, white-haired gentleman with bony hands and shrunken skin, peered over his pince-nez, sizing me up as he outlined my duties as an office boy: opening morning mail, copying letters in the hand press copier, delivering letters to downtown offices, and (what really terrified me) supervising a rather complicated telephone exchange. Up to this time I had never in my life spoken on the telephone. I got the job: eight shillings and fourpence a week, 9 A.M. until 6 P.M., with an hour and a quarter for lunch and half holiday on Saturday.

On my first day delivering letters, accompanied by Tom Williamson, whom I was succeeding, I was introduced to this Artful Dodger's skill of avoiding trouble.

"Always shuffle papers when Old Kerr's head appears," Tom advised. "He has gimlet eyes. Watch out for MacLean, a holy terror when aroused. You will have no trouble with Mr. Fyfe; he's a kind old bachelor. And my advice to you is to get out of this place as quickly as you can. It's a dead-end unless you are apprenticed as a lawyer, and that means going to the university."

It took a year to escape; but all in all, these were happy months. I was able to buy a new suit — on tic. I purchased a rail commuter ticket and Monday through Friday caught the 8:20 A.M. from Maryhill Station, where as a child I had seen the soldiers go off to the war. I recall still the feel of the cold, soot-covered, brass carriage door handle as I swung into the nonsmoking compartment and crouched at the window seat to read a book (or more likely to daydream), and the chug of the train as it thundered through Botanic Gardens Station and accelerated downhill underground to Kelvinbridge, rumbling into the cavernous tunnel to Stobcross Station and, through billowing clouds of sulphuric smoke, reaching the lower level of Central Station with its begrimed white tiles where, climbing the stairs under the vast, glass-roofed concourse echoing with hissing steam and engine whistles, I mingled with a happy sense of community in the hurrying throng.

Six mornings a week, in all weathers, I set out happily on my round of deliveries armed with a black Gladstone bag stuffed full of letters for lawyers, stockbrokers, insurance agents, and shipping companies. Every day was like a voyage of discovery. Glasgow belonged to me as I whistled my way through an enchanting world of sight and sound, of the bells of colored streetcars, the honking of fussy impatient motorists, the rushing pedestrians (they never walk in Glasgow) in what the poet laureate John Betjeman has called the finest Victorian city in the United Kingdom. Outside the office stood the massive finger of the steeple of St. George's Tron, built in 1807 and demarcating the western boundary of the city, and to its left the Atheneum, with its four Ionic columns, the Royal Faculty of

Procurators, a Roman piazza in the heart of the city. Eastward was the massive banded masonry, topped with a majestic central tower, of the City Chambers, through whose main doorway I often walked, over the variegated marble floors of the spacious entrance hall and up the wide Italian marble staircase; one might have been visiting the Doge's Palace in Venice. Before it, facing west, stands the city cenotaph—clean, smooth granite commemorating the dead of the First World War, its two functionally carved recumbent lions sitting sphinxlike, as if recalling "at the going down of the sun, we shall remember them."

George Square is a clutter of monuments raised to important personages whose lives have impinged upon the history of the city. Of course Queen Victoria is there, and Prince Albert, as well as Burns and Gladstone and Peel and David Livingstone and a Mr. Oswald, whose fame escapes me, except that "his top hat in hand [is] an ageless temptation for small boys to lob things into," as Maurice Lindsay notes. Perched on a single fluted Corinthian column, twin to the Nelson column in Trafalgar Square in London, stands the figure of Sir Walter Scott, too far out of sight to note exactly whether, as has been said, his plaid is drawn across the wrong shoulder.

I would dally watching the pantomine at the foot of West Nile Street, where the trace horse boys would haggle about their turn to buckle their horses to the overloaded lorries that had to be hauled up the steep incline toward Buchanan Street station. Wily horses these; they have been known to step to the end of the line when it came their turn to haul the load.

To be an office boy—is there a more pleasant time-killing occupation, demanding not the slightest initiative or drive or ambition? I loved it, and with youth's indifference to the passing of time, I was tempted to be content. That is, until I was suddenly frightened out of this dead-end world by the imperious threatenings of Miss Morrison, Mr. Kerr's middle-aged secretary. Day by day she strode like a sergeant major past me perched on my stool at the high office desk, a sheaf of letters in her hand to be copied, stamped, and mailed or delivered by me. Late one afternoon she broke her silence: "George Docherty. What on earth are you doing here?"

"Copying letters, Miss Morrision," I quaked.

"Don't be sillier than you look, boy. I mean, What are you doing in this office? Do you intend to be like Mr. Smith over there?"

Mr. Smith was seated on his own high stool, a sad-faced, frail, white-haired man, his red-rimmed eyes peering through thick spectacles, his shoulders hunched over an enormous ledger, its edge turned like a wave of the sea, into which he laboriously copied the office accounts. "Mr. Smith has been at that same job for thirty years. Do you want to be doing that for the next thirty years, boy? If not, get out of this office and as soon as you can."

Without awaiting my response (I had none; I was too taken aback) she strode on and never again brought up the subject as she continued her walk at the end of each day past me atop my high stool.

Mr. Smith, a kind of Marley's ghost, disturbed the even tenor of those carefree days. Finally I took action. I went to Mr. Fyfe and explained to him that since I did not intend to become a lawyer but would prefer a job in a shipping office, could he, with his shipping connections, get me a job elsewhere? He returned a not unkind, but quizzical look!

To improve my chances for another job, I attended night classes in Pitman's shorthand, bookkeeping, and commercial French. I resumed the pilgrimage to the Maryhill Public Library reading room, where the line of men reading the newspapers looked ominously longer. Some fellows who had left school with me were still without work; some seemed to have no hope of ever being employed.

I applied for the civil service, but my place in the examination competition was too far down to warrant a job. On one occasion, I was interviewed by the head office manager of the Glasgow Savings Bank in Ingrim Street. He was a Presbyterian elder whom years later I would meet under rather different circumstances.

"Is this the only suit you own? We like our clerks to be well-groomed. Tell me about your home. Bedroom? Bathroom? Let me hear how well you can read. When meeting with the public you will appreciate that we like our clerks to be well-spoken." He reached for a tome of Banking Law and I blundered through a few incoherent paragraphs. "Well, Mr. Docherty, we do like your handwriting and would be happy to see it in our ledgers. Come to the office tomorrow morning at ten for the written examination we always set applicants."

All I recall from this miserable experience was the question: "Spell out '9'; '9th'; '19'; '90.' " To this day I'm not sure which is the number without the *e*. I never found out whether I passed or not, but I did recognize when I passed the bank a ginger-haired fellow, one of the twelve candidates, at work.

Finally, after an otherwise not very memorable Friday night rehearsal of our string ensemble, Alex Livingston, our principal violin, asked me whether I would like a job in a shipping agent's office. It seemed he was employed in an office that had received one of my letters of application. He put in a good word on my behalf. I got the job: customs clerk — with prospects of advancement.

The office of the firm of shipping agents, Messrs. Davidson, Park, and Speed, Ltd., was in the Waterloo Chambers at 19 Waterloo Street, across Hope Street from the Central Station, in a six-story, soot-caked, red sandstone structure with a haunted Dickensian air about it. The main floor entrance was a dimly lit cavern that led to an antiquated self-propelled elevator in an open lift shaft surrounded by a spiral stairway. On the fourth floor, at the end of a dark corridor on a pale frosted glass window door, the name of the firm was painted in black. I knocked and entered a very cramped office. At one of the bay windows sat a girl on a three-legged stool operating a telephone exchange. A pleasant girl, she smiled as she came over to meet me. She was about my own age, too — sixteen.

"You'll be the new customs clerk? I'm Jerry Watson."

Her voice bore no hint of a Glasgow accent; she wore a white cashmere cardigan over a knee-length print frock; hazel eyes sparkled under fair eyebrows, touched up a little with black eyebrow pencil. Her bobbed blonde hair swept away over her left ear, revealing a single pearl earring. She was about five feet tall, and walked gracefully.

In no time I was finding Miss Watson a most helpful colleague.

"Miss Watson, I wonder if you would get me on the telephone the Clan Line . . . Mr. Russell at 20 Queen Dock . . . the Customs House . . . Collins in Cathedral Street. Where are these new *ad valorem* duty forms for F. W. Woolworth?"

I was actually giving orders — and loving it. No longer an office boy running at everyone's beck and call, I was dreaming of better things in the world of commerce and shipping.

My work took me every morning to the Customs House in Clyde Street, where the river is surprisingly narrow and the tidal waters end at the weir. Thence by streetcar, I would wind my way down to the docklands, Queen's dock particularly, to meet ships from Hamburg and Swedenburg, laden with china for Woolworth's and rolls of newsprint paper for Collins, our largest customers.

One year after I joined the firm, we moved to a new office building at 200 St. Vincent Street, more modern and commodious. Our office was on the top (the seventh) floor, commanding a splendid view of the city to the east and of the great Glasgow shipyards to the west, and in the foreground "Greek" Thomson's splendid church, a latter-day Parthenon.

There I spent four years, content, for the most part, as a shipping clerk, a happy life, confined but not confining, and rich in friendships. I lived comfortably on my salary, as my needs were few. I possessed a cat's-whisker wireless set, complete with headphones, on which magically through the static came a human voice or a Chopin nocturne. Our little string ensemble broadcast on the Children's Hour, where, in the BBC's first studio in Bath Street, I first met "Aunt Kathleen" Garscadden, a significant pioneer in the early days of radio. Through the wireless I was also introduced to a new world of melody: the diapason saxophone playing "Ramona," and the tunes "If I Had a Talking Picture of You" and "I'm Dancing with Tears in My Eyes, for the Girl in My Arms Isn't You." My introduction to the rhythm of black music was Layton and Johnson singing "The Birth of the Blues."

Ruchill Church was the lodestar of these maturing days, the center of my little universe. Saturday afternoons and long summer evenings were spent at "Sandyflats," the twenty-acre tract of land on the edge of the city where the River Kelvin meandered near Killermont Golf Course, donated by Ruchill's affluent mother church, Westbourne, for the use of the young people in Ruchill. I played tennis, and could volley with top spin. In the church dramatic club, I played the handsome hero Laurance Blake in a comedy, *Paddy, the Next Best Thing.* Winter evenings were devoted to the Young People's Federation, where, with a rather notorious reputation as a debater, I would make a speech at the drop of a hat. Once I successfully debated the affirmative on the proposition "The Pen Is Mightier Than the Sword."

All of us were working-class lads — apprentice plumbers, painters, carpenters, a baker, office clerks like myself, and some few bound for the university as teachers and doctors. The Federation was the training ground for our growing minds. Walker MacGregor was the experienced Socrates to us young Platos. A sculptor by trade, stolid, and at times taciturn, he was an authority on Robert Burns, and, like so many who have missed the privilege of a university education, possessed a large and well-thumbed library. Behind the daunting exterior burned a deep love for us; even his negative arguments were meant to challenge us to make us think for ourselves.

Two significant lifelong friendships were born out of these years.

Bert Scott was the musician, a fine pianist. We would argue endlessly about the competing merits of the piano and the violin, but when we played together, it was to discover — from the first trivial pieces to Mozart sonatinas and Beethoven sonatas — that the violin and piano are wedded as no other two instruments. Bert, a gentle soul, made music his vocation, teaching in public schools, and on Sundays serving as organist and choir-master in several fine city churches. He carried into manhood a benign aloofness to the brokenness of life, almost as if childhood innocence never quite forsook him. He was a good man who believed that others were like himself. I never listen to Chopin's *Polonaise Militaire* without seeing the thirteen-year-old Bert seated before the antique walnut upright piano by Chappell of London ben the room in his home in Maryhill Road, thumping out the dominant chords with his strong fingers, drowning out the noises in the street below.

Moses Cochrane was the philosopher, my intellectual mentor. When we first met, he was employed in some menial job in a wholesale ware-house in the city and was studying at nights for his Preliminary Examination to the University. He lived in basic poverty, top flat, room and kitchen, in a decaying ashlar tenement with his widowed aunt and younger brother, both parents having died in his poverty-blighted childhood. Chronic malnutrition had left its marks in later life: he was gaunt, almost skeletal, of pasty complexion, and wore thick horn-rimmed glasses, but his soft brown hair was ever carefully groomed, his clothes meticulously cared for. He walked erect, spoke in a fine Scottish accent without trace of Anglice, and in his open face one discerned the reflection of an inward peace, the harvest of much pain. He had no time for games (tennis was a bourgeois horror to him), but kept fit by endless walking — and talking — mile upon mile.

After the evening service in those long summer Sabbaths, Moses and I would stroll along the canal bank or out into the lovely hinterland of Maryhill past little farms and the "Skittery Woods." Moses could strike a Keats-like pose, his long black-and-gold university scarf trailing behind in the wind, a rough-cut ash stick in hand, gesticulating as he argued, sometimes pausing to make a point clear, and displaying the omniscience known only to first-year university students, while I, not so well tutored, valiantly tried to keep up my end.

"Moses, you are talking just a lot of nonsense! Why do you make matters so complicated? It is simply a question of being either true or false."

Whereupon he would stop in his tracks, a look of pitying patience on his face, and place his left hand gently, almost paternally, on my shoulder.

"My dear George! I wish I could make you understand. No question is ultimately simple. You talk of 'truth' and 'falsity.' Don't you realize that Aristotle founded a new science, Formal Logic, precisely to discover what is true and what is false?"

"I know that two plus two equals four. You can't deny that simple statement."

"Ignoring for the moment your comment that two plus two is a simple statement of fact, let me enlighten you, my dear George, that according to Albert Einstein, when you are dealing with Reality at the speed of light, then two plus two equals two."

"Moses, I refuse to be drawn up your philosophical closes."

Frequently we would walk and talk until midnight, treating each other to a "Scots convoy": he would see me to my close mouth and I would return the favor, back and forth until finally one of us reluctantly trudged up to bed.

By this time our family had moved to 38 Hotspur Street, a two-room-and-kitchen flat with a bathroom, hot and cold running water, walley close, and hallway with painted glass door. My mother had made it!

When I was seventeen, I decided to join the Church, to make a commitment to Jesus as savior, and, instead of arguing about the faith, to commit myself to it. I am sure that Moses Cochrane influenced me: the serenity he displayed in a life that ought to have caused heartbreak, his determination one day to "wag his heid in a pulpit," his gift for friendship. There was also Alf Gray, a tall, gangling, lovable fellow. He approached me one Sunday after church: "By the way, George, we need Sunday School teachers and you seem a likely fellow. Of course, we cannot allow you to teach until you attend instruction classes."

A preposterously audacious remark, I thought; I needed no instruction in anything! But Alf insisted. We became friends. I began to learn something of the wonder and majesty of the New Testament. John Campbell, an elder and our Sunday School superintendent, a Highlander from Campbelltown, spoke quietly and persuasively with the slight tang of the Isles. His own certainty in the faith was a bulwark against which I used to throw my half-digested understanding of the Bible.

"I don't care how you rationalize this, Mr. Campbell," I burst out one Sunday as we went over the lesson for the following Sunday. "I just don't believe that an angel came down from heaven and turned a key in the door of the prison where Peter was confined."

Mr. Campbell just smiled. Wiser than I realized then, he knew I was searching for some coherence to my faith. I became a Sunday School department leader.

The Sunday services at Ruchill Church had an abiding influence. Regularly I was in my pew in the gallery along with some hundred other boys of the 69th Boys Brigade. In the pulpit our minister, Mr. Law, loomed large—round smooth face, dark hair glinting under the pulpit light, clerical collar half-hidden behind the white slash of the Edinburgh M.A. hood, his ordination tabs radiantly white against his spacious Geneva gown. He symbolized for me goodness; his diligence and kindness helped to shape for me the ideal of the Christian ministry.

His sermons, I fear, I do not recall, but unforgettable were the services of the Lord's Supper. From my vantage point in the gallery I surveyed the church, the spotless Irish linen covering the backs of the pews, transforming it into a single Table of the Lord. On the hour, as the organist brought his prelude to a quiet conclusion, Mr. Jack, the beadle, appeared through a side door at the pulpit, reverently ascended the steps, pulpit Bible, hymnbook, and psalter in his hands, switched on the light, and with one final adjustment to the Bible on the reading board, descended the steps, where at the bottom Mr. Law was awaiting. When the minister had entered the pulpit and engaged in his private devotions, hand over bowed head, Mr. Jack returned, snecked the door closed, and made his way to a pew nearby, ready for any request the minister might make during the service. In the ensuing silence, Mr. Law rose to his full height, surveyed his people, and with a carrying voice announced: "LET US WORSHIP GOD" (never, "may we?" or "shall we?" as if there were any other purpose for bringing the folk to the kirk).

At the distribution, the elders moved toward Mr. Campbell and Mr. Barclay, seated on either side of the minister, receiving at their hands the plates of bread and the trays of wine, unhurriedly bearing in their hands

35

the mystery of the body and blood of Christ to the expectant faithful. On weekdays these men may have been plumbers, carpenters, bricklayers, motor mechanics, school teachers, or laborers, but on the communion Sabbath they were priests unto the Lord, treading in holy silence broken only by the squeak of an elder's new Sunday boots or the stifled cough of a worshiper.

Those of us lads sitting in the gallery did not "partake," since we were not full communicating members of the church. My own situation was somewhat complicated: I had not been baptized as a child. In those early years, my father and mother had moved much from one job to another, and I suppose as the years passed they had omitted "to get it done," as they say in Scotland. Mr. Law was quite understanding. I was admitted as a full member of the Church of Christ one Sunday morning in the vestry in the presence of two elders by adult baptism. One of the elders, John Campbell, placed his arm around my shoulder—a concession to his Highland shyness—as if to indicate that his wayward prodigal had at last entered the fold of the kirk. He was my father in the Lord. On the back of my now-yellowing birth certificate in Mr. Law's handwriting is the laconic notation "Baptised 18th November, 1928. Harry Law."

Looking back, I am now convinced that Mr. Law was perhaps a bit too accommodating to the mood of those days. Had he challenged me to stand in the face of the congregation, take my vows, and be baptized, it would have been for this shy and sensitive lad significantly more declaratory.

"Ah! You have too many irons in the fire," said Mr. Troup, a kindly officer at the Customs House, as over *ad valorem* duty forms I shared with him the many projects I was involved in in my spare time. "Why don't you do one thing and concentrate on that?" He was right, and I knew it; but what to do? To what was I prepared to give all my energies, my undivided mind and heart?

The presence of Miss Watson in the office was not at all helpful. She was increasingly occupying more of my real thinking. I would consult her about all sorts of such inconsequential matters as lost files or request that she ferret out some obscure account. I found our conversations increasingly exciting. Once I daringly showed her a travel brochure depicting a moorish castle bathed in Spanish sunshine. Perhaps we would one day visit such places?

Every morning I was at my office desk before nine, shuffling papers with one eye on the door, awaiting her arrival. When she swept into the office like a burst of sunshine, she would look over to my desk for the sign: thumbs up if the boss, Mr. Davidson, had not yet arrived; head in hands if he had already been inquiring about her.

Years later, when I read C. S. Lewis's description of "joy," I recognized the bewildering emotions I had been experiencing: "an unsatisfied desire which is itself more desirable than any other satisfaction . . . a particular kind of unhappiness or grief . . . a kind we want . . . [not to be exchanged] for all the pleasures in the world."

I was falling in love. I wanted to sit down and write her long letters describing how I felt, but I always balked at the last moment. I wrote her a short story about lovers, of the lad who was too shy to speak to his girl. She said that one day I would write a great romance.

In the long winter nights I would go out and walk alone down deserted main streets or along the canal bank until, unable to bear the solitude, I would stop at the nearest phone box and dial her number, wondering as it rang why it took her so long to answer. Where was she? Was she ill? Or out? With whom? And when she did answer, I would have to cast about for some plausible reason for calling at 10:30 P.M.

Every night after office I walked her to her train at St. Enoch's Station, bound for the little suburb of Kennishead, where she, her mother, and her brother Jim lived with her Aunt Gracie. I'd watch her board, the quick wave and smile that I cherished until the morrow, then dash over to Central Station in time to catch my own train.

We had a kindred love of drama. In those depressing days of 1929 the theaters were only half filled. We saw *Dear Brutus* and the beautiful Maud Risdon in *Mary Rose*, and at Christmas *Peter Pan*, when I clapped as loudly as the children, to prove I too believed in fairies.

Shortly after my nineteenth birthday, Miss Watson and I decided to celebrate the King's birthday holiday, which falls in May, by spending the day together picnicking. We took the streetcar to Hillfoot, then set off on a five-mile trek through the salubrious suburb of Bearsden and over the winding Stockiemuir road. We reached a wood on the top of the hill commanding a splendid view of the city in the far distance, its shipbuilding cranes and university tower clearly descried in the clear spring air of that sunny day. We scrambled over the roadside ditch, trying to avoid the spreading prickly bramble bushes, through green fern fronds of bracken into the wood, where in an opening beneath silver birches, beech trees, and a towering oak we spread out a tartan shawl on the cold soft moss blanketed with long-dead dry leaves, and watched the sunbeams like glittering lances dappling a shimmering carpet of bluebells. It was like Barrie's wood in *Mary Rose* on the little Highland "isle-that-likes-to-be-visited," except that our May wood echoed with song. All through the timeless day we could hear in the distance the repetitive plaint of an unseen cuckoo.

Miss Watson had brought sandwiches, and tea in a thermos flask. Came dessert.

"A special treat," she boasted. "Made it myself. Marizipan potatoes."

I popped one of the attractive brown-coated confections into my mouth and suddenly gulped as if I had swallowed a pepper pot.

"Oh, dear," gasped Miss Watson, spluttering. "The recipe said 'toss into cinnamon.' I must have tossed them into cayenne pepper."

All the long day, we blethered and laughed together. I must have been talking about me. And the future. And the things I believed. And dreams about castles in Spain.

The sun's rays dipped lower; the virgin green beech leaves rustled in the rising, suddenly chill breeze; the birds ceased their song. My heart was thudding. In the cool silence our eyes met, as if for the first time.

"Jerry, my dear, I want to marry you."

3

Called to the Dignitie of a Preachour

I shall be telling this with a sigh
Somewhere ages and ages hence.
Two roads diverged in a wood and I —
I took the one less traveled by,
And that has made all the difference.
— Robert Frost, "The Road Not Taken"

In this town and church, did God first call me to the dignitie of a preachour.
— John Knox; inscribed in the porch of Holy Trinity Church, St. Andrews

AS I WALKED home from the office one spring evening — it was Wednesday, March 25, 1931 — I decided to be a preacher. I can still point to the exact spot at Charing Cross, despite massive urban renewal in the area, under the *grand horloge* set in the wall of the fine curving facade of Charing Cross Mansions. Once more its gold face tells the exact time, but on that evening the hands were missing, its windworn face corroded with rust. For me also time stood still, though the hurrying Glaswegians did not realize that this twenty-year-old lad in the heather tweed suit, soft hat in hand, head tilted to the side, was striding off the map of his life.

Not that this was an experience of conversion. It was a commitment to the ministry of the Church. It seemed so natural. I was not aware of a voice within me calling, "Come, and I will make you a fisher of men." No ball of light flashed out of the blue heavens casting me to the ground like Saul on the Damascus Road. There were only the noises of city streets: nesting sparrows twittering in the eves, the whine of streetcar wheels grinding their way around the curving tram tracks, and the metallic echo of the hooves of the Clydesdales straining under their heavy loads from the docks.

I envisioned myself henceforth as a tonsured monk in cassock and sandals walking slowly, head bent in his breviary, over the flagstones of a Gothic cloister garth, the music of Ketelby's "In a Monastery Garden" in the background.

A Freudian would immediately deduce that this young man was seeking escape from life; that was partly true. The fact is I had grown deeply dissatisfied with my life, bored with the daily commuter trains jammed with the office crowd, the monotony of desk work with its customs forms and bills of lading. It was an uncommitted life; the specter raised by Miss Morrison, my guardian angel of the lawyers' office, was beginning to haunt me again.

My social life was by no means monotonous. Indeed, exciting experiences at Ruchill Church were actually insulating me from the serious part of life. I was like the Parisian gutter sweeper who, when asked by Robert Louis Stevenson how he could possibly endure such a life, replied, "Ah monsieur, au nuit, nous sommes serieux!"

Now it was quite clear. Like Moses Cochrane, I wanted to "wag my heid in the pulpit." There was nothing complicated about it; I'd be a preacher, a friend to the aged, the sick, and the young. On that happy spring afternoon when the hand of the Lord was laid upon me, sufficient the prayer

> Keep thou my feet; I do not ask to see
> The distant scene — one step enough for me.

After dinner that evening and before mother had time to redd up the dishes, I shared the exciting news with my parents. "I'm going to be a minister! Made up my mind on the road home from work tonight. It'll mean going to the university for six years, but I think I know how I can save on costs. I shall file for unemployment benefits; that'll be 23 shillings a week, though I know it will be less than my wages of 35 shillings. I'll pass my preliminary examination by taking a course at Skerry's College in the evenings and work during the day, at least until September. And there are other ways I can save. I won't need any new clothes, at least not for a long time. I'll be saving the cost of my commuter ticket, three shillings a week. And when I go to the university, there can always be part-time work, and of course pulpit supply. I'll not be able to contribute much to the house, but will try not to be a burden."

The words flowed as in a torrent. Dad was silent at first. Mother, quite overwhelmed, gave me a kiss. "Don't worry, son. We'll manage to make ends meet."

Off I dashed, bounding down the stairs two at a time, to tell Moses Cochrane the great news. I doubt that I paused even to say thank you to two amazing parents; yet I like to think they knew that in my heart I was grateful.

I climbed the worn stone stairs of the turnpike staircase at 13 Chapel Street and knocked at the door first on the left. Moses was seated in the welcoming glow of a kerosene lamp on his desk, its noxious odor mingling with the clammy fustiness of secondhand books.

"Moses," I burst out. "I'm going to be a minister."

"That's great, son," he said, rising and shaking my hand firmly and quite formally ("son" was a shy concession we used with one another in moments of affection).

The next morning at my office desk, I waited with more than the usual impatience for Jerry's grand entrance. I whispered to her beside the cabinets with the travel brochures of Spain and the Mediterranean, "I've got to see you! I've got important news for you."

At noon, above the roar of traffic in Hope Street, I shouted to her: "I'm going to be a minister!" as we hurried for her train.

She started to weep. I could never understand Jerry at times. She wept when she was happy, when she was sad, when she got a surprise, when she attended a movie or a play. We reached her carriage door. As the guard waved the green flag and whistled, I leapt into the moving train and sat down beside her. In that murky third-class G. S. W. Railway compartment I told my tale.

"How long will it take until you are through University?" she asked.

"Seven years, including a year at Skerry's College."

"That's a long time, George."

"Aye!" I replied grandly, "but you'll be a minister's wife and not a shipping clerk's."

By this time Jerry and I had what is called in Scotland an "understanding," a relationship short of official engagement that may not lead to marriage. Our courtship lasted seven years, like that of Jacob and Rachel. Four years later we were officially engaged. However, in those days thoughts of marriage were not to be entertained by a student studying for the ministry until his course was completed. The social mores dictated that you studied, you graduated, you were called to a church; only then were you married in the University Chapel and took your young bride to your first charge. On the lee of the years, I look back with regret, indeed some bitterness, that we should have delayed our marriage so long. It would have been possible when I got a student assistantship. We could have prepared for our life together in some anonymous Glasgow apartment. For reasons I did not really understand then but I can guess at now, our much-too-long courtship was fraught with arguments and tensions. On at least two occasions we came near to breaking up—but we kept together. Both of us realized that Jerry would be marrying the minister as well as the man. It was to be Jerry's calling as well as mine.

Skerry's College was an emporium in Glasgow that specialized with great success in getting the densest dullard through the university preliminary examinations. With uncanny skill, the fruit of years of tutoring, the wise oracles could spot the theorem of Euclid that would come up or the quotation from Shakespeare or Milton the examinee was required to spot, place in context, and exegete.

All that summer long I was every evening at my desk, a drop-leaf oak table set in the parlor bay window, my textbooks spread out in front of me — mathematics, English literature, history — glancing up toward the tip of the university tower in the far distance and upon East Park Church at our street corner: a constant reminder that the steps to the pulpit are disciplined study. Neither the lure of the tennis courts at Sandyflats nor peripatetics with Moses Cochrane enticed me from my self-imposed task of study. Saturday afternoons and Sundays were reserved for outings with Jerry. We went to a movie once every two weeks. We walked the country roads around Maryhill or through Rouken Glen Park or in the upland farmlands of Renfrewshire around Eaglesham. I would tell her of the adventures of the dashing Prince Hal and the colossal Falstaff from *Henry IV*, or the state of England in the days of the Domesday Book. Each Sunday morning, of course, I was in my place in the side gallery of Ruchill Church with the other fellows. Now I watched Mr. Law more carefully, noting especially how he conducted himself in the pulpit. On Sunday afternoons I tried out some new exegesis of Scripture on my Sunday School scholars. But study was never on Sundays, even when there was a Monday morning examination — though I was known to rise at four A.M. on the day of a test.

I resigned from the office in September 1931, having passed the first two subjects of the university examinations. Now I was to devote full-time study to Latin and Greek, endeavoring to cover in one year what the regular student had taken in at least four at High School. Finances seemed to work well. Mr. Stewart, the manager of the local unemployment exchange, which was meeting in our church hall, congratulated me on my decision to study for the ministry and said I was eligible for unemployment benefits until such time as I entered the university; he was satisfied I was preparing for a job.

Twice a week I signed on at the exchange and drew my unemployment allowance, a ritual easy for me, my future bright with some purpose. But for the men I chatted with, men with a haunted look and ironic humor, there seemed little hope. They were part of the 2,600,000 unemployed in Great Britain that year. Their visits to the reading room of the Maryhill Library were an exercise in futility, while billboards along the wayside depicted a pipe-smoking Prime Minister (Stanley Baldwin) assuring us that "prosperity was just around the corner."

Came the "means test," a desperate measure of a government devoid of new ideas. By virtue of the new regulation, one's eligibility for unemployment benefits was determined after taking into account the total combined income of all members of a family. This not only led to reduced unemployment compensation for most families but also imposed a new humiliation upon proud housewives, compelled by law to detail the family's meager income to some bowler-hatted official taking note of these intimate details of the family life. In our case the result was predictable: my father was working — self-employed — and since I was part of the same household, my dole of twenty-three shillings shrunk to four shillings and threepence.

I joined my father, digging alongside him in mud and mire, making it gleam like a Van Gogh landscape, watching him shape the contours of a beautiful flower garden or rockery. Evenings and Saturdays were devoted to the classics.

In September 1932, I sat higher and lower Latin and Greek; I failed all except lower Greek. Preparing for another attempt would delay my entrance into the university for a year. I noted in the fine print of the regulations that since only a limited number of candidates was admitted, a student of twenty-one years might be accepted if his examination papers were of "pass" standard. I promptly filed a claim to the Scottish Universities Board in St. Andrews.

Matriculation day at Scottish universities is the second Monday in October. It dawned; I had still received no word.

Next morning, I was urgently awakened by my mother. "Georgie! Look, son! A letter postmarked St. Andrews." It contained a single printed sheet of paper informing the recipient that he was eligible to attend any Scottish University with a view to graduation in the Faculty of Arts.

By nine, I was one of a long line of rowdy, loquacious students gathered in the Arts Quadrangle awaiting confirmation of their classes. As I completed the appropriate forms, I bumped into Moses Cochrane rushing off to his own classes.

"What are cognate subjects?" I asked desperately.

"Don't argue! Nobody really knows; and don't get into any discussion with Professor Thomson, the adviser of studies. He is a holy terror."

The line moved slowly until at last I found myself looking down at the balding pate, fringed with gray, of a middle-aged man wearing a black academic gown. Head down, he was muttering to himself, letting out occasional blasts at some timid freshman who had erroneously filled in the form. This was the adviser of studies at Scotland's most distinguished university! His advice to me took twenty-five seconds.

"Next," he boomed without looking up, taking my form in his hand. "Name?"

"George Docherty, sir," I muttered, clearing my throat.

"Cognate subjects?"

By now I knew. "English and Moral Philosophy, sir."

"Degree?"

"Master of Arts, sir. Ordinary."

He scrawled an indecipherable signature at the bottom of the page, pushed a small white card toward me and, without looking up, shouted "Next!"

The card read *civis universitatis Glasguensis*. Heady with excitement, I trailed away between the massive pillars that support the undercroft of the Bute Hall, looking for World History (ord.), the adviser's booming voice receding into the distance.

The University of Glasgow was founded by Bishop William Turnbull in 1451, fifty years later than St. Andrews, Scotland's first university. It originally stood in Townhead near the Cathedral and Bishop's Palace, but in 1860 a mercantile town council ruthlessly pulled down the seventeenth-century buildings in High Street to make room for railway sheds. The University was moved to the present splendid site on Gilmorehaill, where it commands a panoramic view of the entire city. All that has survived the vandalism of the town council are the lovely trapezoidal doorway now in the Lodge Gate on University Avenue and the elegant wide staircase embellished with unicorn and recumbent lion at the entrance to the memorial chapel.

At first the leisured life of the student, vastly different from the tightly scheduled routine of office work, went to my head. I strutted the two miles from our home in Hotspur Street resplendent in tweed jacket with leather patches mother had sewn at the elbows, baggy grey flannel trousers, black-and-gold striped tie, and scarf. Yet as soon as I mingled in the crowd of raucous students in the Arts Quadrangle, avoiding the trim greensward over which no student ever trod, I was overwhelmed with a desolating sense of inferiority. I was an incomer, my head crammed with ill-digested crash-program facts from Skerry's College.

"We shall not trouble to read the text of the *Canterbury Tales*, since every schoolboy already knows it almost by heart," announced Mr. Bickersteth of the English Lit. Class. I had not even heard the name Geoffrey Chaucer!

I read voraciously every word of the *Glasgow University Magazine*, edited by the students for students, but never dared to send in a contribution, fearing the knifing ridicule I knew I would be subject to in the next issue's editorial, "The Three Legged Chair." I never joined the Students' Union, not having the cash for the initiation fee, though I did attend union debates on open nights, sitting at the back, quite carried away by the oratory and the humor of the student speakers, dreaming that perhaps one day I might reach such Olympian heights of debate.

Greek was an agonizing experience. Having taken Classical Greek by correspondence, I did not understand even the transliteration of the Greek texts sonorously chanted by Professor Davis, let alone how to translate them. Once I got a zero for an "unseen" of Homer's *Iliad*, Book IX. Indeed, I passed my degree examination in Greek by native cunning rather than any acquaintance with the subject. I discovered in the Mitchell Library, while studying some examination papers of previous years, that Book IX of the *Iliad* appeared regularly at four-year intervals, and that on the previous two occasions the same passage had been given for translation in the degree examination. Now Dr. Davis was about to retire. Was it conceivable that this frail old scholar would, after thirty-five years, choose another passage for translation in this his last year? I hastened home and spent the whole evening before the examination concentrating on this single passage, until I could have translated it into prose, blank verse, or even rhyming pentameters. It was the passage chosen — I passed Greek!

Crowded into amphitheater classrooms, seated on narrow, cold wooden benches with little room for notebooks, some lucky to get a seat in the aisles, students feverishly took notes as the professors, quite unaware of our presence, read out their lectures at dictation speed. Typical was Professor Smart, a white-haired don who had played some part in the formulation of the Versailles Treaty at the end of World War I, his head bent over his lectures, which looked like a book of wallpaper samples, muttering away about the medieval Just Price, or was it the Theory of Mercantilism? In despair, we would shuffle our feet. He would look up in hurt surprise, remove his pince-nez, and inquire, "Is there anything the matter, ladies and gentlemen?"

"Can't hear you, sir."

"May I suggest you make less noise with your feet," he would respond, and resume his mumbling.

On the other hand, Scottish students were hardly docile. When a lecturer was late, he was greeted with a chorus of "Oh, Why Are We Waiting?" to the tune of *Adeste Fideles.* Any linguistic slip was seized upon with gleeful catcalls, the sound of popping corks, or slow clapping or scuffling of feet. One hapless lecturer, fresh from an Oxbridge donship, suddenly broke off one morning, slammed his lecture book shut, announced "Go to hell!" and strode off the platform. There was a mighty roar. We knew he had to return next day, when he was given a rousing reception. When he apologized, we cheered.

Two noble exceptions to this soulless system stand out.

Professor W. MacNeile Dixon, an erect Irishman with the wrinkled face of a *bon vivant,* his torn academic gown faded with age, processed into the classroom with the dignity of a mace bearer, placed his lectures on the podium, surveyed us, and with a solemn sweep of his mortar board, bowed to the class. Adjusting his monocle, he proceeded to lecture on Shakespeare with such authority that one got the impression he had just left the bard at the Mermaid Tavern. Of course, he never noticed or ever spoke to me; intimacy with such a visitor from Olympus was reserved for those taking an Honors degree.

The other was Archibald Allan Bowman, who introduced us raw recruits in philosophy to its technical vocabulary and enabled us for the rest of our lives to think conceptually. He had the Socratic gift; he brought philosophy down from the heights to the marketplace of our little minds.

His crowded class was a rowdy mob, the air filled with bantering catcalls; around our heads paper airplanes soared and nose-dived, and when the Professor was overdue, as usual our feet pounded out *Adeste Fidelis* on the wooden floor. Suddenly, as a symphony orchestra ceases tuning up when the conductor approaches his music stand, a silence dramatically fell on the class as Professor Bowman reached the platform, a little breathless from climbing the six flights of stairs leading to the classroom. He would smile broadly at the reception, apologize for his lateness, and begin his lecture with studied diction and pace. He still walked with the soldierly bearing of an officer of the First World War, but with his sandy moustache, brindle hair thinning on top, longish aquiline nose, and steel spectacles the figure he cut hardly accounted for his ability to cast an almost hypnotic sway over his classes and public meetings where he would protest against the iniquity of the idle rich parading their finery at Ascot in the midst of such tragic unemployment.

Bowman's universe of discourse was a dualism in which he distinguished two fundamental modes of being — nature and spirit, subject and object, self and nonself — held together in a monism in which spirit was always primary and supreme. His dialectic steered me between the Scylla of Berkeley's Subjective Idealism and the Charybdis of naive materialism. He set my course in philosophy and theology forever, enabling me to come to appreciate Sartre, Camus, and B. F. Skinner. In my New Testament studies, his training prepared me for Rudolf Bultmann's existentialist exegesis of the resurrection of Jesus. He set the tone for my generation of clergy.

Professor Bowman suggested to me, in the only personal conversation we ever had, that I should read Honors in Philosophy. But, in a hurry to get into my own parish, I made a decision I have lived to regret. Bowman died in June 1936 at the age of 53.

University life was unreservedly happy. New and lifelong friendships were born in the Student Christian Movement. I joined Christmas caroling in a (borrowed) red undergraduate gown under mist-haloed Glasgow streetlamps. Daft Friday dances in the Students' Union celebrated an end to the winter term, when Jerry and I not only *could* but *did* dance all night, and still we wished for more. Then it was breakfast under the balloons and the Christmas decorations in the Union Refectory, around 7 A.M.

This life was too happy to last. The specter of want soon raised its head that hard winter. My father's little business as a landscape architect was closed down by incessant rains and hard frosts. He was too much of an artist to be a good businessman. On one occasion, for instance, he was offered a contract to design and construct a fine garden. I helped Dad draw up the plans; it would have meant three months' steady work, weather permitting. My father, who never heard of Frank Lloyd Wright, believed that a garden should be an outcropping alongside the house, natural, not superimposed. We awaited his return from the presentation.

"The contract, Dad — what happened?"

"Nothing happened! Who does she think she is? I explained in detail my plans, but she had other ideas and wanted the work done her way. 'After all,' says she snootily, 'it's my garden, and I can do with it what I please.' So I just said to her, 'Well, it may be your garden, but it's my work, and I would be seen dead before I worked to your plans.' The cheek of her! Don't you think so, Georgie?"

Of course he was right — but unemployed.

With Dad idle, the old banter was gone from family meals. Mother burst into tears. "Georgie, we have no money to pay the taxes on our house. How can I possibly get fourteen pounds when Daddy has been out of work for over a month now? We'll all be put out onto the street!"

Dad stood looking out of the window, hands in his pockets, without a word.

I decided to leave the university and go back to work. Perhaps as a policeman, a steady job. I could always study in off hours. After a sleepless night, I got up at four A.M., dressed, and went out into the comforting darkness of the city I had grown to love. My footsteps carried across the splash of streetlamps on the wet pavements toward the West End Park, over the rustic bridge, past the rough-hewn granite monolith of Thomas Carlyle, uphill toward the majestic townhouses of Park Circus. I sat down on a bench under the equestrian statue of Lord Roberts and looked forlornly toward the silhouette of the university against the glow of the city. The dawn coming up behind me revealed it in its full splendor. I joined my fellow students at the eight o'clock service in the chapel choir stalls. At its conclusion I approached the chaplain and requested an appointment. The Reverend Archie Craig was a tall, lanky man with the expressive hands of an artist, stubby black hair, and a warm smile reflecting the life of a consecrated scholar; he was an M.C. in the Great War.

"Why, of course, George. Shall we say ten o'clock at my house in Bank Street?"

He listened to my tale of woe, in the recounting of which I disgraced myself by shedding tears, and responded, "George, on no account must you ever give up — or even contemplate giving up — your studies for the ministry. Now, I'll tell you what you will do: take this letter and deliver it to 105 West George Street, to the office of the shipping company McClay and Company. Ask for Mr. McClay; say I sent you, and give him this letter."

At the office of the shipping company, I was ushered into a comfortable Victorian room where, seated at a large desk, a tall man looked out from under heavy eyebrows with a ready smile and a gracious manner that immediately erased any sense of embarrassment. We spoke awhile about my life at the university, my friends, and some of the professors whom he seemed to know well. A clerk entered the room and handed him an envelope.

"Now, Mr. Docherty, in this envelope there are thirty-five pounds which I wish you to accept. I want you to know that this is not a loan, but a small gift of encouragement in your preparation for the ministry. Now, don't say it, for you cannot pay it back. The life of a minister is hard enough. With this small token go my very best wishes, Mr. Docherty."

Many years later when I preached at the chapel services of the Quarriers Home, Jerry and I were luncheon guests of Lord McClay in his mansion at Bridge of Weir.

It was a red-letter day in June 1935 when my mother and Jerry (my father having surrendered his ticket on her behalf) attended the Bute Hall on Graduation Day. I processed in a long line of graduates. Eventually came my turn. I kneeled before Principal Rait to hear his "Te quoque" as he touched my head lightly with the mortar board. The Bedelus draped over my shoulders the purple M.A. hood, rented for the occasion, which I had been carrying over my left arm.

Before my next adventure—going on for my B.D. at Trinity College, the theological department of the University—a significant event occurred that was to have repercussions for the rest of my ministry: I was approached to become a student assistant to the minister at Kings Park Church, Glasgow. The position carried with it a salary of one hundred pounds a year. Out of my first pay packet I made a down payment on a mahogany-cabinet Pye radio receiver. It was a gift for Mother and Dad. Twenty-five years later it was still functioning well.

I found my studies came easily. From now on I would hold my own with the best.

4

The Pacifist

No military preparedness, no political expedient can guarantee the kind of peace on which the heart of the world is set. The Christian religion backed by a united Christendom and a Church as daring and heroic on spiritual lines as the army has been on military lines, is the only hope of the world, and of the solution of the great problems with which the world is faced.
—General Douglas Haig, Supreme Commander of Allied forces in the Great War, 1914–1918

The only thing necessary for the triumph of evil is for good men to do nothing.
—Edmund Burke

VISITORS APPROACHING GLASGOW from the four airts in 1935 could hardly miss the three square towers of Trinity College on Woodlands Hill, one of the highest points in that city of seven hills. Originally the Free Church College, built some ten years after the Disruption of 1843 that split the Kirk on the question of patronage (what Americans would call the principle of separation of Church and State), since the Union of 1929 it has been renamed Trinity College.

To this divinity school, on the second Monday of October 1935, I made my way. Lightly taking in my stride the four steps of the main entrance under the great tower, I excitedly pushed open the double swing door and found myself engulfed in a noisy group of students gathered together in the fine hallway under the much-too-large statue of David Livingstone, his eyes lifted to distant uncharted African lands, wearing his trademark naval officer's cap and *kapi*. What a contrast this encounter was to the waeful day three years earlier, when as the lonely outsider I set foot on the Arts quadrangle of the University!

Ours was a fine faculty who saw quite clearly their two-fold function: to train ministers of the Church and to provide a solid academic foundation. All had served in parish churches.

W. M. MacGregor, Principal Emeritus, a patriarchal figure, slowly processed the crowded corridors deep in thought, like a wraith. Voices perceptibly lowered when this distinguished New Testament scholar and preacher passed by. Once a month, we savored his brilliant exegetical sermons, illustrated from a vast command of English literature.

Arthur John Gossip, one of the great Scottish preachers despite his tangle of uncombed white hair, untrimmed brush of a moustache, and two large rabbit teeth, taught Homiletics and Christian Ethics. His face was open and alert, kindly eyes twinkling as if savoring a laugh just around the corner; a soft face, born of pain and a deep sadness. He had a voice like a corncrake with a cold, screeching at us with flailing arms: "For God's sake, gentlemen, for God's own sake and the gospel's, I beseech you, take care of your voice! Look what I've done to mine!"

When he preached, words rolled like a Highland burn in spate. Simple Anglo-Saxon words, chosen with the precision of a Swiss watchmaker, brought to life the cold stained-glass portraiture of the apostles and of Jesus himself. Here was a mystic, like all great preachers since Paul, far ben in the life of the Spirit.

He was without doubt the worst lecturer ever to grace a college podium. Entering the classroom with an armful of books which he piled up on his desk, pieces of paper sticking from all corners, he shuffled and teased at a sheaf of dog-eared notes, turning them around as if they were inscribed from every corner of the compass. Intermittently he would refer to the pile of books. Never did I put pen to notebook in his class. I sat back, letting this quite extraordinary impression of what it means to be a preacher sink into my soul; it was learning by osmosis. Every time I sit down for my own sermon preparation the vivid picture and unforgettable words and phrases of this dear man rise up to encourage or warn me. A similar mark was left on three generations of Scottish preachers.

If he had written no other sermon than "When Life Tumbles in, What Then?" Arthur John Gossip would have been remembered still. His session at Beechgrove, Aberdeen, insisted that the sermon, written immediately after his wife's totally unexpected death, which left a stunned preacher in his forties with four bairns to rear, be published. The preacher likened himself to Ezekiel, the prophet to whom God spoke these ultimate words: "Man, I am taking from you at one blow the dearest thing you have." In class on one occasion, this sensitive soul parted the veil of grief.

> As I stumbled through life bearing a burden that made no sense to one who believed in a loving heavenly Father, letters began to arrive over my desk from every part of the English-speaking world, and they all began the same way: "It also happened to me . . . you gave me courage again. . . ." Only then did light stream into the darkness of my aching heart and I cried out to the Lord, "Perhaps, after all, my bereavement has brought courage to others. Let me bear it redemptively."

On the grave in the cemetery in Aberdeen where Nina Carslaw and Arthur John Gossip lie stands a Celtic-cross granite tombstone; no date of death is carved on it.

50

Hardly less influential was Garth H. C. MacGregor, nephew of the Principal. His teaching of the New Testament at a time when such radical form critics as Bultmann were being translated into English gave a balanced sanity to the extreme skepticism of German scholarship. John Mauchline brought the same balanced outlook to the Hebrew Old Testament. Jarvis Riddell, who taught Dogmatics, gave us a masterly survey of the history of theological thought without committing himself to any school. Riddell was a splendid teacher. We would later disagree on the question of peace and war, but we remained firm friends.

Professor Fulton taught Apologetics, a defense of the Christian faith in the broad spectrum of the world's religions. A gentle man with sparse white hair and a brush of a moustache, he was a meticulous scholar. In his class I read widely. Disturbing doubts arose. Evil was understandable when man was the author: self-inflicted diseases, murders, passions, drunken drivers who kill the innocent. But what about earthquakes, droughts, floods, storms, contagious diseases? Not every lily of the field is allowed to grow unmolested, and too many sparrows fall, apparently without divine notice. I had been reading Freud's *Reality of Religious Experience.* For Freud, God was a purely subjective experience, a projection of a primitive father or one's own father, recollected in later life. I floundered, recognizing the apparent truth of Gerald Heard's lines: "Newton banished God from the heavens; Darwin banished God from the earth; and Freud banished God from the last fastness of the soul."

A question about Freud appeared in the term examination. I foolishly decided to attack Freud's thesis and spent too much time on that single question. Undaunted, I went to see Professor Fulton, hoping he would, out of his own vast reading and sincere Christian life, be able to shed light on my spiritual problem.

"Ah, yes, Mr. Docherty, I remember your paper. A very good effort, especially on the Freudian heresy; but it was a pity you spent so much time on it. Having omitted two other questions, you could not have gained more than eighty percent. Then, your writing leaves much to be desired. It does not help the disposition of an examiner when he finds it difficult to read illegible writing. Also, you misspelled 'Brunislaw Malinovski.' It made me suspect that perhaps you were merely returning my lectures and not reading the textbooks. . . ." His voice trailed away, leaving me splashing in the shallows of my own agnosticism.

If people ask me when I became a minister, I prefer to fix the date the week after my graduation as an M.A., although I would not be licensed to preach for another three years. I was appointed Assistant to the Minister at King's Park Church, Glasgow. During my course in Divinity, I assumed all the duties of a minister except officiating at the sacraments.

51

It took me away from my books. That was a mistake: it is not easy to make up for lost reading. However, it brought reality to my studies.

King's Park was an unimaginative sprawl of some ten thousand houses, spawned to meet the housing shortage after the First World War. It lay within what was then known as the "thousand-acre dike," a tract of fine farmland between the ancient Royal Burgh of Rutherglen and the middle-class suburb of Cathcart. In 1932, on a plot of ground beside an inadequate shopping center at Castlemilk Road and under the shadow of a garish cinema, the presbytery had built a rather pleasant Normanesque building, though its rustic brick interior achieved a gloomy effect, lightened only by a radiant blue-red stained glass window of the Ascension. The sanctuary seated seven hundred and already was crowded Sunday by Sunday.

My "bishop," as Scottish students call the pastor they assist, was the Reverend William R. Clarke, their first pastor, called in 1932. He was an Irishman, from Belfast, a graduate of Queens, but without a trace of an Irish accent. In my time at King's Park he was in his early forties, with dark hair and thin lips that moved little when he spoke in his clipped, anglicized accent. His was a challenging task, and he did well to build up such a splendid congregation by dint of careful pastoral oversight and preaching that was good, though never scintillating. Much of what he taught me about liturgics still remains. He and his wife, May, welcomed me into their family circle. I appreciate their friendship all the more now, when I realize how my enthusiasm at times must have seemed to them so much egotistical showing off.

Exuberantly I tackled the daunting task of visiting the two-thousand-member congregation. I set out two days a week after common dinner at the college, often visiting late into the night, sometimes making as many as fifteen visits in one day. Each visit was a unique experience. I found myself saying as I rattled the metal door knocker above the letterbox, "I wonder what new friendship will be born in this visit." I bravely attempted to cope with Scottish hospitality: tea was always served, and it was gravely impolite to refuse. One unforgettable day I consumed four evening meals, each at a different home, at different hours!

I encountered what at first seemed a pleasant problem: the good people wanted to know about their new assistant. I found great pleasure in talking, and even more pleasure in hearing myself talk. Since each visit lasted little more than twenty minutes, I devised a scheme of conversation to take the center of interest away from myself. On entering a house, I would immediately comment on it favorably, a sincere and easy task — these homes were impeccably clean and meticulously tidy.

"How long have you been in this house, Mrs. Stewart?"

"Five years."

"Where were you before you came here?"

"Wishaw, in Lanarkshire."

"Know it well. A coal mining area, I recall."

"Yes, my husband worked in the mines until he had to take an early retirement. The doctor said it was his chest; silicosis of the lung. He enjoyed our new home and grew strong in the fine fresh air of the garden. He loved his garden. It became his main interest, but last summer . . . he just fell over while digging the potatoes. . . ."

I listened to their stories, the kind not recorded in the press, heartfelt, and sometimes tragic — sorrows that would not heal, chronic illness, loneliness, failure in some business project, children unaccountably gone wrong, sometimes broken homes — never discussions that students in college were concerned about, such as C. H. Dodd's view of the evangelist John's "realized eschatology" or the verbal inerrancy of the Bible or the Pauline authorship of the Epistle to the Hebrews. These questions have their place, but at the back of the mind.

I said a prayer in every house, until sometimes at the end of a long day, wearied at the sound of my own voice, I would rationalize why a prayer was not really necessary, knowing when I went out into the night prayerless, it had simply been a temptation of the devil. I do not recall anyone ever objecting to my offer to pray; and more than once the parting comment I heard as I stood at the doorway was "Thank you, Mr. Docherty. That's the first prayer that's been said in this house for a long time."

Most exciting of all, my duties required me to preach once a month. I eagerly threw myself into preparing new sermons. I had already preached my sermon "Faith" twenty-seven times in various Glasgow churches before my appointment at King's Park. My patient Jerry could tell when I had missed an illustration or transposed a paragraph! So enamored of this sermon was I that on one occasion I found myself thinking as I came down from the pulpit, "Well, this congregation has heard the whole gospel in its entirety! Indeed, they may as well close down the church!" I still possess it, its pages sear and dog-eared.

The preacher who influenced me more than any other was James Black of St. George's, Edinburgh. A devotee, I followed him around whenever he was within traveling distance of Glasgow. Whatever the weather, I would join the long line of expectant worshipers awaiting the opening of the church doors. I studied his voice, method, exegesis, and sermon structure as a medical student might dissect a cadaver. I learned that preaching is never abstract, never conceptual; it is *perceptual*, painted in vivid word pictures. Once Black preached on Jesus cleansing the temple of the money changers and merchants; I really saw those merchants flee in fear from the church and swear I heard the coins rattle down the middle aisle! He had four distinct voices: didactic; "winning"; a roar like thunder; and a whisper, perfectly audible even in a Gothic building, for dramatic moments — "I beheld . . . Satan . . . like lightning . . . fall . . . from heaven." I discovered to my own astonishment I had adopted his lisping burr! Black's *Mystery of Preaching* was for me, at that formative period, the classic homiletic textbook.

I was forever experimenting each Sunday I preached. I recall what I was pleased to call my "symphonic period," when I patterned the sermon after a Brahms symphony, its slow quiet opening, its Aristotelian climax, and its beautiful diminuendo whisper to silence. On one occasion, after a very dramatic ending, a member of the congregation observed, "That was a grand sermon, Mr. Docherty. But, if you don't mind me saying so, I didnie hear the ending!"

"You were not supposed to," came my astounding reply.

Nor were these sermons mere ten-minute sermonettes. They ranged upwards of twenty-five minutes, and on one unforgettable occasion for fifty-five passionate minutes. After all, I used to argue, one does not request ten minutes of Beethoven!

During these years at King's Park in the mid 1930s, as the sun of civilization seemed to be sinking, the ominous shadow of Germany's Chancellor Hitler was spreading across Europe. In 1936 he flouted the Versailles Treaty by reoccupying the demilitarized zone of the Rhineland; France stood passively by. The British Prime Minister, Stanley Baldwin, seemed entirely preoccupied by his dread that King Edward VIII might abdicate. Indeed, the only protest Hitler received was from his own generals, who feared another European war.

The question of peace and war had been occupying the councils of the Church of Scotland, and its General Assembly produced a report entitled "God's Will in Our Time" that indicated a split within the ranks of the Kirk. The nonpacifist position affirmed the Church's historic position of condemning war and urging the nations to seek other ways of reconciling international disputes. However, if Britain's very existence should be threatened, it was the duty of the Church to support the nation. The pacifist position held that even at the risk to national security, modern war can never be justified by Christian norms. Total war made the continued use of the terms "defensive" or "aggressive" war wholly irrelevant. Modern war had achieved such demonic possibilities that it would destroy the very values it was seeking to preserve: there could be no greater evil than modern war. I found myself sharing the pacifist position.

Why? Perhaps it was the memory of the lads of the Highland Light Infantry bound for the war at Maryhill Railway Station with a cheery smile and wave. Later came the realization of the ghastliness of the First World War. In the battle of the Somme, more perished in ten days of conflict than were killed in the American Civil War. There were friends, older and wiser: Professor MacGregor, author of *The New Testament Basis of Pacifism*; and Dr. George MacLeod, Dr. A. C. Craig, and Dr. John Kent, all of whom had been combatants as teenagers in the First World

War, but were now among the leading exponents in Britain of the pacifist witness. I found myself signing a document issued by the Fellowship of Reconciliation outlawing war as an instrument of international diplomacy.

Mr. Clarke had asked me to preach on Armistice Sunday, 1936, at the evening service. When I informed him that morning of my pacifist position, he merely remarked that it was perhaps good for the congregation to be exposed to the divergent positions within the Church. He himself was a chaplain in the territorial army.

The church was crowded with worshipers wearing the traditional Flanders poppy boutonniere. Armistice Day services were moving, patriotic occasions. Military parades were the order of the day, the national anthem was sung, and people who normally did not attend church returned to remember the tragic war that was to end all wars.

Mr. Clarke wore his chaplain's uniform under his pulpit gown, his army boots clanking over the flagstones during the procession. Having spent most of the week anticipating his arguments for justifying a Christian war, I found after hearing his morning sermon there was no need to alter one paragraph of my evening sermon, save to omit a rather facetious quotation from Beverley Nichols: "A military chaplain is overdressed: either the uniform or the clerical collar; never both."

I preached for fifty-five minutes to an overflowing congregation, meeting every argument, or so I believed, that Mr. Clarke had presented at the morning service. In the vestry after the service, Mr. Clarke said to me very quietly, "Mr. Docherty, I'm sorry, but I cannot permit you to preach such pacifistic sermons in my pulpit, and I am ordering you never to do it again."

I was stunned. It apparently made little difference that we had already talked about the Church's position and that we had agreed to disagree. If I had preached heresy, it would have been different. Mr. Clarke confirmed his order in writing by first post on Monday morning.

In my mood of bewilderment, I turned to the one man I believed could help. I did not wish to raise trouble in the church over the matter; on the other hand, there was at stake the principle of freedom of the pulpit. I phoned Dr. George F. MacLeod, minister at Govan Old Parish Church in Glasgow, and made an appointment for that Monday afternoon. Thus began one of the deep friendships and molding influences in my life.

George MacLeod is to my mind the outstanding figure of the twentieth-century Church of Scotland, a judgment not shared by all, but one that history might well confirm. He has had a lover's quarrel with the Church; child of its establishment, he has often been a "sair saint" for the kirk. In the thirties, when he was minister at Govan, his voice became known all over Britain through his radio program, "Govan Calling." Like Dick Shepherd in England, he made the medium of radio his own.

MacLeod's greatness is not easy to assess; it is like a Highland mist, all-pervading, yet difficult to grasp. He is an intuitive thinker, not easily identified with any school of theology. Passionately nationalistic, with generations of the Highland blood of the MacLeods of Morven coursing in his veins, he is not a member of the Scottish National Party. Son of a Scottish baronet and an English mother, educated in England (Winchester School and Baliol, Oxford), he was called to Govan to minister to forgotten craftsmen and the poor. Adjutant in the Argyll and Sutherland Highlanders, and recipient of both the Military Cross and the French Croix de Guerre *avec palmes*, he has spent most of his life as a militant pacifist. Son of a Tory M. P., he is a left-wing socialist and in recent years has been elevated to the peerage as Lord George MacLeod of Fuinary, with a seat in the House of Lords. A mystic knowing those things that "never were on land nor sea," he has a flair for organization and administration. A high churchman, he has infused liturgy with a new dimension of reality. (It was at Iona that I first heard God addressed as "You" instead of "Thou.") Like Columba, he was once, and may still be, half Druid. I recall the summer when he triumphantly claimed St. Paul's words "the whole creation groaneth and travaileth until the coming of the Lord" meant no less than that creation itself—rocks, mountains, seas—was redeemed, Eden come back again! I asked the fine New Testament scholar Dr. Manson of Edinburgh, who was on Iona at the time, about this quite astounding exegesis. He replied that George was probably nearer to the thinking of the apostle than other modern exegetes.

Dr. MacLeod is an extremely shy person, as George Bernard Shaw was, his exuberance a cloak of self-conscious Victorian reserve. This publicly austere man with the drooping Highland jowls is extraordinarily humorous, as perhaps only his young associates have discovered.

To Dr. MacLeod's rooms in the Pearce Institute at Govan Cross, where he then lived as a bachelor, I made my way on that Monday afternoon, my controversial sermon folded in my pocket. I first saw him sitting at a large desk. He rose to meet me, his surprisingly small hand outstretched in cordial greeting. I was aware immediately of the impression others had experienced when first they encountered him—that we had been friends for years. Six feet tall, with broad shoulders, military moustache, dark hair with a natural wave, and the small steel eyes of the Highlander piercing into the soul, he was then in his early forties.

As I unfolded my tale of woe, he sat back, hands clasped under his chin, nodding as I spoke, listening intently. When I had finished, he drew himself up, his right hand caressing his military moustache, and replied with a broad smile, "Of course, the trouble with you youngsters, my dear George, if I may say so, is that you just don't quite realize what a very serious business is this question about the Christian and war; you just too often go off half-cocked without knowing too much about the subtleties of the matter."

"But Dr. MacLeod, I have my sermon here, full manuscript, if you would care to read it."

He scanned the pages, his lips moving as if he were reading aloud, occasionally grunting and peering at the manuscript at arm's length as if he had difficulty in reading the typing.

"Well, now. Let me see. Uh . . . uh." The grunts came more regularly, once a guffaw, and then "Yes! Good Lord! Where on earth did you get that quotation from General Haig? Been searching for it for months now."

He handed back the sermon.

"Of course you must not on any account resign your assistantship. You must go bravely on. Let your bishop, Mr. Clarke, haul you before the presbytery if he dare. But don't resign. Never resign. Let them kick you out first; but never resign."

I remained another eighteen months as assistant to Mr. Clarke. I was never allowed to preach in his pulpit again, even during his vacation. I know now I must have appeared to Mr. Clarke a dogmatic, opinionated young troublemaker. It is a measure of the man that the incident did not end our friendship, which would go on long after the war was over.

The spring term of 1938 at Trinity marked for me the end of seven years of study. The occasion was celebrated at the Final Year *conversatione*, as the social was called, when we gathered, with our "steadies" or fiancées, for a night of celebration. Jerry and I joined the others in the traditional climb to the top of the college's two-hundred-foot tower, up the dark, mysterious, cobwebbed stone stairway, each couple bearing a candle flickering in the cold draft. From the corbeled, corniced parapet, a protecting arm around Jerry against the chilling night wind, we gazed over the wrought iron railings toward the dazzling spread of the city around us like an inverted Milky Way galaxy in the clear moonless dark, tracing in the distance the winding pathway that was the River Clyde weaving among the lights.

Above the giggling, some of us were wondering where our first charge would be. None of us could have known then that too soon one of our number would become a victim of the war we prayed would never come. On that night I saw my dream parish, where I had preached only two months before when the minister suddenly fell ill. It stood on the shore of a Highland loch, an eighteenth-century building, the characteristic lantern belfry at its gable, the manse beside it, a back garden that swept up to the heather-carpeted hills, and a wee boat drawn up on the pebble shore, where all day long white-breasted gulls yammered as they swooped over the surface of the waters. I would spend languid afternoons visiting the folk in the glen, dropping in at their but-and-ben cottages for a chat beside the inglenook at a peat fire, to pray and talk of the deep things, the air filled with the repetitive plaint of an unseen cuckoo from the hill forest; it would always be summer, the sweet-smelling honeysuckle climbing the pillared porch of the manse front door.

On April 20, 1938, some thirty of us were licensed to preach by the Presbytery of Glasgow. We received from the hands of the moderator a copy of the King James Version of the Bible, duly signed for the occasion, a reminder that all books begin and end with one.

I recall one conscientious student sitting on the cold stone bench that circles the cathedral where once the aged and lame sat, "backs to the wall"; he was reading a copy of the Westminster Confession of Faith because he had not read it before, suddenly realizing he would be taking vows confessing belief in the fundamental doctrines of the Christian faith contained in the said Confession of Faith of the Church of Scotland. And there was a remark made by an old man, himself rather deaf and therefore nearly shouting, "There's nae enough kirks for a' these laddies."

I left Trinity College with only one prize, but it was the one I coveted: the Dowanhill Prize for Preaching, judged by a panel of the entire student body. Next came the "trial sermon" before my teacher, Arthur John Gossip; his imprimatur would mean even more than the Dowanhill. It was an evening service at New Cathcart Church, Glasgow; I entered the pulpit with suppressed excitement, a new sermon, the ink hardly dry, ready for the great test. During the singing of the opening psalm, mouthing the words, I scanned the thin ranks of worshipers for the well-kent shock of gray hair. With difficulty I spied it half hidden behind a pillar in the last pew under the back gallery.

After class Monday morning, Dr. Gossip requested the pleasure of Mr. Docherty's company in his office, immediately. In response to my timid knock came his kindly voice, "Come in, George. Sit you down, lad!"

There followed a pause as he circled his desk, head bowed, as if finding difficulty in knowing where to begin, all the while chewing the stub of a pencil as was his wont. Suddenly he turned to me pointing a wavering, bony finger and glaring at me out of glinting grey eyes (shades of the Ancient Mariner): "Young man! Don't you think for one moment that you are a preacher. Don't ever get a conceited notion into your head that you can preach — at all! Oh, maybe, I suppose, just maybe, after, let us say, ten years in your own pulpit, with regular weekly preparation, it is conceivable, yes it is quite conceivable, that perhaps — perhaps — you may lay claim to be able to preach what could be a passable sermon! But not yet, young man, not yet! And I beseech you, and I know the Lord himself beseeches you, don't ever believe that you are a good preacher. Man, lad, you have the gift! It's from above, but don't misuse this gift; don't spoil it by believing it has anything really to do with you. If pride and conceit take over, I shall go down to my grave cursing you. You may go now, George; and thank you, lad." He patted my shoulder and put an arm around me affectionately. "Thank you! It was a privilege to sit under your ministry last night in Cathcart."

Several days later Professor MacGregor spoke to me about an appointment as Organizing Secretary of the Church of Scotland Peace Society, a one-year appointment with the possibility of renewal. If I would accept it, the stipend would be raised by voluntary contributions from members of the pacifist movement in Scotland and England. They needed someone of pacifist convictions to rally together pacifist forces and opinion in the country in a last attempt to stave off the frightful movement toward a second world war. Both George MacLeod and John Kent, whom above all ministers I came to regard as my brothers in the Lord, encouraged me to accept this invitation.

It made me very restless. Jerry was not much help; she rarely was when such a question arose. The decision must be mine, she always said; and she would go wherever I believed I had been called.

I shared my problem with Dr. Gossip, who had experienced the horrors of the trench warfare in the First World War as a chaplain and now had little time for what he called "this pacifist imbecility."

"A secretary! A secretary!" he screamed at me, holding his white mop head in his bony hands. "You have before you the whole Church of Scotland and the invitation to some of its fine pulpits. I've already been approached on your behalf; and now you want to be an organizing *secretary*." He spat out the word. "And worse, much worse, a secretary to a group of misguided, woolly-headed Christians."

Professor Riddell was hardly less appalled and went further by wisely reminding me that once I became associated with the pacifist movement the label would stick.

Despite such advice, I became Organizing Secretary of the Church of Scotland Peace Society and the Fellowship of Reconciliation, believing, daft as it now sounds, that I could stop war from breaking out!

Jerry and I were married in the University chapel on June 24, 1938, by the chaplain, Archie Craig. A. M. Henderson played a litany by Schubert as I entered with my best man, Lewis Davidson. Thirty-two years later I would listen to the same litany under a dark shadow, but today I was bemused with unbelieving wonder. When the triumphal chords of Clark's "Trumpet Voluntary" echoed through the high rafters of that beautiful chapel, Lewis and I turned around to see my bride, smiling from side to side of the aisle as she passed our relatives and friends in the choir stalls. Her father, grown old but looking excited, led her slowly toward me; Jacob's long wait for his beloved Rachel was over.

Daringly we went to the Continent for our honeymoon, a package trip to Le Zoute in Belgium. The £35 I won for the Dowanhill made a

down payment on a house, semidetached and newly constructed in Giffnock. An old farm drystone dike was our rear garden boundary. Near it
grew a stunted gnarled oak and a whin bush, whose yellow blossoms bloom
all the year ("kissing's out of season when the whin is out of bloom"),
reminding us of the Broomfields at Largs and the mass of whin on the golf
course at Lossiemouth whose summer blossoms smell like coconut. We
called our house "The Whins."

Homebuilding was such fun! My father helped me plan our new
garden. We bought a mongrel wirehaired terrier, picked from the back of
a cage of yapping pups in a city store because she looked so forlorn—as
well she might: she had fleas. When she scampered over our polished
linoleum floor, yapping happily and skidding at the corners, we decided
to call her "Dopey" after one of Snow White's seven dwarfs. I was beginning to realize a truth the years would bring out: I had married a lass who
was happy to be a minister's wife as well as the wife of a minister. The
ministry, like farming, is a family affair.

When Jerry's father died shortly after our wedding, her mother came
to live with us and would continue as part of our family for the next
twenty-six years.

With characteristic enthusiasm, I set about my work as Organizing
Secretary out of my study in "The Whins." The main thrust was to
organize public meetings across the land to place before the people the real
issues of war as we saw them. I traveled the country speaking to seminars
of ministers and to congregational gatherings of Edinburgh and Glasgow
(where we held many) as well as Kilmarnock, Galashiels, Perth, Dundee,
and Aberdeen. The purpose of the ministers' seminars was to organize
large public meetings, in which I imagined myself making passionate or-
ations in St. Andrews Hall, Glasgow, or the Usher Hall, Edinburgh. When
I had outlined the grand scheme, the invariable reply of the clergy ran
something like this.

"Well, that sounds great, George. We'll plan as large a gathering of
the town as we can. Now, who will be the speaker?"

"Me!"

"But, my dear George, nobody really knows you. The only hope we
have of drawing a crowd and making use of the media is to have a 'name'—
like George MacLeod or Canon Raven or Dick Shepherd."

My work became more and more secretarial, organizing behind the
scenes the interminable details involved in arranging public gatherings:
police, press, local interests, inclusion of denominations other than the
Kirk. I was a P.R. man with none of the undoubted gifts that public
relations requires.

However, I did on one occasion get my chance to speak and share the
platform with George MacLeod himself. It was at Dundee, in the

fine Church of St. Clements. The sanctuary was crowded to the door. This was my moment in the limelight, and I was determined not to let it slip! I had prepared and memorized a forty-minute address that was didactic, reasonable, and passionately patriotic in the name of peace. Never have I delivered the gospel of peace with such belligerent abandon!

At its conclusion I received a standing ovation. Dr. MacLeod slowly rose, stretched himself, and looked around the hall as if not quite certain whether he was in the right meeting. He began quietly: "Ladies and gentlemen, I really don't know why I am here this evening. My young colleague and dear friend George Docherty has said everything that is to be said in what I regard as one of the finest speeches on the subject it has been my pleasure to listen to." He continued in this conversational, almost apologetic, manner for a few more minutes, whereupon he dropped into second gear. A hush descended on the audience as he began in his charismatic way to capture the imagination, the reason, the heart, with telling aphoristic stabs of truth and quotations from the most unexpected sources to confirm his opinion — the Prime Minister, British generals, Gandhi, trade union leaders, the cry of captive Austria, even something from *Mein Kampf*. In the end he had swept them all before him to a tumultuous ovation. Next day in the Dundee *Courier* a whole front-page column was devoted to the evening's proceedings with a fair précis of Dr. MacLeod's address. The last line read:

"The Rev. C. [*sic*] Docherty also spoke."

Revisionist historians of that period tend to lay much of the blame for Hitler's unopposed aggression at the door of the pacifist sentiment in the country, quoting, for instance, the Oxford Union debate on "King and Country" as an example of the lack of resolve among most Britons for another war. The situation was much more complex. Again and again, there could have been a settlement of German dreams of *Lebensraum* without going to war. Indeed, as Liddell Hart, one of the greatest military thinkers of the century, has noted, the real fear in those days among the councils of Britain and France was not Hitler, but Stalin. Even as late as Hitler's invasion of Austria, the British Prime Minister, Neville Chamberlain, rejected Russian proposals that there should be a conference for collective insurance against any further German advances. As late as September 1938, when the Czech crisis was coming to a head, the Russian government made known both privately and publicly its willingness to combine with France and Britain to preserve the independence of Czechoslovakia.

As British newsreels flashed on the cinema screens the return of a triumphant Prime Minister Chamberlain from Hitler's Eagle's Nest retreat in Berchtesgaden, waving in his hand a single sheet of paper and quoting Disraeli from the steps of his plane, "Peace with honor! Peace in our time!" to the tumultuous cheers of a relieved British public, we had no way of knowing that Russia had been deliberately excluded from the Munich Conference that sealed the fate of Czechoslovakia and made the Second World War inevitable.

It was for just such newly aligned peace conferences of all the great powers that the pacifist movement in Britain had been calling. I still possess one of the leaflets produced at the time inviting everyone who could to petition the government for a National Peace Conference. We were supported by churches across the land, by trade unions, educational bodies, civic societies, and a multitude of apprehensive citizens.

In contrast, the Kirk in Scotland was tragically ambiguous and ill-informed. The General Assembly Report, "God's Will in Our Time," still suggested there could be a defensive war, that the coming conflict could be limited: "In time of war, Christian ethical considerations can never become irrelevant; and even when victory seems at stake, the church cannot admit that military operations, whether by bombing or otherwise, which have the civil population, including women and children, as their deliberate object, can ever be brought within the definition of legitimate defence."

I heard no organized protest from the Church when, during 1940 and 1941, the industrial cities of Lubeck, Hamburg, Essen, Frankfurt, Hanover, and Kessel were devastated night and day by what was called "area bombing," but which was quite clearly indiscriminate. The tragedy is that the air staff themselves would later report that it was very disputable whether bombing, by itself, could be a decisive factor in the war. "On the contrary, all that we have learned since the war began shows that its effects, both physical and moral, are greatly exaggerated."

What was perfectly clear to me at that time was a choice between either total war or a new way of reconciliation through international conference. The one realist was my hero, Dr. James Black. When he returned from his Moderatorial tour of Germany on the eve of the war, the old First World War combatant immediately joined the Home Guard and resumed rifle practice!

One practical result of my frequent trips to London was a new appreciation of the churches in England, not least the Society of Friends. In some small way, I saw firsthand the devastation of London during the bombing, though I was fortunate to miss being involved in the firebomb and doodlebug period of Hitler's pent-up fury and fear. It was not without some excitement that I sat in on discussions with the churches in Germany via Switzerland and came to know firsthand the work of Christian reconciliation performed by Bishop Bell of Chichester.

The time came for a reassessment of my one-year appointment. The signs of the outbreak of war had become more and more ominous. I decided I must be in my own pastorate when the catastrophe struck. Accordingly, I gave notice to my committee, grateful that I had learned much concerning the nature of war, made so many new friends in the holy catholic Church, and begun to realize that the witness of the Church is ultimately to be that of the "remnant," that inner circle of Christ's followers who will always be the goad against a self-complacent church, its torchbearer, believing in the "impossible possible" of the Christian way of life.

When the war did come, among the casualties was my old "bishop," William Clarke. Taken prisoner on May 20, 1941, when three thousand crack Germany paratroopers dropped out of the blue Mediterranean skies and captured Crete, he was sent to Germany; he refused repatriation on several occasions. When he returned in September 1944, in an exchange of prisoners of war, his experience with American G.I.s had whetted his desire to serve in the United States. He became minister of the First Presbyterian Church in Louisville, Kentucky.

Thirty years later we met again. I had been visiting at Louisville Theological Seminary, where he heard me preach. I visited his home and met again his wife, May. We talked affectionately about the old days in King's Park. I was happy to feel there had been complete reconciliation. Six months later he died.

5

The War Years

The first day ye preach in your ain kirk, speak a gude word for Jesus Christ.
— Ian Maclaren, *Beside the Bonnie Briar Bush*

NEW YEAR'S DAY, 1939, fell on a Sunday, a date I well remember for the poor sermon that I preached in the perishingly cold church of St. Paul's Milngavie, to a scattering of chilled parishioners. After the service, a tall, slow-spoken man with a warm Border accent introduced himself.

"My name is John Binnie Good, and I have come especially to the service as a member of the vacancy committee of the Sandyhills Church in Glasgow. I want to thank you for the service, and might go so far as to say that I am sure the vacancy committee will be getting into touch with you."

A letter, one month later, explained that the committee wished to place my name in nomination for the charge, but a matter had come to their attention that required clarification. Since I was known to be a pacifist, and in view of the possibility of war, would I refuse to have the national anthem sung at church services; and what would be my relationship with the lads and lasses in the armed forces?

However anxious I may have been to be settled into my own charge, it did seem to me that I was confronted with a matter of principle. Was this censorship of my preaching, indeed my ministry? I replied that as a patriot, I would never in peace or war object to the national anthem being sung in church, after the benediction, on appropriate national occasions, but I must be free to preach as my conscience dictated. My position as a pacifist was already recognized by the General Assembly. Beyond the commitment "to seek the peace and unity of the congregation" and to be a faithful pastor in time of peace and war, I was not prepared to debate the issue when the call of a pastor was at stake.

As sole nominee, I preached before a crowded congregation. The vote of the congregation (750 members) took place on the following Tuesday evening, when I happened to be out of town. Jerry, awaiting anxiously the result of the deliberation, was summoned to the phone around 10:30.

"Mrs. Docherty? This is Mr. Good. I am very sorry to phone so late. We had a very fine congregational meeting tonight, and the attendance was very good. And we have come to a decision about our future minister." His voice was clear but ponderously slow; Jerry was getting more and more anxious. "Well now, I have written down on a piece of paper the results of the voting . . . and if I can find my reading spectacles . . . it is not very light in this telephone booth . . . let me see . . . ah yes, here it is. Are you still there, Mrs. Docherty? *For* Mr. Docherty, 318 votes; and *against* Mr. Docherty, none. So you see, it was a unanimous call and I would like you to know that we are all very happy over the result."

Sandyhills Church stands on the main road leading out of the east end of Glasgow just beyond Shettleston — once "shuttles-town," a thriving village where for centuries the *click-clack* of cottage hand looms could be heard by travelers on the high road to Edinburgh. It is a red sandstone Gothic building with a traditional horseshoe gallery, central pulpit, and pipe organ behind the preacher. Steel bars attached to the beams span the roof, reinforcing the outer walls, which had begun to fall outwards as the land, above abandoned and flooded mines that honeycombed the district, subsided.

The congregation had "come out" from the parish church of Shettleston at the time of the Disruption in 1843. The Sandyhills district had a splendid history of evangelical witness. In the middle of the eighteenth century, Cameronian covenanting congregation (named for Richard Cameron, who had defied Charles II's ordinance against covenanting preaching) had held conventicles on what are still called the "Preaching Braes," the site of the present Sandyhills golf course. A certain Robert Williamson, member of this Cameronian congregation, emigrated to America. His grandson was Thomas Woodrow Wilson, twenty-eighth president of the United States. No doubt the President was remembering his grandparents and their Scottish conventicles when, addressing a gathering at the Mansion House in London on December 28, 1918, he declared: "The stern covenanting tradition behind me sends many an echo down the years."

The manse stood in the quiet residential oasis of North Mount Vernon, located a mere twenty minutes by train from Queen Street Station. Solid villas sheltered among splendid beech trees that screened off the unsightly coal bins and slag heaps of the neighboring mine works. From my study window in the attic, I commanded a panoramic view of the city's lights; often the night sky glowed like the dawn when the great iron ore retorts of Colville's steel works across the Clyde at Cambuslang were tapped.

At our back door lay the foundations of the splendid mansion built by the Glasgow import merchant George Buchanan early in the eighteenth century; it was called "Windyedge." The Buchanan brothers carried on a considerable tobacco trade with the American colonies and indeed owned their own plantations in Virginia, on the banks of the Potomac River. Their Virginia neighbors, the Washingtons, lived on their own 2,500-acre "Hunting Creek." Augstine's son, Lawrence Washington, and George Buchanan-made a compact as a token of friendship: they would change the names of "Windyedge" and "Hunting Creek" to "Mount Vernon" in honor of Admiral Vernon, under whom Lawrence had served in the Caribbean. When Augustine Washington died in 1743, Lawrence adopted and brought into his spacious home his half-brother, George, a shy lad from Ferry Farm on the Rappahannock River. At Mount Vernon, George met the leading figures of Virginia: the Fairfaxes of Winchester and the Carlyles of Alexandria, as well as the Buchanans of Scotland's Mount Vernon.

In the American Revolution, all trade with Glasgow came to a standstill. The Buchanans were ruined, while the shy lad from Ferry Farm became the first president of the United States. As I walked among the ruins of the Buchanans' Mount Vernon, I often wondered about these tales and whether the great arc of beech trees that had lined the drive of the Scottish house was in fact duplicated at the Mount Vernon on the Potomac. As I discovered later, the plan is identical, but Virginia's Mount Vernon has tulip trees in place of the beech trees in Glasgow.

As I assumed my new charge, I was determined to make a good impression, especially in view of the pacifist label I carried with me. I planned to avoid anything that might sound like controversy, at least for the first few years. I was therefore happy that my first meeting of the board of deacons and the session was a delightful social evening, with no business agenda. Jerry and I were most cordially welcomed; Miss Girdwood poured tea from her family heirloom silver service. At about nine o'clock, when the guests were ready to depart, George Donaldson, a kindly but taciturn, well-meaning elder, an electrician by trade, suddenly announced: "I wis jist thinking, Mr. Docherty, since we're all here and it's now coming into summer and we'll no' be meeting until the autumn, there is one item of business that won't take long but might as well be dealt with tonight. It's about the painting of the exterior of the church — the rhone pipes, windows, and doors. We have the quotation here and it seems in order. Maybe I could have the Board's permission to go ahead with the work during the dry summer days?"

His words were greeted with nods of approval. But my heart suddenly beat faster. I had in fact noticed the disreputable condition of the church doors; flaking seasick-green paint obscured the beautiful filigreed wrought-iron hinges, truly a work of the blacksmith's art. I asked, nervously, "What color are we going to paint the front doors of the church?"

"Same as before."

"What color is that?"

"To tell the truth, I jist dinna ken. Jimmy Thomson, whit colors are the front doors o' the kirk? You dinna ken? Jimmy Weir? Green? Bottle green? Weel, I suppose, Moderator, they will be painted bottle green; of course, that is, unless you had maybe anither color in mind, Moderator?"

"Well, as a matter of fact, I had noticed the need of paint. And admired the wonderful filigreed-iron hinges. I thought maybe we could paint the door red and the hinges black; that would bring out their un-doubted craftsmanship."

"Red? Surely you mean Brown?"

"No, Mr. Donaldson. Red, Pillar-box red."

"Weel, Moderator. Eh? Red? Michty me! Maybe we should tak' the matter back to the property committee for further discussion."

So red doors it was. For years after, Sandyhills was known in the district as "the kirk with the red doors."

The summer of 1939 was an idyllic time for Jerry and me. We fell in love with our Victorian grey stone villa. My father helped me once more with the garden. Blackbirds sang in the maple trees in the front garden, and we went to sleep at night with the hoot of the owls from the nearby beeches of the ghostly Mount Vernon estate.

I embarked on a regimen of New Testament study. My books were spread across my desk, including most prominently Huck-Lietzmann's Greek synopsis of the first three Gospels and several English translations of scripture: King James, Weymouth, Goodspeed, Moffatt. It was exciting detective work discovering the similarities and the differences in the three evangelists and their accounts of the incidents and sayings of Jesus. Always I came away with some revealing new thought that had to be preached.

I visited members of the congregation, always on foot (I didn't own a car until I lived in the United States), sometimes to miners' row cottages. I recall Sandy, whose wife of sixty years I had recently buried; at his open fireside he whispered simply and poetically, "Aye, Mr. Docherty, she just left me like the snapping of a thread." New houses were springing up in Sandyhills and Garrowhill and Mount Vernon, whence came a growing membership in Sandyhills parish. I climbed dark tenement stairs in Shettleston and visited lovely red sandstone tenement flats, all of them spotlessly clean. There were the more expansive evenings when we visited our neighbors in Mount Vernon, many of them Glasgow businessmen, like their American counterparts forthright, without class consciousness, and speaking in the good Glasgow Doric. It was as near to Camelot as we ever came.

On Friday, September 1, 1939, the world was suddenly introduced to the new technique of *Blitzkrieg* as Hitler's panzer divisions stormed across a virtually defenseless Polish countryside. We read in the press on Saturday that the British government had issued an ultimatum to Hitler delivered personally in Berlin by the British ambassador. If German forces were not withdrawn from Poland by 11 A.M. on Sunday, September 3, a state of war would exist between the two countries.

On Sunday the church was crowded, fearfully, prayerfully, hopefully. During the singing of the first psalm, John Barrie, the beadle, asthmatically climbed the pulpit stairs and handed me a scrap of paper on which he had scrawled: *Mr. Chamberlain has just broadcast. We are at War with Germany.*

I read this message to the congregation. I prayed that even at this eleventh hour there might be a speedy end to the conflict. I pledged anew my ministry, seeking to be a faithful pastor, and while I would not use my pulpit as a recruiting station, vowed that I would identify myself with those who would be bearing the burdens of the war.

In the afternoon I visited one of our members who had lost a brilliant young husband in the Great War, leaving her with two babies to care for. I asked her, "Mrs. Dunnachie, my dear, what would you, who have lost so much by war, expect your minister to do and be now?"

She returned an understanding smile. "Why, we shall expect you to continue to be our minister in wartime as in peace; we shall need your prayers and your comfort more than ever, and the uplift of the services on Sunday. There will be many grieving hearts now, and what they need most is a trusted friend."

As I was leaving Mrs. Dunnachie's home, the air raid sirens, what Mr. Churchill called "those wailing banshees," shattered the peace of the Sabbath afternoon. Our first experience of an alert, there reigned a terrifying silence. Every moment we expected sticks of bombs to devastate our homes. We awaited the *ack-ack* response of the anti-aircraft guns that encircled the city. Since we were in the east end, the German planes must pass over us first. Nothing happened. The minutes ticked on into hours. Finally, the even tone of the all-clear signal brought its own benediction to the waning day.

Preparations for imminent war had been going on for some time already, some of them since the Munich conference. Food rationing was already the accepted practice. Homes with gardens were supplied with Anderson air raid shelters consisting of four-by-eight-feet corrugated steel sheets bent on one end to fit together into an igloo-like shelter. The householder dug a hole in the garden and half buried the structure, covering it with the excavated soil. It made an excellent baffle. I once held a new communicants class in one for a couple during an alert. Fragile as they looked, the shelters proved suprisingly effective when the massive bombing did come. The blast simply passed over the top, and even if it brought down the house, the occupants of the shelter were invariably safe — except, of course, from a direct hit.

Stout air raid shelters of brick and concrete were erected in the back courts of the tenements, and strong brick baffle walls were built at the entrances to the closes. When invasion became a real possibility, thousands of solid concrete blocks were placed at strategic points along the entire east coast of Britain, especially along beaches. Some can still be seen, immovable even by the wildest storms and tides. I thought at the time how easy it was to acquire and set up concrete and brick in wartime, whereas in peace the government had repeatedly cited the impossibility of rehousing the slums.

The streets teemed with people in uniform: army, navy, air force, air raid wardens, special firemen, police, home guard, and land army girls looking healthy and strong in their fawn corduroy breeches. A *Punch* cartoon of the time depicted two aristocrats walking down Bond Street, the only civilians in sight, saying, "I think we civilians ought to have some sort of uniform, don't you?"

Every open space in the cities became either vegetable garden or public air raid shelter. Most people carried a gas mask. Children were shipped off to the country from the vulnerable industrial areas; some country children near air bases were moved to less vulnerable towns. Some families sent their children to Canada. The blackout was a gloomy curfew, and when Glasgow fogs shrouded the already dark night, streetcar drivers would walk ahead of their vehicles carrying hooded lamps. While out visiting one night, I became helplessly lost in the fog and blackout. I made the interesting discovery that one does in fact walk in circles in such a circumstance; I didn't get home until three A.M.

The sirens continued their nuisance wailing, but no bombs fell. Sometimes we would watch a dogfight between German Messerschmitts on reconnaissance flights and British Spitfires. There was talk that the war might be over by Christmas without a shot being fired. The Americans coined the phrase that best described this lull before the storm: the phony war. Evening church services were moved to the afternoon; attendances fell off. The special noonday services that had been arranged by the council of churches eventually ceased altogether. When one of the district noonday services was to be held in our church, John, the beadle, announced on the stroke of the hour: "There's naebody in the kirk!"

"Ah, John," I replied, as I threw my B.D. hood over my preaching gown and cassock, "God is there. And we'll be there."

John gave me a strange look as I conducted a service of scripture and prayer in an empty church.

My first real grief occurred in these months. My father died. My parents had taken over "The Whins" when we moved to our manse, but my father's retirement was an enforced idleness he could not endure. He was glad therefore when Lord and Lady Weir of Eastwood Estate invited him to take the place of some of the younger gardeners called to active duty. At the age of seventy-two he scythed their vast ten-acre lawn by hand; petrol rationing made the use of power mowers impossible. One day he was found asleep under the large tree, much to his embarrassment; he had to be carried home. The doctor diagnosed angina pectoris. Lady Weir brought him orchids from the orchid house; for my father, it could have been a visit from the Queen with a knighthood.

In the following months I visited "The Whins" twice weekly. Dad and I talked a great deal and were closer than we had ever been; we now had time to talk. He shared with me his early days and tales of his father's childhood in Ireland.

It was during one of my nightly vigils I realized he was leaving us. I called for mother; we watched as a strangely beautiful transformation crept over his tired face, smoothing out the weather-worn lines. He closed his eyes, then blinked them open again, trying to focus. When he saw us both, he smiled his bashful smile.

"A beautiful world . . . beautiful world."

A sigh and then stillness. Mother gently and tenderly closed his eyes, murmuring through her quiet sobbing, "My wee darling; my wee darling."

On the day of the funeral, it rained a hard rain. The Scots have a saying: "Blessed is the man on whose grave falls the rain." We stood around the gaping, narrow trench, sheltering under canopies of umbrellas, shoes mired in the waterlogged grass. I read the service, assuring us once more of the certainties of the faith and the promises of our Lord in John 14. I gathered up a handful of the cold, sodden earth and let it fall upon the unadorned oaken coffin, now lowered deep in its narrow bed, repeating the final words this side of Calvary:

> Earth to earth, ashes to ashes, dust to dust:
> In sure and certain hope
> Of the resurrection to Eternal Life,
> Through Jesus Christ, our Lord.

Under leaden skies, I became aware for the first but not the last time of the sacramental mystery uniting us with the earth, alive and life-giving, changing with the seasons of the passing years, yet ever the same good earth, always abiding while we come and go. This earth my father had nurtured, and it had brought forth bud and blossom; he had moiled and toiled over it in all weathers. This same earth was now falling upon his coffin, in ultimate benediction. I became aware of my father's pristine innocency as never before, like that of Adam, the primal gardener, before the Fall, an uncomplicated life and simple, shared only with saints and the children of God. Now he had entered into the joy of his Lord.

Christmas, 1939, was a melancholy celebration, making the message of "peace on earth to men of goodwill" seem hollow. Hogmanay ushered in the New Year with even more nostalgia for the old days. The early dark of winter gave way to spring's lengthening hours of sunshine and nature's renewal of color and the singing of birds.

Then, on the day after my birthday, May 10, 1940, German panzer corps raced through Holland and Belgium in an arc of fire, thrust through the thick forest of the Ardennes, and crossed the Meuse at Sedan. The way to Paris was open. On June 15, Hitler signed an armistice with France in the identical railway carriage in which a former generation of Germans had signed a surrender in the presence of Foch and Haig, on November 11, 1918. The German armies had accomplished in some six weeks what four agonizing years of trench warfare had failed to achieve in the Great War.

"Jerry, my dear," I found myself saying, "our old world of castles in Spain and *Sentimental Tommy* is gone forever. The New Order which Hitler has been preaching for years is about to dawn. Life can never again be the same. Let's spend an afternoon together; let's get out into the country for a walk—maybe a visit to our May wood."

We spent the day walking together leisurely, a warm June day; the buzz of bees, the song of the birds, the countryside lush with green and gold made the news we had just heard seem unreal. That evening we were called to our radios: Prime Minister Churchill was going to speak to the nation.

> What General Weygand called the Battle of France is over. I expect that the Battle of Britain is about to begin. Upon this battle depends the survival of Christian civilization. Upon it depends our own British life, and the long continuity of our institutions and our Empire. The whole fury and might of the enemy must very soon be turned on us. Hitler knows that he will have to break us in this Island or lose the war. If we can stand up to him, all Europe may be free and the life of the world may move forward into broad, sunlit uplands. But if we fail, then the whole world, including the United States, including all that we have known and cared for, will sink into the abyss of a new Dark Age made more sinister, and perhaps more protacted, by the lights of perverted science. Let us therefore brace ourselves to our duties, and so bear ourselves that, if the British Empire and its Commonwealth last for a thousand years, men will still say, "This was their finest hour."

The speech was all the more remarkable in that Churchill and the British government knew that it was logistically impossible for Britain, standing alone, to defeat Germany. Yet for eighteen months Britain did stand alone, sustained often by the voice of this one man. He alone united the British people at a time when the morale of the nation might easily have swung over to a British Vichy. This was unquestionably Winston Churchill's finest hour.

The British Expeditionary Force performed a brilliant rearguard action until they found their backs against the English Channel at Dunkirk. One of the mysteries of the war is why Hitler personally intervened to call off his troops advancing upon the trapped Allied and British forces numbering 338,000. "The miracle at Dunkirk" they called it in the streets, as thousands of vessels crossed the Channel to pluck the troops from the French coast: warships, merchant ships, tramp steamers, barges, private yachts and motor boats, even dinghies, rowboats, and rafts.

Of all those lads who survived the evacuation at Dunkirk, one cocky, ginger-haired boy of the Glasgow Highland Light Infantry remains vivid in my memory. We met in the Church of Scotland canteen downtown, where I had been taking my turn at night duty. He appeared before me, all smiles, capless, no rifle or respirator, unshaven and bedraggled, his boots covered in caked mud and almost falling apart. On his right shoulder he carried a large wooden case which he laid down very gingerly on the table as I joined him over a cup of coffee.

"Great coffee, Padre! My! I'm that gled tae be hame! Wis at Dunkirk! Boy, It was awful! These stukas coming at ye, about a hundred feet in the air, blasting away, and us lying quaking in our slit trenches. Three days, Padre, can you imagine, until we got onto a boat!"

"What's in the wooden case, son?"

He winked and proceeded to remove the lid, delving among the straw packing.

"Ah! You just wait tae ye see this." He withdrew from the straw an exquisite demitasse and held the cup up to the light that I might see the shadow of his hand through it.

"Whit doe ye think o' that? It's for my grannie. I pinched it in Brussels. And I had a bit of a bother getting it into the boat at the beach wi' me up to the oxters in watter. My grannie always wanted a coffee set of her ain. I know she'll be pleased."

Suddenly history telescoped and I was sitting beside his Scottish mercenary forebears, who had made European wars their daily work, the Scottish soldier of whom the songs had been written. He pinches at Brussels, is strafed on the country roads of Belgium and France, and loses all his equipment, including his rations—while still guarding his precious loot. Bombed on the Dunkirk beach, he shepherds it across the waters to his rescue boat, disembarks in Southampton, boards a train to London and another to Glasgow. Now, over a cup of coffee, he is more excited about the precious gift for his grannie than about his part in one of the great battles of any war.

The following spring came the bombing of the port cities, part of the German blockade of Britain. In our area, Glasgow, Clydebank, and Greenock were all hit—thirteen major air raids in all. Though the raids were not comparable to the bombing of London, still Clydebank was seriously damaged: 1,083 killed and 1,602 seriously wounded. After the raids of

Greenock, our church hall was used as an emergency center for bombed-out families, a bedraggled, dust-covered, dazed group of people, utterly exhausted as they lay down on the rough palliasses thrown on the floor. I can still hear the cry of one sobbing woman: "Where's John? What's happened to John?"

What of my pacifism now? I went to the local labor exchange to register as a conscientious objector but was refused because I was a clergyman. I demanded to see the regulations, which read that among those "ineligible to register" were idiots and ministers of religion.

Downtown I visited George Square to see a German plane that had been brought down during a raid over the city. Unbelievably, a stick of bombs had leap-frogged buildings and monuments leaving a row of gaping craters. In the street outside the city chambers, with its facade of shattered windows, was the downed aircraft. I stood gaping with the rest of the silent crowd. My eye lighted upon the tires; they were marked *Dunlop Rubber Tyre Company.* What would Ayrshire-born John Boyd Dunlop have thought back in 1887 when he invented the pneumatic tire had he imagined his company would use them for this?

This was a different kind of warfare than we had anticipated. Our front garden was the front line, where night after night I watched German bombers passing one another against a cloudless moonlit sky on their errands of destruction. On one occasion, returning in the wee hours after a stint at the downtown service canteen, I distinctly heard the stick of bombs falling, like a long freight train braking. Suddenly, I found myself face down in the cold damp grass at the roadside, having jumped, instinctively, from one side of the road into the ditch on the other. The earth seemed to shake as the bombs landed. I picked myself up to see the ghastly sight of dwelling houses less than a mile away belching flames and smoke and the shadows of people running around against the red glow of the flames.

I joined my next-door neighbor, an air raid warden, as he went immediately on the sound of the sirens to the post in our church hall and motored with him through the deserted streets checking the damage. I took the opportunity of stopping off at places where I knew my members stayed, and visited in the air raid shelters in the back courts, grimly dark, with only a peep of light, crowded with whispering shadowy figures seated backs to the walls. I passed from one to another, a pat here and there, a wee word of encouragement ("Don't worry, my dear, that's our ack-ack guns firing") and always a word of prayer.

"Women are strange folk," as Barrie's Weary World, the Thrums policeman, was heard to remark. Jerry approached me one day to inform me that while the womenfolk appreciated my visits, they felt a bit embarrassed sitting in the bleak shelter, overcoats thrown over their nightgowns, curlers in their hair, and in general not very presentable to the minister. One lady I recall sat hat on head, gloves in hand, wearing her Sunday shoes.

I appeared before the conscientious objector tribunals on behalf of lads I had known to be pacifists. But they got short shrift; all that I was permitted to say on their behalf was that I knew that before September 3, 1939, they had held pacifist convictions. When they did appear before a Law Lord, the counsel offered them the routine alternatives to war service to which they invariably responded "No."

"Will you join the armed forces? Noncombatant armed forces? Ambulance corps? Air raid precautions, such as warden, firewatcher, firefighter? Forestry?"

"No."

"What is your present occupation?"

"Butcher . . . baker . . . teacher . . . policeman. . . ."

"You will continue in your present occupation until the end of the war. Next please."

The ministry was a "reserved occupation," but I was young, fit, and eligible for active service. Somehow I could not see myself as a chaplain, especially conducting services, where I would be expected to pray for victory. Whose victory? I could visualize myself as a soldier, especially a paratrooper, submerging self and identifying completely with the war effort. My present situation — to be neither wholly in it nor wholly out of it — was becoming intolerable, especially when we began to hear reports of friends dying. I will go down to the grave with the scar of these years upon me, never to know whether I was doing the right thing or not.

The memory of Alistair McLemon still comes back. In college nobody would have regarded Alistair as one who would be singled out for leadership in the Church. Tall, bespectacled, possessing a brilliant mind but lacking the ability to communicate with simplicity, Alistair was a rather dull preacher but a saintly, lovable man who would no doubt spend his life in some inconsequential parish. Came the war, Alistair volunteered as a combatant. His troopship was torpedoed in the Mediterranean while attempting to relieve the garrison of Malta. His lifeboat was overloaded. The young officer at the prow of the boat ordered some to go over the side; otherwise the boat would capsize and all hands would be lost. Alistair, a sharp pain in his middle from a shrapnel wound, inobtrusively slipped overboard into the churning oily waters. All the hundreds of sermons I have written, with their purple passages and clever exegesis, are not to be compared with this one shining, living word of Alistair, incarnate in a brave life, the sacrifice of a greater love.

Professor Riddell, who had disagreed with me on the pacifist issue, suggested that one course for me might be to do a spell with the Church of Scotland Huts and Canteens in the Orkney Isles at St. Margaret's Hope, a village on South Ronaldshay, one of the islands that form the Scapa

Flow base, a spread of twenty miles of protected waters and the only naval base, apart from Malta, left to the Allied cause. From here, the North Atlantic fleet joined the convoys to Russia.

I was granted five months' leave of absence in the summer of 1942 and, with Jerry and our puppy Trudie (short for Ermyntrude), a black, crossbreed Shetland collie, set off for the Orkneys. Our work, with the help of volunteers from the village, was to run a canteen, supplying snacks for working parties of the Pioneer Corps, selling cigarettes and chocolates and generally providing a place for the servicemen to relax when off duty, a place where they could play billiards, listen to the radio, and talk, a place for worship and discussion, especially on Sunday nights after the service at the local parish church. At this time, there were 250,000 military personnel on the Isles.

We found the experience emancipating; we were able to laugh once more. Jerry was the perfect hostess for so many lads, many of whom were at times overwhelmed with homesickness and culture shock. Night after night they would spruce up and come along to our hut to meet the minister's wife, sample her home cooking, and, of course, show her their photographs: of Mother and Dad, and "Jenny, my wife; and little Tommy, he takes after me; and Mary, who will grow up I hope to be like her mother." Once a week we held a party. We had no other program than to sit around playing the old-fashioned innocent games we used to play in the manse with our young people: guessing games or Pass the Parcel. Always someone would sing (apologetically) and much of the time was spent telling stories and recalling adventures.

"Jerry, they must be bored with this sort of thing," I ventured one day. "Let's ask along one of those blonde bombshells from the E.N.S.A. party. It'll give the boys a real thrill."

The blonde came, but, apart from her entertainment value, proved to be no bombshell. The next day Jerry was confronted by Ronald, corporal and a church organist back home.

"Mrs. Docherty, I do hope you will not think us forward or ungrateful, but the lads have asked to say that while it was nice meeting Miss 'Rosalee' last night, we really prefer your own parties and hope you will not change them."

With a borrowed bike, I visited far-flung ack-ack and searchlight units poised on the brink of the cliffs, the wind howling around—always the wind in Orkney. I would hold discussion groups, exchange stories, and engage in my own "asking questions" technique, enabling me to search out their doubts and misconceptions about the faith.

The Pioneer Corps was made up of men who fell short of an A-1 physical fitness classification. The corps included a higher than usual proportion of artists, writers, and philosophers. They produced an island newspaper, appropriately called *The Orkney Blast*, edited by professional journalists and writers; the circulation must have been around 100,000. It was a splendid production except for the chaplain's column, a grim, sermonic piece obviously got together without either much thought or much heart. I interviewed the editor and suggested that this was the one poor column in his newspaper. He agreed, as did the chaplain who wrote it, and said it was mine if I thought I could do any better. Hence was born the column "A Padre Prattles." I wrote each week about some incident, adventure, or calamity in the private lives of the boys. The St. Margaret's Hope Pioneers were delighted to read week by week of some incident that had befallen one of their group. When we left, the editor wrote an editorial in praise of it, which I took as no small compliment.

I recall one day over lunch when Charley asked, "Padre, who are you going to write about this week?"

Charley was a Cockney with flat feet whose one purpose in life was to find a way whereby his flat feet might take him out of the services. He spoilt his chances when, in order to please the major, he walked three miles to a farm and back for a chicken.

"Charley, not only am I writing about you in the 'Prattles,' I'm writing a novel in which you are the principal character. Let me read you the opening chapter. 'Lord Charles Escue'—that's you, Charley—'Lord Charles Escue folded his newspaper as he sat before the great fireplace in the library of his country mansion. He rose, stretched, and moved across the thick pile carpet to the vast oaken door to retire for the night. He turned the handle. He never felt the shot that killed him. . . .' "

"Cor!" said Charley, "What a beginning! I say, is that the end of me?"

"Yes, Charley You are the body. It's a murder story."

Our hut stood beside "the dump," an open field littered with piles of building equipment of all kinds. Sections for portable huts were everywhere. I badly needed a chapel. The lads could easily build one from the portable sections, but I needed official permission from the colonel in charge of the entire Orkney engineering operations. I boarded the ferry for the eighteen-mile sail across the choppy Flow to Stromness, having sent word of my coming ahead of me. I was met at the door of the hut by a private, who led me through an office to a lieutenant, who led me down a passageway to a captain, who knocked quietly on a bare door. From the other side came an irritated "Come in," and I was ushered into the sanctum of the chief himself. It was a sparsely furnished room, with here and there some family photographs. The colonel was seated, his head bowed in deep thought over a card table on which were spread out two packs of playing cards.

"Padre Docherty to see you, sir."

"Sit down, Padre."

There was an awkward silence while he slid appropriate cards into their correct slots.

"What's the game, Colonel?"

"Double patience."

"Good way to kill time, I suppose?"

"Kill time, Padre? Kill time? Young man, it is obvious you have never played double patience. Now sit over here beside me and I'll show you."

His concentration was total. He could have been a surgeon engaged in a major operation. It seemed we sat in silence for about an hour. At length I broached the subject of my visit.

"Sir, you will have heard about my request for a hut that I wish to use as a chapel. It seemed logical to me that the parts may as well be assembled into a finished hut rather than simply lie about on the ground. And if it is required, it can be taken down again. The men, who are keen to have a chapel, will erect the hut in their own time."

"Yes, Padre, a jolly good idea. Splendid! Now where the devil is that queen of hearts. . . ."

Soon thereafter I dedicated our new chapel. It proved more adequate for worship and a better forum for discussion. I felt honor bound, however, to keep off the subject of peace and war. The soldiers raised it nevertheless.

"Padre, how do you as a Christian square the present war with the commandment 'Thou shalt not kill?' "

"Well, of course, that Mosaic legislation specifically referred to murder."

"And what do you think modern war is? Murder, ain't it?"

My last service with them was Holy Communion, a card table for the elements, a loaf of bread and some Robina wine. Beyond young upturned faces I looked through the wire mesh window to the ineffable glory of an Orcadian sunset, turning the still waters of the Flow into gold, the silence of the evening broken only by the cawing of swooping gulls around the distant jetty.

Back home in Glasgow, I helplessly watched the crescendo of violence as German industrial centers were pounded night and day by American and British bombers, decimating the civilian population, although — as was later discovered — not making an appreciable dent upon German industrial output or breaking the morale of the German people. I had kept in touch with the Fellowship of Reconciliation and observed firsthand some of the night attacks on London. I visited Coventry after the "baedecker" raid on the cathedral and spoke to Scots workers who had been drafted for war work to that city. At home I kept up my daily discipline of study and conscientiously visited my congregation, especially those whose boys were in service. One family had a son who was a prisoner of war in Germany. In a censored postcard he had written, "I am being well treated here, but of course I'd rather be in dear old Sandymount." The censor could not know that Sandymount was the name of the local cemetery. Jerry and I wrote personal letters enclosed with the parcels of woollens knitted by the women and sent to members in the armed services.

I formed a Youth Community among the teenagers; "Work, Worship, and Recreation" were the key words. Jerry wrote one-act plays for them and the Women's Guild, which we performed for the entertainment of the French and American soldiers who happened to be billeted in the area. Our Youth Community had a memorable two weeks on the island of Iona, where we saw firsthand the beginnings of the Celtic Church, the ancient stone crosses, and the Columban monastery.

But I was flagellating myself at my work. Deep down I was an outsider to events of mammoth historic importance. There was much that I gained from these years, not least an enduring friendship among those who shared my views. Yet at Orkney I had glimpsed a loyalty of men freed from the aggravation of an uneasy conscience about the terrible question of the rightness or wrongness of the war. I shared my anxieties with a friend, an army chaplain; he hooted at me.

"Don't be daft, George. Stop wearing that hair shirt like some medieval monk caught up in the agony of haunting demons. You are in it as much as I am. War contradicts everything any of us ever believed or hoped for."

But his perspective did not entirely relieve my anxious conscience. And these dark moments, when I had doubts not only about myself as a minister, but also about the very faith that I openly confessed in the face of the madness of war, would come back again and again.

But I was blessed in my home life. Jerry was then, as she always would be, by my side whatever the crisis. Only one thing we lacked: there was still no baby. We sought medical advice. Gynecologists did all sorts of embarrassing tests and reported that they saw no reason why we should not have a child of our own. We decided to adopt; it was a pity to have a home such as ours and the adventure of the life in a manse without sharing it with some homeless bairn.

We visited an adoption clinic in Edinburgh run by the Church of Scotland. On our first visit, Jerry saw her heart's desire. True, he was a puny little fellow, barely two months old—but he had the Macpherson name, and we wanted to take him home with us on the spot, knowing that in no time Jerry would have him spunky and healthy. But the sister refused. It was against regulations to let out for adoption a child who did not meet certain health qualifications. We were asked to return the next month. The same report: not ready. The next month, we heard the same tale. The following month we decided not to return home without him.

"I'm sorry," replied the sister.

"But," argued Jerry, almost in tears, "we think the child is not putting on weight because he lacks a mother and the constant handling and care that only a home can give."

"You are probably right, my dear," said the sister gently, "but I have to stick by the regulations. I'm sure he will be all ready for you when you come back next month."

Out into the cold night, Jerry started to weep and indeed was sick, a condition I took to be a perfectly natural emotional reaction.

"Let's go into Princes Street and have something to eat, George; I'm feeling a bit peckish."

I had not the stomach to eat much, but to my surprise, Jerry relished her share of the fish and chips we had ordered.

It was Wednesday, prayer meeting night. When I returned home and inquired about her condition, Jerry said she had phoned Dr. Davidson. He wanted to see her in the morning, but had added that he felt the first step ought to be to cancel any plans for adoption. He was sure we were going to have our own baby.

6

Highland Interlude

In Iona of my heart, Iona of my love,
Instead of monks' voices shall be the lowing of the cattle;
But ere the world come to an end,
Iona shall be as it was.
—St. Columba (521–597)

IT IS MORE than twenty years since I last visited Iona, the little Inner Hebridean isle lying about a mile west of the flat promontory toe of the Isle of Mull, washed by the Atlantic, with nothing westward except Tiree and America.

You take one of McBrayne's boats from Oban. For over a century David McBrayne has been knitting the west coast of Scotland to the Hebrides.

The earth belongs unto the Lord,
And all that it contains,
Except the piers of the Western Isles —
These belong to McBrayne's.

To catch the 9:15 boat at Oban you have to be up betimes in Glasgow for the 4:15 A.M. train, and even that does not leave you much time to meet the connecting boat. Certainly not enough time to admire this uniquely situated town, the curve of its shore set into the craggy Argyll hills and, across the spacious bay, beyond the island of Kerrera, the beguiling prospect of the route to the isles. You dash to the pier where the *Duchess of Argyll* sits majestically in calm sheltered waters, a ribbon of steam at her yellow funnel, her great paddles ready to churn the green waters. A little breathless, you sit down and wait amidst the clatter of milk cans, the bleating of sheep being herded aboard, some lambs carried in the arms of the farmer, and the music of that untranslatable language of the Gael. Two hours later you are still waiting.

"When will we be leaving for Craignure?" you politely ask the officer

80

on watch; and with no less grace he replies, "You will be reaching Craignure about an hour after we leave Oban."

Eventually, the *Duchess* beats her way gracefully and quietly into the
choppy waters of the bay, breasts the dangerous, swirling currents past
Duart Castle, the ancestral home of the MacLeans, until she eases to a
gentle stop at Craignure pier on Mull, where you encounter a rotund
figure in a cap standing beside an ancient, top-heavy, twenty-seat Beard-
more bus. Mr. MacGillivray's greeting has the poetry of one whose English
is a translation from the Gaelic. Four other passengers brave that bus
journey across Mull, careening over the single track road rutted with
winter storms, swaying dangerously as it negotiates hair-pin bends while
you peer nervously out over red-granite rock precipices. Mr. MacGillivray
hums a Highland melody the while and tells of the old days when he made
the journey by horse and cart. After about two hours of some fifty miles
of this winding cart-track road, you alight a little unsteadily at Fionphort,
a scatter of houses. Suitcase in hand, you trudge down the winding pathway along the wrack-covered rocks and onto the concrete jetty where the
longboat waits to take you across the Sound of Mull, a mile and a bittie,
the final leg of the adventure of journeying to Iona.

Before boarding, you pause and look across the crested waves where,
to your surprised eyes, lies Iona. It is about three miles long and low-
lying; its solitary hill, Dun-I, stands some three hundred feet, girdled by
cruel, tooth-edged maroon Precambrian rocks interspersed with inlets of
white seashell sands. Marvelously camouflaged against the terrain of the
island stands the abbey, near enough to hear the dominant boom of its
bell in the eleventh-century square belfry tower. To the north you can
descry a peppering of white-painted stone farmhouses, the green, sheep-
spotted fields corraled by small drystane dikes. To the south lies the Bay
of the Coracle, where Atlantic breakers boom rhythmically upon its
smooth-pebble beach.

The longboat chugs toward the village, a scatter of houses running
down to the water's edge. You step ashore, a little startled when the gun-
wale of the motor boat suddenly pushes away from you, making you
jump onto the concrete jetty. Up the pebble pathway, skirting a small
white-sand shore washed with turquoise waters, you pay your respects at
the post office to Miss Morag Macphail, the postmistress, whose dark
Highland eyes return a smile of welcome. You turn right, past the ruins
of the Gothic nunnery where seven centuries ago black-robed Benedictine
nuns walked and prayed, all of them sisters or daughters of Highland
chiefs. Within its melancholy roofless ruin masses of summer flowers
blossom. Traveling north, you come upon a sudden right-angle bend in
the road, where stands the lichen-encrusted fifteenth-century McLean's
Cross, like a sentinel, about twenty feet in height. This is the junction of
the Road of the Dead, where Johnnie MacMillan encountered on a still

summer evening a silent procession of cassocked monks, hooded heads bowed, hands in their gown sleeves, gliding past him on invisible feet, their white Celtic tunics visible under their grey woolen *camilla,* as they have walked down the centuries at the setting of the sun. On Iona, all things are possible.

You clamber over a stile, the road not taken by tourists, up the original Road of the Dead, skirting the dike along the plowed field, past the solitary St. Oran's Chapel and the Ridge of the Kings — *Reilig Odhrain* — where lie buried fifty-eight Scottish kings, among them, side by side, Duncan and his murderer Macbeth. Against the boundary wall of the burial ground, in stark contrast to the lichen-covered recumbent stones, stand two simple white wooden crosses. The inscription on one tells of a sailor whose body was washed ashore on Iona when his ship was bombed; the other, of a German pilot whose body was recovered from the sea when his plane crashed while making its bomb run — perhaps aimed at the very ship of his companion in death. As you read the words, your heart once more aches at the madness of war, and you ponder the words of the Welsh poet Wilfred Owen, himself killed in the First World War:

> "Strange friend," I said, "here is no cause to mourn."
> "None," said the other, "save the undone years, . . .
> . . . .
> I am the enemy you killed, my friend.
> I knew you in the dark: for so you frowned
> Yesterday through me as you jabbed and killed.
> I parried; but my hands were loath and cold.
> Let us sleep now. . . ."

Thus they also sleep, among kings, in the second most sacred shrine in Britain.

Clambering over the boundary wall, you reach the abbey buildings, passing the wooden huts erected by the Iona Community, and pause once more to admire the noble tower, vast against the blue sky, its quatrefoil tracery in the window, its clock framed by wrought iron, the hour hand a gilded flaming sun, the minute hand a sickle of moon. You look up at the juncture of the ancient cathedral and the new refectory and see the identical cornerstone under which you placed half-a-crown in the cement as you labored on the unfinished wall alongside the master mason, Bill Amos.

You push open the side door that leads into the south transept of the cathedral. Does it still creak as once it did on an eerie midnight in the long ago? At the crossing of the church, you search for the little fern you once saw growing out of the damp between the stones of the arch behind the wooden side pulpit, near the carved face of a soul in torment, tongue bloated and sightless eyes uplifted, placed by its medieval sculptor above the preacher's head in order that the congregation might not miss the vision of the ultimate doom befalling those who would neglect such a marvelous salvation. You climb the three steps leading to the choir, worn down the ages by the feet of kings and commoners come to Iona for grace and pardon.

Your hand caresses the smooth carving of the bishop's mitered head in the sedilia, matching the ancient time- and weather-worn originals, and recall the morning you sat and admired an artist at work, his skillfully gliding chisel fashioning it from a cube of bright sandstone.

You retrace your steps across the choir and the crossing and climb the five steps to the compact nave with the large modern baptismal font at the west door, through which a radiant blue sky, as if washed by summer showers, dazzles your eyes. Before you rises a broad mound, an outcropping of rock covered with grasses and mosses. You climb and look down on the outline of the foundations of a cell with stone pillow and incredulously realize that here Columba spent thirty-three years of his life, transcribing the scriptures and writing poetry. From here he voyaged in his coracle to the Isles and mainland with twelve faithful companions, and once at least back to his self-forsaken home in Ireland. They brought the radiance of the gospel of Christ to pagan Picts, even challenging King Brude himself at the capital in Inverness. The Celtic gospel was the good news of the goodness of God's creation, as well as the salvation that is in Christ. Half Druid himself, Columba called Christ his Druid: all creation holy, every common bush aflame with God — true holiness, haleness.

On Saturday, June 8, 597, while transcribing the Psalter in this cell, he laid down his pen. "Here I think I can write no more; let Baithen write what follows."

In the waning light of that summer's day, he entered the church to celebrate nocturnal vigils for the Lord's Day. Early Sunday morning, before the altar, he raised his thin, work-worn hand in final benediction on his grieving, beloved *familia*. He was seventy-seven, a testimony to his remarkable constitution living at such a time and after a life of unremitting travel. The last words he penned were from Psalm 147:

> The young lions do lack, and suffer hunger,
> But they that seek the Lord shall not want anything.

Half of me, the commonsense half, urges me to accept the gracious invitation to return to Iona and be the guest of Lord MacLeod in the rooms set aside for him and his friends; the other half, the Celt, draws back, afraid that the wonder of the vision I once discovered in this strangely fey island of faith be dimmed by familiarity or that I may never again recapture the feelings of those days of my youth.

A beatific vision came to George MacLeod at a most unlikely time—in the early thirties amidst the Depression—and in the most unlikely place—at Govan, Glasgow, hub of the British shipbuilding industry. Minister at Govan, Dr. MacLeod used to watch daily from his study in the Pearce Institute overlooking Govan Cross the melancholy sight of the faceless unemployed in hodden grey caps and colorless, bedraggled clothes lounging against shop windows, standing at the curb kicking their heels or jumping up and down, rubbing their hands together to keep warm against the whining wind cutting up from the Clyde. They were part of the three million unemployed, an embarrassment to Tory and Socialist governments alike. Down the river in John Brown's yard stood the vast, rusting hull of the greatest ship in the world, unfinished, they said, because of lack of funds (it would be launched later as the Queen Mary). Under the eyes of the traffic policemen preoccupied with directing a few lorries and trucks and yellow clanging streetcars, a bowler-hatted man moved secretively among the crowd, collecting little white pieces of paper from men who had been studying the form of race horses in the Noon Record.

The Pearce Institute was the recreation facility at St. Constantine's Church, a fine, though soot-laden red-sandstone Gothic building. Inside all was calm and cold and dimly religious. On this spot St. Constantine, a disciple of St. Columba of Iona, had erected his wattle church fully a decade before Augustine landed in Kent in 597, a fact that Dr. MacLeod took some glee in recounting to the "Red" Dean of Canterbury, Dr. Hewlitt Johnston, when he spoke to a group of us at Govan. Here at this holy site down the centuries the liturgy of the Church was carried forward. Now in the Great Depression the Word was preached as perhaps from no other pulpit in Britain, and the faithful celebrated the sacraments before going back to the harsh world of economic stagnation, want, and hopelessness.

Worship and worklessness; holy Sundays and secular, empty Mondays; the sanctity of the soul and the secularization of everyday life; the body of Christ and the body of humanity, starving, diseased, or indulged; the breakthrough of the kingdom of God and all its glory and the false utopias of men's kingdoms crumbling all over the world—the contiguity of such contradictions worried Dr. MacLeod until he realized that what we had thought to be the gospel was rather the false traditions of an otherworldly view of the faith. To seek first the kingdom of God did not merely mean believing that beyond the grave we would all inherit eternal life. The first words of Jesus to his own people were to announce that in him Isaiah's vision was fulfilled, the kingdom had come: piety and politics, the sacred and the secular, holiness and health, body and soul, prayer and practice were not separate worlds but were two aspects of the same wholeness of life, the unity of the human and the divine.

What was the prayer of the Church in a day of dole queues, the

"Wee Georgie" Docherty,
four years old (1915)

Thomas Norton Docherty, on the eve of
the First World War (1914)

The Glen Usk in its civilian days as a pleasure steamer out of Bristol. With the advent
of World War I, it was pressed into service as a minesweeper. George's father served
aboard it as a stoker for five years.

Miss Jerry Watson, sixteen years old, secretary in the employ of Messrs. Davidson, Park, and Speed, Ltd. (1930)

George's brother Jackie, seventeen years old, Assistant Steward on the Anchor Line's S.S. California

The customs clerk, hat in hand, walking home after work along Sauchiehall Street, Glasgow (August 1932), near Charing Cross, where he was called to be a preacher on March 25, 1931

Master of Arts (Ordinary), Glasgow University (June 1935)

Mr. and Mrs. George M. Docherty and wedding party on the steps of the University of Glasgow's Memorial Chapel, June 24, 1938

George and Jerry outside the west door of the Iona Abbey, beside the St. John's Cross (summer 1944)

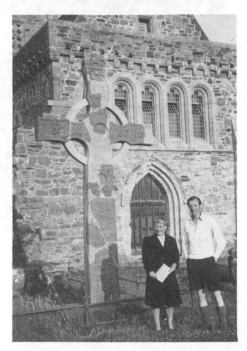

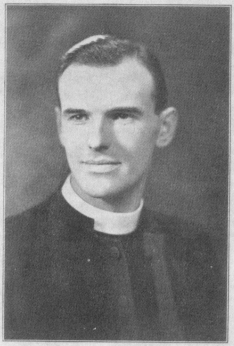

Lafayette

Ordination and Induction Arrangements

On Tuesday, 16th May, 1939, at 8 p.m.

The Presbytery of Glasgow will meet in
Sandyhills Church to Ordain and Induct

The Rev. GEORGE M. DOCHERTY, M.A.

OFFICIATING MINISTERS :

The Rev. J. CLARK BROWN, M.A., . . . Old Rose Street.

AND

The Rev. W. C. LAVALETTE, ... Chryston West.

The cover of the ordination service program

*Peter Marshall at the lectern pulpit in the old
New York Avenue Presbyterian Church (1948)*

George's mother, Jean Macpherson, in her eighty-fifth year

Peter Marshall's Successor
(April 1, 1950)

means test, hopelessness in family life, malnutrition in children, and a growing cynicism about everything? That the Lord return in this day of distress, roll up the map of time and history, and call a halt to this wicked world in final judgment? That the unemployed be given strength to endure the hardships of this world knowing that there is a happy land far, far away where we shall happy be, from sin and sorrow free? Or had the day come once more for the Church to denounce such evil systems as starve children and corrupt human life, and to do so in the name of him who was identified in his life with the poor and in his death with the wicked? We were not reading the signs of the times, and failing this we were opening the doors to a takeover by secular, atheistic Communism or materialistic fascism.

Out of such a beatific vision of the mission of the Church in the hungry thirties, the Iona Community was born. It was no less than a revival within the Church of a *familia*, a community such as Columba had gathered around him, but in terms of twentieth-century culture. If laymen and clergy alike could commit themselves for two years to serve a parish in an industrialized area where the need for mission was greatest, it might not yet be too late to win the people to an understanding of the gospel. Central to the mission would be the restoration of the abbey buildings as a project demonstrating the cooperation of laity and clergy, work and worship. This was to be no Highland twilight sentimental journey. *We Shall Rebuild*, the title of the book Dr. MacLeod in time would write, meant rebuilding not merely the stone and mortar of an ancient abbey but also the body and soul of humanity into the body of Christ which is the Church.

The setting of Iona had much to commend it. Back in 1907 the Duke of Argyll, with the commendable sense of a dedicated, ecumenical proprietorship, gifted, in trust, to the Church of Scotland the Cathedral of Iona, with the proviso that forever the cathedral be a place for all denominations of the Church, where every Christian would be at home. At the same time, the Church of Scotland rebuilt the cathedral, which during the centuries had fallen into ruins, its stones used for the building of crofts, its sacred precincts for the shelter of sheep and cattle—where "instead of monks' voices there sounded the lowing of cattle."

Scotland was stirred with the news that the minister of Govan was resigning and embarking, literally upon an act of faith, the founding of the Iona Community and the rebuilding of the abbey buildings.

The little corrugated iron village hall of Iona was crowded when Dr. George MacLeod announced to the villagers his plans for the future of the abbey and bespoke their blessing on his work. With other students from the four theological colleges in Scotland, I was present at the meeting. We had gathered during spring vacation, 1938, in a retreat made possible by the generosity of Sir David Russell, a dedicated churchman, and led by Dr.

MacLeod and Dr. David Hyslop. Dr. MacLeod shared his dreams, blending tactful humor and startlingly serious innovation. He was accorded a respectful silence. Highlanders, like deep waters, are still, but I am certain that then and since, the islanders have respected and indeed loved the grandson of Dr. Norman; was he not bone of their bone and flesh of their flesh?

Few ventures have started off with such dire portents. The Kirk itself was not united behind the movement; there were the inevitable few, the "we-never-did-that-afore" school. Others regarded the whole project as a sail thrown up in the winds that would not last the next storm. It was the eve of the Munich agreement. In a little over a year, the nation was at war. Such a project as rebuilding an ancient abbey was hardly a national priority. Official government permission was difficult to obtain. The stories concerning the progress of the rebuilding are many; most of them border on the fey. The deck cargo of wood that was washed ashore in a storm by law became the property of the island. The Norwegian timber was supplied by Norwegians in reparation for their violent Viking forefathers who had plundered the island and burned the abbey. But none of the stories is quite so extraordinary as that of the discovery of the well of water within the precincts of the abbey.

From the start, it was obvious that rebuilding could only proceed if water, which was required in almost unlimited quantities, could be found *within* the boundary walls of the abbey. The farmers and villagers had their own water problems. Two water diviners from Glasgow were employed to discover a source of water within the abbey grounds. Day after day they walked every square foot of the precincts, performing their dowsing exercise, divining rods held out horizontally, hoping for the sudden turn of the sticks which, incredible though it may seem, is still the infallible proof of the existence of a source of water. Each day a telegram arrived at Dr. MacLeod's home: "No water." "No water." And finally, "No water, returning."

On the morrow, in the providence of God, the *Duchess of Argyll* was late. To pass the time while they awaited the steamer, the two diviners decided to explore the circular base of what was believed to have once been a Culdee tower. Removing the lid, they delved with pails into the dark recesses of the foundation, bringing up sand, silt, and mud in which they hoped to find ancient coins, artifacts, and perhaps even monastic treasure hidden there during the Viking raids. At length the black smoke of the steamer was visible as it rounded the point at the south of the island. Hurriedly they replaced the round wooden lid; as they did so the surprised water diviners looked into the reflection of their own faces in the darkness. This had been the well of the monks, untouched, unknown, and unrecorded for centuries! It provided abundant water—and still does, years later.

The story of the rebuilding of the abbey ended in June 1965, when the buildings were finally completed. To commemorate the occasion, communion was celebrated outside the west door before an ecumenical gathering. Numbered among the worshipers were members of Govan Old Parish Church.

It must have been around the New Year of 1944 when the voice of George MacLeod came over the telephone.

"George! I want to see you. It's rather important—I've got a job for you. Could you possibly come round to 4 Park Circus Place, shall we say tomorrow, around three? We shall have tea."

Punctually on the hour the following afternoon, I was ringing the doorbell of the splendid townhouse of George's father, Sir John, one-time Tory M.P. for Glasgow Central District. It was now the office of the Iona Community and residence of Dr. MacLeod. To my left, I looked up to the three towers of Trinity College and the baronial tower of the Park Church.

Over tea I was informed that Sir James Lithgow, shipbuilder and churchman, had left a trust fund under the auspices of the community to be called the "Iona Youth Trust." The funds were intended to finance three parish projects in the inner city, specifically among the young, on the principles of the Iona Community. The Barony of Glasgow—the parish church of Glasgow—under its minister Roy Sanderson wished to be one of these parishes. Would I be prepared to lead such an experiment in parish mission?

The technical difficulties were soon met. I saw no reason why I should leave a full charge to become an assistant; I was made Minister Co-adjutor, an episcopal term meaning "assistant to an aged bishop with a view to succession"! For the sake of the experiment, I desired to retain my seat in the presbytery. This was accomplished by making me Minister Emeritus of Sandyhills, an honor surely without precedent: Minister Emeritus of my first charge, at the ripe age of thirty-four!

With great regret but clear resolution, I left Sandyhills Church and took up my new duties on the eve of the Second Front in Europe, June 5, 1944.

The Barony Church stands in the parish of Townhead beside the Western Infirmary, where Lord Lister did his experiments in antiseptics, across the square from the cathedral. The congregation of the Barony originally worshiped in the sixteenth century in the crypt of the cathedral. In the background stands the hill of Glasgow necropolis, dominated by a statue of John Knox in the midst of substantial granite vaults, where many of the merchant princes of Victorian Glasgow are buried.

Social conditions in Townhead in the mid nineteenth century were grim; one contemporary writer notes, "jollity was everywhere absent; sheer loathsome, swinish inebriation prevailed." Conditions had certainly improved since those Dickensian days, yet housing still was deplorable. Ninety-six percent of the home had no hot water nor an indoor bathroom. For many, sanitation consisted of outside water closets in the back court. In Collins Street across from the Barony stood what were called "The Galleries": the close opened up into a wide courtyard surrounded by four stories of galleries. On each floor, four families shared the single cold water sink.

Back in the grim days of 1851, Dr. Norman MacLeod, the grandfather of George, had been called to the Barony and immediately set about tackling the appalling social conditions of the parish. He built a "chapel of ease," which would become the MacLeod Church on Parliamentary Road. He started a men's club and initiated a savings bank, one of the first in the country. To break down the social distinctions of the Victorian church (his own congregation in the Barony were largely affluent, living in the west end of the city), he introduced a rather unique qualification for attendance: only women with a shawl (a wrap against snell winds and a blanket for baby) and men wearing moleskins (cotton fustian trousers, the hallmark of the laboring class) were admitted. It became known as the "moleskin kirk." Lady Fraser Balfour, a notable churchwoman and the daughter of the Duke and Duchess of Argyll, arrived one Sunday evening to attend this new "chapel of ease" that her friend Dr. Norman had built. Alighting from her carriage, assisted by the footman, she swept with haughty air toward the entrance only to be stopped by an extended grimy, calloused hand.

"I'm sorry, milady, only women with shawls admitted."

Whereupon Lady Fraser crossed Murray Street toward a group of curious women standing at a close mouth astounded at the sight of so grand a lady. Doffing her spacious hat, she requested of one of the women the loan of her shawl and marched with dignity into the church for the worship of God.

The object of the Iona Youth Trust experiment was to revive within the parish a viable connection with the MacLeod Church, since most of its dwindling membership now lived in the scattered suburbs of the city. We would begin with the young. The old MacLeod Church was to be turned into a modern youth center.

The traditional horseshoe gallery was extended across the sanctuary, making two floors. The underside of the gallery was filled in to provide side rooms for a crafts class, a worship, and a complete kitchen where housekeeping would be taught. The center area was left open, a gathering place for talk and informal discussion. The only other place these young folks could gather together was at a street corner, where they were at the mercy of the police; it seemed a good idea to provide such an informal meeting place. (Even so, they insisted on talking in the vestibule and by the front doors!) Upstairs in the remodeled sanctuary the chapel occupied the center space, large enough to hold the entire membership. Side rooms were constructed for other classes, such as art, musical appreciation, radio listening, and debate. At the far end of the chapel stood the billiard table. I believed that if we could not worship with a billiard table at the end of the chapel, our worship was lacking reality; and if one's billiards was vitiated by the presence of a communion table, then surely there was something substandard about the game. (It did not work out; a curtain was drawn across the rear of the chapel separating the sacred from the secular.) The old church hall was refurbished as an up-to-date gymnasium with showers and two sunken baths large enough to accommodate teams after a session of basketball, touch football, or gymnastics.

Membership in the Barony Kirkhouse, as I named the center, was open to all boys and girls from six to eighteen, with preference given those who lived in the immediate parish. The club was open six days a week (all day on Saturday) and closed on Monday. My staff consisted of three full-time colleagues: George Hunter, who would later study for the ministry; Jean Macgregor, who would later marry my successor, the Reverend John Sim; and Edith Mustard, who would become the wife of the Reverend Bill Smith, now in Toronto, Canada. The hope was that scores of volunteers would augment the paid staff.

"Work, Worship, and Recreation" — this was the trinity of purpose. The "work" was simply doing what the "boss" (my informal title) told them to do or to help in renovating, cleaning, and painting the premises, running the canteen, or playing in the band. Chapel prayers were compulsory. Even on Saturday nights after the weekly dance, the community retired upstairs for worship. On Sunday evenings we gathered in the gymnasium where, apart from business and canteen, we held a service of worship. I always preached.

I was soon to learn the truth of Jesus' words that whoever does God's will shall know his truth. In a group engaged in a common activity the true nature of belief and faith arises. Compulsory chapel raised a profound theological problem as well as the question "What makes a community Christian?" Some believed that chapel should be voluntary, that members would come to know the meaning of glorifying and enjoying God of their own will. I called this "Christianity by osmosis," by the atmosphere of the club. On the other hand, I believed that worship was central to any definition of the Christian faith and new members would soon recognize that Christian worship was the feature that distinguished this from secular clubs. Membership in the club was a commitment to a trinity of purpose.

On the other hand, no one could compel a lad or lass to become a member of the church. Profession of faith in Christ was a personal commitment that could spring only from within the heart and mind of the person. It had been my hope that in time the club members would seek to become communicants of the Barony Parish Church. Here I encountered two problems. The Barony Church was remote and beautiful and strange; here amid the familiar laughter and fun and seriousness of purpose of this old church ("desecrated to the glory of God," as one cleric described it) was a center of true fellowship and faith. The Kirkhouse was becoming a church. When, in time, a couple who had met in our club wished to be married, we knew that it *was* a church. In due time came requests for baptism and possibly even the Lord's Supper.

Two gangs were among our most devoted and excited members; I knew they would never have the courage or nerve or perhaps even inclination to join the church on their own. The Kirkhouse met all their present needs. I knew if I harangued James and Bill, the leaders of the two gangs, like a sergeant major ("Next week you all will join the church or you are out in the cold"), they would immediately rally, would take any vow without knowing anything about its implication for the faith, if only they were allowed to continue as members of the club that meant so very much to them.

I decided to consult an authority, Professor Burleigh of Edinburgh, a noted church historian and a leading authority on St. Augustine. He listened to my dilemma. "If I wait, they will never become part of the fellowship of the church; if I order them, they will, but that would be the Emperor Constantine's way — Christianity by edict."

The good man paused, rubbing his chin, and sighed with a shake of his shoulders: "Ah! I'm afraid I cannot help you, Docherty. You see, my period ends with Augustine."

I was to meet even heavier weather in sorting out distinctions between what is secular and what is sacred.

Our boys were being swamped on the soccer pitches every week. I refereed two matches each Saturday on Glasgow Green, that nursery for some of the great players in the game. But our Kirkhouse boys needed practice badly.

"What about Sunday, boss?"

"Can't. You'll disturb the neighbors; we should take care that how we spend our Sundays does not prevent others from enjoying peace."

"What about practice in the gym then?"

Or what do you do with youngsters on a Sunday whose only Sunday School had been the street gambling school?

"Table tennis? Yes! Billiards? No!"

"But, boss, what's the difference between a white celluloid ball being hit over a net with a bat and a white ivory ball being hit with a cue over a green baize table?"

"Billiards is associated with gambling!"

"But, boss, you know we don't gamble in the club."

"What about music on Sunday afternoon, boss?"

"It must be classical; no jazz or that sort of stuff."

"What about Bing Crosby singing Brahms' 'Cradle Song'?"

"Boss, I can get you a supply of wood and sheet metal and one or two tools for the crafts class; the club is running short, you know."

"How would you get them?"

"At my work. I'd pinch 'em."

"No, you must never steal from your work. Mind you, if you asked permission of the foreman to take them, that would be all right."

"Foreman, boss? Foreman! Why he steals more than the rest of us."

Should the band have to pay the shilling for admission to the dance like the girls who did the cooking? The band said No — they were entertaining. I said Yes, they must pay; they were no more important than the rest of the club. The band refused to play; we played records for the dance.

Could the girls cook in the cookery class ovens on Sunday afternoon for the Monday night dance? They had learned some fine new recipes. No! That would be breaking the Sabbath day. Could they take home the flour, sugar, and other ingredients and bake in their own homes on Sunday afternoon?

I began to appreciate the burden Moses carried as he sought to interpret the Ten Commandments; no wonder he required two stalwarts on either side of him, to uphold his arms!

The abiding value for me, and I believe for the whole Church of Scotland, was George MacLeod's reinterpretation of the calling of the ministry. MacLeod inverted the traditional concept of the ministry. Heretofore our careers followed an almost foreordained pattern. We graduated and took a small country parish where we would spend long hours with our books, drinking deeply of the classics, not least the mystics, in our preparation for the pulpit Sunday by Sunday. Then, perhaps, we would move to a provincial town like Perth or Kilmarnock to await the hour when we would be called to the great preaching pulpit of Wellington, Glasgow, or St. George's West in Edinburgh, where our undoubtedly effective ministry would blossom with the usual rewards of a D.D. from our *alma mater* and even the prospect of the Moderatorship of the Church. George MacLeod turned that idea on its head. Get into the city, the inner city, where the need is greatest in this urban industrial age, when you are young enough to climb the tenement stairs and idealistic enough to believe in the wonder of the saving grace of the gospel! Too often the mission of the inner city was left to pastors who had returned to the city in their middle years and spent hard-working days with increasing pessimism, visiting their flock who had "bettered themselves" and moved out of the parish to the enlarging suburbs of the cities. Theirs was a thankless task at a time in their lives when they were simply no longer physically or spiritually able to cope with it.

George MacLeod brought romance to the mission of the downtown church. He believed that our best young minds should be working there, that large staffs were needed not for the famous suburban or west-end congregations, but downtown. The old class-conscious strategy of supporting a "mission among the poor" was outmoded.

For me, it seemed a peculiar challenge; as a lad from the tenements, I believed I had an entree into the lives of the working class, so called. Only the nineteenth-century aristocrat Matthew Arnold could pen such patronizing lines as these while walking "the squalid streets of Bethnal Green":

> I met a preacher there I knew and said:
> "Ill and o'erworked, how fare you in this scene?"
> "Bravely!" said he; "for I of late have been
> Much cheer'd with thoughts of Christ, *the living bread.*"

Thus the pitiable preacher to the poor can set up this "mark of everlasting light":

> Not with lost toil thou labourest through the night,
> Thou mak'st the heaven thou hop'st indeed thy home.

We believed that the energies of the Church, spiritual and moral and financial, should be loosed for those who saw Christ not only as the living bread of sacrament, but also as the bread that feeds the multitude, until there are twelve baskets full left over.

Six nights a week and all day on Saturdays! The work demanded every ounce of physical strength and every thinking moment of the day. And of course, the experiment could hardly succeed after over a hundred years of neglect, of being relegated to second-class status by a bourgeois church. I buried more babies in those three years than I have done in the rest of my ministry. I watched a boy go down to death with tears because he regretted he could not play for the team on Saturday. I've visited a home where on the bed, under a blanket, lay a lad, dead, fished out of the canal. I've knocked at a door in "The Galleries" opened by the lovely girl of the house who blushed and shut the door behind her, lest I see the poverty she was forced to live in. We wallpapered the kitchens of aged folk in tenements fit only for the demolisher's ball.

The Barony Kirkhouse is now gone; "The Galleries" are no more; and where a duchess strode into church in a borrowed shawl, new highrise homes have been built—not by a God-fearing city whose motto is "Let Glasgow Flourish by the Preaching of the Word," but by a secular town council. The Barony Kirk is a shadow of its former glory and is working on a merger with a neighboring church. But the people are still there. New problems in those high-rise apartments abound, awaiting a renewal of that vision given once to me—the romance of the inner city.

Highland Interlude

Youth leaders, like athletes, have short lives. Too soon we are out-of-date, as I was to be reminded by the redoubtable Davie Brown when once I applied my usual authoritarian certainty to a discussion of modern music.

"But Mr. Docherty, you are no' even of oor generation."

How right he was! I was double his age, and I knew the time had come to move. Besides, I was yearning to preach; the pulpit of the Barony was occupied Sunday by Sunday by either Roy Sanderson or his assistant.

One pivotal memory from those days in our flat in 196 Walton Street. A bleak December, 1944, a Saturday night or rather Sunday morning, when still at my typewriter, I was finishing off the prayers for the service I would take on the morrow. I was typing the call to worship:

> How beautiful upon the mountains are
> The feet of him who brings good tidings,
> Who publisheth peace.

The telephone rang.

"It's a boy, George, and mother and child are well. Congratulations!" It was Oliver Springer, our beloved doctor, a Jamaican who would in time turn to the church as a minister.

I went out into the dark, starless night and walked along a deserted Great Western Road, the streetlamps making dull pools of light on the damp macadam sidewalks, the limp bare trees of the Botanic Gardens making slow moving shadows across my path. I was stunned with happiness, a strange, unbelieving elation after our six years' wait. And I recall thinking, "Well, my son, you are coming into a world that will have got rid of Hitler and war forever."

We called him Garth; the name means "cloister garden."

Eighteen months later his brother David was born.

7

Grey Granite

Bon Accord
—Motto of the city of Aberdeen: "Happy to meet; sorry to part; happy to meet again."

IT WAS NOW OCTOBER 1947, and I was beginning to feel somewhat apprehensive about my future. I had resigned from the Barony Kirkhouse in June in order that my successor, the Reverend John Sim, could have time during the summer months to prepare for the heavy schedule of the winter. I was unemployed—for the second time. On Sundays I had been preaching in various Glasgow pulpits, mostly of friends, and on several occasions there had been a vacancy committee in the congregation. The war was over, but the label *pacifist* was dying hard, or so it seemed to me, as Professor Riddell had warned me some years before that it would.

The telephone rang in my study at Wilton Street, the flat we had occupied during Kirkhouse days. At the other end of the line I heard the two copper coins drop, the crunch as button A was depressed, and a broad, youthful Glasgow voice, "Is that you, Mr. Docherty?"

"It is."

"This is Christopher speaking!"

"Why, Christopher, I'm delighted to hear your voice again! How are you, son?"

"Oh! Ah'm jist fine! But I thought I wid jist phone you. To see if you hid got a job yet."

Christopher, an undersized fifteen-year-old, had been the Kirkhouse billiards champion. I had taken up the game seriously and tried hard to beat him, but I had never prevailed. Just as well perhaps, for his mastery over the "boss" round the green baize table gave him an unaccustomed kudos in the eyes of the other members.

It was Christopher who on one occasion hid under the billiard table after the Saturday night dance in order to avoid our traditional chapel prayers. I had taken him firmly but gently by the scruff of the neck, led him unresistingly to a back seat in the chapel, and strode on pontifically towards the Holy Table, where I made the call to worship:

Grey Granite

Except the Lord build the house . . .

and I caught the mischievous sparkle in Christopher's eyes as he in mock
solemnity responded,

They labor in vain that build it.

There is no evidence that Christopher ever made a full confession of faith —
or indeed that any but a few ever came into membership of the Church —
yet that telephone call, costing that lad twopence and the resolve to master
the intricacies of the British telephone system, made me believe once more
that perhaps the work of the Kirkhouse had not been entirely in vain.

I decided to telephone the interim moderators of vacant churches that
might plausibly proffer me a call. Beechgrave, Aberdeen was no longer a
possibility — they were about to call Tom Torrance (later to become a professor and one of the most distinguished Scottish theologians). I called
Professor John Graham of Aberdeen University regarding the vacancy at
the North Kirk, Aberdeen — a rather dicey move that was frankly born of
desperation.

"Why it's most interesting to hear from you, Mr. Docherty. Only
last night we had another meeting of the vacancy committee of the North
Kirk. Frankly, we are at a standstill. Two men we asked have refused us.
We have decided to go back over other men we had heard, and your name
came up. You will no doubt be hearing from me about coming up to preach
in Aberdeen before the whole committee. Tentatively we have made arrangements for you to be heard in St. George's Church."

I did preach at St. George's, Aberdeen; I was appointed sole nominee,
preached before the North Kirk, and was duly called and inducted — December 16, 1947.

Aberdeen, the "silver city by the sea," faces the grey North Sea,
perennially buffeted by snell winds from Norway. It stands between two
salmon-fishing rivers — the Don to the north, the Dee to the south; between them stretches a splendid two miles of beach where for generations
happy holiday makers, especially from Glasgow, have enjoyed its sunshine
and braved its arctic waters. The city has a population of about two hundred
thousand, and its magnificent natural harbor where the Dee flows into the
sea is one of the largest in Britain. As a fishing port it is second only to
Lowestoft in England. Behind the sands lie the windswept treeless links
on which golf has been played for as long as it has in St. Andrews. Westward lie the good farmlands of Aberdeenshire, and the little red granite
towns of Kintore and Inverurie. Some fifty miles along the North Deeside
Road stands the little town of Ballater, where royal families since Victorian
days have alighted at the railway station, thence by carriage to Balmoral
Castle, built and beloved by Queen Victoria. Nearby stands Crathie Kirk,

where royalty, who by statute become Presbyterian in Scotland, worship when they travel north across the English border.

In Ptolemy's map, Aberdeen is demarcated as *Devana*, "town of the two rivers." More likely the name is derived from the Gaelic *Grianan*, "sunny drying place," where women folk bleached their washing on the links or perhaps laid out their fish for drying. It is *Apardion* in a twelfth-century Norse poem ("The King destroyed the peace / Of the dwellers of *Apardion*"), from *aber*, "mouth of the river," and *da-awan*, "the two streams."

Old Aberdeen on the banks of the Don to the north grew up around the Christian settlement there in the fifth century. St. Mochrrieha, a missionary from St. Ninian's monastery down in the Solway Firth, settled his Christian mission on the *machair*, "the level ground near water." By the fifteenth century there had arisen a noble granite cathedral where the bend of the river resembles a bishop's crook. The twin towers of St. Machars Cathedral are still a landmark; nearby is King's College Chapel, around which grew up the ancient Aberdeen University. Old Aberdeen had increasingly become integral to the University, with spacious students' residences growing up around the Old Manse.

The North Kirk is situated in the more modern city above the harbor behind the splendid seventeenth-century Tolbooth in the Castlegate, now unhappily hidden from the street by a nineteenth-century "balmoralized" granite-turreted townhouse at the confluence of Shoe Lane, Queens Street, and King's Street. It was a Free church, its congregation "coming out" from the Toon Kirk, St. Nicholas, at the time of the Disruption in 1843.

At the turn of the century, the congregation of the North Kirk embarked on what now must be regarded as a remarkable venture in Christian evangelism. A group of young men drawn from the trades and professions of the city decided that the age-old invidious distinction between "mission hall folk" and the more bourgeois kirk people should be abolished. The Mealmarket Mission of the church where the "orra folk" worshiped Sunday by Sunday was demolished and the old North Kirk was itself taken down as well. In its place a new building was erected that had none of the features more commonly associated with churches, such as Gothic arches, stained-glass windows, choir stalls, and pipe organs. Willie Gauld, the architect and one of these young men, designed the new building along the lines of the Manchester Methodist Central Hall, with a horseshoe gallery like a concert hall, a podium on a large platform for a pulpit, and a floor slanted like that in a theater. Nor was there a pipe organ; the praise on the Sabbath was led by a brass and string orchestra in which many of the town's leading musicians played. It became affectionately known as the "Fiddlers' Kirk."

Among the church's succession of distinguished scholar preachers, the Reverend David C. Mitchell was quite outstanding. He was tall and rather heavy-built with a smallish round balding head, a pugnacious pacifist, an avid teetotaler, nonsmoker, and an unrepentant Christian socialist. His pleasant tenor voice often graced his services with song, and his rather thin treble preaching voice at times rose to a pitch of controlled passion. When he arrived after the First World War, the North Kirk was firmly established, and he was able to rally round him many of the veterans returned to the land, "fit for heroes to live in" albeit suffering massive unemployment. The Sunday afternoon meetings of the brotherhood, led by the orchestra, were an immediate success; the 850-seat church was consistently filled to capacity. In his ten-year ministry (1920 to 1930), "D. C." added no fewer than 1,557 first communicants. The congregation itself increased from 1,350 to 2,576.

By 1947 a new age had dawned. Around the church's doors the fetid slums of Shoe Lane and other dark alleyways had been demolished. Indeed, the social witness of the congregation had played a leading part in the transformation. The Brotherhood, on the other hand, was a ghost of its former glory, its Sunday afternoon meetings attended by only a handful of sleepy veterans who were coaxed into song by an aged Willie Gauld, the same who had designed the sanctuary. And the fiddlers were gone. Even the sanctuary had undergone some changes. A former minister had installed a hideous Picassoesque stained-glass window behind the platform. Later it was mercifully hidden from the eyes of the worshipers when a new pipe organ (itself an innovation) had been installed. But there still remained a dynamic group of old North Kirkers such as Garden Swopp, their Socrates, Donald Fraser, the session clerk, and Duncan Fraser, who became Lord Provost during my ministry. They and their successors, all Christian socialists, made a deep impact upon the life of the city. So many were elected to the town council that when I constituted the session, I could have been opening a meeting of the council. Several of them became Lord Provost. Under their witness, urban renewal became a priority. The city, with its thousands of rosebeds on highways and open spaces, has annually been voted The Most Beautiful City in Britain.

The old and the new joined hands in the North Kirk to create an exciting city ministry and a great preaching pulpit. Of its two thousand members I could count on the complete dedication of life and service of a strong nucleus of nine hundred. The pastoral responsibilities were heavy, however. For the first year I had no assistant; my professional secretarial help was limited to one morning a week when a pleasant lass came in to take dictation. The Scottish parish system gave all residents in the parish a certain claim on the minister for such pastoral obligations as sick visitation. Two afternoons each week I spent at Forresterhill Hospital trying to visit from fifteen to sometimes forty patients, most of whom had no connection with our church beyond perhaps a grandparent who had been baptized there.

Some of my duties were more joyful. One Sunday morning after a Parish Mission led by D. P. Thomson and Tom Allan, I baptized eighteen babies. Weddings were always great occasions. The poorer the bride's parents, the greater the celebration. Not for these folk those cocktail affairs with people walking around aimlessly gabbing, with paper napkins and wafer-thin sandwiches; these receptions were almost always sit-down affairs — three courses in one of the city's posh hotels. Formal toasts were offered, beginning with a toast to the King, before which no one was allowed to light a cigarette. The minister was the factotum. He gave the toast to the bride and bridegroom, who suitably replied. He encouraged the best man, obviously uncomfortable in his rented morning suit, to say a pretty word on behalf of the bridesmaids. There were toasts for the parents of the bride and the bridegroom and suitable replies by the respective fathers. And always at the end, just before the tables were cleared for the dancing, a shy man, no doubt a distant cousin who had attended such occasions before, rose and proposed a toast to the minister, which was greeted with cheers and to which I modestly replied. Then, on with the dance into the wee sma' hours! Jerry and I would dance one or two dances before leaving. On the Monday following (weddings were always held on Saturday afternoons), Jerry would meet a neighbor who would recall how grand was the whole affair: "And you know, Mrs. Docherty, we had a great time after you and the minister left."

There would be about one hundred funerals every year, and sometimes as many as three in a single afternoon. One such afternoon remains vividly with me. The funeral director of the second service I performed told me that we would also be together for the third, but he regretted that he had no limousine available for me. Would I care to travel with him to the other house of mourning in the hearse? It seemed a reasonable request, except that I didn't want to arrive three quarters of an hour early at the house, where there was little a pastor could do but sit with the other black-robed mourners in the little tenement parlor denuded of all furniture save the chairs, some borrowed from neighbors and placed around the wall, while in the center of the floor the simple open wooden coffin rested on a movable tressel around which a slow procession of grieving folk passed in awed silence. I suggested that he drop me off at 9 Canal Place, where I would pay a call on Mrs. McIntosh, a nonagenarian and a rare soul of the old North Kirk days.

Thus on that bright afternoon, as Mrs. McIntosh sat at her bay window looking through the lace curtains as was her custom, watching the world pass by, she was startled at the sight of an empty hearse stopping at her front gate, out of which sprang an alert young minister, top hat, puritan black clerical coat and collar, gloves, and service book in his hand, who approached the door with a quick step and rang the bell.

"Michtie me, Mr. Docherty!" she shouted, holding her apron up to her face in mock horror, trying to smother her laugh. "Michtie me! Come awa in! I kent I was auld, but I didn't think I was deid!"

As the minister's wife, Jerry found herself involved in the life of the church. Her mother had been with us since Jerry's father died, six months after we were married. "Friendly," as I called her, filled the role of adored grannie for our two boys and of a most welcome babysitter for their busy parents. Jerry became the chairwoman of the Woman's Guild and the Mother's Meeting, by edict of the women themselves.

"Weel, Mrs. Docherty, it's jist like this. We a' ken each ither sae weel — we gaed tae school th'gither — and we will take orders from nane except the menister's wife."

The Woman's Meeting was the gathering place for the folk of the parish, few of whom were members of the church. There they would enjoy a cuppa and a blether together every week in a gathering that brought much happiness and fun to their dreich lives. We visited those who were not always able to attend the meetings, such as Mrs. Cheyne, the blind woman whose sensitive fingers passed over Jerry's face as we sat in darkness in her wee cottage. She loved to hear the gossip of the kirk and town.

My predecessor John Symington had laid a foundation for a Youth Club, assisted by a church sister, Betty Pullar. A new generation of North Kirkers was arising who would in time be the leaders of the church. Coming as I did from the youth work of the Barony Kirkhouse, I believed that I was not without experience of how to run a Youth Club.

These were the days when tape recorders were coming into general use. We had used them not without success at the Barony, especially for the production of religious drama. About this time the BBC had ruffled puritan sensibilities by producing Dorothy Sayers's play *A Man Born to Be King*. To hear even a great actor articulate the words of Jesus in a play was a shock that I encountered with some reservations, though the production was impeccable and sensitive. My idea was to stage a passion play *without an actor playing the part of Jesus*. The main characters would be light, color, and readings of Scripture against a background of music — Wagner's *Fire Music*, Sibelius's *Swan of Tuenella*, and of course Handel's "Hallelujah Chorus."

In the beautiful chancel of the Barony in Glasgow I had produced such a play once for a crowded Holy Week audience. Our young people were dressed in colorful saris borrowed from the India Club of the University. We had called upon a ballet teacher to help us teach them how to walk and move as in the crowded marketplace scene in Capernaum. No one played the part of Jesus. When it was announced over the loudspeakers "Jesus came to Capernaum," there was a sudden change of mood in the music; everyone stood stock still; every eye was fixed upon the entrance and followed in unison the progress of a slowly walking invisible figure. Similarly, soldiers on Golgotha's Hill simulated the cruelties of beating a victim carrying a cross, kneeling to hammer nails through hands and feet, and lifting the invisible cross up into place. Out of the darkened church came my reading, *"Eli! eli! lama sabachthani!"* Wagnerian music climbed to a new climax. In a strangely sacramental way, the invisible victim had become the Real Presence. It was this experience I wished to repeat at the North Kirk.

A University student, Andrew Gray, who was embarking upon radio and recordings as a career, was able to acquire for us a remarkable set of rejected surplus R.A.F. equipment — three loudspeakers, a record turntable, microphones, a ham radio transmitter/receiver, and tape recording equipment: price, £100! I successfully made a case before the city's Education Authority that this was as necessary a sort of youth equipment as footballs, handbars, barbells, and the other gymnastic equipment provided through the government's Youth Scheme. We built a radio kiosk in the hall. All was set for the opening performance.

"It'll no' work, Mr. Docherty," said the apprentice electricians who were supervising the work. "The equipment works from AC current, but the church is still on the old DC current."

I called on the manager of the Electricity Board in the city and explained our dilemma.

"I'm sorry, Mr. Docherty. It is true that we are re-laying the entire city with AC cables, but the North Kirk is not due for another two years. Actually, the new cables have come as far as Queen Street, but they stop short of the North Church by two hundred yards."

"I was hoping something could be done. Much of our youth work depends upon our having AC current," I replied.

A couple of weeks later I had difficulty approaching the church. Queen Street was closed to all traffic; workmen were busy with mechanical shovels digging up a long trench five feet deep, creeping nearer and nearer to my church! The sympathetic manager of the Electricity Board was a scoutmaster in his own church!

Our radio drama was ready — except for the stage. An architect had drawn up plans for a proscenium stage that could permanently be built on the fine platform of the large hall, with overhead lighting operated by a rheostat dimmer (included in our R.A.F. equipment); Stewart and Lloyds, the steel works in Glasgow, promised structural beams for the construction of the proscenium.

I brought the matter before the kirk session with understandable enthusiasm, outlining the whole project, and noting that we would no longer have to call upon Jack B— — for the dimmer he so faithfully made available for us every Christmastide, an ancient three-porcelain-jar hydro-dimmer, a fire hazard with every use, which was in any case not the property

79746

of the church. My exciting news was received with discomfiting silence broken eventually by Jack himself, a detectable sadness and regret in his voice.

"Weel, Mr. Moderator, as one who is not unacquainted with the functions of electricity, let me congratulate you on a fine idea, a very modern idea, I may add. My old dimmers, of course, are out-of-date; but mind you, Moderator, for these past twenty-five years they have worked very well, and many a Christmas pageant has been greatly benefited by them. But I see that is all in the past now. One grows out-of-date. But let me say, Moderator, if in any way I can be of service to you, please do not hesitate to call upon my services."

The subject was tabled until the next session meeting. After the meeting, the Lord Provost offered to drive me home, and en route drop off at his home for a cuppa. Duncan Fraser was a remarkable man. He had come from Grantown in the lovely Aberdeenshire countryside, a lonely lad, to the big city of Aberdeen, where he had worked in a draper's shop. In time he took over its management and now owned the business, which he ran along the socialist lines of shared partnership with his staff. A dedicated churchman, he gave the welfare of the North Kirk his constant concern. His persuasive speaking skills and strong will had brought to him business success, the highest honor in the city, and universal respect.

"Do you take sugar in your tea, George?" he asked as we sat before a crackling open fireplace, the wind howling down the chimney. "Milk? Aye, it was an interesting session meeting." He sat back, his pipe in hand, a small man with a fine face and light brown hair, choosing his words with obvious care. "You know, Jack B — — has been a member of the North Kirk all his life — was baptized in it. . . . He's been an elder for, I must imagine, nearly fifty years. We were lads together in the old days. Aye, a fine man. Loves the kirk. . . . Always eager to help us, especially the Sunday School. . . . You know, George, that dimmer means much to him. He's looked forward every year for us to ask him to use it at the Sunday School Christmas pageant. I think it would be wise to drop the whole business of the Passion Play and new proscenium altogether. . . . My! winter must be coming. I feel it in my bones these days. . . ."

Open-air preaching is an art surprisingly neglected by mainline churches in the United States. It seems this ageless method of evangelism has been ceded to the lunatic fringe of self-professed Christians. When I visit the New Jersey shore, I lament seeing no open-air preaching on the boardwalks, an ideal context, with large numbers of vacationing folk milling in the pleasant sunshine, in which to proclaim the message of the gospel. In Britain, where freedom of speech is something more than just a catch phrase, every town has its open-air stance and an accompanying bobby standing by to make sure there is no breach of the peace. In London it is Hyde Park; in Edinburgh, the Mound; and Glasgow has its Green. In Aberdeen, it was the Marketplace, a natural amphitheater of some six acres in a setting of drab, grey-granite four-story tenements.

My own introduction to street preaching was a baptism of fire — or rather water. When at Trinity College back in the thirties, I went with some other students on a Gospel Mission to Port Glasgow, a shipbuilding town on the Clyde, under the leadership of D. P. Thomson, an inimitable preacher who made proclamation of the gospel the goal of his long life. He started seaside missions at almost every coast holiday resort in Scotland. A scholar and a passionate preacher himself, he declaimed biblical decision-making sermons free from the myopic exegesis of the traditional fundamentalist preacher. From him I learnt the art of streetcorner preaching — the choice of stance, the reiteration of the message necessitated by the escalator audience, the methods and tricks of drawing a crowd. "Down with the King," he used to shout out to startled passersby who stopped to hear more; "Up with the red flag!" At Port Glasgow we spoke in the open air at work gates meetings and in the square at the railway station. The prospect scared me. To my relief, on the Wednesday night when I was due to speak, a monsoon of sorts struck the town. "D. P." was not about to let a mere flood deter us. Right on schedule, he summoned us to button up our coat collars and get out into the night to witness to the Lord. "After all," he insisted, "we did scrawl on the pavement of the Square that the students of Trinity College would hold a meeting at 7:30. You wouldn't want the Communists to turn up on a night like this to check whether we had the courage of our convictions, would you now?"

"D. P." erected the little portable platform under dark heavens from which came down raindrops big as hailstones, sparkling like diamonds in the lamplight. He announced my name as speaker. My coat collar vainly buttoned against the torrent, I gingerly climbed up onto my wobbly pulpit.

"Friends!" I called out desperately into the inhospitable night. Not a friend was in sight save two figures in caps and hodden grey clothes, the smoke from their pipes swirling in the air as they stood in the safe, relatively dry shelter of the railway station about two hundred yards away. I bent forward, to feel nearer to them — in defiance, unfortunately, of the principle of cantilever. The portable platform collapsed and sent me hurling into the gutter, the chill muddy waters rushing around my legs and the seat of my pants. I spluttered, half-blinded, trying to rise. Above the confusion the stentorian voice of "D. P." reached my ears:

"Stay where you are, George! You'll draw a crowd!"

I resolved then and there that I would never again speak at an openair meeting and was therefore ready a few years later when I was minister at Sandyhills Church and the voice of the Reverend Ralph Fairway came over the telephone. Ralph was the chairman of the Glasgow Presbytery

102

Committee on Evangelism and belonged to the more evangelical school of the church.

"George! We want you to preach at one of the summer open-air services that we hold every week at the corner of Argylle and Dunlop Streets."

"Not on your life, Ralph."

"Do you mean to tell me, George, that you, a minister of the gospel, are refusing to stand up and make a public confession that Jesus is your Savior? How can you continue to preach Sunday by Sunday in Sandyhills when you refuse to witness to the world without the safe guardrail of the pulpit? How can you turn your back upon the passerby? 'Is it nothing to you who pass by . . . ?' "

On the appointed day, I ambled along Argylle Street to Dunlop Street, a cul-de-sac that constituted the perfect place for open-air services: there was no through traffic and our stance was only two hundred yards from Glasgow's busiest thoroughfare. Ralph welcomed me and introduced me to a handful of folk, a tiny sea of smileless faces and drooping lips typical of some grim Glaswegians. Fumbling with my topper, rolled umbrella, and gloves (I had just conducted a wedding), I tried to summarize the three points of the previous Sunday's sermon, encouraged by a Land Army girl who had stopped in her stroll along Argylle Street and had come nearer to hear what I was saying. After seven eternal stuttering minutes, I came down from the soap box. Ralph proceeded to field the questions the sullen crowd was asking until one man shouted indignantly, "Why is it that when I go to church in England I can go after the Sunday service to a pub and drink my beer, and yet I cannot do that in Scotland, because the pubs are closed on Sundays?"

"Over to you, George," said Ralph blandly.

I tried one of Professor Allan Bowman's tricks, the way of the philosopher: you begin at a point furthest from the subject and move rapidly in the opposite direction. I cited the French Revolution and the Russian Revolution. I compared the secularization of our day with that of the Sabbath described in the book of Exodus and chronicled its development in Old Testament times, making a ringing case for a Sabbath holy unto the Lord. Other questions came. Some were personal.

"What do they pay you?"

"You tell me what you get paid and I'll tell you what my stipend is. And I'll bet you get a bigger wage than I do." (Cheers.)

On I went, Ralph holding my topper and gloves until suddenly I straightened my back and looked out at the gathering. The street was crowded with people; there must have been more than three hundred. For over two hours I had been fielding their questions. In the end I begged them to go home. They elicited from me a promise I would return next week at the same time and same place. One workmen in overalls and a rust-covered cap approached me and in a confidential voice said, "Mr. Docherty, you'll have to come hame wi' me. I was on my way hame frae work when I stopped for just a minute to hear you and lost track o' the time. Now, if I say I was standing at a street corner listening to a minister, the wife'll certainly no' believe that tale!"

It was therefore quite logical when I was called to the North Church that I should hold in the spring, summer, and autumn open-air services in the marketplace in Aberdeen after my regular evening services. It started out as a project of the Youth Club, who passed out tracts and formed the needed nucleus of the crowd before I began. We shared the marketplace with two other groups—one a black-suited evangelical crowd gathered around a wheezy harmonium singing Moody and Sankey hymns, the other a group of working-class fellows listening to a stocky man with close-cropped hair engaged in impassioned oratory under a banner announcing them as the "Aberdeen Communist Party." After a few weeks, only the kirk and the Communists were left, standing over against each other, a parable of the real contemporary conflict between a brave theistic democracy and militant atheistic statism. I always saw to it that our open-air meeting outlasted that of the Communists, and was delighted when they joined us after concluding their own meeting to ask me the threadbare, biased questions about the veracity of the Bible and the morals of the Church. After some weeks, one of their number approached me with a proposition: "Mr. Cooney would like to have a public debate with you."

My first meeting with Bob Cooney was over a cup of coffee in the students' lounge of the University of Aberdeen. It was a meeting of kindred souls, even though we were poles apart dialectically. Bob Cooney, by his puritan life, shamed me. A man of complete integrity, he neither smoked nor drank nor indulged himself by taking holidays, except for a few days with his devoted wife and three children (whom he allowed to take the Bible Knowledge classes at the local school—not because he thought it was good for them, but because he did not want his own beliefs to stigmatize them in any way). He had joined the Hunger Marchers in their trek to London in protest after the First World War. He had fought with the Reds in Spain. He had worked in a factory in Moscow. And year after year he ran—unsuccessfully—for a seat in the town council of Aberdeen.

There would be two debates, the first on Communism, and the second, to be held the Sunday following, on Christianity. I laid everything aside in preparation for the Communist debate, reading Marx and Engels's *Manifesto*, battling through some of the interminable turgid prose of *Das Kapital*, consulting the Webbs and Shaw and Richard Crankshaw until I could have sat a degree exam on the subject. We advertised the debate in the *Aberdeen Press and Journal*. The town responded in force: more than eight hundred people showed up. I found Bob to be a brilliant dialectician and a controlled but passionate public speaker. By the time he summed up the whole debate two hours later, I was limp and weary.

"How did I get on, Bill?" I asked one of my elders who had turned up to see St. George face the Dragon.

"Well, Mr. Docherty, let me put it this way: you were out for the count. But you were still on your feet! Shoemaker, stick to your own last."

The following Sunday evening, I was more at home with the topic at hand — Christianity. Bob brought up all sorts of cliches about Church history and persisted in *ad hominem* arguments instead of getting down to the substance of the Christian faith. I easily countered his superficial understanding of the early Christian communal living described in Acts 4 – 5. Ready for the *coup de grace* when it came my time to sum up the whole debate, I rose confidently to answer all the Communist arguments. A bright flash charged the leaden sky and a dramatic peal of thunder cracked in quick succession. In minutes torrential rain cascaded out of the night sky, sending the audience scampering for shelter and leaving only Bob and a few of our supporters to hear my brilliant summing up. I found myself murmuring the prayer of St. Theresa: "Dear Lord, no wonder you have so few friends. Look how you treat them."

A childhood spent in city streets had taught me the need for knowing more about nature. When at the Barony in Glasgow, I had tried to rent a church in the country where my city-bred Kirkhouse young folk might enjoy the beauty of the countryside over a weekend. In exchange, the country children could see the life of the city. I found an empty church in a delightful town only twenty-five miles north of Glasgow, but the kirk session feared rowdy Glasgow "keelies" running around their town on the weekends and did not follow through. Years later I saw what had become of the building that might have been our country youth retreat: the abandoned church building was now a garage. Evidently the smell of gasoline was more acceptable in a place where once the sacrament was celebrated than the uninhibited voices of healthy, spirited children.

I was to be given a second chance in my pursuit of this ideal. One day I read in disbelief an advertisement in the *Aberdeen Press and Journal* — "For sale or to rent: old Durris Free Church."

Durris parish comprises a scattering of houses eight miles along the South Dee Road. At the top of a winding road commanding a royal view of the River Dee stood the wee Free Kirk built back in the Disruption days. Now empty, it had been used as a grain storage depot during the war. It stood in an acre of grounds with a solid manse built of fine red granite beside it. Some fine pine pews were still in place in the gallery. Here, I dreamed, we would build our retreat center, with side rooms, rest rooms, and a large rustic fireplace in a spacious lounge. In time the gallery would make a splendid dormitory for overnight weekend stays. Around us were woods with unseen brown burns singing in the still air — "a lovely place, God wot."

The minister and session of Durris refused several better offers in favor of ours, welcoming the proposed center and hoping that Durris in the country and the North Kirk in the city would in time form a special link together. It could be ours for £7.10 per annum!

Once more the starry-eyed dreamer, I presented the Durris Country Retreat Project to the session. The questions came quickly. How much would it cost to refurbish the building? Had I drawn up plans for making it a suitable place to live in even for weekends? Did I realize how very expensive it was to buy beds and kitchen equipment for such a project? Finally, a vote was taken. The project was defeated by a two-to-one majority. I'm afraid I blew up. It is always a mistake to do so.

"Then if the North Kirk session will not sponsor this scheme, I shall run it myself, assisted by such members of the session and the church as believe that the project is worthwhile, especially for our aged and our young folk."

Jimmy Mackie gave me £35; others rallied round. Each Saturday a group went out, transforming the former barren grain store into a well-furbished country retreat. One man, a bricklayer, built the rustic fireplace. Carpenters made the pews into partitions. The little kitchen, with water from the well, was soon producing light snacks. Our young people eagerly visited it. Our Woman's Meeting, made up of women from the parish, spent a sun-kissed day amidst the loveliness of the newly planted forests, the smell of pine resin, the buzz of summer bees, and the song of blackbirds. A group of ministers came to an all-day retreat that closed with the celebration of the Sacrament under a majestic pine tree that might have remembered the humble beginnings of the Free Kirk in that parish.

But Durris was still-born; another more distant voice was calling to me. Some years ago I retraced my footsteps up the steep winding road. The kirk was gone. The proprietor had exercised his right to take the building over should it ever cease to be used for church purposes. The old manse that Jerry and I had dreamed might be our country house is now a shooting lodge.

At summer's end, I read a notice in the *Press and Journal* that the Reverend Erskine Blackburn would present to his congregation a color slide lecture entitled "My Visit To America." I attended the lecture and watched his travels with fascination: Fifth Avenue Church in New York City, a retreat outside Chicago, Massanetta Springs Bible Conference in Virginia, Montreat in North Carolina. I was determined to visit the United States. Almost every Scotsman has an uncle in America; I had four uncles and an aunt in Chicago. On the Monday morning following, I visited Erskine.

Of medium height, rather portly, his fair hair now receding, he was always impeccably dressed in black clericals, his cherubic smile and merry eyes reminding one of Chesterton's Father Brown. In his day he was one of the masters of the Scottish pulpit. With a wide grasp of literature and history and an uncanny simplicity of style, he drew large crowds to the great Renfield Street Church in the heart of commercial Glasgow.

"Actually, George," he told me, "a trip to America will be quite simple to arrange. I shall write my old friend Harry Holmes, who is chairman of the Pulpit Exchange Committee of the Council of Churches in New York City. I will tell him that you are the greatest preacher in Scotland."

"Now, Erskine," I remonstrated, "you and I know that's simply not true."

"Of course it's not true, my dear George. But that's the only language they understand in America."

My old teacher Professor Arthur John Gossip must have forwarded a flattering testimonial on my behalf, however, for Mr. Holmes, who knew Dr. Gossip through his printed sermons and regarded him as one of Scotland's great preachers, soon wrote to me confirming a preaching tour and asking me to name the places I would like to visit. Where indeed? Chicago of course; and New York City.

Thus it happened. For the summer months of July and August 1949 I was set to be a guest preacher in the United States.

Some weeks later I received my itinerary: I was to speak at Bible conferences at Cornell University and Thousand Islands on the St. Lawrence River and at the annual meeting of the Christian Endeavor in Toronto, Canada, and preach at Montclair, New Jersey; Hyde Park, Chicago; and the First Presbyterian Church in Newark, New Jersey. And after conferences at Massanetta Springs in Virginia and Montreat in North Carolina, there would be two Sundays (August 21 and 28) at the New York Avenue Presbyterian Church in Washington, D.C.

8

George in Wonderland

"Well, in *our* country," said Alice, still panting a little, "you'd generally get some-where else—if you ran fast for a long time as we have been doing."

"A slow sort of country!" said the Queen. "Now, *here*, you see, it takes all the running you can do, to keep in the same place. If you want to get somewhere else, you must run at least twice as fast as that!"

—Lewis Carroll, *Through the Looking Glass*

ARMED WITH A portable typewriter and overnight bag, I struggled and squeezed my way down the narrow aisle of the plane past fellow passengers who were packing the overhead racks with Scots tweed coats, scarves, and tartan shawls. Eventually reaching my place, I scrambled over two pairs of legs and subsided into the narrow window seat on the port side of the four-prop constellation, where I was to spend eighteen tedious hours. I placed my typewriter on the floor as a footrest. With a sigh I looked out the window at the spread of concrete runway, and beyond to the green fields of Ayrshire, tinted with the salmon-pink glow of a Turner sunset on that memorable day: June 27, 1949.

Directly above my head, a neat sign announced "No smoking: Fasten seat belts." What, and where, was a seat belt? My puzzled expression must have been noted by my fellow passenger.

"You're sitting on it," he growled in that querulous Scottish accent that indicates the person being spoken to is a bit of a dolt. I was to hear his voice throughout the long night; it became more kindly with the passing hours. I never learned his name; Scots are diffident about revealing such intimate details.

Out my window I could see the single-story temporary wooden terminal buildings of Prestwick. Somewhere among the patchwork of heads and fluttering handkerchiefs were our cousins the Craigs, who had come down from Glasgow to see me off. Jerry and our two boys had stayed at home in the manse, now far away to the north in Aberdeen. We had taken soulful farewells that morning as I boarded the train, Jerry teasing, "Don't forget to come back to us." Garth, now four, and David, three, had joined me in an inspection of the locomotive, a green-painted giant, hissing steam, their tiny hands gripping mine confidently. The guard's whistle echoed shrilly under the glass-domed roof; we hurried back to my compartment. The boys, so small and solemn as they looked up at their father, waved their pudgy little fingers. An awkward silence. We kissed. From the distance, a roar of steam, two blasts of the engine's whistle, a jolt of carriages, and slowly the train moved on its way.

"Don't worry," I shouted above the din. "I'll write as soon as I arrive. I'll phone from Prestwick. Goodbye. . . ."

The train was gathering speed as it rounded the curve of the platform. I watched the receding figures waving, Jerry holding a handkerchief to her left cheek. The train clanged over the steel girders of the bridge that spans the River Dee, in which stood, as always, the solitary fisherman, waders up to his armpits, casting a line for the salmon a man may catch in the very heart of this city. I felt a sudden stab of homesickness and the same cold loneliness I had once known as child on a long-ago Christmas Eve. Jerry and I had known many partings, but this one was somehow more portentous.

A series of spluttering reports jolted me back to the present. Our plane was thunderously revving up. It bumped across the tarmac, turned around, and hurtled down the runway at an accelerating speed calculated to end in ruin upon the characteristically stout Scottish stone boundary wall that I knew lay ahead of us. Suddenly, my seat pushed up beneath me and we were airborne, the boundary wall receding into the distance, stonily staring and unmoved.

We soared into the summer sunset, the lands of Ayrshire laid out below us like a patchwork quilt of neat green and brindle fields bordered by dry-stane dikes where cattle idly chewed the cud. Over grey stone farmhouses and byres we rose, over the green fairways of St. Nicholas Golf Course, the bunkers looking yellow against the brown and purple gorse of the roughs. I was able to map out the contours of the Ayrshire coastline curving below, the slate-blue waters of the Firth of Clyde leisurely casting a ribbon of white breakers upon the sallow sands. Higher yet, over the Cumbrae Islands with Millport, the little seaside town where Jerry and I spent our first vacation with her family, tucked away in the horseshoe bay of the Big Cumbrae. Upwards and over Goat Fell, the "Sleeping Warrior" mountain that dominates the skyline of the Isle of Arran, looking now like a vast brown cloud floating on steel grey waters.

As we reached our cruising altitude, I relaxed, removed the earplugs supplied by the steward, and sat back, savoring the enjoyment of this novel experience. Twelve thousand feet above the Atlantic Ocean! And bound for America!

Gradually the steady hum of the engines and the comfort of the cabin lulled me to sleep. I recall nothing of our touchdowns at Reykjavik or Gandor, Newfoundland. At Boston we were cleared through customs before reembarking for our final destination. In a short time the self-assured, clipped BBC voice of the captain announced our imminent arrival at Idlewild Airport, New York City.

As the plane descended, I eagerly anticipated a stirring view of the Statue of Liberty and the Empire State Building. I saw instead a vast stretch of brown muddy water dotted with many tiny white sails and a dark brown shoreline crisscrossed by numberless geometrically clustered streets and homes.

"Long Island Sound," confided the Scot's voice, with the air of one who knows. "You'll no' see Manhattan yet; it's awa' west o' here."

Just when I expected a fatal splash into the sea, a runway appeared from nowhere, a vast grey concrete pavement streaking past my window. There were two gentle bumps, a round of applause from the passengers, and we wheeled round and taxied toward huge terminal buildings.

Gathering up my typewriter and overnight bag, I eased myself along with the crowding passengers toward the open door of the plane — and walked straight into Dante's Inferno! Gasping for breath in the stifling heat that engulfed me, I stumbled across an endless tarmac. My Scots tweed trousers were sticking to my perspiring legs; a merciless sun bore down through a grey haze upon a trail of hapless Scots, dutifully carrying their tweeds, scarves, and shawls.

No one had ever mentioned to me that American summers were hot. The lovely movies of New York City one saw gave no clue to temperatures. This was worse than tropical Africa — ninety degrees of heat and eighty percent humidity. Feeling faint, I pressed on towards what I hoped would be a cool haven in the terminal building.

Everything was vast. Everywhere were people. A booming loudspeaker emitted quite incomprehensible noises. I waited uncomfortable ages for my baggage, until it was finally disgorged from a moving belt circulating from some mysterious region behind black rubber flaps.

Lugging an overpacked suitcase, I wearily trudged outside into a bedlam of people and the unrelenting heat. In vain I looked for a taxi; only enormous automobiles moved past in unbroken procession. I began to realize that these yellow monsters must be taxis, though they looked to me as large as buses. My bag getting heavier and my clothes growing more sodden, I stumbled on toward a nonchalant fellow leaning against a yellow cab, a stocky, black-haired Italian with the stub of an unlit cigar firmly fixed in the corner of his mouth. He was so very sensibly dressed — no coat, no tie, a short-sleeved white shirt, and dark blue summer-wear trousers that bulged at the middle as if he wore an inner tube under his belt. He portrayed an air of total indifference to the weather, or anything else for that matter.

"Wharyagawn?" he muttered, without removing the cigar, as he took my bags and placed them in the trunk of the car.

Where indeed, I thought, as I got into the front seat beside him. Where does one go when one has arrived for the first time in New York City? The address of the Council of Churches offices was safely packed in the cool of the trunk, in my bag. I muttered the first name that came to mind: "Grand Central Station."

The cab moved off noiselessly and sedately, slowly carving a way over the crossovers, sending the clamoring people scampering like frightened sheep on a Highland road. He was obviously driving on the wrong side of the road, but everyone else seemed to be making the same mistake.

Gathering speed, we careened around cloverleafs, tires screeching, racing like Nero's charioteers, four abreast, down concrete-paved boulevards bordered by bottle-green leafy trees limp and dusty in the summer heat, past gigantic red brick apartment complexes and, on our left, the grey waters of Long Island Sound. Suddenly we swerved off the boulevard, racing uphill to a towering road built on dizzyingly high steel girder supports; the tops of houses whizzed past beneath. We raced up a mammoth bridge (the Triborough) arching upwards to the smoggy sky and down again at a breathtaking speed into the canyon skyscrapers of Manhattan Island. The limestone buildings were beautiful, as clean as if they had been built yesterday. I gaped out of the cab window, craning my neck at the soaring structures. Abruptly, we drew to a halt outside a row of large plate-glass swinging doors through which poured crowds of people in both directions.

"Grand Central Station," muttered the driver, the only fragment of conversation he had made during the forty-minute ride.

It was cool as I walked up the wide marble staircase that opened up into a vast foyer, its high vaulted roof painted to represent the starry heavens. After placing my baggage in a terminal locker, I looked around for a barber shop. I hadn't shaved for forty hours, and I wanted to present myself to my hosts "looking respectable," as Jerry would express it. I jostled with the crowds through an arcade of shops until I finally espied the red and white striped revolving sign.

A smooth-spoken, affable barber welcomed me with a wide sweeping gesture toward a high chair that pivoted as he tucked me into the large white sheet he deftly threw around me. His fingers felt cool around my perspiring neck. I had the sense of being encased in a straitjacket—which turned out to be a not inappropriate metaphor.

With professional dexterity, he sheared my locks. That concluded, he muttered something about "hot olive oil," and before I could voice any opinion, a stream of warm, glutinous liquid poured over my head, which he proceeded to massage thoroughly with the tips of his strong fingers. That completed, he poured on another liquid; my head frothed as if I were wearing a white turban. He then jerked my head towards the wash basin in front of me, rinsing off the turban in alternately hot and cold water.

A furious rubdown with a hard towel preceded an attack of hot air from a whirring gadget, ruffling my locks like a harvest breeze over a ripened field of wheat. He then massaged my scalp, a vibrating machine attached to the back of his hand. My body quivered all over. Next I was eased backward to a reclining position — it was pointless to try to escape — and a hot shaving brush stabbed vigorously at my two-day growth. With the last stroke of the open razor, my assailant threw a scalding hot towel over my face, wrapping it around with a neat sweep of his hand, leaving only a small aperture around my nostrils to forestall certain suffocation. With the grace of a ballet gesture, one hand withdrew the towel while the other poured over my smooth face a tingling, stinging potion. I felt like Gulliver tied on the beach, defenseless against the Lilliputian arrows showered upon his face. This was mollified with a soothing syrup, restful and cool. Perish the thought, he powdered my face! I smelt like a baby after a bath. The chair suddenly came bolt upright and I found myself looking into a mirror reflecting a smiling Leonardo da Vinci face poised beside my own. To be honest, I was impressed with what I saw, and felt greatly refreshed. Meanwhile, my Leonardo, with sleight-of-hand skill, folded the towel over his arm, released me from the straitjacket, and slipped into my hand a piece of paper.

"Next time you're in Grand Central Station, sir, drop in again. Remember my name — Mike. Ask for Mike."

"Mike, I'll never forget you!"

Somehow I reached the Fourth Avenue offices of the Council of Churches. I recall standing before a spacious wooden counter and striking a bell. A young woman appeared.

"I'm George Docherty," I announced.

The young lady let out a high-pitched squeal.

"My sakes!" she called to someone behind a glass partition. "Mr. Holmes! Mr. Holmes! It's George Docherty! We have been waiting for you all day," she explained as she came round the counter and bussed me — a welcoming kiss that, after all these years, I have not forgotten.

A grey-haired, slightly built man in his fifties dressed in a seersucker suit, with a serene smile and the soft face of those who have known pain, came forward to me, both hands outstretched in welcome.

"My dear George. Do come in! We were indeed getting a bit worried about you."

It was one of those moments when one does not know rightly whether to laugh or to weep.

After a Coke — the first I had ever tasted — Harry Holmes got down to the business of checking my itinerary and reassuring me that everything was in order. "But you must come upstairs," he said. "There is a forum of rather distinguished clergymen I'd like you to meet."

Upstairs, I found myself in a salon where a meeting was already in progress. In the room was a group of men, none of whom looked like a clergyman—not a clerical collar in sight. In the center of the group stood the speaker, a tall middle-aged man with thinning hair and thick-lensed spectacles, his thumbs dug deep into his waistcoat pockets. He spoke in a monotonous, unmusical Yankee drawl, lisping his consonants through his back teeth. He was apparently talking about the Marshall Plan.

"If, for example, we give financial assistance to Belgium, let us say, to manufacture shoes, these will then be exported to Holland. In the meantime, we shall have financed Holland to manufacture machinery which in turn will be exported to Belgium to make available modern shoemaking machinery. If the economy of Europe is stimulated by the input of American capital, we shall have a solvent Europe and that will bring new economic growth to the stagnant world economy. We cannot trade with a continent bombed into ruins after a devastating war. America in the end must gain. . . ."

"Who is this?" I whispered to Harry Holmes.

"John Foster Dulles," he replied offhandedly.

At dinner late that evening in the University Club, Fifth Avenue, I asked nervously about my preaching assignments. Harry reassured me, "George, a Scottish accent is a great asset to a preacher. We in America hold Scottish preachers in high esteem. You are entering into a great tradition. That's why we invited you over this summer. You were a new Scottish voice, and we wanted to hear some of the younger men from the Old Country."

Later that night, after Harry had left me at my hotel, I looked out from the twenty-ninth floor on the beady eyes of a thousand lighted windows peering at me out of the darkness; I felt alone.

I unpacked, typed a letter to Jerry, and sketched out the first draft of an article, "Mike: My Friend the Barber at Grand Central Station," which was later to appear in the *Aberdeen Press and Journal*. There seemed nothing else to do but to go to bed. To bed? In New York City? A desecration of time! Jacketless, shirt-sleeves rolled up, I left my room and was soon walking down the few blocks to Times Square.

Nobody seemed in a hurry; the summer-attired crowd sauntered leisurely in the cool night air—so very unlike Glaswegians, who are always in a hurry. Between towering canyons I strolled, around me walls of electric lights, music blaring from every doorway, little shops crammed with leather goods and cheap pottery, cameras, gramophones, flashy costume jewelry. I paused for a moment to listen to an ageless woman preaching the gospel; nobody noticed her. I gazed through the windows of steak shops, flames rising from the grills as a dexterous cook flipped over the smoking steaks. On either side of Forty-Second Street the marquises of half a dozen movie houses competed with one another. Colored lights chased one another round and round on the sides of buildings.

In Times Square, a comet of lights rose up the side of a building, the flashing reds and yellows spelling out in rhythmic curves the word *Coca Cola*. In the center of another billboard was a man's face, gigantic and ruddy, out of whose mouth came, at intervals, puffs of smoke, while a caption flashed the message *Smoke Camels*. Racing across another building a ribbon of flashing white lights spelled out the latest news, including the mysterious message "YANKEES WIN DOUBLEHEADER."

I gaped in wonder. This was better than a dozen Guy Fawkes Days rolled into one. The crowds moved slowly on, unimpressed, quietly, unhurried. A policeman, his baton held in his two hands behind his back, glanced my way.

"Wonderful place, sir," I called out.

He nodded in silence.

I recalled how G. K. Chesterton had stood in perhaps the same place, gaping as I had gaped, nose puckered in the middle of his full-moon face, peering through his pince-nez with their black ribbon, and finally exclaiming, "What a glorious garden of wonders this would be for anyone who was lucky enough to be unable to read!"

Back in my hotel room, I retired, but tossed and turned, too tired to sleep. I offered a quiet prayer of gratitude for a safe landfall and for the wonderful day it had been, and asked a blessing on my little family far away, it seemed now at the ends of the earth.

Many British writers, from Dickens to Dylan Thomas and almost all members of the British press, seem to derive a certain caustic satisfaction in denigrating the American scene. Even G. K. Chesterton, in his essay "What I Saw in America," was not free from condescending journalism. "Everybody that goes to America for a short time is expected to write a book," he said. "Nearly everybody does."

Those who have lived in America for any length of time realize that such books can be written only after a short visit, when everything seems so clear-cut, so raucously obvious, so vulnerable, so very un-British. As the years pass, the way of life we call "American," like the tortuous banyon tree, becomes contradictory, more complex, and always startlingly innovative.

In that memorable summer of 1949, I was the eager young Scot on the loose, so confident in my opinions, which much wiser and more mature minds than mine listened to with a respect far beyond their deserving. I was tasting the heady wine of a new world and its startling difference. Deep down I remained nonetheless grateful to a kindly Providence that had provided this magic-carpet adventure — all expenses paid.

The first American pulpit I preached from was the First Congregational Church in Montclair, New Jersey, a magnificent neo-Gothic church built in 1915. Mary and Alan Lorimer and their daughter Mary welcomed me to the spacious white manse in the church grounds on Saturday afternoon. After supper I retired early, but not to sleep. The heat was intense. I lay and watched the humid air billow the lace curtains at the open window, my single linen bedsheet becoming stickier and stickier as I anxiously contemplated the Sabbath.

Over breakfast, I confessed I was scared.

"What am I to preach? How am I to preach? What's it like to preach to an American congregation?"

"George," said Alan soothingly, "we are all the same people wherever we live, needing the same word of salvation."

I entered a crowded sanctuary to the reverberating sounds of the doxology played on a splendid pipe organ and sung by a large choir, filling the vaulted roof with song. It took a little time to get used to the colorfully dressed summer congregation, so different from the grey tones of Scottish kirks — women attired in summery frocks and floral hats giving the appearance of an herbaceous border, men in white and seersucker suits, all gently fanning themselves with the morning church bulletin. I have no recollection of what or how I preached.

"What did you think of my sermon, Alan?" I ventured to ask later as we shared dessert and iced coffee in the screened porch of the manse.

"Well, I'll tell you, fella. It's like this. I was seated up front with one of my deacons and when you had finished preaching, he reached over to me and in an awed voice whispered, 'Alan, what is it that these Scotch preachers have?' 'It's the mystic!' I whispered back."

I spent the afternoon visiting a shriveled old white-haired man, sitting under the shade of a mighty maple tree in the large garden of his Montclair home. Archie Black, the Minister Emeritus, had once been, with his famous brother Hugh of Union Theological Seminary and James of St. George's West Edinburgh, a denomination of their own within the Church of Scotland. Their father had been a baker in Rothesay. No baker had ever produced such yeast of the gospel! They were magnificent preachers.

The little man was kind and gentle, and drank in all my news of his homeland so far away in time and space. "And they won't let Jimmy visit me," he complained. "Said he had a heart condition and that travel would be too tiring. It's all nonsense. No one ever walks in these parts."

From New Jersey, it was on to Toronto, where I spoke at the International Christian Endeavor Conference. As the overnight train pulled slowly into the station, I was astounded to see a vast poster exhorting the world to "Drink Canada Dry." Here I met for the first time Dan Poling, editor of the *Christian Herald*, a broad-shouldered, athletic man with heavy brooding eyebrows and a deep voice that belied a gentle, almost childlike spirit.

It was the Chicago trip that excited me most. My childhood, unlike that of Dylan Thomas, had included no gathering of uncles in our house, no Auntie Hannahs singing of bleeding hearts and death. My uncles and aunts were in America. Now I was to meet them for the first time.

The Macphersons (my mother's side of the family) had been Banff-shire stonemasons. Back in the 1880s, when the buds began to show in the wild rose bushes by the roadside and the snell winds of Moray Firth were tempered by the onset of spring, the men of the family traveled by train to Glasgow, where they would embark upon one of the Anchor Line ships that sailed weekly to New York harbor, thence by train westward to Chicago. My Uncle Alex—the one who never settled down anywhere—would often "hobo it," beating his way on freight trains, precariously perched between the wheels of the cars.

Chicago in the late nineteenth century was a mecca for stonemasons. Long after the Great Fire of 1871, it was still being reconstructed. Grand-dad, with some slight exaggeration, used to boast that he had rebuilt the new Chicago practically single-handed. He did in fact work on the new Rockefeller-endowed University of Chicago in the 1890s. In 1917, he and my uncles were the master masons who built the majestic Gothic Fourth Presbyterian Church on Michigan Avenue.

Sleeplessly I tossed, caught up between excited anticipation and the swaying, jangling, rumbling of the train as it threaded its way through the westward darkness. Laden with my typewriter and suitcase, I staggered down the high steps of the sleeping car into the great concourse at Chicago's Union Station, wearily weaving among friendless strangers, vainly searching for faces I only knew from photographs. As near panic was about to take over, a voice from heaven, a great booming voice like that of God in Cecil B. De Mille's epic *Ten Commandments* echoed through the vast station.

"Will the Reverend Docherty please come to the information desk?"

And like Browning's thrush, lest I might not capture the first fine careless rapture, the voice sang its song once more. There at the information desk, I was soon enfolded in the arms of Aunt Ella shyly smiling and weeping. Cousin Nettie, whose photograph in the kilt had graced our mantelpiece at home, now a plumpish middle-aged woman with a warm midwestern American accent, embraced me lovingly. Uncle George, portly and baldheaded like Grandfather, stood awkwardly silent, trying to laugh. And I knew then what Mother meant the many times she had said, "Aye! blood's thicker than water!"

America had suddenly become home, but for all of that, a home unbearably hot. These dear ones propped me up in a deck chair surrounded by bottles of Seven-Up beside the fan in the screened porch. It was as if we had known each other all our days.

Uncle George began to tell me all about "God's own country," here in the Midwest. As a stonemason he had done well and was now comfortably retired. He expatiated on the superiority of America to the Scotland he had left, forgetting that the Scotland he had left no longer existed: for good or ill it had changed with the times. I soon realized Uncle George was simply the emigrant Scot seeking to cope with the incurable ailment of homesickness by an effort to forget the past and to begin anew — as if one could! Aunt Ella, on the other hand, would later confess that for forty years there had never been a day in her life, especially in those humid summers, the trees limp and listless, when she would not recapture again with her mind's eye the deep green of the firwoods, hear the whine of the wind in the creaking branches and the carried wash of the tide over the rocks and harbor wall of Buckie in Banffshire. But Chicago was her home now; here bided Malcolm her Highland husband, a dear, lovable mystic, and their four children, all grown up now with Irish, Czech, Danish, and Scottish spouses, and around her feet happily the voices of a new generation of American children calling out to Grandma.

Uncle George took me by streetcar to see the sights along the seventeen miles of Lakeshore Drive: the Planetarium, where I beheld as in the book of Genesis the starry heavens above; Michigan Avenue where stood the majestic Fourth Presbyterian Church; Rockefeller's University of Chicago with the inscription from Lord Kelvin above the archway — "What I can measure, I know" — carved in a block of stone no doubt by Grandpa's hands. We boarded the elevated railway to visit a favorite haunt of Uncle George, the world's largest abattoir, down at the stockyards. I stood in a line of awe-struck spectators watching a slowly revolving assembly-line belt of squealing, struggling pigs suspended by the hind feet. Beside it waited a man dressed in a blood-splattered white coat. As the panicking pigs reached him, with a deft flash of a poised knife, he slit their throats, and the blood spouted out into a swirling red channel below. The hapless creatures vanished from sight, still kicking, but silent. At another stall a long line of black Aberdeen Angus steers grunting in protest were being corralled into a narrow pen, stamping and struggling to escape (as if instinctively aware of their oncoming fate) the figure of a man who calmly placed a metal bell against the head of each beast as it reached him. There was a muffled bang; one after another the animals slumped and were dragged off by the chain belt — still kicking, but quite dead — to be immersed into a vat of boiling water. Uncle suggested that we visit the finest steak house in the world, but I felt somewhat queasy.

I was to meet with St. Andrew's Society Scots, who showed me the other side of the coin of emigration. Hungry for news from the lips of a home-bred Scot, they responded with much laughter and not a few tears as I recounted the many strange funny-tragic stories of Scotland, and about Glasgow's Suachiehall Street and how the Glasgow Rangers were doing this soccer season. I assured them that the *Eagle III* still sailed from the Broomielaw in Glasgow "doon the watter." I read Scots poems from Burns, and "The Whistle" by Robert Murray in the Aberdeen dialect (which I can speak like a second tongue), and Stevenson's

> In the highlands, in the country places,
> Where the old plain men have rosy faces,
> And the young fair maidens
> Quiet eyes. . . .

That was the Chicago I visited in 1949. My family are all gone now, except for second-generation cousins. Even the stockyards, they tell me, are no more.

Cornell University commands a magnificent view of the Finger Lakes of upper New York State and consists of a noble campus of perpendicular Gothic buildings. I preached in the Sage Chapel. At the conference a well-dressed young man named Walter Reuther spoke impressively and quietly about the need to improve relations between the nation's management and labor forces, challenging the Church to be relevant by proclaiming the principles of justice and freedom so compellingly demonstrated in the life of God's people in holy scripture.

I tired the sun and the moon and the stars in an all-night session talking with a young black man called Bayard Rustin, who opened my eyes to the tragic plight of the black community in the South. My sheltered life in homogenous Scotland had its own class struggle within proletarian Glasgow, and beyond our boundaries, instinctively, like most British, we suspected the devious French and Prussian Germans. Japanese and Chinese (between whom we made no distinction) were likewise suspect, their narrow eyes bespeaking dark oriental intrigue. All I had learned of foreigners came from the movies. Toward black Africans, we held a paternalistic affection. Did not we sing in Sunday School about "Where Afric's sunny fountains roll down their golden sands," before we took the offerings to send Bibles and clothes to naked black children? Of course Stephen Fletcher was a movie funny man, with his slavery stutter and stupid loping walk, an object of fun, like the minstrel shows we laughed at on holiday at the Clyde Coast beaches — black faces, enormous white lips, and a "banjo-on-their-knee" singing "Swanee, how I love you, how I love you," the large white eyes rolling grotesquely. Now, for the first time in my life, I was alone in a room with a black man, whose beautiful brown face reflected every mood of the tragic tales he was telling — the chain gang insults, the cell he had shared with about thirty other inmates with no room to answer a call of nature, the road work with ankle chains, the friends in jail who disappeared and were never heard of again.

"But what was the Church doing all the time?"

"Well, brother Docherty, I'll ask you the question. What is the Church doing about it now?"

How could I possibly realize then that this stranger, quietly and unbidden, had introduced me to the sufferings and tragedy of his people, and that the cause of racial injustice would become a burning issue that was to save my preaching from fatal fluency and empty oratory. It was another sixteen years before I was to see Bayard Rustin again, when he would be seated alongside Dr. Martin Luther King, Jr., on a platform set up on the square in front of the statehouse in Montgomery, Alabama. I would be one of the twenty-five thousand gathered from all over the country to celebrate the conclusion of the march of the black community from Selma to Montgomery. I would recognize him immediately — the warm smile, the round handsome face; only his greyed hair would bespeak the passage of many years between our memorable meetings.

Thousand Islands Park on the St. Lawrence River is a delectable place to spend a vacation. Here I met an old man of Scots origin who had something to do with Quaker Oats; maybe he founded it? Early Sunday morning service was held on the bank of the wide river, where, unlike the gospel story of Jesus preaching to the crowds on the shore from a boat, the preacher on the shore preaches to a congregation of motorboats on the river — some one hundred, at least. What better sermon in such an Elysian setting than "The Silence of God"? I lifted my hand towards the blue sky arching that cool Sabbath morning as around me weeping willows kissed the gently lapping water, still as the grave save for the song of summer birds.

"Listen, my friends, to this silence! What is it telling you? Is it not telling you that God is here?"

Suddenly there burst into the holy silence the thunder of an approaching high-speed motorboat, half submerged between the two walls of froth-crested waves its bow was cleaving. A noisy latecomer for church, I thought. Every head turned around indignantly, scowling at the intruder. The boatman, sizing up the nature of the gathering, panicked, turned tail, and fled, his accelerating engine booming into the hazy distances of the river. The backwash produced a miniature tidal wave; the boats rocked against one another like a thousand clapboards crashing. With elbows on the stone podium (a memorial to the good man who had inaugurated these services before), I began to laugh; my congregation, bobbing about as if caught up in churning rapids, began to laugh also — some cheered.

My next stop was Newark, New Jersey, where I preached at the First Presbyterian Church, a sedate Georgian building in a part of the city once affluent but now an island of neglect. In the vestibule stands a framed

Charter of George II granting to the colonial congregation the land on which they were to build their church. I noted its old Scottish style of pew with doors at the ends to enclose the worshiper. A stout, ornate balcony curved halfway around the interior (quite empty); only a scattering of worshipers sat in the area. The atmosphere carried a pall of forgotten things; it was like preaching into a velvet curtain.

I followed the practice of greeting the congregation in front of the pulpit at the conclusion of the service, a happy custom eschewed in Scotland. The people were gracious and solicitous about my visit, and those with some Scottish connection, however distant, seemed happy to be identified with the brogue of their morning preacher.

I found myself shaking hands with a white-haired man with a goatee on his chin and a twinkle in his eye, speaking slowly in a midwestern drawl. By his side stood a little lady, white-haired and beaming, whom he introduced as his wife, Helen Edgington. "We are from the New York Avenue Presbyterian Church in Washington."

"What a coincidence!" I replied. "I'm due to preach there this August."

"I know you are. That's why we motored sixty miles this morning from Milford, Pennsylvania, to hear you. That was a fine sermon, young man! I wonder if you would give us the pleasure of preaching it again when you come in August?"

"Well, that depends! I must be in the mood!"

It was a conceited remark, indeed flippant. American flattery was rapidly catching up with me.

That same evening I was aboard a parlor car of the Southern Railroad thundering south through the darkness. I recall looking out through my sleeper window as we lumbered through a sleeping Washington, over the railroad bridge across the Potomac, eastward toward the distant white dome of the Capitol Building, majestic against a grey sky already streaked by the dawn.

My destination was Asheville, North Carolina — Thomas Wolfe country — sheltering in the lea of the Great Smoky Mountains, lush with trees and so unlike the bare heather-covered hills of home, the first russet brush strokes of autumn among the dark greens of the pines.

A young man approached me at the railroad terminal and addressed me by name; it seemed so natural, yet magical! In his station wagon, we were soon hurtling over roller coaster roads strewn with apples along miles of roadside orchards — red apples, too, large and ripe. I was getting the feel of the prodigality of American soil. On the following Sunday, when after dinner at the home where I was guest, my hostess called out to a pouting, disobedient twelve-year-old, "Now Billy, I have told you for the last time; go right out into the yard and rake up those pecans from the lawn into the baskets. You know I might turn my ankle on them!" Baskets of pecans! A far cry from those World War Two days when I would consider myself fortunate to crack open a single pecan and pick out the tasty gnarled treasure from its tough shell.

I was one of the speakers at the lovely Montreat Conference Center of the Southern Presbyterian Church (carved out of Black Mountain, complete with light-filled, spacious auditorium capable of seating two thousand) and the Assembly Inn, built with rustic quartz stone beside a mountain lake. Hidden in the cool of the woods, hundreds of summer cottages nestle, the happy vacation homes for generations of Presbyterians.

Sunday morning the auditorium was filled to overflowing. At the conclusion of the service, an enthusiastic line of worshipers pumped my hand and commented on my wonderful Scots accent and praised the sermon they had just heard. I lapped up this heady stuff!

One worshiper was a tall, dark-eyed, bushy-browed gentleman dressed in a neat grey suit that contrasted with the short-sleeved and light-hued summer suitings of the others. Dr. Jesse Baird of San Francisco Theological Seminary wanted to talk to me about the possibility of my coming out to become their Professor in Homiletics.

Almost every Scottish preacher hopes one day to be the professor of preaching at a seminary; the invitation exceeded my wildest dreams. Nevertheless, I had only recently been called to the city of Aberdeen, and I saw clearly that my future lay in the North Kirk. Had I been offered the chair at Glasgow, I would have given it more serious thought, but as for America — it would still be there in years to come, when I hoped to return for a visit with my family. Only St. George's, Edinburgh, or Wellington Church in Glasgow could ever induce me to move from Aberdeen.

The Saturday overnight train took me to Washington, where I was due to preach the following morning at the New York Avenue Presbyterian Church, whose minister Dr. Peter Marshall had recently died. I was booked in at the Washington Hotel overlooking tree-lined Pennsylvania Avenue, the spacious Ellipse and the White House nearby, resembling, it seemed to me then as it still does, the Hyde Park Corner area of London. No sooner had I entered my room than the telephone rang.

"This is Bob Bridge, the Associate Minister at the church, George. Welcome to Washington! I'm just checking your safe arrival. You've cut the time rather tight. It probably says nine o'clock on your watch. Actually it's ten o'clock — daylight savings time here in Washington — and the service is at eleven."

I showered and, skipping breakfast, raced up the incline of 14th Street to the church. A hot haze hung over the city. Was there to be no escape from this sauna-bath climate? On a triangle at the confluence of New York Avenue, H Street, and 14th Street stood the church — a colonial building of pleasant weathered maroon brick with a splendidly proportioned tower, surrounded by some dilapidated two-story brick and frame Victorian buildings. Already at 10:45 a serpentine line of visitors around the church was awaiting admission, the congregation having the privilege of having their pews held for them until 10:55. I entered by the New York Avenue entrance and was immediately engulfed in the hallway by a milling crowd of chattering laughing people. I roamed in total bewilderment until a friendly grey-haired man with an English accent reached out his hand and said, "Come in, George. I'm Bob Bridge. Welcome to the kirk." An Englishman, he chuckled at his daring imitation of a Scots accent. "Let's go upstairs to Peter's room."

Together we climbed a narrow winding stairway to the second floor and entered a smallish office lined with books, the window looking out onto broad New York Avenue. In the background, I could hear the swelling cadences of the organ playing the prelude.

"Bill Watkins, our organist, is one of the finest in the country. Indeed, he won a nationwide prize recently. The sanctuary is on the second floor, after the colonial tradition of Presbyterian churches in America. You have about five minutes to get ready. The service begins on the tolling of the bells in the tower — a gift from Robert Todd Lincoln. You know that Abraham Lincoln worshiped in this church? You will notice his pew, about seventh from the pulpit on the left. A red sash ropes it off. We only use it when the church is already crowded. And this is Dodson."

I looked up into an olive brown, ageless face and neatly close-cropped white hair cupping a shining balding brown head. He had large sad eyes, but around his lips were the creases of a permanent chuckle that easily erupted into shoulder-shaking laugh when Mr. Bridge remarked that "Dodson is our sexton. He's been here since Lincoln's time, or so it seems!"

A sudden change of expression clouded his features as the distant chimes tolled out the hour. Dodson drew himself up, whispering "Will you please follow me, Mr. Docherty."

With a limping gait he preceded us until we reached the door that led into a three-arched apse, where three large ecclesiastic chairs made of dark oak and padded in regal red velvet stood before a resplendent brass eagle lectern, wings outstretched.

I looked out to a crowded congregation waving bulletins vainly against the stifling humid air, the ladies in summer frocks and floral hats and many of the men coatless. At my feet, a whirring fan did little to temper the heat.

At the time of the announcements, I took the occasion to thank the congregation as representative of the many American friends who had provided for me such heartwarming hospitality during an extraordinary tour. I recounted something of my travels and adventures in their land. I spoke about my family, and how our elder son, Garth, according to the last letter from home, had painted our cabbages red — "a not inappropriate color, may I add, for the garden of a Socialist minister." That remark would be remembered!

I preached the Newark sermon requested by Frank Edgington — "A Sacramental Universe" — on 2 Samuel 23:13–17, how David, not yet king, hunted by King Saul, a wanted man among the hills, had poured out on the earth as an offering to God the precious water his three mighty men had brought to him from "the well of Bethlehem, which is by the gate," at the peril of their lives. Water bought at such cost was too precious to slake a passing thirst.

The temperature that morning actually reached ninety-five degrees. My head was tight. My pinstriped black morning-suit trousers clung to my legs. Faces swam in and out of focus as I stood shaking hands at the conclusion of the service, my jaws too stiff to make any intelligent response to their questions.

"I'm Catherine Marshall," said a young, dark-haired woman in a small floral straw hat.

"Why yes, of course, of course," I stammered. "I'm so pleased to meet you. Want so much to hear more about your husband. I read a write-up about his ministry in *Life* magazine. Must have been a remarkable man."

"Why don't you come round to the manse this afternoon for a 'cuppa,' as you say in Scotland? Shall we say about four?"

The cab sped over the Calvert Street bridge that spans Rock Creek Park past the old Wardman Park Hotel on Connecticut Avenue, climbing the gentle incline of Cathedral Avenue past a large white frame mansion in a green park bordered by ancient tulip trees (it was the summer White House in Lincoln's time) until I reached 3100.

"Milk?" asked Mrs. Marshall as we sat together in the airy lounge that opened up into the dining room. "You Scots, I believe, do not take cream with your tea? No sugar? Do you realize there was an overflow crowd at this morning's service? They said about four hundred. The ushers keep tabs on the attendance. And do you know that the telephone has hardly stopped ringing since I got home? They are all saying the same thing: they want you to be Peter's successor."

Her sudden and frank statement made sense of many things that had been happening to me, why the Edgingtons had motored from Milford, Pennsylvania, to hear me at Newark. I was not merely flattered; I was scared.

"Oh, I'm afraid not, Mrs. Marshall. I've been called two short years ago to the North Kirk. Besides, there is work to be done in our war-wearied Britain. I don't think Americans quite realize the devastation of the Old Country — not merely the physical destruction but the spiritual malaise. Our people were almost broken by the juggernaut of war; we are only slowly rebuilding our shattered country and seeking to recover Christian values. As an unrepentant socialist, I believe the British Labor movement requires the spiritual dynamism of the Keir Hardies who brought it into being; otherwise it will degenerate into a materialistic statism. I'd like to be in on that rebuilding."

"Did it ever occur to you that my husband, as minister of a significant congregation just three blocks from the White House in the heart of the nation's capital, far more than he ever realized, not only kept the gospel before the nation, but by his accent and words and thinking served as an unofficial spiritual ambassador for the Old Country?"

I put the question out of my mind by pursuing further the life of this Coatbridge lad who had come across the sea to settle, as so many Scots had done before him. I wanted to know more about this man: his life-style, his Christian convictions, his view of the ministry and the Church.

Between Sundays, I was guest preacher at Massanetta Springs Bible Conference lying in the lush valley of Virginia, abounding in peaches and turkeys. Here I met for the first time the remarkable man who had founded the Conference a quarter of a century before. Dr. Hudson, tall, with a wrinkled ascetic face and a slight build, was a kindly man and gentle — until he got behind the wheel of his ancient automobile; then he drove like Jehu. I noted several members of the New York Avenue Church among the audiences at the Conference, including Susan and Bill Kerr. Bill was the typical émigré Scot, happy in his new life in the States (he was a typesetter for the *Washington Evening Star*), even though he often felt the tug of the Old Country. Completely at home as an elder in the Presbyterian church, he was stubborn at times, but once he gave you his friendship, he was loyal to the end. Bill took me aside after lunch one day and in the confidential tones of one who was in the know said, "Lad, they really want you to be their minister. A dozen or so here already approached me to sound you out — confidentially, of course — for we are still in the process of the vacancy. Man, it would be great if you could be persuaded to succeed Peter Marshall!" A very flattering compliment, but I repeated my concerns regarding the fact that I had been only two years at the North Kirk; I was happy there and eager to meet the challenges of the depressed life of the city's drab tenements.

The following Sunday, my last in the States, I was again preacher at New York Avenue Church: once more the overflow congregation and sti-fling heat. After the service many wished me bon voyage. From the sea of faces emerged that of a grey-haired gentleman with the soft gnarled face of a young Carl Sandburg — thin pursed lips, strong mouth — who spoke with a kindly rounded Tennessee accent. There was the slightest suggestion of a courtly bow when he stepped up to shake my hand firmly.

"I'm Judge Sam Whitaker, Mr. Docherty. A few of us would like to have lunch with you tomorrow, a sort of farewell affair. Perhaps your host, Mr. Kerr, would be able to bring you to the Metropolitan Club. Shall we say about twelve noon?"

Monday morning the faithful Bill Kerr took me down to the Internal

Revenue Office on Constitution Avenue. It seemed I had to declare my earnings and pay tax thereon before I would be allowed to leave the country. Since most of my honoraria had been swallowed up in travel and hotel expenses, there seemed little sense in charging income tax on a net balance of some $200. But how to categorize me, that troubled the inspector. Leafing through a large tome of regulations, he triumphantly spied what he was looking for. Pointing to the place on the page, he said, "Got it, Mr. Docherty. I'll tell you what I'll do. I'll write you off as a 'traveling entertainer,' and there will be no tax." Whereupon he stamped my form and bade me a pleasant trip home.

Everybody knows what I did not then realize, that the Metropolitan Club of Washington is about the most exclusive fraternity in the city. Years later, President Kennedy would set off a minor earthquake by resigning from its membership because it excluded Negro members. Recently I returned to that place so significant in my story with Chem Oliphant, now eighty-seven, one of two survivors of that ten-man group who had invited me for lunch. The spacious dining room was unchanged; even some of the same waiters were quietly moving from table to table addressing the members by name. The faces had changed, however; no longer did one see Dean Acheson, though there must have been some cabinet members, congressmen, bankers, and perhaps "Scotty" Reston of the *New York Times* among the many heads bent in serious conversation over their vichyssoise and prime rib. But on my first visit, now so remote, I sat among a group of serious Presbyterian laymen, enjoying an ease that I was never again to know in that place, prepared to answer their questions with adolescent glibness.

"Why did the British people not reelect Churchill in 1945? After all, he had saved the nation and was a great statesman."

"Oh," I replied airily, between stabs at the large steak I was consuming, "that's easy! Mr. Churchill was the great war leader, the greatest Prime Minister since the younger Pitt. But he was Edwardian, living in an age of Empire and Kipling and all that sort of stuff. Any statesman who could say that he would not preside over the liquidation of the British Empire was still fighting the Boer War and the Indian Mutiny. So with tears in our eyes, we elected a Socialist government as the best solution to our postwar problem. I myself voted Socialist. In fact for the first few years of the war, I was a pacifist."

On and on I blethered, my words flowing like a streetcorner orator's, not realizing that these men were shrewdly listening and noting with keen experienced perception what kind of fellow was lurking behind those facile words.

After lunch I walked with Judge Whitaker toward the Ellipse, where we could call a cab. He talked about the city, pointing out the brick Octagon

House nestled among newer characterless stone-faced structures. He paused at the curb.

"There were really two reasons that we wished to have lunch with you today. You had assured us you soon would be leaving for home in Scotland; we wanted to make this occasion a sort of farewell, bon voyage luncheon, with the hope that you will one day return to these parts, and to assure you that there will always be a welcome to our pulpit. On the other hand, these men with whom you dined today are among the most significant and influential in our congregation. They have asked me to put this question to you. If you were called to be the minister of the New York Avenue Presbyterian Church, would you accept the call?"

Quite simply, I replied, "Sir, you flatter me, and indeed I am honored. I'm tired and wearied, almost sick by the heat of your American summers; and I'm homesick to get back to my family. My mind is in a whirligig at the moment, and I've always remembered Morrison of Wellington's advice never to make a major decision at three o'clock in the morning. I'm sort of sleepwalking at the moment. But there is as little chance of my becoming your minister as the man in the moon; though if you were to ask the man in the moon, and if he were a Scotsman, I believe he might think twice about remaining up there in the darkness."

The Judge smiled and gave my shoulder a friendly pat.

"That's all I was wanting to know. Have a pleasant trip back home."

By this time a cab had drawn up and I was on my way back to Bill Kerr's to get packed in preparation for the journey to New York, thence to Idlewild Airport, and by B.O.A.C. "over the sea to Skye" and home. A bumpy, unhappy flight it was. I had contracted a head cold; my sinuses were clogged. As the plane reached its cruising altitude, lightning bolts of pain darted across my forehead.

After an eternally long journey, I was able to look down on the grey-crested waters of the Irish sea, and through wisps of scudding clouds to the neat emerald green fields of Ayrshire. With a circling movement, we were soon over the racing ground, breaking in with a roar on Scottish soil.

For this family reunion after such a long parting, I had dressed in the special new light-weight pastel summer suit that Rupert McGregor had purchased for me at Montreat and a broad-rimmed caramel-colored Stetson. Reaching toward the open doorway, I inhaled once more the stimulating Scottish caller sea air and blinked up at the bright sunshine piercing a cloud-streaked August sky. There, quite unmistakably, I espied Jerry among a small group of people at the airport barricade, awaiting the arrival of the plane. Chewing gum, and waving my hat ferociously, I tried to attract her attention, but she had no eyes for me. Later, she was to explain that when a gentleman beside her had pointed out a man waving his hat at her, she had replied, rather indignantly, "Not that American! I'm waiting for my husband."

It was a joyous reunion, though our two boys were a little daunted by the American outfit of their father. We had planned to spend a few days at Largs, a holiday resort town on the Ayrshire coast where Jerry and I had spent so many happy times before.

Next day we took the boys out in an outboard motorboat across the sound to the Millport shore of the Cambrae, where we would picnic. As I steered the little boat, I asked Jerry what she'd think of going to a church in America.

"Why?" she asked.

"I think I'm going to be called to be the minister of the New York Avenue Presbyterian Church in Washington — you know, Peter Marshall's church."

"Did they hold a congregational meeting?"

"No."

"Did the vacancy committee approach you?"

"No."

"Did they state anything in writing?"

"Not really."

"Then we'll just wait and see."

"But Jerry . . ."

"We'll wait! Don't lean too far over the side, Garth, or you'll fall in. David, stop trailing your hands in the water."

9

American Interlude

God moves in a mysterious way
His wonders to perform.
— William Cowper

THE ANNUAL MEETING of the New York Avenue Presbyterian Church is held on the third Wednesday in January. It provides opportunity for the whole congregation to survey the work of the previous year, hear reports on finances, and discuss the mission of the church; plans and budget projects for the following year are also presented. The 146th Annual Meeting, held on January 19, 1949, was eagerly awaited; plans for the new sanctuary had to be accepted or rejected by the congregation.

It was obvious to everyone that the old building, constructed in 1859 with wooden beams, had become a fire hazard. Nor was it adequate to meet the expanding mission of the congregation or to accommodate the congregation that had been growing since the arrival, some eleven years before, of a young Scots preacher, Peter Marshall. Its eight hundred seats were not enough to meet the needs of visitors from all over the land who lined the sidewalk waiting to hear at the two morning services his forthright preaching.

A crucial question that had held up a final decision on the new sanctuary was whether the architecture ought to follow traditional colonial lines like the present building or break with tradition in favor of a modernistic Frank Lloyd Wright structure. A compromise had been submitted by the architect, Delos Smith: the traditional Georgian colonial lines would remain, but a square apse would replace the normal three arches, the ceiling would be paneled, and recessed lighting would be installed. While the sanctuary would remain on the second floor, as was the custom in colonial America for Presbyerian meeting houses, a large hall would be constructed on a fifth floor above the sanctuary, and a spacious basement would be made available for youth work. The floor space of the building would thus be doubled. The project was estimated to cost about one million dollars. After some characteristically heated debate, the compromise was accepted and the meeting adjourned, finally, just before midnight.

A weary pastor had pronounced the benediction, commending their decision to the blessing of God, and then made his way to his study through the Lincoln Room, in which the President for whom it was named had met with others for the midweek prayer meeting during the dark tragic days of the Civil War. In the half dark, Peter Marshall encountered a familiar figure, Frank Edgington.

Despite the late hour and the strain of the meeting, he had one more matter to clear up before retiring, he said, something that had been on his mind for some time: the summer's pulpit supply. A letter from Harry Holmes of the Exchange Committee of the Council of Churches in New York City had been awaiting his attention for much too long, and before things went any further, he meant to unburden himself of it. The letter mentioned one George Docherty, minister at North Church in Aberdeen, Scotland. He hadn't heard about the man personally, but he knew his church in Aberdeen, and Holmes wrote that Docherty was highly recommended. In any case, he hoped the pulpit supply committee would extend an invitation.

Before retiring that evening, Frank Edgington mentioned his conversation with the pastor to his wife, Helen. It seemed strange that Peter had never before suggested a name for pulpit supply; he had vetoed an occasional nomination, but had always left the final selection in the hands of the committee.

On Friday the 21st the pulpit supply committee met to arrange for the summer supply, and Frank brought up Peter's suggestion. They too were surprised but very pleased; they wrote immediately to Harry Holmes in New York to say that they would be happy with such an arrangement and to ask if it would be possible for the young Scotsman to preach for them on the 21st and 28th of August.

Sunday, January 23, was a particularly heavy day for Peter Marshall. He taught an Adult Bible Class at 9:30 and preached at 11:00 to the usual overflow congregation. In the afternoon he shared in evensong at the Washington Episcopal Cathedral, and then was back in his own church in the evening by 8:00 to preach a sermon entitled "All or Nothing."

Monday morning he was at home at his desk, writing out in his bold cursive handwriting the prayer for the opening of the United States Senate that would take place at noon. That completed, he got into his green Oldsmobile in the garage at the back of the manse at 3100 Cathedral Avenue, drove down the Rock Creek Parkway, along broad, tree-lined Constitution Avenue up the incline to Capitol Hill, and in the space reserved for the Chaplain parked his car under the portico of the Senate wing of the Capitol, giving a friendly nod to the Capitol police officer. In the anteroom of the Senate Chamber, he chatted, as was his daily custom, with the President of the Senate, who happened to be Senator Arthur

Vandenberg, acting *pro tem* for Vice President Alben W. Barkley, who was out of town.

The afternoon was spent with his son, Peter John, downtown at the Mayflower Electric Shop in L Street, trading in some old Lionel model trains for new ones.

Monday evening, his night out, was spent at the home of John Danley in Foxhall Road, near the American University campus where for the previous two Monday evenings they had been engaged in tight games of bridge with two young men of the congregation, Bob Dean and Lyle Mershon. Peter had earned a reputation for being a gamesman; he loved to win and hated to lose. Tonight John Danley and he were winning the rubber in a canter. Around nine o'clock his host noticed Peter wince a little as he spread out his cards.

"What's the matter, Peter?"

"Oh nothing, nothing at all!"

"Wrists sore? Pain kind of streaking up your arms?"

"A wee bit."

"Well, that settles it, fellows. I'm sorry but we'll have to call a halt; the game's over. Peter, you are going straight home to bed. Like yourself, I've had a heart attack and I know the symptoms."

"But John, we're winning! First time in three weeks! And it's only nine o'clock. Never been in my bed at this hour in my life."

"Now Peter, be a good fellow and don't argue. Let me help you into your coat. Sorry, lads, about this, especially since we were winning. We'll have another rubber sometime."

"It's all a lot of nonsense, but to please you, John, I'll go home and go to bed. My, it's been a grand evening, lads. And thank you for your hospitality, John."

Peter Marshall sauntered out into the bleak, dark night, down the concrete path of the front garden. At the gate, he turned, the streetlamps swaying in the wind reflecting his smile. He waved.

"Never mind, John. Tonight I sleep the sleep of victory!"

In the manse, some five minutes away by car, Peter and Catherine drank a cup of tea quietly before retiring for the night. About three A.M., Catherine heard groaning at her side.

"Catherine! It's my chest! Terrible pain! Can hardly breathe! Will you please call the doctor?"

The pain eased somewhat after the doctor's injection. Soon an ambulance drew up to the front door. Two orderlies gently and professionally eased their patient down the rather narrow winding stairway into the small hallway and out into the darkness. They paused at the door. Peter looked up from the stretcher at his wife and smiled. "Good night, darling. See you in the morning."

At hospital there were more injections. The patient was now sleeping soundly. The night nurse took his pulse periodically. Doctors came in at frequent intervals. At eight o'clock the next morning the nurse was aware of a strange silence in the room. Her patient had stopped breathing. It was January 25, 1949, the anniversary of the birth of Robert Burns.

The casket containing the earthly remains of Peter Marshall was placed in the sanctuary of the church in front of the platform he had graced with such powerful proclamation of the gospel. For twenty-four hours before the funeral service around the flower-draped catafalque there stood at attention a guard of honor consisting of members of the board of deacons and representatives of the St. Andrews Society of Washington in full Highland dress (Peter had at one time been their president). Bill Watkins, the organist, sat at the console in the gallery throughout the day playing softly and with incisive deep feeling.

Washington can be a soulless city. Too many world-shaking decisions are made there, too many national figures live there for it to hold long the remembrance of ordinary citizens. But the death of Peter Marshall was noted in the press as if a national figure had passed from the scene. For more than twenty-five years afterwards, the New York Avenue Church would be called Peter Marshall's church.

The stunned congregation bravely set about the slow, complicated, and at times frustrating business of calling a Presbyterian minister who would continue the work Peter Marshall had begun with such distinction. A vacancy committee, representative of the entire congregation, took up its task. It studied the dossiers of ministers from all over the States. Members of the committee traveled north and south and as far west as Texas and California to hear preachers about whom they had been informed.

The months passed. Winter gave way overnight to spring as it does in the city; soon the azaleas, forsythias, cherry blossoms, and dogwood faded. Summer settled in with its windless enervating heat, leaving nature limp and people seeking shelter in the shade of the great trees. Frank and Helen Edgington had for years escaped from this unbearable climate to a cottage in Milford, Pennsylvania, among the cool hills. In the gathering darkness one evening as they sat rocking on the porch sipping iced tea, Frank suddenly said to Helen, "A nagging thought just won't leave me, Helen, though it sounds odd I know. Do you think Peter was appointing his successor when he suggested that we hear Mr. Docherty this summer? I've decided to get into touch with the Council of Churches in New York City. I'd like to hear that young fellow before he arrives at our church in Washington."

And so it happened on a Sunday morning in the half-light that these two septuagenarians set off over the tortuous sixty miles of the Appalachian Trail mountain roads, crossed the Delaware River into the flatlands of New Jersey, skirting Paterson and Montclair, those dormitory appendages to New York City, until they reached the sprawl that is Newark, where they picked their way in the Sabbath stillness through rundown streets whose red brick townhouses, once the homes of the affluent, were now subdivided into flats for the poor, arriving on time for the morning service of the Old First Presbyterian Church to hear Mr. Docherty preach.

What I did not know then, what I learned only a year afterwards, was that Frank had on their return to Milford that afternoon sent off by Western Union the following cable to Harry Blake, a Scot and chairman of the Vacancy Committee of the New York Avenue Presbyterian Church:

> We heard Docherty at Newark today. Dramatic forceful preaching. Logical clear thinker. Attractive personality. Sense of humor. Deeply spiritual. Excellent voice. Accent not too much pronounced. Strongly urge full committee be notified to hear him as he merits serious consideration. Edgington.

By September of 1949 I was back at my work in Aberdeen after my remarkable American safari. The spontaneous welcome I had received from so many churches gave a boost to my self-confidence. Discounting the extravagant praise, I nevertheless believed that my preaching had been productive and helpful. One day I hoped to return and repeat the trip with Jerry and the children. I wanted them to meet my relatives in Chicago and to sample the wonderful family holiday that Massanetta Springs and Montreat had provided. Maybe in another two years?

With renewed energy and my vision of the Church greatly enlarged, I was back in my attic study in the manse pounding out new sermons. It was a joy to see our two boys grow up. Garth graduated from nursery school and passed the intelligence test for the Grammar School, founded about the fourteenth century, an institution that had sent many generations of Aberdonians to serve the Empire around the world.

Have you, gentle reader (as the Victorian novelists used to express it), ever accompanied your firstborn on his first day of school? The undertaking was handed over to me by Jerry, who was too emotionally upset to face up to the pivotal and sad *vale* to the babyhood of her first child. Suddenly he looked every bit a grown boy as he awaited his dad at 8:30 dressed in his dark blue school cap and blazer adorned with the school crest (*gules, three towers triple supported by two leopards; in escroll above: "Bon Accord"*), grey shirt with matching school tie and stockings, black shoes, and school bag (empty). As we walked the long mile to the school in silence, he held my hand tightly. We paused outside the tall wrought-iron gates, thrown open wide in welcome, and gazed over the vast playground, in the center of which stood a heroic statue of Lord Byron (a former pupil), and beyond to a three-story, grey-granite, turreted, balmoralized mid-Victorian building. Crowds of youngsters brushed past us excitedly to join the rushing, screaming bedlam. Garth looked up at me. He seemed so very small. Did I detect fear in his eyes? He bravely marched forward to join the mass of boys, all of them dressed exactly like himself. He looked round once and timidly waved his fingers. I have known happier moments.

After a melancholy day, I was back promptly at three. He came flying to me, pushing other lads out of his way, shouting and laughing, all in a rush to recount his first day, which we celebrated over an ice cream in Cattelli's. I heard all about the large gym and all its equipment, and about the prefects you had to look out for, tall fellows in long trousers, too high and mighty to notice him, and about the other boys in his class, and about the new friendships he had made.

Abruptly into this settled and happy life came letters from across the Atlantic postmarked Washington, D.C., or Maryland or Virginia, all of them kind, generous, and appreciative, and all of them ending in the same formula: please, would I come back and be their minister at New York Avenue Church? Some gave thumbnail sketches of the history of the church; some extolled the virtues of living in Washington; some challenged me with the opportunity of serving a significant church in the heart of the nation's capital, standing three blocks from the very center of political power, the White House.

With secretarial help limited to just one morning a week, I was soon inundated by the scores of letters that began arriving. The best I could do was to return a short acknowledgment and words of thanks. One letter, though, from a lady who was apparently somewhat concerned about the doctrines of the Virgin Birth and the Second Coming of Christ, called for a lengthier response. I wrote her that such deep problems could hardly be adequately discussed by transatlantic air mail and that she ought to seek help from a neighboring minister — and, in any case, if her letter were in fact a questionnaire to test my position relative to what she regarded as orthodoxy, I declined to answer on the grounds I was already a B.D. and had sat my last theological examination.

One letter did elicit a serious reply. Judge Samuel Whitaker wrote saying that my name was being considered along with others and that some members who had been present at the luncheon given for me at the Metropolitan Club on the eve of my departure wanted to know precisely what I meant when I had stated that I was a socialist and a pacifist. Eager to return to the States and aware already of the problem of being labelled "pacifist" and "socialist" (I learned too late that the latter term was, in the States, considered to be virtually synonymous with "Communist"), I replied in ten pages, outlining differing positions of pacifists and nonpacifists in the Kirk in Scotland concerning modern war. I pointed out that British Socialism, the strongest bulwark against militant Communism (and fascism), consisted of three types: the Fabians (Shaw, the Webbs, and Harold

133

Laski), the Trade Unionists (their leader Keir Hardie, a Scot, had founded the Labour Party), and the Christian Socialists among whom were several clerical friends. It was the third of these types with which I associated myself, a political party comprising a large majority of Britain's Christians, among them some of the best ministers in the Kirk, a party that believed a democratic socialism representing both freedom of the individual and justice in the community could best translate Christian ethics into the political arena. No fewer than thirty-five of the Labor M.P.'s were former Methodist ministers.

I was now really concerned. My off-the-cuff remarks at a luncheon were being interpreted as something far more serious than I had intended. It appeared I was a candidate for the vacancy and being given official consideration. I took into my confidence one of my elders, a dear friend. John Murray is a tailor whose shop in Aberdeen may be wee, but whose influence as a churchman in the North Kirk and whose example to the community place him among the most significant men in the city. We motored, I recall, on his half day off, along the road by the River Don to Kingseat Asylum, where two members of my Kirk were patients (my visits there justified my use of a car during a day of petrol rationing). We talked long under a tree, the fingers of autumn around us.

"Man, lad, dinna dae a thing aboot it. And certainly dinna bring up the matter before the kirk session. Suppose you tell the kirk session, and suppose the New York Avenue Church does *not* call you? Why, the elders will think you are anxious to leave, and it will create an unsettlement in the congregation. Now, if they do call you, then you will receive a letter from Washington. That will be the time to bring the matter before them for discussion and you can make up your mind as you think best. Mind you, between ourselves, if the call came, I'd tak' it. That's a big job, man."

On the morning of October 20 around seven, the telephone rang while I was shaving. It was the voice of Erskine Blackburn, always an early riser: "George, have you read the *Press and Journal* this morning? Your name is on the front page. In fact, there is half a column devoted to you. Let me read it out to you. Heading. 'Washington Church Rejects Aberdeen Minister: Voted Socialist at the Last Election.' "

The item stated that on the evening of October 19 the congregation of the New York Avenue Presbyterian Church in Washington, D.C., had met to deal with the name proposed as sole nominee by the vacancy committee — the Reverend George M. Docherty, minister of the North Church, Aberdeen. A stormy meeting ensued that broke up in some disorder around midnight. Objections were raised to having a foreigner as pastor, and a pacifist and socialist to boot. A leading judge, Mr. Leach, had declared, "The only difference between Communism and socialism is that the Communists say their theory must be enforced by bloody revolution. I don't want a socialist in that pulpit."

When the voting finally took place, 391 voted Yes and 167 voted No; abstentions amounted to 187. Since less than seventy-five percent of the communicant members present had approved, the call was not sustained.

This news had reached the desk of the editor of the *Aberdeen Press and Journal* via UPI wires at two o'clock that morning. This Tory newspaper was only too happy to publish. If America would not even call a Socialist minister, what chance was there for cooperation between the two countries?

The following Sunday from my pulpit I tried to explain that the word "rejected" seemed to imply that I had applied for the position but that this was not the case. At a meeting of the kirk session after the service, I set out in detail the events that had led up to the announcement in the press. The elders sat stolid and silent except for one who eventually came up and with a quizzical smile said, "You know, Mr. Docherty, I really *do* believe you!"

Around seven on the morning of November 3 Erskine Blackburn's happy voice was once again at the other end of the telephone.

"George, this is Erskine. Your name is back on the front page of the *Press and Journal,* together with your photograph. Let me read the column to you. 'The congregation of the New York Avenue Church in Washington, D.C., known as the Church of the Presidents, has extended a unanimous call to the Reverend George M. Docherty of the North Kirk, Aberdeen.' George, let me be the first to congratulate you. And of course you will accept the call."

"Not on your life, Erskine. Not after all this carfuffle."

It was indeed headline news in Scotland. The *Scottish Daily Express* announced in bold letters, "Aberdeen Minister Called to £3,000 Pulpit" (the stipend of the minister of St. Giles Cathedral—one of the highest in the church—was only £1,000). In the *Daily Record* it was "U. S. Calls Scottish Minister." The *Daily Mail* had a banner headline, "Scots Minister Wins Fight for U. S. Pulpit: Kathy Swings the Vote."

That afternoon in our lounge were gathered at the same time press representatives from the BBC, the *Glasgow Herald,* and the *Scotsman.* Photographs were taken. I was invited to go on radio to explain my position.

Within a week I received a letter telling the full story of this second meeting which had nullified on constitutional grounds the findings of the October 19 meeting: "Silent members, unless excused from voting, must be considered as acquiescing in the majority decision." With the large number of abstentions (187) included in the total, it seemed that eighty-seven percent had voted in favor of the nominee. A new vote was recorded after many emotional speeches, including a plea from Katherine Murray: "How many in this room are pure Americans? How many are Navajos? Don't you remember the portrait of Jesus in Sunday School surrounded by children of every race and color?"

The final vote was Yes, 512; No, 142. After the vote, Judge Leach moved that it be made unanimous. "I have no retraction to make, but I am a Presbyterian — I am a New York Avenue Presbyterian. I therefore move that the vote be made unanimous."

Understandably, I had now no intention of going into a situation that had caused so much turmoil in the congregation. In light of the circumstances, I wanted simply to remain in my own Scottish downtown kirk even though I would like to visit the States again. It did occur to me, however, that it would be difficult to express this without there seeming to be an element of pettiness in my response. As the days passed and the official call arrived, Jerry and I prayed much about it. I tried to foist the responsibility onto Jerry's shoulders, but she simply said, "Whither thou goest, I will go."

A call extended to a minister at any time is a solemn undertaking, and, like the marriage vow, it must not be taken "lightly or thoughtlessly, but reverently and in the fear of the Lord, and with due consideration of the ends for which it was ordained." We listened carefully to the honest advice of good friends, most of whom said that we should go. I canvassed my elders, most of whom agreed that I ought to go. After a month, we came to our decision. We did not wish to say Yes, but we dared not say No. We would go with an open mind, and if it did not work out, after five years we would return to Scotland. After all, I was only thirty-eight.

In the spring of 1950 there set sail for the United States from Southampton on board the *Queen Elizabeth* our little family, a father with two boys (Garth, just over four; David, three); a mother-in-law; a black mongrel cocker spaniel, Trudie; and a mother who was expecting our third child sometime in August. We were buoyed at the prospect of our new life, brokenhearted at leaving home. For me the worst moments came while I was standing on deck at Southampton looking down between the ship and the pier, watching the swirling muddy waters intently, until at last the pier appeared to move ever so achingly slowly away from the ship. Would we never really get going? The space between ship and land widened: we were on our way. In the evening Jerry and I watched the double lane of churning sea following the ship in the midst of the Atlantic, no land in sight, the great ship plowing heavy seas on her way to a pinpointed landfall. We struck rough spring neap tides, the worse for my poor Jerry! Seasickness added to her already unsettled disposition. It was a painful trip for her; seldom did she leave our cabin. In contrast, the boys loved it. Trudie, unaware of the purebred company she was keeping in the dog pen on the top deck, was exercised by me and the boys twice a day. I met the film star Van Johnson at the barbershop and in the swimming pool. He was the Robert Redford of these days, and Jerry, a star-struck movie fan all her days, was almost beside herself with envy.

Approaching the narrows outside New York Harbor, the pilot's cutter drew alongside to guide the great ship to her berth. There was a knock at our cabin door, and there in the room stood George Worthington and Verne Bonesteel, two elders of the church welcoming Jerry to the States with a grace they would always accord to the manse family. They had been delegated to meet us and were given special permission to come aboard with the pilot. Because of their presence and the special category in which they seemed to stand with the authorities, there was no custom examination of our personal luggage (our furniture would arrive later). When we met the Immigration Officer, we were received like royalty; our passports were stamped and we were sent on our way with his best wishes.

"By the way, Jerry, there's Van Johnson," I said. Standing in a long line with the other first-class passengers was a tall, fair-haired, handsome young man. Jerry gave him a smile which he returned cheerily.

Our first place of residence was a suite at the Wardman Park Hotel at Connecticut and Cathedral Avenues, where we spent three days because the manse was not ready for us; painters had not quite completed the redecoration. We were rather wearied after the four-hour train journey from New York. Only hazily do I recall my Scots friend, Bill Kerr, urging me to "come and meet another Scot, Sir Alexander Fleming."

A smallish, quiet, shy man extended his hand. I took the opportunity of saying after we spoke a little about Scotland, "God bless you, sir, for the miracle of penicillin you have uncovered."

Quietly we celebrated Jerry's birthday, March 31. I was ready for my first Sunday on schedule—Palm Sunday, 1950.

Looking back, Janus-faced, these thirty years, I am still amazed at my temerity, my *amour propre*, daring to accept the challenge of such a call. I can think of only a few less qualified to assume the multifarious duties that a congregation in the heart of the nation's capital demanded. I seemed, now, the young fool rushing in where angels fear to tread. Yet the wonder of those days remains with me still, of a generous and kind people so eager to meet our every need, so understanding of the pain it must have meant for us to leave Scotland and settle as immigrants in their country.

At the welcome social, a steel-haired gentleman, tall and courtly, approached us with a cordial greeting and a handshake. He was smiling and had that aura of calm that seems to have surrounded every judge I have ever met.

"I'm Judge Leach. I voted against you, sir, at first, but I want you to know that I want to get to know you better and I want to like you and to assure you of my complete support in this great new venture you have embarked upon."

On our first visit to the manse at 3100 Cathedral Avenue, where only the previous summer I had enjoyed afternoon tea with Catherine Marshall, we were met at the door of the empty house by a tall, dark, handsome man, an apron around his middle and a broom in his hand, apparently industriously engaged in sweeping up stray slivers of wallpaper and wood shavings left behind by workmen hurrying to complete redecoration for the new minister and his family.

"Daddy," Garth whispered behind his little hand, "Daddy, is this your man?"

Bud Stott, one of the leading businessmen in the city, would recall with a chuckle Garth's remark ten years later at a social gathering celebrating our anniversary: "I was indeed his man then; and I am still his man now!"

But it gives me no joy to realize that many of these dear folk are no longer with us. Only two of the original twelve who talked with me at the Metropolitan Club—Bill Willard and Bud Stott—are still alive.

Frank Edgington, my session clerk, however, would live until his ninety-seventh year, a tower of strength to me, a superb churchman and an authentic Presbyterian. Sometimes as we spoke together on Friday afternoons after staff conferences, he would recount again, with a sense of wonder in his voice, the story of that long-ago summer evening when he sat with his wife rocking in chairs on the porch of their cottage among the Pennsylvanian hills protecting their beloved Milford village, around them in their garden the dahlias of which he was so rightly proud: "Do you think, Helen, that Peter Marshall was appointing his successor?"

10

A Man Called Peter

A man walks on through life—with the external call ringing in his ears but with no response stirring in his heart, and then suddenly, without any warning, the Spirit taps him on the shoulder. . . . The true minister is in his pulpit not because he has chosen that profession as an easy means of livelihood, but because he could not help it, because he has obeyed an imperious summons that will not be denied.

Such was my tap on the shoulder.

—Peter Marshall, *Mr. Jones, Meet the Master*

MORE THAN THIRTY YEARS after his death, I am still asked what it was like to succeed Peter Marshall. My reply has always been the same: "As a fellow Scot acquainted with the early life of Peter Marshall and as his successor reaping the harvest of his great ministry, I was too proud of his achievements to have room for jealousy or to fear intimidation. Besides, the Lord who in his infinite wisdom does not make two sheep alike, nor two identical daisies, surely calls each preacher to be his own man." I recall little of the welcome social at New York Avenue Church, except for one point I made; I informed the congregation that the only man's shoes I was going to try to fill were my own. The remark was met with a standing ovation.

The life and ministry of Peter Marshall over the years has been a fascinating study to me. I believe I could present a Ph.D. thesis on the subject! We never met face to face, although we came close to it when, many years ago, I attended the Atheneum Theatre in Glasgow. The Nessie Knight Players were presenting Barrie's *Quality Street* on behalf of her husband's medical mission in Africa. I learnt subsequently that Peter Marshall was also there, helping with direction and props on stage behind the scenes.

I have lived in his home, worked at his desk at the church, preached from his pulpit, and come to know on several visits back to Scotland both his God-fearing mother, Mrs. Findlay, and his sister Chrissie when we visited them in their lovely home in Coatbridge. They told the story of a boy, a typical Scots lad, brought up in a religious home, somewhat conservative; who was a member of the church, the Buchanan

139

Street E. U. Congregational; who ran around with lads and lasses in the church, played tennis and cricket in summer, and was goalkeeper on the local Y.M.C.A. soccer team in the winter; who was a Sunday School teacher, a scout master, and a drummer in a dance band — this last a little daring perhaps — a strong boy, full of healthy animal spirits, and a non-smoker and teetotaler to boot.

Literally scores of friends and at least one teacher at Decatur, Georgia, shared with me tales of Peter Marshall. That he was thus remembered is itself testimony to the impact he made upon everyone. I have read every sermon he wrote as well as his addresses, gathered together in *The Exile Heart*, which a Scots group in the congregation headed by the devoted Bill Kerr published. I have watched home movies of him bantering with his board of deacons and listened to his voice on records.

His wife, Catherine, remained in the congregation for some years after his death. I have rejoiced in her skill in simple, direct, unadorned prose and her extraordinary success as an author. *A Man Called Peter* headed the national best-seller lists for over a year; sales of her books have reached, I believe, around fifteen million volumes. I remember their son, Peter John, first as a lonely little boy who returned almost every day to his old home at 3100 Cathedral Avenue to play with our two boys, as if reluctant to give up the happy days he had known there. I have watched him grow to manhood, graduating from Sidwell Friends School, Yale, and Princeton Theological Seminary, tall and handsome, a fine preacher, though without his father's charisma; and I have grieved with him over the sorrows in his otherwise happy married life.

Peter Marshall was an authentic preacher. He "had the gift," as they say in Scotland, though he was the last person to agree with such a judgment, which is maybe as it should be. Preaching was agony for him — and maybe that is also as it should be. His intimate friends, who were in time to become my own colleagues, Dr. Clarence Cranford of Calvary Baptist Church, Dr. Edward Pruden of the First Baptist Church, and Dr. Albert Shirkey of Mount Vernon Methodist Church, would recall as they met for lunch at the old S & W Cafeteria on New York Avenue how Peter would sit with them, as I now sat with them, of a Friday, and lament that his Sunday sermon had not got far beyond a text and a title, and that the heavens seemed as brass to his entreaty for some inspiration. Yet when the hour struck Sunday morning, he was ready, his sermon manuscript written out in full in his splendid cursive handwriting, the lines uniquely arranged as if in blank verse. When *Mr. Jones, Meet the Master* was published, Sara Leslie, one of our members who helped in the arrangement of the manuscript, suggested that it be set in type just as Peter had written his manuscript, line for line. It created an extraordinary breakthrough in written sermons, almost as if the reader could hear Peter's voice in poetic cadences reiterating the truth he was proclaiming.

When I shared with my own members questions about Peter's preaching, a not uncommon comment was that his sermons were poetic, almost too flowery in language, that he preached in pictures, making startlingly vivid not only scenes from Scripture but anecdotes he would share. One member said, "While Peter was preaching, we were captivated, hanging on every word, yet later over Sunday dinner, it was not always easy to say exactly what Peter had been saying."

Yet what more can be expected of any preacher Sunday after Sunday than that he should for a brief twenty minutes hold the attention of his congregation? (Would we all had that gift!) In authentic preaching, as opposed to an essay or an address, the preacher and the message seem one, the words an extension of his thought. We address ourselves to the subconscious mind. The congregation is aware of an event, a happening in the pulpit, a parable, a picture of the majesty of God and the love of Jesus. The preacher responds to their demand "Sir, we would see Jesus." It is the task of the theologian to portray the Christ-event in syllogistic terms.

Around a dining table or engaged in a fireside chat with friends, Peter seemed reticent, almost tongue-tied, I am told, content to listen; yet in the pulpit all inhibition was absent. On one occasion, preaching in the great Fourth Presbyterian Church in Chicago on the topic of Joshua's challenge to the people of Israel to choose between Yahweh and the baalim of the heathen, on his proclamation that, "as for me and my house, we shall serve the Lord," Peter closed with the startling peroration "Well, there it stands, my friends! There you have the choice! Either you go to heaven, or you can go to hell!"

One is tempted to suppose Peter Marshall fits the mold of the typical American folklore hero — the poor Scots lad who emigrates from his home across the seas, lands at Ellis Island penniless, and after much hardship rises to become Chaplain to the Senate of the United States, finding fame if not fortune. The picture of an impoverished childhood, especially in the movie *A Man Called Peter*, based on Mrs. Marshall's book, did not go down well with his family and friends in Scotland, not because poverty was something to be ashamed of, but because it simply was not true.

Peter was raised in a solid Scottish stone house. If his family were not affluent, he certainly lacked nothing of the necessities of life. His stepfather, Mr. Findlay, was a traveler for Stewarts and Lloyds, the great Scottish steel company, and a member of the local golf club. In the tube works where he was employed, Peter, an intelligent, enterprising lad, was soon promoted from machinist to charge hand (what we would today call "shop steward") when he was only about twenty-one, and he remained in this position for six years, until he emigrated to the States at a time when unemployment was plunging toward the depths it reached during the Great Depression. The three pounds a week he received was a good wage for any worker at that time; it was exactly double what my own father was then earning.

The struggle that dominated Peter Marshall throughout his life was quite different. The Scot may even boast of "honest poverty" (Burns), but he finds it hard to forgive either in himself or in others intellectual indolence. The scar Peter carried was the memory that he had failed to pass the entrance examination to the University of Glasgow. Like Icarus, he fell when his waxen wings melted before the sun of the entrance examination, even though they did serve to keep him afloat in the waters of an American college.

Yet failure in the entrance examination to a Scottish university was hardly the sign of intellectual indolence. Passes were expected in Greek or Latin, Advanced English Literature, Higher Mathematics, and in the History of the British People. To attempt such a stiff curriculum by correspondence course at Skerry's College, Glasgow, was itself a brave endeavor. (I know!)

When our boys graduated from the fine Woodrow Wilson High School in Washington, D.C., I considered sending them over to Glasgow for their college courses. I was informed that unless the boys personally presented themselves for the entrance examination, they would be required to show evidence that they had completed a sophomore year at an "A" college with a pass mark no lower than B.

Dr. George Buttrick of the Madison Avenue Presbyterian Church in New York City once told me of an occasion at Montreat Bible Conference when Peter was sharing a soft drink with Dr. Jim McCracken of the Riverside Church and himself after the morning meetings.

"Peter," George said, "I would like to think that I preached this morning as well as I shall ever preach. And Jim here, I have never heard him preach better. But man, Peter, you went up to that platform and swept the congregation with you. It was a magnificent sermon, lad."

"Thanks, George, thanks," Peter said with an embarrassed shrug, "but you see, you fellows have got a degree."

During his several visits to Scotland, not once did Peter preach in such prestigious pulpits as Wellington, Glasgow, or St. George's, Edinburgh, which would have been honored by having him as a summer pulpit supply. The place where he preached — by his own choice — was the Tent Hall, a brave little evangelistic mission in the Cowcaddens of Glasgow, a dreary district.

Peter made no claim to originality. Who can? Dr. William Barclay in his autobiography writes that he had not one original thought in his life. Peter "kindled his lamp at another man's lou" (glowing ember). But he made dull thinking come alive with telling phrases ("We must stand for something or we shall fall for anything") and lively description (a Scottish tree-covered mountain was like "a regiment marching down to the lochside"). He had the gift of being able to say what oft was thought, but ne'er so well expressed, as Pope described true wit. On one occasion, when vacationing in the South, he heard a dedicated but dull preacher seek to expound a great text. On his return to Washington, Peter rewrote the preacher's sermon and preached it to his own congregation. In those days the De Witts, founders of *The Reader's Digest*, were members; De Witt demanded that the sermon be handed over for publication in his magazine. Peter got $800 for the sermon. He sent a check for $400 to the country preacher in the South, telling him that this was what he had done with his sermon!

Peter Marshall was already a national figure in church circles, on demand from coast to coast as a preacher, and particularly a speaker at Scots gatherings, even before the publication of Catherine's book *A Man Called Peter* or the release of the film that was based on it.

When the book and movie were made public, Peter Marshall became a figure of worldwide reptuation, his fame as a preacher second only to that of Billy Graham.

A Man Called Peter is a remarkable movie, still to be seen on the late show some thirty years after its production. It captured the idealistic imagination of a generation of young people. When Richard Todd, who played the part of Peter (in his own brand of Scots accent), was depicted standing in the pulpit of the Naval Academy at Annapolis peering down under heavy eyebrows and announcing to the assembled cadets, "Let us pray," it is reported that all over the world movie audiences bowed their heads in prayer!

Those of us who knew the real story of Peter Marshall and New York Avenue were not at all happy with some of the myths the film created. The scenes of poverty in which Peter was supposed to have grown up rightly infuriated his family and friends back home in Coatbridge. The identity of the dowager in the film who showed aloof indifference to the needs of servicemen in Washington was easily recognized—but this was a cruel parody of the woman on whom the character was supposed to be based: she was in fact the one above all others in the congregation who each Sunday after the service sought out servicemen attending the church and entertained them in her own home for Sunday dinner. And it would be quite out of character for Peter to have suggested to a married couple that they spend their nuptials in the church's Lincoln Chapel, where Mr. Lincoln had attended mid-week services of prayer, as the film has him doing; if there was no room in the overcrowded Washington hotels, he would have invited them home to the manse. The movie also gives the impression that Peter succeeded to a congregation in a very low ebb—a cruel falsehood that does a great disservice to the outstanding ministry of Dr. Joseph Sizoo, his predecessor. Indeed, Joe Sizoo did what neither Peter nor I ever succeeded in doing: he packed the Sunday evening services with brilliant sermon lectures. The conflicts the film has occurring between Peter and his boards are quite exaggerated. Peter did have conflicts, but there were no more than what every authentic minister endures.

During a visit to Hollywood shortly after the movie's release, I shared my unhappiness with the film's producer in the Fox studios. He heard me out patiently and then said quietly, "Dr. Docherty, conflict is the essence of all drama. Of course we exaggerated the conflicts; it made the movie more dramatic. On the other hand, this movie was perhaps the most remarkable production Hollywood has ever made. Do you realize that we included twenty-seven minutes of prayer and preaching? And we got away with it! Audiences throughout the English-speaking world loved it. Indeed, yours is the first adverse criticism I have listened to among the thousands of letters of approval that have reached my desk; and mark you, all of them from young bobby-soxers."

I felt like George Bernard Shaw when he was haled to the stage with cries of "Author! Author!" on the opening night of one of his brilliant plays, receiving ovation after ovation. From the upper gallery came one resounding raspberry. Shaw immediately responded with a wave, saying, "I agree with you, old man, but what are two of us among so many?"

After talking to those who knew him best, I am convinced that Peter Marshall and I shared something more than just the concerns of the New York Avenue pastorate. We were both stricken with an unhealable homesickness. Both of us were moved by the Lord to serve him whithersoever he led us. In America we both found fulfillment and happiness loving America, its people and its ways; yet, never a sun set behind the hills but thoughts wing back home, where

> Blows the wind today, and the sun and the rain are flying,
> Blows the wind on the moors today and now,
> Where about the graves of the martyrs the whoups are crying
> My heart remembers how.

The tragedy of Peter Marshall is that he was dead before he reached his forty-seventh birthday, in the prime of his ministry, and having laid the groundwork for the building of a new sanctuary and an even greater ministry in the heart of the nation's capital.

He was buried at Fort Lincoln Cemetery. Over his grave stands a grey granite stone on which is carved a Celtic cross with the everlasting pattern, the eternal intertwining of the human with the divine. The cross was patterned from a pew carving in the St. Leonard's Church, where we now worship in St. Andrews. The headstone was subscribed by a group of admiring Scots headed by Mr. William Kerr. Always when I conducted a funeral service at Fort Lincoln, I directed the driver to detour past Peter's grave, where I tarried a while, always with a prayer of thanksgiving. This little pilgrimage became our closest encounter this side Calvary.

Bill Kerr, chairman of the Peter Marshall Scottish Memorial Fund, elder of New York Avenue, and perhaps the closest friend Peter had in the church, approached me with the suggestion for a memorial to Peter's ministry. I suggested the Peter Marshall Bursary. An invitation could be extended to a licentiate of the Church of Scotland, a graduate of Trinity College, Glasgow, to spend a full year in the United States. The year would begin with a semester of study at Princeton Theological Seminary, where the bursar could choose his own subjects (though classes in Church Administration and Mission would be essential, since there is much American churches can teach about running a kirk). The remainder of the year would be spent in service on the staff of a Presbyterian church where, working under the senior minister, the bursar might receive invaluable firsthand experience of the operations of a great parish. Thus was born the Peter Marshall Bursary. To date about twenty Scots have profited by the experience. Dr. McCord, the president of Princeton, has cooperated most generously. Dr. William J. Wiseman of the First Church of Tulsa and Dr. Ernest Somerville of the First Church of Philadelphia are two among many others who have enjoyed participation in the work of the Bursary and whose congregations have opened their hearts to these young Scots from abroad.

11

The Church of the Presidents

Thou, Lord, my allotted portion, thou my cup,
Thou dost enlarge my boundaries;
the lines fall for me in pleasant places,
indeed I am well content with my inheritance.
— Psalm 16:6

ON A SUNNY SPRING MORNING in 1950, pedestrians hurrying along the sidewalk near the corner of 14th Street and New York Avenue in Washington, D.C., were not likely to take much notice of a preacher in black coat, striped trousers, and clerical collar leading by the hand two irrepressible boys in kilts, accompanied by their mother, who, discerning folk might have noticed, was with child. The little family paused beside the shell of what once might have been a red brick church. From its gaping roofless interior, the skyscraper crane's ruthless wrecker ball, swinging precariously at the end of a long steel hawser, was rhythmically pounding the remaining walls in a cloud of dust.

"Daddy," asked the elder boy, Garth, who was old enough to have remembered such sights in bombed Scotland, "Daddy, has your church been blitzed?"

We retraced our steps to Pennsylvania Avenue where stands the majestic Greek-columned Treasury Building. It is said to have been built at this place when an impatient, irascible President Jackson, wearied by the delays in choosing a site for the building that would replace the one burned by the British under Admiral George Cockburn in 1814, had left the White House stick in hand and said, "Build it here!" It pushes an elbow into Pennsylvania Avenue, which otherwise runs in a straight line from the Capitol, disrupting the master plan of the French architect and military engineer Pierre Charles L'Enfant, who had envisaged a *route nationale* to the White House. The proud portico of the White House facing Lafayette Square was originally meant to be the rear entrance.

We walked the short distance to the White House, a splendid Georgian colonial mansion, and paused to look through the high wrought-iron railings across the lush Kentucky bluegrass lawn with gushing fountain and

146

flower beds almost ready for the glorious carpet of yellow daffodils and crimson and white tulips. Before this spacious mansion was built, my congregation, a group of Scottish stonemasons, worshiped regularly each Sunday in the carpenter's shop on the grounds.

In 1792 President George Washington laid the foundation stone of what was then called the President's House, and shortly afterwards wrote to a man named George Walker, who was about to sail for Britain, exhorting him to facilitate the importation of Scottish stonemasons to complete the building. Undoubtedly, Mr. Walker would sail from New York to Glasgow. I am tempted to believe that he may have signed up some of those same Cameronian covenanters who had met in conventicle on the preaching braes of my old Glasgow parish of Sandyhills. What is certain, Scottish stonemasons did complete the White House; and the records show that a group of Cameronian covenanters belonging to what was called in Scotland the Auld Licht (Old Side) school did worship in the carpenter's shop.

In 1795 the Presbytery of Baltimore sent down to this little group of Scots a young minister, James Brackenridge, as pulpit supply. For reasons not fully disclosed, there was an immediate split between the young minister and a majority of the group, who moved to a wooden schoolhouse in F Street where the Roman Catholic procathedral of St. Patrick now stands. I am quite sure the personal friction that arose must have stemmed from a theological disagreement. Theology in those days was no abstract discipline, but the very guide and guardian of the lives of the believers. The exclusive singing of the metrical Psalms at worship; the conviction that all mankind is from the very beginning totally depraved and without hope except for the grace of God; the belief that only some can be saved from the burning fires of hell and that the elect are already chosen, predetermined from the foundations of the world, were all woven into all their thinking and doing.

It is not without significance that when in 1801 this struggling little group in the schoolhouse felt strong enough to support their own minister, they petitioned not the Presbytery of Baltimore forty miles away, but the Synod of Philadelphia, which had in 1842 expelled from their membership those who had been caught up by the revival known as the Great Awakening, headed by Gilbert Tennant and influenced by the powerful preaching of George Whitfield. These ministers, the "New Side" as they were called, had exhibited "heterodox and anarchical principles" and had "industriously worked on the passions and affections of weak minds." I fear the unhappy Mr. Brackenridge must have been a liberal evangelical!

The response of the Synod of Philadelphia was to send, in 1803, a twenty-six-year-old Scot, the Reverend James Laurie, accompanied by his new bride Elizabeth, née Scott, cousin of Sir Walter. Together they braved the long coach journey over dirt roads and through virgin forest. In his diary Mr. Laurie noted that he "enquired of the coachman how long it would be until we reached Washington and received the reply that we had been in Washington for the past two miles." He would remain as their pastor for over fifty years.

Laurie was a graduate of Edinburgh University, and as a candidate for the ministry of the Relief Church had no doubt received his theological education by means of private tutoring from ministers in their manses; both students and clergy were few at the time. The Relief Church had been founded by Thomas Gillespie, who has been described as a gentle preacher and a tolerant man. He had corresponded with Jonathan Edwards in New England, who himself had tempered his theological views after the Great Awakening. Mr. Laurie may well have sat at the feet of Gillespie, a not inconsiderable theological training!

The Celtic wanderlust seemed to have held sway of the heart and mind of the young preacher. He traveled as far north as Boston and as far south as Savannah, by boat, gathering funds for the building of his new sanctuary. An elegant structure capable of seating five hundred, it was erected in 1807 at the corner of F Street and 14th, where the Willard Hotel presently stands. This building was the first Protestant place of worship in the District of Columbia. Of course back in 1780 Georgetown Presbyterian Church was formed, but Georgetown had not yet been incorporated into the District of Columbia by 1807.

For those who have a taste for historical origins and are not unduly influenced by a sort of Presbyterian "apostolic succession," the records do show that what is now the New York Avenue Presbyterian Church was the first Presbyterian congregation in the District of Columbia. The splinter group that was left in the White House grounds under the leadership of Mr. Brackenridge (whose trials and tribulations seem to have continued) struggled on until in 1812 they, too, were in a position to build a sanctuary. It was known as the "Little White House under the Hill" and stood along South Capitol Street. Described as the First Presbyterian Church under the Baltimore Presbyery, its first pastor was not formally installed until 1818, when they called the Reverend Mr. Rubin.

In October 1885 a group of fifty-six elders and members of the New York Avenue Presbyterian Church were granted letters of dismission, "having expressed the desire to withdraw from the church, and . . . unite in forming the Church of the Covenant," as our session minutes note. A fine Normanesque building was constructed on Connecticut Avenue near Dupont Circle, where, according to records of that time, "top hats had chosen lots for residence . . . a majority of the residents being of the wealthiest class [and] some of the best Presbyterian people."

In 1930 the First Presbyterian Church left its site on Capitol Hill and united with the Church of the Covenant to become the Covenant-First

Presbyterian Church. In 1947 the united congregation renamed itself the National Presbyterian Church; but that is another story altogether.

My mother often said, "Aye! It's a guid thing we dinna ken what lies afore us!" Only now do I blush at the audacity of accepting a call from a congregation of whose work and mission I was totally unaware, of pulling up roots irrevocably from Scotland and arriving in a deceptively foreign land, of thinking that I could lead such a charge, situated three blocks from the White House in the capital of the United States, whose building was being razed to the ground, and whose congregation was to be dependent upon the movingly wonderful hospitality of sister churches of almost every denomination during the twenty months until the new sanctuary would be completed!

George Washington University granted us use of the Lisner Auditorium, a splendid modern spacious 1,700-seat hall for our services. Sunday by Sunday I walked onto the vast platform, our hundred-voice choir behind me, and from a podium delivered sermons both mornings and evenings. A large fire curtain on the stage depicted a collage in Calvinistic colors applied, it seemed, by the pailful. I dubbed it "The Chaos," which was in the beginning; it reflected not inaccurately my state of mind.

The church staff was housed temporarily in an office building at 1406 G Street that now, like so many buildings in the area, sadly is no more. My Associate Minister was Bob Bridge, a Methodist by background and an Englishman by birth, whose calm wisdom made him a much-appreciated tower of strength in those unsettling days. Jim Bryden, a Pennsylvanian and the son of a preacher, took from my shoulders the entire responsibility of Christian Education. Jim Patton was called the financial secretary, but he was no less a colleague in the ministry; his knowledge of the congregation and his simple, forthright ways enabled me to appreciate something of the fine outreach and mission program of the congregation.

Bob Bridge introduced me to my new office. I sat down in a swivel chair behind a finely polished mahogany desk on which stood two wooden trays marked In and Out, both empty — for the last time! Around the wall stood empty bookcases. They would remain empty, for I had made up my mind to continue the Scottish custom of using a room in the manse as my study, where I would prepare for my services and do my reading. (I have never been able to fathom how the average American minister is able to do any sort of creative writing in an office set in the center of an inevitable clamor of callers, phone calls, and endless interruptions.) Opposite the desk stood a comfortable green leather armchair. Someone had placed a vase of flowers at the window. I could look down from this fourth-floor vantage point upon the rhythmic bustle of Washington traffic; I can still hear the sudden erupting roar of city buses as they move away from their stops in first gear.

Gingerly I pressed an extension button on the telephone. It was followed immediately by a gentle tap upon the door. Before me stood an attractive smiling brunette with notebook and pencil at the ready. She sat down in the green armchair, alert and ready for her first orders.

"Mary Anne," I said to Miss Jackson my secretary, "why don't we both have a cup of tea?"

Once you know the layout of the city of Washington, it is easier to get around than most any other city of its size — but it does take a while. On one occasion I found myself completely bewildered by the circles that L'Enfant had placed at strategic locations where the avenues cross at forty-five degrees to the right-angled streets (I believe he did this with an eye to providing defensive positions in case of an enemy attack). Du Pont Circle, which consists of double concentric circles, vanquished me on one occasion. I found myself going round and round a slow-moving honking carousel trying to get to 18th Street, quite sure I would spend the rest of my ministry there.

Having known a little of controversy, I resolved to raise no disruptive issues, certainly not until my people had come to know me better, when I thought and hoped they would appreciate some of the things on my mind, such as the Order of Service that they had been following, which seemed to me at first sight not very liturgically satisfying. Frank Edgington had told me that the order of the service was entirely in my hands and that I could do as I thought best.

"Oh, the service is fine, Frank; except for one feature. I notice that the benediction comes immediately after the sermon. Now, it would be much better, don't you think, if the sermon were followed by a hymn, rather than the benediction?"

"Ah! A pity you raised that! You see, we have been accustomed to going out after the service with the words of Peter Marshall's sermons ringing in our hearts."

"But that means that the congregation are seated at the benediction."

"Well, ask them to stand!"

I did, at the conclusion of my first service.

"The congregation will be upstanding!"

Nobody stood! Nor did they stand on the following Sunday. I suggested to Jerry that this might be some sort of defiance. Nevertheless they must be taught that one either stands or kneels at the benediction.

On the third Sunday, after a few here and there in the crowded auditorium had stood up, a little ageless lady approached me.

"Mr. Docherty, may I be permitted to ask a personal question? When you say, 'The congregation will be upstanding,' what do you mean?"

"That they should stand up!"

"That's just what I said to Mabel, but she said that was your benediction."

The following Sunday after the sermon, I asked the congregation please to rise. Everyone immediately snapped to attention as if I had been a sergeant barking out an order to raw recruits. Yet the incident was not yet finished. George Worthington, who had met us on the boat in New York Harbor, said that he had noted that I now used the verb *stand up* instead of *be upstanding*.

"My mistake entirely, George. You must be patient with me; it will take time to learn American idiom."

"On the contrary," he said. "It is we who must learn from you. Go on saying 'upstanding' now that we know what you mean. Besides, many of us like it!"

Thus it is that, in the end of the day, perhaps the most arresting word I have ever spoken is *upstanding*. I have noted a member nudge a visitor as the service ended as if to say, Here it comes! One of our members, dear Millie Muggeridge, took a snapshot of the manse family in the garden, and when she gave us a print, we found that she had written on the back "The Docherty family downsitting."

I had to learn a new hymnary and strangely worded tunes. The Reverend Samuel Francis Smith's national hymn "My Country 'Tis of Thee" is sung to the tune of the British national anthem. During the singing of this fine hymn on one Sunday, perhaps a little homesick, I suddenly burst out, rigidly at attention, head high, "God save our gracious king," blissfully unaware that latecomers assembled in the vestibule until the end of the first hymn were doubtless somewhat startled to hear above the great singing of a large congregation a Scottish voice imploring that the British king might "be victorious, happy and glorious, long to reign over us."

One Sunday, while using the Church of Scotland *Book of Order* for my prayers, and making the appropriate emendation where the name of the king was used, I solemnly prayed, "We pray for the President of the United States, the Honorable Harry S. Truman. O Lord, long may he be granted health and strength to rule over us." The congregation lapped it up. When I appeared on a very warm Sunday morning, having forsaken my Genevan black gown, cassock, hood, and stole for a dazzling new white suit, they applauded!

I make no apology in stating that for the first six months I preached sermons I had delivered in Aberdeen, changing only such details as "Union Street" to "Pennsylvania Avenue," and so on. The essence of any sermon is, after all, timeless. I came to realize that the message I had delivered to douce Aberdonians was not entirely lost upon an American congregation. However, sooner or later, the sermons had to be made more contemporary, more specifically relevant to a vastly different situation — especially with the junior Senator from Wisconsin igniting a prairie-fire fear of Communism that spread across the nation and even reached the solid phalanges of the Pentagon.

At a political rally in Wheeling, West Virginia, Senator Joseph McCarthy claimed to have in his possession the names of 205 people known to be Communists by the Secretary of State, Dean Acheson, and the Pentagon—all conspirators who were now working at the State Department making policy. To dramatize his discovery, he held up a piece of paper for the television viewers to see. No one will ever know what was actually written on that piece of paper, but whatever it was (his laundry list?), it had the power to initiate a witch hunt that was to overshadow American politics for a decade and engender a dangerous widespread irrational fear of the Soviet Union that is with us even yet. Of course the Senator was fundamentally right—the great plum for Soviet imperialism is the United States—but to meet the challenge of a Russia that prides itself on its genius for chess and long thoughts nurtured through endless winters will require more than irrational fears, demagoguery, and the sort of language manipulation that itself subverts truth in favor of drama.

Senator McCarthy attacked not only the Secretary of State; he turned against the greatest American general of the Second World War, George Marshall, implying that he was a traitor to his country. I recall General Eisenhower as a presidential candidate especially eager for votes in the Midwest, standing smiling behind a beaming Joe McCarthy, conspicuously silent with respect to a defense of his wartime colleague and friend.

I had seen demagoguery similar to the Senator's from Oswald Mosely and his Black Shirts just before the war in Britain, and recalled how Plato had warned that when democracy fails, it gives way to dictatorship. I preached on the subject. After the service I was met by an attractive young woman.

"Mr. Docherty, my mother was born in Scotland, and I know the difficulties you must be encountering settling into a new land, but I would advise you to keep off politics until you have been here for a few years at least. You really do not know all the facts about Senator McCarthy and the Communists."

My defense was that I too had been paying considerable attention to the press and the other media. Perhaps she worked at Capitol Hill and therefore had a biased view of the situation. "I expect you work for a Republican Senator?"

"I do. I'm Senator McCarthy's executive secretary."

Jean Kerr would later marry Senator McCarthy.

It was an extraordinary era dominated by a Senator who even held President Truman at bay over the Korean War, which could have ended by 1951 except that the terms might have given McCarthy more ammunition for his witch hunt. The President was later to confess, "I would have been crucified for that armistice."

Secretary of the Army Robert Stevens, who was to feel the whips of the Senator's scorn, was one of our members and would remain a lifelong friend. I often saw Mr. Stevens alone in the Lincoln Chapel in the middle of the day, silently meditating during those turbulent days.

The entire nation was drawn into the tense drama of the Army-McCarthy hearings by way of an extraordinary television public service program. It ran thirty-five days — 187 hours of television presented to an average of twenty million viewers in that late spring of 1954. With the rest of the country, I watched as the New England country lawyer Joseph Linden Welch finally turned the tide of the Senator's heretofore almost irresistible ascendancy. When McCarthy stooped to attack Welch's junior colleague for what clearly seemed to be no more reason than gratuitous slander, Welch indignantly seized the opportunity.

"Until this moment, Senator, I think I have never gauged your cruelty and recklessness. . . . If it were in my power to forgive you your reckless cruelty, I would do so. I like to think I am a gentleman. But your forgiveness will have to come from Someone other than me."

From conversations I had with Mrs. McCarthy, I have concluded that as a husband he was a gentle, considerate man (one could guess this when the name Jean came to his lips). He sought in his home life to be worthy of his wife and their adopted child, Tierney Elizabeth. As his will was sapped by the sickness that would take him away from the arc lamps under which he had spent so much of his career, he often expressed the desire to retire with his wife and child to a small cattle spread in Arizona. A tragic figure, his own worst enemy, he brought, during his time in the lights, darkness into both his own life and the life of the nation. The last time I saw Jean was at her aged Scottish mother's funeral. Jean died in 1974. She was fifty-seven.

Came the Washington summer of 1950 as it always does, overnight, shriveling the all-too-short radiance of spring flowers. There would be no vacation for us as Jerry awaited patiently and wearily at home. On the evening of August 15, I told her I had to visit Mr. Danley (Dr. Marshall's old bridge friend) who had just returned from hospital. Jerry suggested that she tag along; she had a book to read — Eleanor Roosevelt's autobiography as I recall — and she'd be happy to stay out in the car reading. It was a lovely cool evening. When we arrived home, Jerry retired for the night while I sat downstairs watching television. As I was uncoiling in the wash of its welcome soporific murmur and flicker, a voice filtered down from upstairs. "George, I think I've got an attack of indigestion."

I dashed out to the car and we were soon on our way to the maternity ward of George Washington University hospital, careening through Rock Creek Park and reaching our destination at exactly two minutes before midnight. I assisted Jerry into the waiting hall and when she was seated approached the counter and rang the bell for attention. I seemed to be ignored by the only person in sight, a man bent over a deskful of papers, entirely preoccupied. I rang again and again and finally bawled out at him, "I say! There's a lady here who may give birth to our baby at any moment."

Slowly he arose from his desk, fished for some forms in a drawer, and in a very apologetic tone said, "Sorry to have scared you, but I didn't think you'd want to fill out these forms until after midnight. Two minutes earlier would have cost you another day."

In the corridors upstairs we encountered a nurse whom we recognized as one of our members. She was just about to go off duty, but when she saw Jerry she took charge immediately, saying she wouldn't miss the event for anything. Later—it must have been around 1 A.M.—she phoned a number of homes in the congregation announcing that the minister's wife was in labor and asking that she be remembered in their prayers.

I returned home with a strange feeling of relief and fear. I took the dog out for a walk, informing my mother-in-law that I would go to bed when I returned, for I had a busy day on the morrow and would need all my sleep. I returned to find a distracted mother-in-law crying, "Quick, you have to go to the hospital immediately."

Back at the maternity ward in a few minutes, I found myself in a smoke-filled waiting room shared by three or four other males, all of them looking very young and haggard. With the nonchalance of the experienced father, I sat watching the silent gnawing anxiety written all over the faces of my companions in labor. The door opened. A doctor appeared.

"Mr. Docherty? You are the father of a lovely daughter."

"How very interesting," I gasped as, light-headed, I slumped into a chair and wept.

When mother and child returned home, Garth ran down the pathway to meet us, and despite our fearful protests, gathered his little sister in his arms and bore her into the house. I have a photograph of Jerry in bed, her baby in her arms and the two boys clambering over the counterpane. Jerry never looked lovelier, not even on our wedding day.

We called our little girl Mairi Janet Grace. She was baptized in the Lisner Auditorium by George Johnston, who traveled all the way from his college in Hartford, Connecticut, where he taught New Testament. More than ever we now felt that the family of the congregation was indeed our family.

It was time for the cornerstone of the church to be laid. I raised the question before the session of who would do so.

"You will, Moderator."

"Not I! I shall be master of ceremonies."

"The Moderator of the General Assembly."

"He will pronounce the benediction."

"Who would you suggest, Moderator?"

"The President of the United States, Harry S. Truman."

There was a stunning silence. I had forgotten that the Presbyterian church has been described as the Republican party at prayer. This was the first of many curious reactions from the congregation that I was to receive to the idea of Mr. Truman laying the cornerstone. Nerved with the naive temerity that emboldened me in those days, I made an announcement from the pulpit the following Sunday:

"It has reached my ears that some objections are being voiced by the members of the congregation against the arrangements to have the President of the United States lay our cornerstone. Let me say this to those who feel that way: in fifty years, we shall all of us in this church be dead and forgotten except by our family and a few loyal friends. In a hundred years many Americans might not recall the details of Mr. Truman's presidency, might not even remember that he was the thirty-second President of the United States. But in two hundred years' time, people who walk past our church will note that the cornerstone was laid by the President of the United States and such was the status and witness we held in the nation's capital. Now I want to hear no more of such talk."

Accompanied by George Worthington, I visited the Oval Office for the first and last time, to finalize plans. Mr. Truman would lay the cornerstone of our church at ceremonies to be held in H Street on April 4, 1951.

The President sat back, left foot crossed over his knee, his bright, alert eyes looking at me, and the crease of a smile not far away.

"Yes, I remember now. I signed a bill giving you a piece of federal land on which your church had been squatting since 1859."

"Quite correct, Mr. President, except that you did not give it to us; we *bought* it for one dollar. As a Scot, I'm not likely to forget that."

A bill had indeed been passed to correct a surveyor's error made back in 1859, so that we didn't have to pay the considerable sum of money for the additional four hundred square feet on which the new church would stand.

H Street was closed off for the ceremony. Police were stationed at every corner and on each of the unfinished floors of the church. Only weeks before, Mr. Truman, then living temporarily at Blair House, had been threatened when some nationalistic Puerto Ricans rushed it, killing a policeman in their unsuccessful attempt to assassinate the President. A special podium was lifted by a crane onto the large wooden platform that had been erected for the special guests. Long cables trailed from this heavy steel podium. At the sign of the least suspicious movement, Secret Service agents could press a button and a bulletproof screen would immediately spring up into position between the President and the audience.

"Suppose a bullet should be deflected from the armor-plated podium? Remember I'll be sitting at the right hand of the President."

"Sorry, Mr. Docherty, that would be just too bad; our job is to protect the President."

When the Masonic Lodge of Alexandria refused for reasons known only to themselves to allow the President to use the trowel that had been used by George Washington at the laying of the cornerstone of the White House, and that had also been used at the laying of the cornerstone of our church in 1859, Mr. Truman had a new silver trowel made. It was suitably inscribed for the occasion and placed in a small glass case, the frame of which was made from timbers of the White House, which during his administration was undergoing extensive alterations.

Mr. Truman was a member of the splendid First Baptist Church. I would like to think that it was the remembrance of the stone-laying ceremony that prompted him to invite me to offer prayer at the ceremonial lighting of the national Christmas tree the last Christmas he would spend at the White House. I was aware at the time that Mr. Truman was "no' speaking" to his minister. Dr. Edward Pruden had courageously (and rightly) opposed the appointment of an American ambassador to the Vatican. "Even my preacher is agin me," the President had lamented.

In the gathering dusk of that December day, I arrived at the White House. Mr. Truman appeared promptly and introduced in the spacious vestibule his guests to his wife, Bess, and daughter Margaret. He set off with characteristic speed into the gloaming toward the Ellipse. At its center stood a hundred-foot Christmas tree felled in a Wisconsin forest and towed all the way to Washington. The Marine Band was entertaining an audience of about two thousand from a specially erected platform. This annual ceremony is broadcast from coast to coast, symbolizing the Adventide lighting of all Christmas trees.

The ground was heavy. Mr. Truman strode on, the distance between him and his family widening perceptibly. On his arrival at the platform, the Marine Band immediately struck up, *fortissimo*, "Hail to the Chief." Mr. Truman removed his soft hat, and, smiling, placed his hand over his heart. He looked around. His family was about forty paces behind him. Concern removed the smile from his face. When his wife and daughter eventually caught up, their high heel shoes covered in deep mud, we were to witness a unique sight. The most powerful man in the world was being delivered, in public, a domestic dressing down by two index-finger-pointing women, a look of abject contrition on his face, while in the background the reverberating brass of the Marine Band continued to blare out "Hail to the Chief"!

Amidst great rejoicings, our new sanctuary was dedicated on Thursday, December 20, 1951. The Moderator of the General Assembly, Harrison Ray Anderson, and the Moderator of Washington City Presbytery, C. Stewart Mackenzie, officiated. The Church of the Presidents was now in its third home. It had been witness to the growth of the nation's capital from "a city of magnificent distances," as the sophisticated Charles Dickens called it, to what I believe is the most beautiful city in the world. Fourteen of the sixteen Presbyterian presidents have worshiped with or been members of the congregation. While a member of the Board of Trustees, John Quincy Adams loaned the struggling church $5,000. Abraham Lincoln, although never an official member of any church, worshiped there with his wife Mary and the children, little Willie and Tod. The church's pastor, the Reverend Dr. Gurley, was present at the bedside of the slain President in the modest home of William Peterson, tailor, across the street from Ford's theater, where the President was shot. Dr. Gurley also gave the funeral oration both at the White House and at Springfield, where the President was interred.

At the dedication of the new building, a question arose that ought to have alerted me to the growing problem of the institutional Church identifying itself with civil religion. The Moderator, Dr. Anderson, insisted that not only for this occasion, but always thereafter, I ought to display the Church flag on the right-hand side of the preacher's platform, as dictated in the recommendation of the General Assembly. I was happy to comply. Some of the elders noted the change, however, and raised the issue at the next session meeting. Despite my defense of the priority of the Church flag and my citing of the recommendations of the General Assembly, they voted unanimously to restore the national flag to the position of preeminence at the preacher's right. I requested that the Moderator's name be included in the minutes as dissenting from this judgment.

The following Sunday I was approached by Admiral Wotherspoon, a veteran of the First World War who had met both Lord Jellicoe and Lord Beattie, and had seen action in the Pacific during the Second World War.

"The Church flag is in the wrong place," he muttered out of the side of his mouth.

"Well, Admiral," I said sweetly, "it seems that Congress came out with new regulations in 1946 about locating the national flag in public, decreeing that it must be placed to the speaker's right if it is on the level of the speaker, and to the audience's right if it is on the floor level. And there is only one exception: during a service of worship at sea, the Church flag will be unfurled above the national flag."

"I am well aware of the regulations, Doctor. I wrote them myself! I was quite specific that in any service of worship, God comes first and that this is symbolized by flying the Church flag above the national flag during a service at sea. It was my intention that the naval practice be considered as representative; that is certainly how I view the matter, wherever I may happen to worship."

One cold sunny afternoon in the fall of 1953 found me in my study in the manse struggling over a sermon. I felt it ought to deal with a subject appropriate to the visit of the Washington Pilgrimage, a group that had chosen our church in which to worship. The Pilgrimage was the brainchild of Dr. Harold Dudley, a Methodist layman. Over five hundred pilgrims from across the nation converged annually on Washington to rekindle their patriotism by visiting the historic places in the nation's capital. At the dinner in our Peter Marshall Hall, a Clergyman and a Layman of the Year would be chosen from those who had shown significant Christian witness, particularly in national affairs. I was mulling over possible topics when suddenly, as if struck by a whirlwind, the study door flew open and our elder son Garth materialized in the doorway, a mischievous gleam in his eye and a monstrous sandwich in his hand, glad to be rid of school for another day.

"Well, son, what have you been up to today?"

"School."

"And what did you do there?"

"Nothing."

"Come on, you must have done something. What's the first thing you did in class today?"

"Said the Pledge of Allegiance," he replied distractedly, his interest having apparently already flown to his brother and sister, who at that moment were doubtlessly playing in the little treehouse perched in the huge century-old maple tree that dominated the back garden of our home. My own thoughts remained with the Pledge, however.

Since its official adoption in 1942, it had read, "I pledge allegiance to the Flag of the United States of America and to the Republic for which it stands; one Nation indivisible, with liberty and Justice for all." It so happened I had been reading the Gettysburg Address, in which the vision of Mr. Lincoln is of one nation *under God*, and it occurred to me that in the Pledge there was no such reference to the Almighty. The founding fathers had believed the nation's destiny to be divinely ordained: "We have entered into a covenant with God for this work," Thomas Winthrop had preached on board the *Mayflower* in 1620; the Declaration of Independence speaks of "Laws of Nature and Nature's God," and claims that "all men are created equal and are endowed by their creator with certain inalienable rights," and its peroration makes an appeal to "the Supreme Judge of the world for the rectitude of our intentions." Even today coins are engraved "In God We Trust," and sessions of Congress, both federal and state, are opened with prayer. Without the words *under God*, the Pledge of Allegiance seemed to me quite secular; it could have been repeated by any little Muscovite who cared to replace the phrase "the United States of America" with "the Union of Soviet Socialist Republics."

I had found my sermon! It was received by the Washington Pilgrims with acclamation. David Cook, founder and editor of the *New Century Leader*, said that "the Scottish minister of the New York Avenue Presbyterian Church saw through American customs we had taken for granted since our childhood; it took a man from Scotland to show us the weakness in Pledge of Allegiance." But after the congratulations and the ceremonies of presentation, the Washington Pilgrimage did nothing about it.

I decided to rewrite the sermon for February 7, 1954 — Lincoln Sunday — when I knew that President and Mrs. Eisenhower would be sitting in the Lincoln pew. As I was escorting the President from the church at the conclusion of the service, he voiced his agreement with my thesis.

One of the advantages — and dangers — of being a preacher in the nation's capital is the ease with which a given sermon, such as one preached when the president is in church, can be given front-page headlines in the press. My sermon was given national coverage. The reaction of Congress was immediate. By Monday morning, secretaries of Senators and Representatives were phoning the office for copies. It was printed in the *Congressional Record* in full, and two thousand copies were sent to the church for distribution. Representative Charles Oakman and Senator Homer Ferguson introduced joint bills to the House (H.J. 371) and Senate (S.J. 127) respectively, and quoted liberally from conversations with me over the telephone when they made their speeches.

The May 23 *New York Times* reported that "Congress is being flooded with mail, but on a subject far removed from the McCarthy-Army hearings that hold the headlines. The letter writers by the thousands daily are demanding that Congress amend the pledge of allegiance so that the pledge is made to 'one nation under God.' . . . The churches backed it. So did veterans groups, civic clubs, patriotic organizations, fraternal clubs, labor unions, trade associations. Newspapers, individually and by chains, backed it editorially. Radio commentators plugged it. . . . The widespread support the bill is receiving must bear testimony to a religious revival of significance."

On June 14, Flag Day 1954, the new Pledge of Allegiance to the flag was repeated in the House of Representatives amidst much pomp and circumstance. The Singing Sergeants of the official Air Force Choral Group, accompanied by the Air Force Band, introduced a newly composed song for the occasion, "The Pledge of Allegiance to the Flag"; it was sung by Ivan Genuchi, one of my choir members. Two weeks later I received a letter from Congressman Louis C. Rabaut of the Fourteenth District of Michigan, who had been in charge of the ceremonies:

I sincerely regret I was not able to contact you that morning, since I am sure you would have enjoyed attending the precedent-shattering proceedings that took place on the House floor. It was the first time that the House of Representatives officially recessed to pay homage to Old Glory.

Sic transit gloria mundi.

In retrospect, I am no longer so sure that the event deserved such celebration — or, indeed, that the change was entirely valid. Objections were raised, but at the time I did not think them significant. Religious (and nonreligious) minorities, for instance, among them some of my Jewish friends, their tragic history of religious persecution behind them, feared the implications of the newly phrased Pledge. I answered them by pointing out that the Pledge merely mentioned the name of God the Creator of the universe, who could be identified with Yahweh or the pantheistic gods of the Eastern religions.

It was also feared that the newly worded Pledge forced new atheistic citizens to pledge allegiance to God. I argued that they pledged allegiance not to *God*, but to a *flag*. The phrase *under God* describes the historic fact that the nation was founded by men who held a profound belief in divine providence. The Constitution preserved the individual's right to the free exercise of religious faith and guaranteed the right to observe *no* religious faith if one so desires.

I still consider my reasoning to be valid, but the times should have overruled my philosophical arguments as irrelevant in light of the greater issues at hand. A false patriotism was being aroused by the bogus threat of Communist encroachment; McCarthyism darkened the airwaves; superpatriots were prone to ask not whether they were on God's side, but whether God was on theirs. As such, the new Pledge unfortunately served as one more prop supporting the civil religion that characterized the institutional Christianity of the fifties. There was no evidence of a "religious revival of significance," as the *New York Times* had suggested.

The early fifties were the golden age of the institutionalized Church, when it was claimed that a cornerstone for a church, chapel, or synagogue was being laid on the average about once every hour of every day. It required two morning services to accommodate comfortably the crowds who flocked to our church, taxing sometimes the fourteen hundred seats in the sanctuary. Every Sunday, two hundred to five hundred visitors attended. No preacher was ever given such encouraging auspices to commence his ministry. The choir numbered each Sunday about one hundred. Our organist, Bill Watkins, was a superb musician. Our music director, Stephen Prussing, who came less than a year after me, would remain until I left twenty-six years later. Steve, who reminded me of a young Gary Cooper, was a Renaissance man. No choral work was too grand or too offbeat to be tackled, from Verdi's *Requiem* to a Mariachi mass. He arranged themes from Mozart string quartets to appropriate words for the

"Seven Last Words from the Cross" Service that we held each year for a quarter of a century, after he had used all other available music (such as Haydn and Berlioz). This Good Friday service lasted from noon till three; it was divided into seven consecutive services, each with music and sermon. In the fifties, as many as three or four thousand would take time off from their lunch hour to participate. I cannot ever recall that Steve and I quarreled about the music of the church — surely a high compliment to Steve.

By the end of the decade our congregation had reached its highest membership — around two thousand. Life was fulfilling and exciting. I had been chosen by *Life Magazine* as one of the ten outstanding Presbyterian preachers in the country. Our little family was growing apace. No man was ever so blessed.

My uncle Alex (the one who hoboed across the States, who had fought in both the Boer and Great Wars, and who on his deathbed had asked that I scatter his ashes around the cairn at the summit of the Binn Hill of Cullen, where he had run about as a lad) used to say to me when I was a child, "Georgie, when you have harried what I have plowed, you will be able to say that you have traveled the world."

I have tried. My ministry became a magic carpet of air travel. From Toronto to Bogota, from Washington to Los Angeles, the invitations to preach arrived. Because of my commitments to my congregation, I had to be delicately selective; yet the travel provided a unique insight into the life of the nation. I discovered that the family of the holy catholic Church contains other Christians than Presbyterians! America is not a melting pot, but a salad of Europeans and others who have pulled up their roots for personal, selfish, or humanitarian reasons, emancipated themselves from ancient enmities, from feudal class systems and warring nationalisms, without losing their distinctive and diverse ethnic character — *unum in paribus*, to the third and fourth generation. In my session, I was able to distinguish German, Swedish, Dutch, Italian, English, and, of course, Scottish traits.

Once, in Chicago, I preached at the baccalaureate service of the McCormick Theological Seminary, held in the majestic Gothic Fourth Presbyterian Church. Prior to the service, as I walked down the spacious center aisle with the minister, Harrison Ray Anderson, he noted that Scottish stonemasons had built the church back in 1917.

"I know, Ray," I said. "My uncle George, who is here tonight, told me. He and his brothers worked on it; and my grandfather was the master mason of the entire project."

It is a stone pulpit. Before I preached, I paused for a moment, caressing the meticulously fitted stonework, admired the Gothic arches, without keystone, and gazed up into the darkness of the lofty vaulted ceiling. My mind traveled back to Scotland down the years, to the Kelvinhaugh quay, Glasgow, where my grandfather, recently widowed, took me up in his arms, a ten-month child, his namesake, before he turned away heavy-hearted up the gangplank for America, "the land of opportunity," bidding a sad final farewell to Scotland.

A visit to the Holy Land, where I led a party with our son Garth by my side, brought life to my Bible studies. When our bus at last reached the top of the hill on that fifteen-mile journey from Jericho to Bethany, I felt like a scientist confirming a theory: Jesus *did* look down upon Jerusalem (though I had always pictured Jerusalem as a city set upon a hill). Nor was I entirely put off by the gawdy liturgical furnishings of the Eastern and Roman Churches at the significant places of the gospel story. Here in this Church of the Nativity had stood a caravanserai where a fourteen-year-old lass had given birth to her firstborn, assisted by an unknown midwife, her husband by her side. At Nazareth I peered down into a subterranean cave where no light of the sun ever reached and realized that here this maid and her husband and family of four children had eked out a living from the little carpenter's business on the upper floor. Here the firstborn Son, who had succeeded his father, fashioned wooden plowshares, yokes, cross-shaped spade handles, and rough furniture. In the Church of the Holy Sepulchre, behind a dazzle of liturgical decorations, was a tomb hewn from a rock. I could guess what it looked like as I visited General Gordon's garden, where stood a tomb, the stone rolled away from its entrance, the flat slab where once a body had lain, and above it a scarred escarpment, the weatherworn gaping holes of which looked like the eye sockets of a skull.

I spent the summer of 1963 as guest preacher at St. Stephens Church on McQuarie Street in Sydney, Australia, where Gordon Powell carried out an astoundingly popular ministry, both over the radio and in crowded Sunday services. I was put up at the Royal Sydney Golf Club; my bedroom looked out over the first tee, the sort of view a golfer imagines could be literally heavenly. I met some Australians who were more English than the English and more Etonian than the Etonians, one of whom, with bush moustache, monocle, and fawn jacket with silk cravat, I recall in particular.

"You Americans are having a pretty rough time of it, eh? I mean, with all that Negro revolt business. Just can't understand it."

"Yes, it's pretty bad — indeed, tragic. By the way, how are you getting on with your own minorities? They tell me that not one Japanese has become a naturalized Australian since 1904. And what about your native Australians, those that survived the Tasmanian massacres — Maoris, I think you call them — are they citizens of Australia?"

"Tell the truth, I hadn't thought about it. I say, Fred? Are these Maori chaps citizens? No? Really?"

But the Australians I met at church were a unique type, possessing still the traditions of the mother country and not yet having lost the pioneering spirit that once characterized the West.

It seems that I am always in a hurry to make deadlines and rushing to keep schedules. It is incredible now to realize that in my eagerness to arrive in Sydney on time, I should have spent no more than four hours in the Fiji Islands (2 A.M. to 6 A.M.) at the airport, where I met a customs officer who had at one time been a member of my church. Nor did I take the time to go on a side trip to Samoa and visit Vailima, where Robert Louis Stevenson died, or climb the hill where weeping natives carried the body of their beloved Tusitala to the resting place, "where he longed to be, the sailor home from sea."

We celebrated the birth of the New Year 1958 as we did every year, at the Watchnight Service. A little band of Scots attended this Hogmanay service as faithfully as they did the Christmas service, and afterward they'd come back to the manse for ginger wine, shortbread, sultana cake, and a crack long into the morning about the old days. We reminisced about the Glasgow we loved, where five hours before we knew there had gathered a jovial crowd around the statue of King William of Orange ("King Billy who slew the papish crew") at Glasgow Cross, awaiting the striking of the Tolbooth clock at the numinous midnight hour, when there had been a sudden and uncharacteristic outburst of Scottish emotion, and many a tear, "A guid New Year to ane and a', and mony may ye see." Once more the peerless words of Burns were pledged, never to forget auld acquaintance, for the sake of auld lang syne.

On Jerry's suggestion, we left town for a couple of days after the New Year festivities to visit the reconstructed colonial town at Williamsburg, the great battleships at Newport News, and beautiful Virginia Beach. The weather was mild and kind. We threw stones into the incoming combers on the beach.

As we were driving the forty miles back to our hotel in Williamsburg, the headlights of the oncoming traffic suddenly seemed to start wobbling from side to side, as if the drivers were drunk. I was overcome with nausea, but managed to steer the car to the side of the road before I passed out. I recovered sufficiently to get us back to the hotel safely, but when I attempted to climb the stairs to our room, my legs became rubbery and buckled under me. An ambulance rushed me the forty miles to a hospital in Richmond, Virginia, where I dimly recall being carried up stairs on a stretcher under the supervision of a bespectacled young intern who pulled down my bottom eyelids and then called out, with a degree of anxious urgency in his voice, for "A unit of whole blood — stat. We've got a bleeding ulcer here."

Two weeks and five pints of blood later, I was back in Washington, suddenly an old man unable to walk without a stick. Within three weeks,

I was back in the pulpit, but not without a stern warning from Dr. Latimer.

"George, you realize you nearly died? You were going into shock. The only reason you felt no pain was because the duodenal ulcer was located on a nexus of blood vessels; had it been on some nerves, it would have been more painful, but at least you would have gotten a warning. From now on you'll have to submit to a strict diet and get plenty of sleep."

But, a regimen of bland food and restricted activity notwithstanding, I was to collapse at the insistence of the ulcer twice within the next two years. The second occasion was serious enough to bring my physician Dr. Latimer to the conclusion that a stomach resection was called for.

On the eve of the operation, Dan Borden, a member of New York Avenue and a leading surgeon, dropped by my hospital room to announce that I'd be receiving a couple of antibiotic injections to clear up my system a bit. A smiling nurse, her demeanor as starched and sanitized as her clean white uniform, soon showed up to make good on Dr. Borden's promise.

"Roll over, please," she chirped; "it's time for your injections."

"No nurse," I implored. "The arm, please — not the buttocks. I've got a slipped disk, you see, and I know from experience that if I get a jag back there, I'll go into spasm, and that wouldn't be pleasant for either of us. It's very painful, you know, and when I feel pain I get angry, and you wouldn't really want to see me when I'm angry, now would you?"

"I'm sorry, sir. I have my orders. Please roll over."

I did as I was told; the result was just as I had predicted: no sooner was I under the covers than I went into complete spasm. It felt as if a knife had slashed me in two. As I lay bathed in pain and perspiration, I bawled between my teeth for four hot water bottles and four aspirins. This time the nurse heeded my request. With those ministrations applied, I was soon relaxed enough to sink into thankful sleep.

Dr. Latimer dropped by later that night and woke me to find how I was feeling. I told the story of my recent travail, but instead of sympathy, I got a reprimand.

"Who said you could have aspirin?"

"Always take aspirin," I replied chirpily. "Been doing it for years. Best thing I know for killing the pain."

"But you told me that you haven't been taking any medicines."

"Aspirin is a medicine?" I inquired weakly.

He shook his head at the depth of my ignorance. "George, I'll stake my medical reputation on the likelihood that you've managed to reopen your ulcer with that aspirin. And if that's the case, of course there can be no surgery tomorrow."

He was right. I spent a nightmarish night, only to be greeted the next morning by Dr. Borden and Dr. Latimer conducting rounds with a group of interns. His comments seemed as much directed to me as to the students: "Now, we have here the sort of patient you have to watch out for. He thinks he knows all about medicine, and yet he overlooks the obvious, conceals vital information from his doctor, and bullies his nurses into doing his bidding. Don't let a patient deceive you into believing that he's intelligent about your profession just because he happens to be intelligent about other matters."

If by any chance that dear nurse who was bullied by me should read this tale, I hope she will let me know her name so that I can more adequately convey my thanks to her. Without her intervention I would have spent the rest of my life with only half a stomach.

That summer we returned to Scotland on vacation. While we were there, I was told that my stepfather, George Bullivant, was terminally ill. George had been a lifelong friend of the family—he had taken me to my first soccer match at Hampden Park in Glasgow when I was ten—and it seemed quite natural after Father died that he and Mother should get married and spend the happy eventide of their lives together. I knew I would never see him again after I returned to the States. We made the most of the days we had left together, going on walks along by the "Pencil" monument at Largs, making long runs into the country, dining at good hotels. Toward the end of our stay, I went one day on impulse into a pub in Largs called The Suez Canal and ordered a fifth of whiskey and a large bottle of port wine. It was the first time I had set foot inside a pub since I was a boy, when I had returned empty beer bottles for the penny-on-the-bottle. I gave the whiskey and port to George—as a farewell present. He died that winter. But to the end, I am told, he continued to marvel that Georgie, a minister, should have gone into a pub for him.

The following year we brought my mother back to the States, where she celebrated her ninetieth birthday. She seemed to take everything in stride. When reporters gathered around this ninety-year-old who had flown the Atlantic, she seemed at her best.

"Oh, I think America is just marvelous. I think you are all wonderful."

"Mother," I said to her after they had gone, "I never heard you use such extravagant expressions before."

"Auch, I know. I just said it to please the laddies. They were so nice and so well-spoken."

We celebrated her birthday by gathering a group of some twenty Scots at the manse, where we danced Highland dances in the recreation room, sang Scottish songs, ate fish and chips Jerry had specially prepared, and spent a long and happy evening telling funny Scots tales. When the guests departed at about 2 A.M., we had our usual cup of tea before going to bed.

"Well mother, how did you like your ninetieth birthday party?"

165

"Oach, it was nice! It just breaks the monotony!"

She flew back British Airways alone, from Kennedy, where we motored her. I was given permission to come right onto the plane and see her seated comfortably. I instructed the stewardess to insist that she go to the bathroom, because I knew that she would be too modest to make such a request.

My brother told me she arrived in great style, accompanied by a uniformed B.A. steward who escorted her through passports and a customs officer who merely raised his hand as she swept past him dressed in a flowery hat and fur cape Jerry had bought her. When she met my brother with his little Ford Escort automobile, her first words were, "Well, Jackie, our Georgie has a much bigger car than you! And your steering wheel is on the wrong side, anyway!"

She was admitted to an eventide home at Giffnock, Glasgow, run by the Church of Scotland, where she was happily looked after and regularly visited by my brother. On one occasion the night nurse found her in the early hours of the morning fully dressed in her flowery hat and fur cape, her bag in her hand and her gloves on, apparently awaiting the arrival of someone.

"And where would you be going at this time of the morning, Mrs. Docherty?"

"I'm going to Washington, D.C. That's where my Georgie has a big church near the President's house."

She slipped away quietly, painlessly, not long after that. She was in her ninety-second year.

The tenth anniversary of our arrival in our new church and home drew near. Life was becoming increasingly fascinating and the church ever more challenging. The question then facing us was whether we would dig deeper our roots or pull up and return to Scotland. To remain and be in any way relevant to the life of the church and nation would necessitate our becoming American citizens — or so we decided. There were emotional blocks. It is not easy to put pen to paper, "renouncing allegiance to all foreign potentates" (though this did not seem to trouble Jerry, since there was no mention specifically of the British queen!). By becoming an American citizen would I be proving false to my native land, a turncoat? Would I be less a Scot if I voted in the U.S.A.?

As it turned out, this latter issue remained academic so long as I continued to reside in the District of Columbia, which became known as "the last colony." Its citizens had no vote to begin with: they were governed by a committee of Congressmen who made it their fixed aim to refuse to grant home rule to Washington, D.C., lest (and their fears were amply justified) the nation's capital might elect a black mayor.

What of my calling as a preacher? Did not Paul write "to the Jew I became like a Jew, to win Jews; as they are subject to the law of Moses, I put myself under that law to win them. To win Gentiles who are outside the law, I made myself like one of them, although I am not in truth outside God's law"? Of one thing I was sure: a relevant preaching ministry would increasingly involve me in questions of national import, and my identification with the nation as a citizen would lend a greater validity to anything I might have to say. We applied for citizenship.

We read again the history of the founding fathers, the articles and amendments to the Constitution, and braced ourselves for a *viva voce* examination before a constitutional lawyer. My examination consisted of only one question: "Who was Abraham Lincoln?"

Old hand that I was at examinations, I immediately recognized a catch question. Lincoln was a Congressman from Springfield, Illinois, but what was the date? Was he the sixteenth or seventeenth President of the United States? I took the plunge.

"He was President of the United States."

"Correct!"

When the interview was over I asked the examiner whether she realized she had asked that question of the minister of Mr. Lincoln's church.

"That may be, but last week when I asked another examinee the same question, he said that Lincoln was the mayor of Richmond."

Not all the steps toward citizenship were so easily taken, however. The process brought me headlong into a dilemma that has plagued me throughout my ministry. I was expected to sign a document that affirmed my readiness "to take up arms in defense of the United States." Inasmuch as I was forty-eight, it was hardly likely that I would at some future date actually be trusted with a gun in my hands; yet I saw no reason why I should bind myself to support some future war of the United States without first considering whether I believed it came under a category that would have the blessing of the Church. Besides, no natural-born American is asked to take such an unqualified vow. I did not see why I should be excluded from the option, guaranteed by law to all other citizens, to declare myself to be a conscientious objector to war if I chose. Members of such churches as the Brethren and the Society of Friends are automatically given conscientious objector status.

"I cannot sign the form as it stands," I said.

"Then you cannot become an American citizen," I was told.

One of my sponsors, Samuel E. Whitaker, a federal judge, sat through this conversation muttering under his breath, "Doggonit, I have been watching this morning a crowd of semiliterates hardly able to speak our language becoming without question American citizens, and here is my own preacher, a stubborn Scot, making all sorts of unnecessary difficulties for himself."

On appeal, I submitted a twelve-page memorandum that clarified, to my thinking, the issue of peace and war. My case was heard before a special sitting of the court. As the judge solemnly read through my brief, my other sponsor, Dr. Rowland Kirks, whispered, "Do you have a corn on your toe?"

"No. Why?"

"Just wanted to know the foot to stomp on if you dare try to open your mouth and make a speech."

Since it was then my belief that any future war would be atomic, in which all distinctions of pacifism or not would be obliterated along with civilization, I regarded the question from an academic point of view. Successfully. On April 1, 1960, Jerry and I became American citizens, a step we would never regret.

12

Samson Agonistes

Presently he [Billy Graham] sat down on a stump, surrounded by tall pines darkly lifting into a secret murmuration of night wind under the sky's frost of stars. . . .
"Lord, help me. I don't have the knowledge. I'm placing myself completely, heart *and* mind, without intellectual reservations, in your hands." And he stood then, lifting his Bible in the faint icy twilight and said, "Oh, Lord, I *do* accept this as your word! Come what may, without question or falter, I *believe* in this your holy word."
—Marshall Frady, *Billy Graham: A Parable of American Righteousness*

IN THE LATE SPRING of 1952 I received a communication from the "Billy Graham Washington Campaign" announcing a series of meetings to be held in the Uline Arena (now the National Guard Armory) and inviting me to be present at the opening service on a Sunday afternoon and to take my place together with other clerical members of a distinguished platform party.

I had never met Billy Graham. I had heard of his evangelistic campaign in Los Angeles in 1949, had read the publicity blurb about "America's Sensational Young Evangelist" in that city of empty spaces and immense distances, of a "Dazzling Array of Gospel Talent" to be held in the largest tent in the world, a "Canvas Cathedral," with six thousand seats (admission free). I have never understood how that maestro of the American press, William Randolph Hearst, then in his eighty-sixth year and retired to San Simeon, his astounding Disneyland castle keep, should have suddenly issued to his chain of newspapers a memo that carried with it the imprimatur of a papal bull — "Puff Graham!" It was to be decisive in Billy's breakthrough to big-time evangelism.

I am suspicious of all forms of mass evangelism. I doubt very much those elaborate claims of "commitment to the Lord" made in the heady emotionalism of an evangelistic meeting. Lax of Poplar, London, used to make an appointment the following morning at five with those who had responded to his altar call, believing the cool of the dawn would confirm their "hour of decision." I was skeptical about my church identifying its mission with techniques more akin to that of Madison Avenue than the Acts of the Apostles. Was I simply being used by the Graham organization?

169

They knew nothing about me personally. I suspected I was being invited as a minister of one of the leading churches in town to adorn the platform with some sort of ecclesiastical respectability — as well as to bring along a large contingent of my own members to the meetings.

In this highly critical mood, I took my place on the platform. A choir two hundred voices strong, culled from city churches, was singing hymns under the enthusiastic direction of Cliff Barrows, whose hands reached up to the rafters and then swept downward in an encompassing arc, as if embracing the robed choristers. A huge banner stretched across the back of the hall behind us, emblazoned in red with the words "The Way, the Truth and the Life." At the side of the platform, at the console of an electronic organ, sat Ted Smith, blending in anonymously with the music, accompanying, tremulant stop full out, the reverberating basso profundo voice of George Beverly Shea, who was inviting us to come to the garden while the dew is still on the roses . . . where we would walk with Jesus and talk with him and be told we are his own.

I became aware of a figure looking down to me, his hand outstretched.

"I'm Billy Graham. I believe you are Dr. George Docherty. I am so glad you have found the time to be with us this afternoon."

I rose my full six feet to look up, and into, the deep-set steely eyes of a handsome, impeccably dressed young man, his dark suit setting off a broad smile radiating from a tanned face crowned with a shock of fair hair like a comber before it breaks on the shore. He had the high cheek bones and prominent nose characteristic of portraits of the Duke of Montrose. As I listened to his warm southern voice, the vast hymn-echoing barn-like drill hall lost its remoteness. It was as if we were old friends meeting again after years of absence.

"I believe you are from Scotland. I've visited your country, and I love it. Of course, my own ancestors came over here sometime after the Forty-Five Rebellion." And then in mock Scots brogue, "Aye, it's a bonnie land!"

Before I could respond, he had moved on to greet the other members of the platform party.

Came the time for the sermon. Billy had been reclining statuesque, a Lincoln figure, his long legs crossed, in one hand a large black soft-leather-bound King James Bible, and in the other his chin, cupped in graceful fingers. As soon as the choir anthem stopped, he started into life, moving quickly to the podium, where he stood for a moment surveying the vast crowd now filling the hall. He raised his hand as if to begin with a benediction, his voice booming from the amplifier like the rumble of a distant spring thunder.

"I am going to ask you now . . . that there be no walking around, no movement of any kind, no talking." He folded his Bible in both hands against his breast and bowed his head, his eyes intensely closed, waiting in the ringing silence for the quiet he was seeking, and then launched into his sermon, firing clipped, unadorned sentences as if he were lobbing mortar shells into enemy territory.

"We're here in the nation's capital. . . . It is the capital of the most powerful nation in the world. . . . At this very moment, we are at war . . . in Korea . . . where even now American boys are dying. . . . To this United States capital comes the Christ, as long ago he came to Jerusalem, the Holy City, a city set on a hill, where prophets of old believed that one day the nations of the world would gather in peace . . . their swords beaten into plowshares . . . and when Jesus beheld the city, we read in Luke 19:41, he wept over it. . . ."

The words began to flow like a cataract of rain on a tin roof. Only occasionally did he glance at his manuscript. His gestures were sweeping and theatrical; his outstretched arms fanned out like a V, lashing the air as if he were about to cleave the podium in two. Loose-limbed, he would step back, then forward; he would galumph across the platform to his right, return to the center and be off again in great strides to his left. Sometimes his right hand would sweep over the vast audience; at other times he would point, left-handed, toward the front seats, where I could observe the frightened eyes of hapless souls who gave the impression that they wanted to flee from it all, if only they were not riveted to the metal folding chairs. Fascinated, I watched from behind the speaker the reactions of the audience, reflecting the moods of Billy's face, like a windblown wheat field beneath racing clouds, darkened when he scowled, lit up with smiles when an amusing aside slipped into his sermon.

I became preoccupied by the behavior of Cliff Barrows sitting next to me. In his hands he held a long cord connected to a lavaliere microphone around Billy's neck. When Billy raced to the right of the platform, Cliff would let out the cord like a fisherman playing a caught trout in a Highland pool. When Billy returned center, Cliff frantically hauled in his line, only to play it out again when the proclaiming figure darted past him towards the other end of the platform. This charade continued during the entire twenty minutes of the sermon.

Billy's text was taken from the Revelation of St. John the Divine where the seer shares with his readers a vision of the City of God "that lieth foursquare and the length is as large as the breadth; and he measured the city with the reed, twelve thousand furlongs. The length and the breadth of it are equal. And he measured the wall thereof an hundred and forty cubits, according to the measure of a man, that is, of an angel."

Billy took this apocalyptic vision of the final beatitude of the redeemed in glory realistically and literally. Bewildered, I vainly tried to imagine a city built as a cube, each side 1,500 miles, surrounded by a wall, built of jasper, as high as the Washington monument!

"The Bible says, 'And there shall in no wise enter into it any thing that defileth, neither whatsoever worketh abomination or maketh a lie but

171

they which are written in the Lamb's book of life.' " He paused and looked around him, scything the air to the far-flung bleachers of the auditorium. "Are your names written in the Lamb's book of life?"

And turning to those near to the platform with an accusing left forefinger, "is yours . . . yours . . . or yours?" he demanded.

Then (center stage) he called out in a ringing voice of ultimate conviction, "I thank God that I can! Here and now I can say that my name is written in the Lamb's book of life. For 'I know whom I have believed and I am persuaded that he is able to keep that which I have committed unto him against that day.' Second Timothy one and twelve."

As a preacher I was both bewildered and dazzled by this display. Never had I heard any preacher whose flow of words cascaded at such speed, so perfectly enunciated, almost without pause. I myself would have stopped for a moment, or slowed down, especially over an anecdote. Billy sped on like a television commercial, as if afraid of silence. The voice was like the overture to *Die Meistersingers*, with French horns, trumpets, and bassoons blaring in my ear. There could be no climax—and all the while, Cliff Barrows frantically winding and unwinding his line, himself perhaps half afraid that Billy might disappear at any moment over the end of the platform.

Then it happened. To this day I cannot articulate the nature of the emotion that was slowly, imperceptibly, but surely beginning to take me over. The marvelous voice and its ringing sincerity were beginning to seep into the inner ear of my soul. The fantastic exegesis no longer seemed important. Behind the words I could hear another Voice, in an accent I shall never know this side of Calvary, saying to me above the *diapason* of the preacher in a still small voice, "And how stands it with you, my son?"

In Billy's presence I was seeing my own ministry and preaching, and what I was looking at was not very pleasant: the conceit that was an excuse to cover my shyness; eagerness to achieve, another name for pride; the damning sophistication I seem to have inherited, which makes so many Scots rub others like sandpaper; the analytical logic of our minds, the negative logical skills that break down every argument into its basic weakness or fallacy, till all that we are left with is the triumph of analysis. In dissecting Billy's exegesis, I had forgotten the Word hidden within the words of Scripture. My own sermons, indebted for exegesis to Rudolph Bultmann and Joachim Jeremias and Oscar Cullmann, were much more academic than Billy's, better composed and structured, and flecked with pseudo-poetic prose. Before the innocent certainties of this preacher whose back, mercifully, was turned towards me, I felt shame and unworthiness. I tried not to recall what James Denney had indignantly asserted—"No man can exalt Christ and himself at the self-same moment."

Could I confess, like Billy, to my congregation that "I know whom

I have believed. . . ?" Were the Gospels the creation of the first-century Church or the *verba ipsissima* of Jesus? Such academic baggage had for too long stifled what I had been longing, but had hesitated, to say — until this fearful *kairos* of self-realization. All I wanted to do at that moment was to "Come to the garden alone, while the dew is still on the roses / And the voice I hear, falling on my ear, the Son of God discloses." No longer was I hearing what Billy was saying. The muddy waters of my mind were clearing. There was a sense of release. Like Christian in *Pilgrim's Progress*, I felt the burden had rolled off my back. A strange sense of joy possessed me. The choir was singing "Just as I am without one plea, but that thy blood was shed for me," and above the singing I could hear Billy's voice as he spoke, slowly now with long pauses, his head bowed upon his breast, his arms folded around his Bible.

"I am going to ask you to come up now. It may seem a long way to come from the back of the auditorium . . . but the steep hill of Calvary was a much longer journey . . . and Jesus traveled that way for you. . . ."

"Just as I am — thou wilt receive, wilt welcome, pardon, cleanse, relieve."

Silently they were moving forward, young people in summer attire, middle-aged men and women, here and there an elderly person with a stick — on they came at Billy's bidding. And there sat I, scared to move, embarrassed by my own emotions, my heart thudding so loudly I feared Billy would hear it, rooted to my chair without even an articulate silent prayer in my heart, miserably alone again in a vast world, with the fog of my childhood coming down around me as I beat again upon our tenement door, once more "wee Georgie," trying to get back home and finding the door shut against him, the cold Christmas winds whining up the stairwell.

I reassessed the impact of the Billy Graham campaign in the solitude of my study at the manse. This was no evanescent experience. It was yet another mutation of the spirit, another breakthrough of the sort I would like to think is experienced by every Christian, a "growing in grace" as the old theologians called it, "sanctification" no less. I began to rethink what Sunday by Sunday I was seeking to share with his people. It sent me back to my ministry with a newfound zeal. After thirty years and more, the memory of that first encounter with Billy is still fresh, still cherished.

When Dr. Powell Davis, the brilliant English pastor of All Souls Unitarian Church, wrote a letter to the *Washington Post*, correctly pointing up the dangers of mass evangelism, I found myself immediately defending Billy.

"Billy Graham," he wrote, "brings a sense of guilt to the minds of young people."

"The guilt was there before Billy Graham came to Washington," was my reply.

On the day my letter was published, I received a telephone call.

"This is Billy Graham. Could we have lunch together today, Dr. Docherty?"

We met in a hauff called the Vineyard at Fourteenth Street and New York Avenue that I visited with some regularity.

"Dr. Docherty," I heard Billy saying, "I want you to know that the encouragement you have given me at this time, when my ministry is passing through a crucial stage, is a kindness I shall never forget."

He kept his word. Across the years, despite his peripatetic ministry, we have been able to meet frequently in Washington. Often when he was guest at the White House during both the Johnson and Nixon administrations, we would have tea in my study and talk. I offered to help in his various campaigns. I spoke to ministers at Charlotte and Raleigh, and offered prayer in Madison Square Garden during the 1957 campaign. When Billy returned to Washington for a second campaign in 1958, our church served as one of the counseling and instruction centers.

After I knew him a bit better, I told him, "Billy, you know you will never really be able to call yourself an evangelist until you hold a campaign in Scotland. You owe it to your Scottish forebears." As I looked at him, I noted again the resemblance to one of Scotland's hero-martyrs, James Graham, Marquis of Montrose. He has the same prominent nose and deep-set eyes as those in the Honthorst portrait of the Marquis. He rose to my challenge to go to Scotland. I wrote immediately to Tom Allan, who at that time was heading up the "Tell Scotland" movement in the Scottish Kirk.

The name Tom Allan is a household word in Scotland to this day. He hailed from Ayrshire, which has produced many gifted ministers of the Kirk, as might be expected from covenanting country. Tom was of average height for a Scotsman, about five feet six, and dressed impeccably. He wore rather thick-lensed glasses. An artless curl in his hair gave him a boyish appearance. He spoke deliberately with an unalloyed Scottish accent, without a trace of his native Ayrshire flatness. He laughed readily, even when he was parrying a thrust in an argument. His logic was ruthless, always reinforced by the *mot juste*. He possessed that elusive quality common to all great preachers, independent of personal appearance, timbre of voice, and gesture, and even of scholarship itself—the inner serene certainty that Christ is Savior that overflows in passionate proclamation. Tom's was always sustained passion, never wordy emotionalism.

Within five short years he had amazingly transformed the mundane witness of his first charge, North Kelvinside Church in Glasgow. His pulpit ministry led logically to parish missions. He gathered around him a body of men and women and a dedicated group of young people who fanned out into a parish visitation mission. Out of this ministry came his book *The Face of My Parish*, a classic that was translated into a score of languages.

Granted permission by the Presbytery of Glasgow to demit his charge of North Kelvinside to become organizing secretary of the Tell Scotland movement, he soon found himself organizing parish missions and preaching sermons across Scotland — evangelical sermons that kindled once more the fires of spiritual revival dormant in the land.

It was this Tom Allan that I was urging Billy Graham to meet when he visited Britain for the London Crusade of 1954. Nothing could be more natural, more providential, than the meeting of these two dissimilar yet kindred souls — the tall, laughing South Carolinian and the stocky lad from Ayrshire, both gracious and warm-hearted, with similar smiles, and infectious laughs, superlative preachers from vastly different traditions and training, yet one in their passion to declare Christ crucified and risen.

Scotland seemed ready for the wind of the Spirit to blow over the land in this year of grace 1955. The postwar years found both kirk and nation still somewhat numb mentally and spiritually. The British people, who had once proudly boasted an empire upon which the sun never set, were slowly beginning to realize a golden era had passed forever beyond their grasp. It was difficult to accept the dawning truth that Britain was becoming a second-rate world power.

Meanwhile the built-in establishment of the Church of Scotland in Edinburgh, an oligarchy of "high-heid-yins," was trying to maintain outmoded ecclesiastical machinery and stereotyped parish structures as they existed before the war. On the theological side, many of us back in the 1930s had doubted the ethical and theological validity of being asked to confess as our standard of faith a Calvinistic creed written at Westminster in 1647. Revisions of this Subordinate Standard of Faith of the Presbyterian Church continued to be brought up each year at the General Assembly without any decisive action being taken. Scottish preaching on the whole seemed to lack the essential fire of a New Testament evangelical faith: it had none of the urgency of Paul's affirmation to the church in Corinth — "I resolved that while I was with you, without the display of fine words and wisdom, I would think of nothing but Jesus Christ — Christ nailed to the cross."

In this atmosphere the Tell Scotland movement was launched, initiated by that core of solid, faithful, and dedicated ministers and laity that kindled again the dormant fires of spiritual growth. A Billy Graham Scottish campaign seemed to Tom and his committee a fit complement, or perhaps even climax, to their parish-structured missions to the Church. It received the blessing of the General Assembly. When Billy returned to the States from the London Crusade of 1954, I was excited to learn, over the inevitable cup of tea in my study, that a Scottish Crusade had been planned for the spring of 1955.

Marshall Frady is the author of a revealing biography of Billy Graham. However, his treatment of the Billy Graham Tell Scotland Crusade misses the mark concerning both the relative significance and the essential nature of the tour. "In Scotland," he writes, "[Graham] reconstituted into polyethylene blandness all the fierce theologies brought by his own ancestors from these very heaths and moors." I am sure Mr. Frady does not quite realize how this heath-and-moor stereotype, this Harry Lauder "Wee Hoose among the Heather" cliche makes the average Scot blush and burn inwardly, and drives the modern Scottish nationalists as wild as those ancient clansmen of two hundred years ago.

Billy Graham was visiting no pastoral moorland to the skirl of bagpipes, but rather one of the great industrial cities of Europe, the seed-bed of labor radicalism, epitomized in the term "Red Clyde," a region that has suffered more economic hardship than any other part of the United Kingdom under the administration of the London-oriented Parliaments that still look upon Scotland as one of the "Provinces."

Glaswegians — and here I write with some feeling as a "Glasgow keelie" myself — are soft-hearted, hard-headed, hard-working, and, alas, too often "at ease in Zion" regarding the Kirk. Institutional religion in Glasgow has too often in popular esteem been identified every first of January with the raucous partisan spirit of the terraces of Ibrox or Parkhead soccer grounds, where the so-called Protestant "Rangers" meet the no less Roman Catholic "Celtics" in a gladiatorial clash that revives feuds born in the ancient Battle of the River Boyne north of Dublin fought on July 12, 1690, when the Protestant William III defeated the Roman Catholic monarch James II and ended finally the fear of a Roman Catholic monarchy in Britain. In Glasgow the battle is fought over again, amidst blasphemous shouting addressed either to his Holiness the Pope or King Billy's Scottish Kirk by spectators with bacchantic Ne'erday hangovers — a rabble disowned by the respectable Christian community, both Catholic and Protestant.

Tom Allan and the organizing committee believed that only the Kelvin Hall in Glasgow would be adequate to accommodate their prayed-for response to Billy Graham's visit. Kelvin Hall is a sprawling low-lying edifice brightened by a warm red-sandstone-pillored frontage on the west end of Argyle Street, facing the baroque towered Glasgow Art Gallery and the majestically poised Gothic tower and buildings of the University of Glasgow upon Gilmorehill. Kelvin Hall is associated by every Glaswegian with automobile shows, housing displays, Christmas carnivals, and world championship boxing. Just two weeks prior to the opening service, this soulless cement-structure barn was transformed. Crews from Scaffolding Great Britain worked night and day, using some nine miles of steel tubing to build a rectangular terraced floor. Eighteen thousand newly painted green chairs were supplied by the Corporation of Glasgow. The spacious auditorium was artistically decorated with palms and ferns to greet the visitors. On the vast platform, accommodating a thousand-voice choir and platform party, a cornucopia of the loveliest flowers came daily from the Botanic Gardens. Behind the platform hung a banner proclaiming "I am the Way, and the Truth and the Life." Outside, flapping in the grey skies of Glasgow, a floodlit banner proudly displayed the original ancient motto of the city: LET GLASGOW FLOURISH BY THE PREACHING OF THE WORD AND THE PRAISING OF HIS NAME.

The sound equipment of Templar Film Studios, coordinated with the British Broadcasting Corporation, was able to relay the addresses clearly across the vast auditorium (with closed-circuit television in an annex reaching an additional 2,500) and nationwide by television to some thirty churches and halls across the country. Billy told me himself that it was perhaps the finest public address system he had ever used.

From the start, an air of expectancy was everywhere. Billy Graham and his party were greeted at the Glasgow Central Station by three thousand well-wishers singing "Blessed Assurance, Jesus Is Mine." I doubt that that old station ever witnessed anything quite like it before.

In the afternoon an official reception was held in the city chambers attended by the Lord Provost, magistrates, city officials, and leading citizens.

The Crusade opened on Sunday with a service of dedication in Glasgow's medieval cathedral when the Very Reverend Nevile Davidson declared that in any movement of the Spirit there is "A Moment, a Message, and a Man," and that "in the visit of Dr. Graham these conditions were truly present."

For six weeks (March 21 to April 30, 1955) it was estimated that 1,185,350 persons attended Kelvin Hall and the satellite places of worship where services were concurrently held. In the Kelvin Hall alone, seven hundred thousand passed through the doors. In Aberdeen, buffeted by bleak nor'easters and an onding of rain, some twenty-six thousand unemotional Aberdonians on the exposed terracing of the city's soccer ground at Pittodrie braved the elements, singing

> Just as I am without one plea
> But that thy blood was shed for me.

Sir Hugh Fraser the Scottish businessman underwrote the costs of travel, board, and lodging of every minister in the western Highlands who wished to avail himself of the invitation to attend the Kelvin Hall meetings.

Billy spoke to audiences in army barracks, churches, town halls, student halls of the four Scottish universities, and to gatherings of clergy. It was a unique experience for Scotland. The topic of religion and especially

177

of the events of the Crusade was on almost everyone's lips, even among people who had no intention of going near Kelvin Hall.

At the closing rallies, over sixty thousand crowded Ibrox Soccer Stadium; at Hampden Park, the largest (and most famous) soccer stadium in Britain, a hundred thousand douce Scots fervently sang the metrical psalms and such hymns as are woven in the tapestry of the liturgical life of the Kirk, such as "Rock of Ages" and "Abide with Me: Fast Falls the Eventide."

Before Billy left for Scotland, I had asked him to visit my aged mother in Glasgow. On one occasion when mother was shopping at the grocery store, the shopkeeper picked up the topic of conversation he must have been sharing with all his customers.

"Well, Mrs. Docherty, what do you think of the Billy Graham Crusade? Have you been to hear Billy Graham yet?"

"Oh, no!" said mother, putting on her tight-lipped, eyebrow-raised haughty look that silenced adversaries and endeared her to friends. "Oh, no!" There's no need for me to go to Kelvin Hall. Billy Graham is coming to see me! My Georgie, in Washington, has arranged it all."

Everyone gaped; it was obvious the dear little lady was getting somewhat confused.

Marshall Frady suggests that "while the BGEA documentary of that Crusade was rather ambitiously entitled *Fire on the Heather*, subsequent scrutinies found only marginal smolderings," and notes that there was an actual decrease in church membership from 202,430 to 202,035 in the Glasgow area a month after Graham's services. But every preacher knows that sterilized statistics concerning the work of the Spirit can be dangerously misleading.

Some 26,457 came forward and were counseled by the two thousand counselors who had been trained for weeks before the Crusade began. My own inquiries when I visited Scotland a year later revealed that so far as the Church of Scotland was concerned, Billy Graham was not everybody's cup of tea, that many of the ministers and sessions were actually hostile to his visit. Because of this coolness, only a minority of the churches that received names from the meetings followed up in any way, either by visiting or providing training classes for those who had stated the congregations of their preference. Such a poor follow-up was contrary to Billy's intentions. He had explained his mission to a ministers' gathering in Renfield Church, Glasgow, at the beginning of the Scottish Crusade.

"I'm a farmer's son from North Carolina. My early years were spent assisting in some small way my father as he plowed the hard red earth, harrowed it, and weeded it with back-breaking labor. Sometimes the young crop would be washed away in the semi-tropical spring rains and there had to be replanting. Sometimes a burning drought would wither it away. Nevertheless, seedtime and harvest never failed. And at the time of harvest, our neighbors would join in to help, as we would help with theirs.

There would be a great harvest banquet for all, rejoicing with prayer, and celebration for the Lord's bounty. We all know that the real work was not the harvest, but the months my father spent plowing, harrowing, and weeding. I come among you to enjoy your harvest of the gospel; I know that the real evangelistic work is done by you patient, dedicated ministers charged with the plowing and harrowing and planting. The true labor is yours, and the glory must be the Lord's."

Billy Graham is really a revivalist rather than an evangelist. He revives the wilting faith and gives new vision to the faithful, to the already committed church members. No doubt many have for the first time caught a glimpse of God's grace through his preaching and been emancipated from broken lives and broken homes, alcohol and dope. Billy himself has always asserted that about ninety-five percent of his audiences are already church members — and judging from the panning television camera shots of the listening multitudes, most have brought with them their Bibles, black leather-bound Bibles too, doubtless the King James Version.

On his return from Scotland, Billy called to see me. "Many of your friends, George, have sent their warm regards to you. And I want you to know that I have in my files about a hundred letters from ministers of the Church of Scotland, all of them speaking highly about the Crusade."

I read some of those letters; there was nothing private about them, inasmuch as the writers had already made it known from their pulpits what the Crusade had meant to them. All of the names I recognized; most of them I knew quite intimately. I could hardly believe what I was reading! They reiterated how they had found new strength and power for their ministry as the result of Billy's preaching.

I think I solved the mystery. These preachers, graduates of Scottish Universities, had been exposed in their New Testament studies to form, source, and redaction criticism of the four Gospels, searching behind the canon to the oral tradition and earlier written sources of the first and second generation of Christians. They had been taught that the resurrection appearances of Jesus recorded in the four Gospels were "legends," products of the first-century church, that not all the words recorded came from the lips of Jesus, some being *logia* or parables created by the early church. Under such training, their preaching was bound to take on a certain degree of historical skepticism. Did Mary in the garden in the half light of that first Easter Day really encounter the risen Jesus, or was the figure actually the gardener at work early in his garden, which had been disturbed by the pallbearers at the interment on Good Friday? Suddenly this American evangelical declares with absolute certainty, "The Bible says . . . the Bible says. . . ." His authoritative proclamation hid from them his fundamentalist exegesis! We had accused plenary-inspirationist preachers — "the letter killeth; the Spirit quickeneth." Perhaps in their monumental scholarship, these Lower Critics had lost touch with the Spirit in their concentration on the words.

"The Spirit blows where it wills," writes John the evangelist. Was not the Holy Spirit speaking through the proclamation of Billy Graham as he had spoken through the servants of the Church down the centuries, and often in spite of their limited grasp of the gospel? Paul, the greatest of them all, seemed to be silent concerning the corrupting system of slavery, only mentioning it in a letter to his friend Philemon. Saint Augustine, in his youth a roistering lad, held to a fantastic allegorical interpretation of the parables, especially that of the Good Samaritan. The Holy Spirit spoke through a superstitious medieval monk called Martin Luther who hated the Jewish race and believed a thunderstorm to be an epiphany of the Lord. The Holy Spirit spoke through a stubborn priest called John Knox, who regarded the medieval church of his day as the "kirk of Satan." The Holy Spirit has spoken down the ages through a blind, arrogant Church whose corruption led Bishop Woodburn in the eighteenth century to declare, "The Church is the Ark of God; in it are snarling, fighting, biting animals; but outside is the Flood." The Holy Spirit still speaks through a Church myopically adhering to outmoded medieval shibboleths such as manual apostolic succession, a stumbling block to true ecumenicity. The Holy Spirit spoke through the untutored Dwight L. Moody, one of the wisest saints in Christendom, who believed there was only one author of the book of Isaiah. And I believe that when Billy Graham preaches, the same Holy Spirit speaks through him despite his belief, for instance, that Jonah was physically swallowed by a whale and remained in its belly for three days — and might even have died and risen again, like the Savior. No matter! My own sermon on Jonah is saying exactly what Billy is preaching: man cannot flee from God who will pursue him "down the arches of the years."

The role of the Holy Spirit in preaching, especially in the preaching of Billy Graham, is something many critics have failed to grasp — not least among them Charles Templeton.

I first met Chuck Templeton in the early fifties at the Massanetta Springs Bible Conference. Friends asked "Have you met Chuck Templeton yet?" as if this were to be one of the great experiences of my life. It was. When my friend Bill Wiseman introduced us, I found myself facing a tall, good-looking young man with black eyes that bored through me, a restless curl in his black hair, and the suggestion of a permanent smile puckering his lips. And there could have been a dimple. He had to be an Irishman. I had seen them by the score — the innocent, open, childlike face masking the blarney that tripped so easily from their lips. There was a half-sob in his pleasant-timbred voice, and I was immediately aware that his incongruous Gaelic humor had not been entirely laundered away by Canadian respectability.

Our first conversation went on like Tennyson's brook, never-ending. A brilliant raconteur, he would tell tall tales of his early days with Youth for Christ, a movement that proved to be vastly successful both on campuses and off, backed up financially by millionaire capitalists such as William Randolph Hearst who in those days of the Cold War were prepared to pay any price to save the youth of the American continent from the taint of Communism. Chuck and Billy would sally forth, knights in armor, to do battle against the dragon devil. With a half-amused smile, he once told me, "You know, George, I discovered Billy Graham."

The "Gold Dust Twins" as they came to be known, together with the Youth for Christ Team, a Hearst reporter, and a *Life* photographer, once flew to Europe via Newfoundland, where on the stopover, Torrey Johnson assembled a large gathering at the American Air Force base. When the servicemen discovered that these guys were not entertainers, but rather a troup of religious nuts unaccompanied by any girls who might kick up their legs to cheer their arctic desolation, they hooted them off stage and began throwing chairs around.

"I can still see Billy," Chuck recalled, doubled over with laughter, "out of the side of my eye, in the wings, as I was trying to restore order, on his knees in prayer, his closed eyes directed toward the heavens for deliverance."

Once they engaged Soldier's Field in Chicago for a peace rally. Billy planned to conclude the meeting with a passionate declaration to the seventy thousand gathered there that "The choice is clear: either it is the atomic bomb or the dove of peace." Chuck had ordered a hundred pounds of photographer's flashpowder and twelve white doves for use as props, but all that could be obtained was a small signal flare used by ships in distress at night and twelve anemic pigeons!

Came the cue "Either the atomic bomb!" A tiny squib of light popped up and was immediately lost in a sky still lit with the traces of a sunset. Billy shouted "or the doves of peace!" The lad who had been paid five dollars beforehand to eject the pigeons from their wicker basket so terrified the pitiable craturs that only feathers emerged! Billy later reported that at least one pigeon must have escaped: it flew past his head with one wing quite featherless, flapping at double time to keep its balance!

Billy was struggling at this time with the question every preacher must face: Is the Bible a book every word, every jot and title of which comes from the mouth of the living God? Is the Bible the ultimate source of all knowledge? Was the world in fact created in six twenty-four-hour days? Is the Book of Revelation a spiritual foretelling of contemporary history? Is, for instance, the possible seizure of Middle East oil by the Russians already foretold in the visions of St. John on Patmos? Or is the

Bible the Word of God in the sense that "the Scriptures, given under the guidance of the Holy Spirit, nevertheless are the words of man, conditioned by language, thought forms, and literary fashions of the places and times at which they were written," as the United Presbyterian Church stated in its 1967 Confession of Faith.

Chuck Templeton had at one time been minister of the Church of the Nazarene, but their plenary inspiration theory of scripture became intolerable to him. He resigned and went to Princeton Theological Seminary to study for the ministry of the United Presbyterian Church. President John McKay claimed that Chuck Templeton was the most widely read student who had passed through his hands. He was appointed Director of Evangelism of the denomination, holding his own vast preaching missions across the country.

Chuck became *advocatus diaboli* when Billy Graham was struggling with the question of biblical authority. Billy was no match for Chuck's brilliant dialectic.

"Chuck, I can't answer your questions. I just know what belief, without question, without reserve, has let God do in my life."

Billy never quite recovered from these discussions. It drove him to make another surrender that would have permanent results in his future ministry. His first surrender had been to Jesus as Lord on that autumn night back in 1937, on the golf course that skirts the campus of the Florida Bible Institute, when, numbed by the broken heart of rejected first love, he declared, "All right, Lord! If you want me, you've got me. If I'm never to get Emily, I'm gonna follow you." This new surrender was made in 1949 under tall pines at a conference retreat in the San Bernardino Mountains that was run by the First Presbyterian Church of Hollywood (and at which Chuck Templeton was one of the speakers!). It was in a wood, where so often men have found the presence of God, that Billy cried out, "Lord, help me! I don't have the knowledge. I'm placing myself completely, heart *and* mind, without intellectual reservations, in your hands. . . . Oh, Lord, I *do*! accept this as your word! Come what may, without question or falter, I *believe* in this as your holy word."

We have all struggled with the question of the authority of the Bible, ever since our minds moved out of the myth-laden world of childhood into the sacramental universe of the holy scripture. My mutation of insight came to me when as a teenager I visited the British Museum in London and listened to the august learning of an ascetic white-haired archaeologist talk about recent discoveries in the ancient Bible lands.

"Have your studies proved to you that the Bible is true?" I asked naively.

"My dear boy, the Bible does not require to be proved; only explained."

Professor Henry Drummond, prince of preachers, taught Geology at Glasgow's Trinity College when the first theological implications of Darwin's theory of evolution seemed to loosen the pillars of biblical authority and tear the Christian Church apart. Drummond was fascinated by Dwight L. Moody when he visited Britain. They became staunch friends.

"Come over to America, Henry," Moody wrote on his return home. "Come with me in the circuit. We would do well together as a team."

"My dear Moody, I would only embarrass you," Drummond replied. "Don't you realize that I believe there were two Isaiahs?"

"Please come over, Henry," was Moody's prompt reply. "There are millions of Americans who do not know that there is one Isaiah."

I had hoped that Billy Graham was the one person who would be able to heal the breach between the Bible Belt South and the more liberal North. It was a vain hope.

Intellectually it meant the parting of the ways between these two remarkable young men. Hereafter for Chuck, Billy Graham lived on a different wave length, a different universe of discourse. In time Chuck would doubt the authenticity of the doctrine of the Trinity. He was too honest to go on preaching an anemic Unitarian gospel. I recall when he preached his last sermon at Massanetta Springs Bible Conference. I sat up most of the night arguing and hoping that he might alter his decision to resign from the ministry.

Since those long-ago days back in the fifties, Chuck, the Renaissance man, has distinguished himself in the fields of television, the press, national politics, and as an author. He is also an inventor. He even played golf well! But the real Chuck Templeton, whose friendship I shall always treasure, is a very private man, most at home when alone with his typewriter in his log cabin on Lake George, discovering as we all do that in the universe of the self lie the mystery and magic and miracle of human existence. "It will never be easy," he has said, "but I have found [in writing] what I want to do finally, and if I have to, I will do it to the exclusion of all others."

He has already published two brilliant best-selling novels — *Act of God* and a revealing semi-autobiographical work, *The Third Temptation*. How can Chuck Templeton fail with the blood of a sober Brendan Behan in his veins, the agonizing imagination of a Charles Dickens, and the neatly disciplined life of an Anthony Trollope?

President Lyndon Johnson once said to Billy Graham, "Billy, you stick to religion and let me stick to politics." The wily politician was quite aware of Billy's conservative stance and his status quo—ism. Back in August 1965, after hearing the news of the fearsome burnings and riots that destroyed Watts, Billy told me over a lunch at Montreat Bible Conference that he had it on the authority of the editor of the *Los Angeles Times* that the riots had been instigated by Communists. His communo-phobia, no doubt nurtured by his close contacts with the White House, influenced his judgment of the basic causes of the Vietnam War. And his genuine friendship with Richard Nixon colored his judgment of the Watergate affair: he refused to accept the facts, and when the truth that the nation was suspecting finally broke, Billy was genuinely crushed. It is symbolic of Billy's integrity that in the end his word to the press was "Richard Nixon has been a longtime friend of mine, and he still is my friend."

Billy Graham has been called "a court priest of Caesar," but he certainly never sought the office. The court of Caesar was only too glad to use Billy Graham for its own purposes. Henry Luce's *Time* magazine was always happy to print his views of almost every subject pertaining to the conflicts within the nation. The network cameras followed him everywhere he traveled; he was good copy. To his credit, he made such publicity occasions a time to "say a word for Jesus," to use the old Ian McLaren phrase. I recall Jack Paar, delighting in his own affability as a host, joshing with Billy, was suddenly brought up short when Billy called his bluff with the question "Jack, when were you last in church?" But if he had only learned the magic phrase "no comment," it would have saved him from making pronouncements on almost every issue before the country, from starvation in India to America's future policy with a monolithic Kremlin. In October 1957 he declared "on good authority" that a faction within the Soviet Politburo was demanding an attack upon the United States within two years.

However the preacher may vote as a citizen (and, indeed, he *must* vote), it is not the place of the pulpit to espouse a particular candidate, especially in a Presidential election. "A plague on both your houses! Is this all you have to offer the nation?" is the stance any prophetic preacher will take. But Billy had no qualms about identifying his position with the candidate of his choice. Of course he would support his friend Richard Milhous Nixon, but to appear among an audience of his supporters on national television at a crucial talk-back session sponsored by the Republican Party on the eve of the 1960 presidential election was surely to add to the support of Mr. Nixon at least two million voters. Billy did not need to speak—he was there.

Nevertheless, he never courted the great and the powerful as so many of us Washingtonians must confess to having done. When General Eisenhower was a presidential candidate, I hoped that he might become a member of my church, which after all stands only three blocks from the White House. And the prospect of Adlai Stevenson becoming one of my members if he were elected was at the time for me (an ardent Stevensonian) a pulse-quickening prospect.

Billy Graham, on the other hand, did not attend the court of Caesar unless he was summoned. Despite his public opposition to the prospect of a Roman Catholic in the White House on the grounds of a conflict of interest between his oath as President and his religious allegiance to the

Vatican, Billy accepted an invitation from President Kennedy to play a game of golf in Florida soon after his election. Lyndon Johnson repeatedly invited Billy to stay at the White House (it was said there was a special bedroom set apart for him). He was an overnight guest on the last night Lyndon Johnson spent in the White House. And at the family's request, Billy traveled to Texas to preach the funeral sermon at the grave on the spacious Lyndon Johnson ranch.

Billy Graham was closer than any other clergyman to President Eisenhower. On his deathbed at Walter Reed Hospital, the weakening President asked him "How can I know that I'm going to heaven? How can I be sure, absolutely sure, that my sins are forgiven?" To this conqueror of Hitler's armies, Billy read once more the sure and steadfast promises of the scriptures, leaving the President to face with peace in his heart the journey to that bourne whence no man returns.

Why should Winston Churchill ask Billy Graham to come to his office in 10 Downing Street during the 1955 Billy Graham London Campaign, and for almost an hour discuss with this young American evangelist the numinous mystery of immortality and the fading hope for mankind, in which Churchill, now an old man, professed a dwindling faith?

Why should Bernard Baruch suggest to Henry Luce that he must see Billy Graham? (When they met at the Governor's Mansion in South Carolina, Luce spoke with Billy until two in the morning about — of all things one would imagine of a hard-nosed editor — prayer!)

What was it about Billy Graham that attracted in a very extraordinary way Her Britannic Majesty Queen Elizabeth II? At a garden party in Buckingham Palace where some ten thousand upper-crust guests mingled with one another on the billiard-table-groomed lawns, Billy, off on his own supping tea under an ancient oak, suddenly heard his name announced over the loudspeaker system, as a voice commanded him to attend the Queen and the Duke in the royal tent. There the Queen, smiling, cordially took his hand in both of hers, remarking, "The Duke and I will never forget your sermon delivered at the Communion Service at Glasgow Cathedral at the conclusion of the Scottish Crusade."

Charisma? Perhaps if we use the term not in its secularized sense of the empty charm of film stars or wildly dressed gyrating rock stars, but in the New Testament sense of *grace*, the external radiance of a heart that is redeemed, what Barrie once described as "charm," "a bloom upon one."

Billy symbolized to the mighty that authentic purity of heart found in the utterly dedicated life; his was the nobler life that they all once dreamed of but that had gotten lost in the rush of the long grasping egotistical years as they lusted after power or fame or wealth.

He reminded them also of a voice, almost certainly a mother's voice, now silenced, that had tried to convince them of the value of the pearl of great price.

Dwight Eisenhower was a country boy raised in a godly home among the River Brethren Church. Richard Nixon was the poor son of a Quaker family. Lyndon Johnson came from the backlands of Texas. Henry Luce was the son of missionary parents, a heritage he was never to forget. Bernard Baruch was brought up on the East Side of New York, working his way through school until, consulted by presidents, he held the power of the nation's purse; he was nurtured in those far off days in the faith of Moses by a mother in whose eyes he saw the light of holiness. Not least was Winston Churchill, who to the end of his days looked last thing at night at a photograph by his bedside of a nanny who was more mother to him in his childhood than his radiant mother Jenny Jerome had been.

Portrait artists spend their time studying faces and peering into the soul behind the eyes. Frank Salisbury (1874–1962) was in his day perhaps the most eminent portrait artist in the world. His subjects included kings, queens, presidents (Roosevelt and Coolidge), czars of commerce (Andrew Mellon), and, in the short Indian summer of his power, Benito Mussolini. When he had finished his portrait of Billy, Salisbury remarked, "Never have I been so conscious as when painting Mr. Graham of being in the presence of holiness."

Yet there is also the Billy Graham his friends know, the man away from the platform and the microphone, what we like to think of as his true self. When he visited my mother in our manse in Washington, she remarked, "He's just like an ordinary laddie." He remembered our Mairi's birthday when we were together at Montreat with a little white leather-bound copy of the Bible. Jerry loved it when she drove with him to the East Los Angeles Stadium through the milling crowds on the road; she knew what it was to be Queen for a Day! Nor was she simply handed over to some anonymous aide when they reached the vast stadium: Billy personally escorted her through a crush of autograph seekers and laughing people, over the grass to her place on the wooden platform, all the while apologizing for the inconvenience of the crowd.

His biographers have not yet caught the real man. Frady is too iconoclastic, Stanley High too self-serving. The authentic Billy Graham I never really met. Beyond the still-handsome face (though the hair is now streaked with grey), I am carried in imagination back down the years to a farm in North Carolina, where a tall skinny loose-limbed lad with a tree stump for a pulpit preached across the bogland of his father's farm toward the weeping willows, a lad truly "called of God," as was Elisha when Elijah cast his preacher-prophet robe around him, called "to the dignitie of a preachour," as John Knox wrote of himself. They have a saying in the Highlands: "He has the gift."

13

The Third American Revolution

The whole history of the progress of human liberty shows that all concessions yet made in her august claims have been born out of earnest struggle. . . . Those who profess to favor freedom, and yet deprecate agitation, are men who want crops without ploughing up the ground. . . . This struggle may be a moral one; or it may be a physical one; or it may be both moral and physical; but it must be a struggle. Power concedes nothing without demand.

—Frederick Douglass, 1863

THE FIRST AMERICAN REVOLUTION, 1776, did nothing to ameliorate the plight of the Negro slave. In the list of charges in the Declaration of Independence against King George III, Thomas Jefferson had accused the King of "keeping open market where men should be bought and sold"; in the final draft, this clause was omitted.

The Second Revolution, the Civil War, 1865, was ostensibly fought to free the slaves; yet this issue was secondary to preserving the Union. The social status of the slaves was in fact not much changed by their official "emancipation." Indeed, it was not until 1870 that the Fifteenth Amendment to the Constitution granted former slaves the right to vote. Even that right was for almost a century hedged around with all kinds of subtle but real obstacles. Blacks continued to be second-class citizens until the Voting Rights Act of 1965 was passed by Congress.

The Third American Revolution may be said to have broken out December 1, 1955, in Montgomery, Alabama, when Mama Rosa Parks, tired after her long day's work, sat down gratefully in the empty seat in the front of a public bus. She was ordered to give up her seat to a white passenger and go to the back of the bus "where she belonged." She refused, was arrested, jailed, tried, and fined ten dollars plus costs. Her attorney eventually appealed the case all the way to the Supreme Court, which ruled in her favor.

Irate black women subsequently organized a mass meeting calling for a boycott of Montgomery buses, and the black community rallied to the call. They chose as speaker the new minister of Dexter Avenue Baptist Church, a twenty-seven-year-old graduate of Boston University's doctoral

187

program—Dr. Martin Luther King, Jr. Locally, the boycott was an overwhelming success, but it became a matter of national interest when white citizens bombed the house of Dr. King with his wife and children in it on January 30, 1956. The horror of the act reverberated throughout the country. The newspapers and the new mass medium of television dramatically confronted America with the evil of segregation. It led to the formation of the Southern Christian Leadership Council.

A new day had dawned for the black community and for the black churches, which for over two centuries had been virtually quarantined, made to worship in unpainted wooden shacks in the countryside and in storefront churches in the cities, their only hope the vision of a new Moses who would lead them to the promised land some day. Now a remarkable group of young Christian leaders, all of them Baptist preachers, came forward to take their places in the forefront of American history, among them, Ralph Abernathy, Andrew Young, and James Bevel, to be followed in the sixties by such men as Stokely Carmichael, H. Rap Brown, and Malcolm X. Like the Christians in Thessalonica mentioned in the Acts, they "turned the world upside down, . . . [doing] contrary to the decrees of Caesar, saying that there is another king, one Jesus."

The black community united like a tidal wave, but the surge did not go unchallenged. In Nashville, Tennessee, students defying a segregation order at a Woolworth cafeteria counter had their heads beaten before a boycott of all downtown lunch counters ended the policy of discrimination. In 1962 a young James Meredith would need the help of federal troops to enter the University of Mississippi.

A new minister in the nation's capital, himself a stranger in the land, soon began to realize that the Third Revolution had spread within the shadow of the noble spire of New York Avenue Church.

The sidewalks of the neighborhood surrounding New York Avenue Church, which had once held crowds of the nation's wealthy and elite seeking entrance to worship services, now hosted a radically different population. The overcrowded Victorian row houses that had not yet felt the wrecking ball stood like diseased teeth amid gaping sockets. Opposite the church an adult movie house did a brisk business, attracting a steady stream of furtive, self-conscious males, collars upturned against detection, for an afternoon of voyeuristic pleasure. On the corner of 14th Street stood a pornography emporium claiming to be the largest in the world. In the delightful little triangular park in the shadow of the church's 180-foot colonial tower, dandified pimps strolled openly, and the flotsam of society slept off the horrors of the night before on wooden benches. I once observed a man urinate against my church only a few yards away from the cornerstone that had been laid by a president of the United States. One army colonel described our church as "an island of morality battered by a turbulent sea of sin."

Valiantly our congregation sought to meet the challenge of this deplorable environment. We protested the sale of pornographic literature,
but found corporate action difficult in the face of the First Amendment,
which guarantees freedom of the press without spelling out the difference
between freedom and license. As my mother used to say, "The mair you
tramp on dirt, the further it spreads." My staff and our board of deacons
patiently tried to help the "undeserving poor" who called daily at the
church; we gave them food tickets that could be exchanged at a fast-food
restaurant down the street, but I fear many of them were exchanged at
cut rates for cash for booze — or worse. We assisted a remarkable group
of Roman Catholic priests in their extraordinary experiment in "containing
the ghetto" by opening a soup kitchen (from which the news-hungry press
and curious onlookers were forbidden). They called it "Lazarus Place."

This was my parish! I preached a sermon on Lazarus, the gangrenous
beggar who sat outside the home of the rich man, happy to eat even the
scraps from his table, his sores licked by the curs of the street. The analogy
was obvious, especially when I shared the statistics gathered by a splendid
group within the church who saw clearly the new mission challenging us.
The Lazarus of our streets consisted of ten thousand people, seven thousand of whom were black. In forty percent of their homes there was no
private bath, no indoor toilet, no running water. Some 650 families lived
in houses already condemned by the authorities as unfit for human hab-
itation. In one third of the black households the mother was the bread-
winner, the men having been shut out of a system still blatantly
discriminatory.

The year was 1960. It brought an end to the postwar boom in attendance among the mainline churches. The crowds who once thronged New
York Avenue Church likewise faded away. What had brought them to
church in the first place is not easy to fathom; in any case, so soon as the
true mission of the Church dawned on them, they either fled to suburban
churches in which questions of civil rights for blacks remained comfortably
remote, or else they simply fell by the wayside, the searing sun of affluence
having scorched them up. Our membership had already reached its highest
level, just over two thousand; from that point it gradually dwindled, until
by the next decade it stabilized at around thirteen hundred. Four downtown
churches in the Presbytery simply closed down, bankrupt. Others sold out
to the growing affluent black community.

The depth of social disintegration of the parish was brought home
when two hundred of our members, after the manner of the Gospels, went
out by twos, visiting homes in the parish on two consecutive Sunday
afternoons. All of them returned with a new sense of commitment, many
in a state of mild shock, angry or bewildered by what had met them when
they stepped out of the light of a sabbath afternoon into the grey squalor
of basic poverty. In these homes they found brave, hard-working (when

work could be found) families, the husband holding down two jobs when he was able, living in ill-repaired, rat-infested houses, people in despair, paying exorbitant rents and heating bills, shopping at supermarkets whose prices were higher than those in the suburbs, while the food was clearly inferior. One house was a brothel. In another, a couple still in bed, enjoying to the lees a lost weekend, asked the visitors to join them.

To meet the task of ministering to this greatly abused community, additional professional staff was required to supplement the work of our already wonderfully dedicated army of volunteers. Carolyn Matthews and Thelma Odom came to us assisted by General Assembly mission funds, and the Reverend Philip Newell, a Harvard man, became my first Minister of the Inner City.

A black woman, Blonnie Thomson, asked to be affiliated to our congregation. I could simply have accepted the letter of transfer from her Baptist church as a matter of course, but I decided that the session ought to become involved in what I hoped would be a precedent for many more. A committee of three was appointed to meet with the young lady. Before the interview I made it clear that we would ask only questions normally put to anyone seeking membership.

"Blonnie, why do you want to become a member of our church?"

"I liked Peter Marshall. He came to our college when I was a student."

"But aren't there other Presbyterian churches nearer your home than ours?"

"But I love New York Avenue, especially the choir."

"Your husband is a Baptist deacon. Why not join his church?"

"The preacher talks too long there. I can never get Sunday dinner in time. Besides, my husband is quite content that I should be happy here."

One of the committee members was an elder from Arkansas who had as a child seen a black man lynched and whose brother-in-law had been stabbed in a brawl by a black gang. At the session he spoke up: "I believe the Spirit of the Lord is guiding this young woman, and I move on behalf of the committee that the session accept her into our membership."

Thelma Odom is a minister's widow and perhaps the most authentically dedicated Christian I have ever known, walking always with a quiet unhurried calm, the sign of real grace, and a patience that is the fruit of much hurt. With my wife, Jerry, she organized a Women's Fellowship group that met regularly in the church. Some thirty black women, all of whom were members of a storefront church, attended on Sunday afternoons after our morning service. This undoubtedly was Jerry's happiest experience in a church where so much was exciting. In addition to the warm Christian fellowship it fostered among the other members, this group provided a basis for some of the church's social outreach. We were able to rehouse every family in the group except one that preferred the house they had. On one occasion when one of the families was literally thrown out onto the sidewalk, two of the girls stayed at the manse for almost two years, to the great enrichment of our family life.

One of our neighborhood families, whom we shall call the Gibsons, lived in a dark, moldy basement heated by a solitary kerosene lamp. The front door locks were long broken; the children sallied out at will through the creaking door into a dangerously busy and crime-infested street. John, the husband, was a hard-working laborer holding down two jobs to meet the extortionist rents charged by the absentee landlord through a vindictive agent who raised the rents when any repairs or paintwork was done. The first time Mrs. Gibson entered the church and joined the meeting of the women, she stood apart, head bowed like a shy schoolgirl, too afraid to feel at ease in the mood of laughter and song. Yet within the month she joined in with the others, bringing her own intelligent and humorous opinions and advice.

We were able to help the Gibsons get out of the hovel that they had sought to make a home and moved into a fine three-bedroom apartment in a new public housing area. When Jerry and Thelma Odom visited her, they were met at the doorway by a radiant Mrs. Gibson, flushed a little with suppressed excitement. She ushered the ladies into one of the bedrooms, where they put their coats. A tour of inspection of her new home followed; it was sparsely furnished, but meticulously clean — new drapes, homemade, on the windows, new cushion covers hiding the drab second-hand furniture.

"Would you like a cup of tea, Mrs. Docherty? I believe you prefer tea to coffee?"

She entered the dining-cum-sitting room, her white apron starkly contrasting with her dark Sunday dress, bearing proudly a tray on which were a teapot enclosed in a tea cozy, chocolate biscuits, cut cake, plates, knives, and paper napkins.

"Do you take sugar, Mrs. Docherty? No? Milk? Thelma? . . ."

Over tea the conversation flowed around the little matters that make up the heart of life — her three children and their problems with homework and colds and baseball; her husband, tired at the end of the week, working late hours. They were saving up for new furniture, would try not to shop in those stores with exorbitant interest charges. They had never noticed how drab their furniture was until it was set against the yellow walls of their new apartment.

It came time for the ladies to make their next visit. Jerry kissed Mrs. Gibson. There was the suggestion of a tear.

Outside in her car, Thelma turned round to Jerry and said, "Jerry, dear, never again in your whole life will you ever do anything so wonderful as you have done this afternoon. You have restored to this woman her self-respect and belief in herself. She actually entertained the Pastor's wife to afternoon tea in her new home without feeling ashamed of her surroundings; and with tea from a pot with a cozy! As long as she lives Mrs. Gibson will treasure in her heart this afternoon. My dear, don't you think this is really what we are all seeking in life — to meet as friends, to talk and laugh and love, with dignity?"

One spokesman for the Women's Fellowship was Mrs. Jackie Greene. (Her son would become one of the most popular pop stars on TV in the Washington area.) Jackie was a natural orator and a character of whom one day I shall write more. On one occasion, when she and some of the other black women were due to visit a well-to-do white suburban church to tell the story of our inner-city work, Jerry asked Jackie about her subject and how long she would speak.

"I jes' don't know how long I'll be speakin' and I will say jes' what the Spirit leads me to utter."

The evening of the meeting, a large group of church women had gathered in the spacious air-conditioned church hall. A reception committee was on hand to greet them. Jerry was, as always, received with a cordial handshake; Jackie and the other black women were given a somewhat embarrassed smile and a polite bow. The chairwoman welcomed them and introduced Mrs. Jackie Greene, who was led by the Spirit to say, "Ma dear friends, I jes' want to ask you one question. How many of you want to go to heaven? Come on now! Put up yo' hand if you want to go to heaven! Fine, that's fine! I'm glad to see so many want to go to heaven. Well, let me tell yo' all, some of you folk ain't not agoin' to go to heaven at all! No ma'am! No indeed! 'Cause when I came here tonight, some of you white folk didn't want to shake my black hand in welcome. Let me tell yo' . . . the Lawd Jesus, he don't like that sort of thing; he certainly don't, 'cause he says we ought to love one another — not jes' white folk lovin' white folk and black folk lovin' black folk, but everybody lovin' one another, 'cause the Lawd Jesus loves us all. An' let me tell you, if yo' don't shake hands with black folk, yo' goin' to go to hell, right down there with the devil! And let me tell you, down there in hell, there's a lot o' niggers, Lordy I know that, an' they are real bad — that's why they are in hell. So you folk had better start gettin' along with us black folk here and now, 'cause it will be the worse for you down there with all those bad black niggers!"

The rather radical transformation taking place in the traditional witness and work of the church caused concern with some of our members. Church folk tend to resist change in the traditional ways, which are deepseated and real. There was, for instance, some resistance to the fact that our many-faceted program so fully taxed available space: the basement, with its gymnasium and club rooms, and the side halls were in constant use for all kinds of meetings, and the fifth-floor kitchen was busy three nights a week with congregational dinners. In passageways one met people of all ages, including Koreans, who had made us the center of their own church life. One elder complained to Jerry that he could not hear the Bible read at the mid-week prayer meeting in the Lincoln Chapel for the noise of roistering youngsters racing up and down stairs and at times taking over the two elevators.

"Ah, John," she replied sweetly, "you should have joined them in their games. I believe I saw the boy Jesus chasing them along the corridors!"

One distinguished member, greatly in sympathy with all that we were doing to make a significant witness among the people still living around our doors, believed that the work could be done more adequately if it were housed in a building separate from the church. He was prepared to donate $40,000 toward such a half-way house. The offer was tempting; there was at that moment a funeral parlor up for sale that would have made an admirable center for the rehabilitation of alcoholics, a bureau for housing and counseling, a bridge between our church and the community. But there was one condition with the gift: no children from the half-way house could become members of our church. What would I do if even one child had come to me confessing Jesus as Lord and requesting membership with us? This was the ultimate goal of all our work. I turned away from the offer.

We inaugurated, under the government-sponsored scheme Project Hope, a secretarial school for teenage mothers. It was the brainchild of two gifted secretaries who had found their work in the White House hardly enlightening. Into two of our fourth-floor rooms came secretarial equipment — dictaphones, twenty-four I.B.M. electric typewriters, and tape-recording teaching machines. Young women were taught shorthand, typing, bookkeeping, and basic English. Over a period of six years I watched each autumn as there arrived at the church young, self-conscious, perhaps suspicious, and very shy young people in pairs, making their way to the elevator in this strange church that was also a commercial college. Ten months later these same girls would appear in academic robe and hood at their graduation in the Peter Marshall Hall, where family and friends had gathered, walking in procession, no less self-conscious, but heads a little higher now, to receive diplomas enabling them to be employed by any who wished to have first-class trained secretaries. Over punch and cookies they laughed and joshed like a crowd of Vasser graduates. This splendid program was later axed by the penny-pinching Nixon administration.

The church also organized a study hall. It met every Thursday evening after basketball in the basement gymnasium. Some seventy volunteers met with as many boys and girls, ostensibly to assist them with their homework. Few of the volunteers were professional teachers. We were more interested in creating new relationships by breaking down mutual distrust and by showing "the perfect love that casts out fear." One volunteer, a teacher, met with a student whom he taught daily at a local public school. We found the boy had been held back in school not because he lacked intelligence, but because he had an emotional problem. With the tutor's help, he skipped through three grades! We helped some students, mostly boys, to complete high school by scraping together much-needed financial assistance. And although it took seven years, the study hall was able to boast its first college graduate.

One triumph remains unforgettable. Willie had been brought along by his pals for basketball and was coaxed into coming upstairs. Once there, however, he sat through the hour study hall session with his back turned toward his tutor, Bill, a State Department whiz kid on the Yugoslav desk. The same charade took place for the next three weeks — Bill patiently talking to the back of Willie's head until the bell rang. Then on the fourth occasion Willie gave Bill the faintest suggestion of an over-the-shoulder glance and a smile as he left. The ice was broken! The following week Willie approached Bill happily; they laughed, joked, and continued their studies together. Willie was simply terrified of all whites. His only experience of them had been via the police, the courts, social workers, and debt collectors.

It is not without significance that the majority of the tutors were members neither of our church nor of any other. Indeed, one of our best, gentlest, and most regular tutors was an atheist. We joshed together. He would have none of the "Christian stuff." I would tell him, "You're following Jesus already, but you just haven't quite got hold of the name." Once a specialist teacher came to watch a tutorial closely, asking all manner of questions about it. In the end she turned on her heel. "I'm sorry," she said. "This work is not for me. I don't mind teaching; in fact, I'm rather good at that. But it's obvious that these tutors love these black children. I could not do that."

Since 1960, literally hundreds must have participated as students and volunteers in this tutorial program, most with monastic discipline. Perhaps none has shown such consistently patient and dedicated witness as Virginia Cochran and David Brown; theirs has been the burning heart of love. May 26, 1983, was designated by the District of Columbia Council as "Virginia Cochran and David Brown Day" to recognize and honor them "for their exceptional work with youth in initiating and leading New York Avenue's Community Club Program." The resolution noted that the program "involves more than 100 students and tutors, boasts four college graduates and seven current college students who participated in the program and enjoyed financial assistance from the several scholarships that the Church initiated" (not least among which is the "Mary Shirlaw Docherty Scholarship Fund"). The citation goes on: "the entire Washington community joins the New York Avenue Church and the Community Club in mourning the loss of Virginia, whose spirit 'lives on and motivates everyone to carry on her good work.' "

The plight of the American blacks was not basically that of poverty; I had witnessed worse poverty in the Townhead district of Glasgow. The evil lay deeper. The poor of Glasgow took pride in their freedom to vote, challenged anyone who would dare to question their civic and political and personal rights. The folk around us in downtown Washington were enduring not merely self-perpetuating poverty but a vicious entrenched racial hatred, surface appearances to the contrary. Second-class education ill fitted them for higher employment, their civil rights were manipulated, and their dignity as persons could be achieved only after much hardship. We were not surprised by the protests of the new generation of blacks ashamed of the "Amos and Andy" image their parents and grandparents had been stuck with; they understandably protested, at times too much with a haughty disdain and disregard for anything that was associated with a slave mentality. Proud of their heritage, they proclaimed to the world that black was beautiful, and in dress and hairstyle emulated the fashions of black Africans. Their courage was awesome at times.

What we were doing was at best symbolic, shoveling a mountain of sand with a teaspoon, nor could we hope to solve all the social, political, and educational problems.

By a strange paradox, the work of the inner city saved New York Avenue Church from deteriorating into what I had seen in so many cities — a noble building whose future was in the past, a symbol of bourgeois Christianity that would eventually be sold to the highest bidder. Young couples with growing families came to be part of us, all of them college graduates, lawyers, government personnel, the "backroom boys and girls" — the speech writers, the creators of policy for the government, servants of the State Department with worldwide experience — these joined us. All of them said when I sat down to talk about membership, "This is a church that is doing something." They were tired of suburban white elite Christianity. Today they constitute the strength of what I make bold to believe is the most significant congregation in the broad United States. I was to remember the word of scripture, "I will honor those who honor me."

It was a time of exciting intellectual stimulation, and I was reading anything I could lay my hands on, finding there were too few Sundays in the year for the many ideas clamoring to be preached. Peter Berger and the French sociologist Jacques Ellul were baptizing sociology into the Christian faith. Bill Hamilton was announcing the "Death of God" (he said it occurred in 1914, when I pressed him for a date), while Thomas Altizer was preaching the gospel of Christian Atheism. Dietrich Bonhoeffer, still with us in spirit, went on reminding us that Jesus came to abolish religion, and Paul Tillich was officiating at the marriage of Christ and Culture. Joseph Fletcher was suggesting that the tablets of the Ten Commandments had once more been crushed to dust, and Paul Lehmann, espousing contextual ethics, was finding the final authority of Christ in the fellowship of the

Church. A symposium assembled by John Hicks was announcing that the Incarnation was a myth, the logical conclusion as well of Rudolph Bultmann's microscopic scholarship into the sources of the gospel allied with the existentialism of Martin Heidegger; in response, Michael Green was asserting the Truth of God Incarnate. Coming to new life in English translation, Kierkegaard was saving us from the humanistic pessimism of John Paul Sartre and Albert Camus, yet he himself, assailing the straw man of his own Danish state religion, seemed to be attacking the Church from the sidelines only to die with a good confession in its arms. Harvey Cox was making out a good case for the redemption of the Secular City while Pierre Teilhard de Chardin's mystical creationism was perplexing virtually everyone.

It is almost impossible now to recapture the emotional furor that swept across the country in that summer of 1960 when the Democratic Party, meeting at Los Angeles, nominated as their candidate a member of the Roman Catholic Church, John Fitzgerald Kennedy, Senator from Massachusetts. Back in 1928, Alfred Emmanuel Smith, the able governor of New York, had been defeated by a lesser man, Herbert Hoover. Even the endorsement of Franklin Delano Roosevelt could not stem the surge of prejudice against the "Happy Warrior" for his being a Roman Catholic.

Some months before the Los Angeles convention I had been invited as principal speaker at the Fourteenth Annual Protestant Reformation Festival sponsored by the Detroit Council of Churches. Aware of the political atmosphere, the organizers had made it a point to announce to the press that the occasion would be kept to its traditional high plane and that politics would be avoided. It seemed to me a vain hope; any lecture on John Knox, who regarded the Roman Catholic Church as the "kirk of Satan," could not but be interpreted as hostile to contemporary Roman Catholicism.

"Since I agreed to make this address last February," I began my speech, "much has happened, especially in Los Angeles. I came here with the explicit purpose of speaking about John Knox and not John Fitzgerald Kennedy. However, I want you to know that if I were not a citizen of America's last colony and had a vote in this presidential election, I would cast that vote for Senator Kennedy."

The immediate reaction was a stunned silence. The press had a field day. The next day's Detroit headlines read "Washington Preacher Uses Reformation Festival to Canvass Votes for Catholic President." The Presbytery of Detroit sent out an official request for my presence to respond to their official censure. I ignored it.

Nor will many recall the meeting that took place that extraordinary summer at the Mayflower Hotel in Washington, sponsored by a group calling themselves "Citizens for Religious Freedom." I had never heard of the group until I received a long-distance call from Houston asking if I would be willing to act as the chairman of a meeting of Protestant ministers and laity. In answer to my probing I received little satisfaction about the organization's background; they seemed to be an ad hoc group of Protestants who were concerned about religious freedom. While a chairman must be impartial, he will inevitably be identified with any gathering that he chairs. I refused to be their chairman, but offered to give the invocation at their luncheon.

Dr. Norman Vincent Peale, the distinguished minister of Manhattan's Marble Collegiate Church, was contacted by telephone while vacationing in Ireland. He accepted the chairmanship. I doubt that the 150 clergy and laymen who gathered in one of the dining rooms of the Mayflower Hotel realized the implications their deliberations might have.

I offered the invocation and then took the liberty, since at that time Washington, D.C., had no elected mayor, to welcome them to the nation's capital.

From the beginning, Dr. Peale set a distressingly partisan tone for the meeting, launching a diatribe against the Roman Catholic Church. He began with some offhand caustic remarks about His Holiness the Pope. He claimed that the future of American culture was at stake in the coming election; he would not predict its demise, but it would never again enjoy the freedom of religion that the founders envisaged were Senator Kennedy to be elected President.

Dr. Harold Ockenga of Boston's Park Street Church claimed that the methods of Rome and Moscow were not dissimilar: if elected, Mr. Kennedy, like Premier Khrushchev, would be captive to the system.

The delegates issued at the end of the meeting a statement suggesting that the Vatican would undoubtedly sway any Roman Catholic President on such matters as foreign policy, education, and the relationship between church and state.

Naively, the organizers had banned the press from the dinner. At least three of the waiters were members of the press in disguise! Protestants were embarrassed. Roman Catholics were enraged. Both the Nixon and Kennedy campaign organizations were infuriated that the religious question had been so gauchely injected into the campaign.

The unfortunate Dr. Peale disengaged himself from the whole affair. The *Philadelphia Enquirer* dropped his weekly column. He went into retreat, offering his resignation from the pulpit of his church. (It was refused.) He also submitted his resignation to Citizens for Religious Freedom, declaring that the people had the right to elect a man of any religion — or none at all — as president. "I was not duped," he told a *New York Herald Tribune* reporter; "I was just stupid."

It was a very close presidential race, the most closely contested of the century. Mr. Kennedy won 303 electoral votes, compared to Mr. Nixon's 219, but in a popular vote of some 68,000,000, Mr. Kennedy's margin was a mere 118,000. Analyzing the results, *Time* magazine later attributed Mr. Nixon's defeat mainly to two events: the televised debates between the candidates and the Citizens for Religious Freedom meeting at the Mayflower Hotel.

I met a member of the press who had been present at the meeting disguised as a waiter.

"Suppose I had accepted the chairmanship of the meeting instead of Dr. Peale?"

"That's a fascinating question. I certainly cannot imagine you making such inflammatory statements about the dangers of a Roman Catholic president and the future relationship of our country with the Vatican. These remarks must have hurt Mr. Nixon. Who knows? You may in some small way have contributed to his defeat!"

November 22, 1963, fell on a Friday. Our staff were gathered together for our weekly conference. The telephone rang.

"President Kennedy has been shot. The news is on television."

Unbelievingly, we rushed to the church's television set. Walter Cronkite, the ever-objective reporter, was describing the scene outside a hospital in Dallas. A further note was handed to him. A pause. His voice broke.

"News has just arrived. . . . President Kennedy has died. The time was exactly one o'clock Dallas time."

Since the Kennedys had taken up residence in the White House, all of us were aware of the subtle transformation. For the Americans who have a subliminal desire for royalty, the Kennedys were the nearest thing to it. Camelot had come to town. His inaugural address had set a new tone of challenge to the nation. "Ask not what your country can do for you; ask what you can do for your country." True, he left a legacy to his successor of eighty-seven bills unsigned, but such domestic politics is swallowed up in the image of the world figure who faced up to the shrewd Khrushchev. After he spoke in the square outside the Schoneberg City Hall in Berlin, declaring "as a free man, *Ich bin ein Berliner*," one German official is reported to have said that Hitler at the peak of his popularity and power had not attracted a crowd so large and warmly emotional. Now Camelot had returned to legend.

I recall ordering that the great bell of the church be tolled at ten-second intervals and that the doors of the church be thrown open. Folk came in, not many, in ones and twos, slowly, silently. I remained there throughout the whole day and evening. Few spoke to me, and when they did, all we could do was to embrace. I read from the Psalms and for some reason browsed through E. L. Mascall's *Secularisation of Christianity*.

Jerry joined me about eleven. We sat together until midnight. When the tolling ceased, we went out into the dark, mild evening, walking towards the White House, stark in the white glare of great arch lamps positioned in Lafayette Square, transforming the fountain on the front lawn into a strange, eerie, chilling spray. On the sidewalks stood little groups, quite silent, just watching. Automobiles moved along the Avenue slowly, in a whisper of sound. Police stood of the ready along the curb. A strange awesome silence reigned — the sort I had not experienced since hearing the all clear after an air raid. We went back for our car, parked in the Capitol garage, and drove northwest to Bethesda Naval Hospital, where the body of the stricken President now lay in one of the many lighted rooms of the towering building. The hospital entrance was ablaze with floodlights. Guards closely questioned everyone who drew up to their booth. Wisconsin Avenue was lined with parked cars. We turned around and came home.

The White House, the scene of pomp and power for most of the nation's history, had suddenly become like any other home of mourning — an empty rocking chair, a pair of slippers by the hearth, a walking stick in the hall stand, a large desk suddenly lonely.

I never had the honor of meeting President Kennedy. The week previous to his visit to Dallas, he had entertained members of the St. Andrews Society, complete with massed pipe band, on the White House lawn. Jerry and Mairi had stood quite close to him as he mingled happily with the very Scottish crowd. But I was at home, meeting deadlines again, finishing off some little article for our congregational magazine, *New York Avenews*. "If only I had known" — it's the saddest of phrases.

14

This Was Selma

At times history and fate meet in a single time in a single place to shape the turning point in man's unending search for freedom. So it was at Lexington and Concord. So it was a century ago at Appomattox. So it was last week at Selma, Alabama.

—President Johnson, introducing the Voting Rights Act to a ioint session of Congress, March 15, 1965

THE JANUARY 1965 meeting of the Washington City Presbytery included among its many announcements about area church meetings, special committees and gatherings, and other ecclesiastical events of dubious importance an invitation from the Southern Christian Leadership Conference signed by Dr. Martin Luther King, Jr., to ministers and laymen to join a voter registration drive planned for Selma, Alabama.

Later that evening, relaxing over our usual bedtime cup of tea and toast, Jerry suddenly burst out, "George, I've decided to go to Selma in response to that appeal. Thelma Odom and I have been on the phone discussing the matter. I'm getting a bit wearied talking about integration and civil rights and hearing about all those committees and task forces that are being set up to have 'dialogues' with the black community. It's time we did something about it. I believe Selma is it. Come, dear; let us go down together."

I became immediately defensive.

"Selma? Alabama? Have you forgotten that next week the annual congregational meeting takes place? I've got to remain here. You know this meeting is crucial for our witness to the inner city. There is going to be a lot of discussion about budget for inner-city work. They think I'm too much involved already, too active in civil rights."

"Well, my mind is made up. Thelma and I are going."

Two days later, I found myself driving these two very improbable soul sisters to the airport. I lingered awhile watching their plane take off into the grey wintry skies and felt a cold loneliness within me. It was more than the usual emptiness we felt at partings. I was concerned. There could be danger for both of them. I turned on my heel homeward, still trying to justify my staying back at such a time.

A crisis of mission was growing within my congregation. Starry-eyed liberals, mostly young people, were beginning to feel I was dragging my feet, failing to make a definite commitment to the social involvement of the congregation. Established members felt I was going too far. They longed for the return of those days in the fifties when we had been enjoying large congregations drawn from all over the metropolitan area and the hundreds of visitors each Sunday from across the nation. Attendance was dwindling; membership was, by attrition, falling off; budget demands were rising. Preaching on the basic themes of the gospel — without social involvement — was what the orthodox members wanted. Hints of unhappiness were reaching me from close friends.

Now alone, my wife somewhere in the deep South, I sat idly watching television until after midnight without really hearing or seeing the program. The telephone bell roused me out of my reverie. It was the well-kent voice.

"Oh, George, I do wish you were here in Selma. Thelma and I have been enthralled by a meeting in Mrs. Boynton's house. Dr. King is here. And Ralph Abernathy and Andy Young and James Bevel. They are all marvelous. So calm and balanced in their discussions. This is the first meeting of the Selma Voter Registration Committee. They are unanimous about the boycott action to be taken. What courage! The upper room in Jerusalem on the day of Pentecost must have been like this. Thelma and I have signed up. We'll be here for I don't know how long. My dear, this is the most wonderful experience I have ever known in the life of the church. You simply must come down."

The story Jerry told me on her return ten days later, stunned me. Out of some 15,000 eligible black voters in Selma, only about 346 had managed somehow to be registered, most of them sponsored by Emelia Boynton. Barriers of every kind had been raised against the voting rights of the black community. There was the poll tax, a heavy enough burden, but one that could be met. More invidious was a sophisticated literacy test. (Later when federal registrars took over the task, it was found that some of the state registrars themselves failed the test!) There was the "grandfather clause" requiring each eligible voter to name both paternal and maternal grandparents, where they were born, and dates of birth. After these questions had been satisfactorily answered, the applicants' names were included in a list read out on the first and third Monday afternoon of each month at the main entrance to the Dallas County Courthouse in downtown Selma. If the voter was not present, his name was relegated to the bottom of the list. When a black asked permission of his employer for time off to go down to the courthouse, as often as not he was met with the callous response, "Now nigger, don't you go getting mixed up in all this politics business — that is, if you want to keep your job here."

On Sunday evening, Jerry and Thelma were present at Brown Memorial African Methodist Chapel to hear Dr. King launch the march for the following day to the courthouse.

"At the rate they are letting us register now," boomed Dr. King amidst a crescendo of response from the crowded congregation, "it will take us a hundred and three years to register all of the fifteen thousand Negroes in Dallas County who are qualified to vote."

THAT'S RIGHT! THAT'S RIGHT! SPEAK!

"We don't have to wait that long."

THAT'S RIGHT! THAT'S RIGHT!

"Today marks the beginning of a determined mobilized campaign to get the right to vote everywhere in Alabama. If we are refused, we will appeal to the Governor, George Wallace. If he refuses to listen, we will appeal to the legislature. If they can't listen, we will appeal to the conscience of the Congress in another dramatic march on Washington. We must be ready to march."

THAT'S RIGHT!

"We must be willing to go to jail in thousands."

THAT'S RIGHT!

"Our cry to the state of Alabama is 'Give us the ballot!' When we get our right to vote, we will send to the State House not men who will stand in the doorways of universities to keep Negroes out, but men who will uphold the cause of justice.

"Give us the ballot!"

THAT'S RIGHT!

"We are not on our knees begging for the ballot. We are demanding the ballot."

The congregation were on their feet cheering and singing and clapping their hands.

On the following day, Monday, the first march to the green-mottled marble structure of the Dallas County Courthouse took place. Jerry, the only white woman present, was chosen to walk by the side of Dr. King as they left Brown's Chapel. She kept noticing two black youths keeping very close to her who seemed to be regarding her with a rather watchful eye, one of them a massive lad, James Orange. She noted also that when the white citizens lining the sidewalks called out unprintable epithets, foreign to the ears of the douce wife of a minister, about "that white woman," the two lads moved over between her and the protesters. She began to realize they had been delegated as her bodyguards.

When the procession of some three hundred arrived at the courthouse, they were confronted by Sheriff Jim Clark and a large posse of helmeted police, batons in hand, forming a circle around the entrance. Clark appeared to be deep in conversation with Police Chief Baker. The procession stopped. Dr. King approached the sheriff and made known his business: these folks had come to register to vote. There was more talk with Baker.

Then Sheriff Clark came over to Jerry.

"And what's a white woman doin' in this crowd? You ain't come here to vote, are you? Eh?"

Silence! Jerry was sure everyone could hear her heart beating. Clark drew nearer to her, his baton in his right hand. He placed his left hand under Jerry's nose and suddenly brought the baton down with a thump into his upturned hand, missing her nose by about one inch. He repeated the charade several times. Meanwhile, Jerry stood her ground silently. She had remembered well the lessons of nonviolence that had been discussed before the march: do not speak; never move; never push, lest it be interpreted as an assault.

I was listening to this tale with mingled fear and anger. I realized then that I could never have responded to such a situation as passively as Dr. King had so consistently done in his own lifetime.

"What happened?" I blurted out.

"Well, I just looked him in the eye. And I remembered the Scottish missionary, wee Mary Slessor, and how she had withstood the big African tribal chiefs, who called her "The Great White Ma," lecturing them as if they were first-grade children. That gave me courage. I think Clark realized I was outstaring him, for he suddenly stopped, and with a rather sheepish scowl moved back to Baker."

Jerry and Thelma then decided to test the civil rights legislation that had been passed by Congress several months before. The proprietors of Selma's cafes and inns and hotels had largely ignored the public accommodations section of the bill. This was also being tested by the King strategy. They entered the Silver Moon Cafe in Franklin Street and ordered coffee. Jerry was aware of loutish stares around her and disdain on the faces of several ladies who evidently frequented the place. A surly waitress served them. As she received the check, Jerry asked, "Is there a ladies' room?"

"White or black?"

"Black."

She was led through a dark passageway at the back of the cafe to what Jerry presumed were toilet facilities of the black kitchen staff, a foul-smelling place, its concrete floor awash with stale water. After what she described as a "reasonable interval," Jerry flushed the toilet, and with head in the air marched with Thelma out into the morning sunshine. At the doorway they lingered a moment talking. This was the spot where later a white minister was to be mortally clubbed to the ground.

Terror and rage and indignation were now possessing me.

"Never again will you go back to Selma without me," I said.

However, it was one thing to "make a witness" to the needs of the black community from the safe pulpit of a downtown church in the nation's capital, preaching fiery sermons about integration, visiting the homes of the black community, and periodically on Sunday afternoons preaching in their pathetic little storefront churches. This was to be expected of any white minister in those days who wished to appear "relevant." On the other hand, to travel to Alabama, to embark on protest marches, perhaps to clash with the police, and generally to be regarded as somewhat fanatical by one's colleagues and by some of the members of one's congregation — this was quite another matter. (Looking back, however, I am not aware of ever having flinched at anticipating violence; and while spending time in jail did not appeal to me, having visited on at least one occasion the drunk tank of Washington's First Precinct jail, the possibility did not really daunt me.)

The crucial struggle lay within, in the deeps of my soul, where I was aware of an aching tension between a token witness that would preserve my position and safeguard the institution of the Church, and a complete identification with the righteous fight for social justice upon which the black community had embarked that day in 1958 when Mama Rosa Parks had protested her being shuttled to the back of the bus in Montgomery, Alabama.

The remembrance of that significant meeting with Bayard Rustin came back to haunt me from what now seemed to be so very long ago, when I first visited the Cornell University Campus in 1949, a young Scots preacher let loose on a preaching vacation. I recalled Bayard sitting with me in his room in the men's dorm, captivating me long into the night with tales of his experiences as a young man in the chain gangs in the South. I listened, at times awed, as he quietly unfolded the tale of unbridled cruelty perpetrated by vicious white guards upon hapless black convicts, cursing the bridled chain gangs working along the roadways and in the fields. He painted pictures of the overcrowded cells rank with the smell of human excreta, told of the disappearences of friends he would never again see, and evoked the cowed sullen silence of almost beaten manhood. What in heaven's name has been generated in the psyche of the white race against their brothers whose skin is a different pigmentation; what lies behind this sadistic cruelty?

I recalled that shortly after Dr. King delivered the "I Have a Dream" speech to a multitude in front of the Lincoln Memorial in 1963, I had invited James Bevel of Dr. King's staff to meet with a group of ministers in my study at the church. He outlined for us the strategy and tactics of the Southern Christian Leadership Conference, emphasizing that the choice was between either the nonviolence of Dr. King or bloody revolution brought about by the Black Muslims.

During the question period, one of my colleagues asked, "Mr. Bevel, could you please tell us preachers the relevance this social revolt, these protest marches, have to the gospel?"

"Relevance! Relevance!" Bevel's eyes began to flame as his voice rose. "I'll tell you the relevance. You whites have been treating my people in the same manner as the authorities of his day chastised St. Paul. He was hounded, he was stoned, beaten with rods, thrashed with the lash, and thrown into jail where they forcibly poured a cathartic down his gullet until he excreted all over the floor of his cell. And when that happened, he scooped up the shit in his hands and scrawled it over the walls, writing 'though I speak with the tongues of men and of angels and have not love, I am a sounding brass. . . .' Until you white preachers realize that this lovely Elizabethan-sounding prose was written not only at the cost of blood but with the shit of imprisonment, you will not begin to see the relevance of the gospel to my people who are being bludgeoned as they struggle to realize their divine calling as children of God, let alone their constitutional rights as American citizens which have been denied them since 1776."

On February 21, 1965, two weeks after Jerry had returned from Selma, we boarded a plane after Sunday morning service to go back there together. As the plane roared south over the Potomac, I felt that I had finally crossed my Rubicon! My perennial conflict between preserving peace within the institution of the church and getting involved in political and social affairs was at last resolved. My course became as clear as the blue sky around us and the glittering winter sunshine on the cumulus clouds below. I still believed that the institutional church must always be witness to Christ, and that organization is important. I realized my trip would be an offense to many of my members, especially those from the South, of whose personal history I was still lamentably ignorant. I was taking a risk. Some did reduce their church pledges as an economic sanction against my visit; others left the church. I no longer seemed to care. Once more I was the happy student of my Glasgow days, taking to the streetcorners to preach the gospel.

I went to Selma at the Lord's bidding, and it was indeed a wondrous trip! If it meant the end of my New York Avenue ministry, so be it! I was now convinced that if I did not go to Selma, I could no longer face my people Sunday by Sunday with unsullied conscience. "Consensus," so dear to the heart of Lyndon Johnson, may be the lifeblood of politics, "the art of the possible," but it has no place in decisions of the soul. I was seeing anew into the heart of John Masefield's sinner to whom the "Everlasting Mercy" was revealed:

> O the glory of the lighted mind.
> How dead I'd been, how dumb, how blind!
> The station brook to my new eyes,

Was babbling out of paradise;
The waters rushing from the rain,
Were singing Christ the Lord has risen again.

At the Montgomery Airport we were met by two youths from Selma's Student Nonviolent Coordinating Committee (SNCC). "I'm George Baker," said a lad, no doubt recognizing my clerical collar. "And this is Willie Loman. Welcome to Montgomery. Let me have your bag. We've still got over fifty miles to go to Selma. My car is outside."

We noticed as he bent down to lift the bags that there was a bald patch at the back of his head showing two painful red weals.

"What about a snack first? I'm rather peckish."

We entered a federally operated airport restaurant. A minister is always aware of welcoming smiles when, wearing a clerical collar, he enters any public place. To my surprise I was receiving uncharacteristic scowls and blank looks. The waitress seemed to be pouting about something. Perhaps we had committed some unknown indiscretion?

"What's the trouble, George? It would seem that Dracula had just entered the restaurant."

"It's Willie. They don't like colored folk in their restaurant."

"But it's a federal restaurant," I protested.

"Doesn't mean a thing."

I did not pursue the matter. I looked across at Willie; he was sitting head bowed in an embarrassed silence.

Soon we were heading south again through the chill dark night down undulating Highway 80 and over the rolling lands of Lowndes County where the road narrows to two lanes. After about an hour we saw the glow on the horizon of the lights of Selma and were soon racing along a four-lane highway, up and across the modern Edmund Pettus Bridge that spans the Alabama River, and into Broad Street, still neon-lighted despite the Sabbath day, but deserted of people. We turned off into an anonymous dark street lit by bleak flickering gas lamps, bumped over the railroad tracks, and slowed down along an unpaved ghostly street pierced by shafts of light gleaming through the partially closed curtains of elevated wooden shack-houses, pulling to a stop before a brightly lit bungalow that seemed out of place in such sordid surroundings.

An open door flashed its welcoming light upon us. Jerry was soon enveloped in the embrace and cuddle of a laughing, shouting woman waving her arms and talking in a brogue beyond my comprehension.

"I'm her husband," I ventured after this initial wrestling bout.

"I'm Emelia Boynton. Any friend of Mrs. Docherty is welcome, and her husband sure is doubly welcome! Do come in and meet our young friends."

The room was alive with young people crowded into chairs and lounging on the floor; it seemed a dozen conversations were going on at once.

"This is our committee of fifteen and other friends. They are just breaking up. Been talking all night. Too much talk sometimes, I say."

I had time to look around a beautiful modernly furnished house. We were led into our bedroom.

"It's my own bedroom," Mrs. Boynton announced. "Nothing too good for the preacher and his wife."

There was a portable television and radio, expensive curtains, and furniture of modern design. We felt beneath our feet a thick carpet. Big business at least did not believe in segregation, except perhaps the real estate business, which had forced this successful businesswoman, because of a closed housing policy, to live on this unpaved street in an aging bungalow, with off-plumb walls, no doubt long ago the dwelling of a white family.

As usual, I was to forget names immediately as we shook the hands of this group of young people, half of whom were black. As they were making their exeunt, I stood listening to some background music; a male voice accompanied by guitar and mouth organ was wailing out a refrain, "The answer, my friend, is blowing in the wind."

A pale-faced lad with a patient smile came over to me, his hand extended in greeting. He introduced himself as Chuck Fager, another of Mrs. Boynton's overnight houseguests. He had classical features and spoke slowly and deliberately. He told me he was with SNCC and that he had been in Selma for about two years working in the library of Selma University (black) indexing and building a more adequate collection for the students. He had been receiving books from all over the country. For this he was paid at the weekly rate of $25. He had quit college to work for the movement.

"Who's the singer?" I asked, indicating the gramophone.

"Bob Dylan."

"Never heard of him. Dylan Thomas, yes, but who is Bob Dylan?"

"Ah," said Chuck slowly and patiently and with a twinkle in his eye as he looked at my clerical collar, "he's the theologian of the movement. Theology-in-folk-music. So much simpler than Thomas Aquinas. Take this song, 'Blowin' in the Wind.' Listen to it and you will perceive what St. John meant when he wrote 'The wind bloweth where it listeth, and thou hearest the sound thereof.' "

By this time we were in a corner together. Jerry and the other women were talking and laughing like women returned home on market day.

"Tell me what's happening down here, Chuck."

"Our strategy, adopted by SNCC, is to divide the city up into wards. Once established by us, they elect their own chairmen. From then on, they are on their own. The people discuss the problems for the blacks voting in Selma. They are becoming aware of what voting means and have learned neither to fear it nor to stand back from it, though many are still afraid of reprisals if they become too much involved in politics. Briefed and educated by this simple organization, the people are prepared to hear any call to action that comes from Dr. King and the movement."

"Who are these students?"

"None is a member of any church, except perhaps Tom over there, who is Presbyterian."

As he spoke, I was wondering where all my own brave young Christians, brought up through Sunday School, were. No doubt in college chasing after a degree and a good job, looking to become members of the white Anglo-Saxon Protestant elite.

"You must be tired," said my hostess, Mrs. Boynton, laying a hand on my arm. She was most perceptive.

Selma is a pleasant market and manufacturing town of some forty thousand inhabitants on the banks of the Alabama River. Once known as Moore's Bluff or Landing, its name was changed when it was incorporated in 1820 by William Rufus de Vane King. The name "Selma" appears in Ossian's Gaelic songs; there must have been some Scottish connection. Chuck Fager showed us around the town in Mrs. Boynton's car. We visited Brown's African Methodist Episcopal Church, where Jerry had first heard Dr. King speak at the launching of the Voter Registration Drive, a garish red brick structure bordered with white bricks, its twin tin-covered steeples reminding one of the onion domes of the Orthodox Church.

I had wanted to meet the minister of the First Presbyterian Church and was cordially welcomed by him in his study, where he shared his concerns. Our registration drive had his wholehearted support, but he had to live with a session that had raised a storm when some black members had attended church at his invitation. His was a tale of a ministry persecuted not by a repressive state but by his own membership. He told of a fraternity of ministers that had tried to pray and think through some kind of strategy to deal with segregated churches. When the officers of the different denominations learned of these meetings, they clamped down on them. A young Methodist, for instance, who had been vocal in his protest, was suddenly sent to a mission station in Africa by his presiding bishop; he was told that he would have ample opportunity to meet with blacks there.

We visited the parish house of Father McCrawley, a gentle cleric who was lending such support as he could to the drive short of taking part in processions. This his Bishop forbade. He took us to see his newly constructed million-dollar R. C. Hospital for Negroes and its annex for the aged.

Broad Street was an attractive busy thoroughfare thronged with folk who came in from the neighboring counties of Lowndes and Wilcox. But another sight met us once we crossed the railroad tracks and bumped through the dust of the unkempt dirt roads of the black community, past rows of unpainted wooden shacks with rusting corrugated tin roofs, standing precariously on foundations of brick pillars. The streets echoed with the happy voices of children at play who ran alongside our slow-moving car, waving and smiling to us; on recognizing Chuck, they shouted and laughed. Men and women, old before their years, sat quietly swaying in rockers on the wooden porches or squatted on the wooden steps of their homes. Lines on suffering faces creased into smiles as they waved to us. As we left the city beyond the railroad station, we drew near to the town dump, its acrid yellow flames dissolving into a black column of smoke in the still air, standing sentinel against the blue sky. Next to it stood the black cemetery, sprinkled with white headstones and wooden crosses, simple folk who had seen their day, now at last beyond life's humiliations, its "heartbreak in the heart of things" and "life's immemorial pain." The tragic irony did not escape me: The city fathers had placed their garbage dump beside the final resting place of those they had referred to as "colored trash."

The main topic of conversation when we arrived in Selma had been the shooting of Jimmie Lee Jackson at Marion in Wilcox County, some thirty miles away. The lad was now lying critically ill in the Good Samaritan Hospital in Selma.

Chuck Fager, with his reporter's eye, wrote up what happened the Thursday night before we arrived:

James Orange, Jerry's bodyguard, was arrested in Marion for "contributing to the delinquency of minors." In fact, he had been heading up a drive in Perry County to get the people and the school children to march in support of the registration drive. A deputation under the leadership of the Reverend C. T. Vivian, who had just been released from Selma prison, went to Marion to speak from the pulpit of the Zion Methodist Church. The plan was to walk out of the church the hundred yards or so to the jail, kneel and pray for James, and thereafter to return to the church. When the congregation, led by the preachers, came out of the door, they found the sidewalk lined with helmeted state troopers, long billy clubs at the ready.

"This is an unlawful assembly," the police chief announced over a public address system. "You are hereby ordered to disperse. Either you go home or go back to the church."

"Just then the street lights around the square went out," wrote Fager, "and troopers began clubbing the Reverend James Dobynes, a black preacher in the front line. The panicking crowd tried to get back into the church, but the doors were already jammed by people spilling out of it. They scattered, taking cover wherever they could. The troopers came after them with clubs, splitting scalps and smashing ribs as they advanced. Two or three dozen rushed through the doors of Mack's Cafe nearby, seeking refuge in its crowded dark interior. Among them were Jimmie Lee Jackson, a young man of twenty-six, his mother Viola and his grandfather, Cager, who was eighty-two years old. The old man had been caught and beaten behind the church and was bleeding from the head. His grandson was helping him out of the door of the cafe to go for medical assistance when a squad of troopers came toward them, chasing and beating people before them and forcing the two men back into the cafe. When one of them hit Viola Jackson and knocked her screaming to the floor, her son, Jimmie, lunged at him. The trooper struck him across the face, and young Jackson went careening onto the floor himself. Then a trooper picked him up and slammed him against a cigarette machine while another trooper named Fowler drew his pistol and calmly shot Jackson at point blank range in the stomach."

The bullet passed through his body and embedded itself in the wood-paneled wall of the cafe. Later, when an inquiry was made, it was found that the bullet hole had been judiciously covered over.

N.B.C.'s Richard Valeriani had been clubbed along with the others in front of the Zion Church. From his hospital bed in Selma that Friday, while still dazed from shock and sedation, he broadcast to millions of television viewers, thus dramatically bringing home what was happening in the South. People saw with their own eyes the violence that was being perpetrated by the police.

On Monday morning, the day after we arrived, an angry protest meeting was being held in Selma at Brown's Chapel. Dr. King came straight to it from the hospital bedside of the stricken Jimmie Lee Jackson, where he had said prayers for his recovery. It was my first meeting with him. He approached Jerry with a diffident, shy, yet warm smile, and, taking both her hands in his, he said to me, "You should be proud of your wife. She showed great courage in coming here. We shall not readily forget her calm before the intimidation of the police. She is a symbol to our people that we are not alone in this struggle for social justice."

Every night that week we would fill Brown's Chapel for worship. Here I was to listen to preaching, eloquent and passionate, from country pastors who had never even heard of Rudolph Bultmann and were quite unaware of Wellhausen's theory of the Pentateuch. Extempore prayers, written in the heart, rang out like Gregorian chants. The wail of the hymns echoed the cry of the solitary soul whose only hope was the new heaven and the new earth the Christ would bring. I was impressed with the similarity between their songs and the no less poignant melodies of the Scottish bagpipe pibroch, grace notes and all. Perfect love had indeed cast out fear. The resolve to protest and march, to be hauled off unresistingly to jail, to be beaten up and come back for more, had its birth in this chapel in a dynamic Christian faith. The preacher was a latter-day Moses leading his flock out of a new Egyptian slavery to the Promised Land of freedom, and freedom *now*. Brown's Chapel was their Calvary, where they watched once more their crucified Lord, bearing in his body their sufferings.

They applauded Jerry when she rose to pledge our solidarity with their cause. They received my inadequate words with undue respect, responding with heart-warming Amens when I made a point that had a scriptural basis. For Jerry and me this house of prayer and preaching became none other than the gate of heaven. Here we were to learn for the first time the song that was to become the battle cry of the black community. Now many years later, I cannot listen to it without recalling those remarkable Christians standing together, heads high, hands interlocked, swaying from side to side like a wheatfield before a gentle harvest breeze.

> We shall overcome, we shall overcome,
> We shall overcome some day,
> Deep in my heart I do believe
> We shall overcome some day
> We are not afraid . . .
> God is on our side . . .
> We shall overcome some day.

These meetings also provided the occasion to learn of community plans for the following days — of marches and gathering places, of the addresses of ward chairmen in which detailed instruction concerning filling out the voter registration forms was to be made available.

Prior to the evening services at Brown's Chapel, Jerry and I visited several ward meetings in Selma, usually held in the halls of black churches. On one occasion we arrived in time to share some of the problems that arose because of a boycott the black community had launched against the town. Mini-buses had been acquired to take the people to work. But what happened to the bus that did not turn up that morning at 7:30 to take the group of workers to the Craig Air Force Base? The boycott of shops owned by whites raised further complications. Suppose the black druggist did not have a prescription in the case of serious illness? What happened when the black butcher ran out of beef? James Bevel sat silently through these long discussions then rose to his feet and said quietly, "Now brothers and sisters, this year we want no unnecessary spending. Is it too much to ask you to give up your new spring bonnet for him who gave his life for us at Easter? If the butcher runs out of steak, buy hamburgers. If there's no hamburger, we'll buy corn and beans. We survived the Depression on chittlins; we can survive again. You remember the Depression? We were hungry then, but we got through, and we're gonna get through again."

Monday had been declared Freedom Day. My first assignment was to accompany Dr. King on a tour through Lowndes County, where not one black voter had been able to register, and where 120 percent of the white population was on the rolls, many long at rest in the kirkyard, others having left the county years before.

At Haynesville, twelve brave blacks, the first in sixty years, had endeavored to register at the courthouse. They were contemptuously turned back and directed to the local jail two miles away. They trudged through the heavy spring rains only to discover the jail barred against them, at least for registration purposes. They had retraced their steps and were still huddled around the courthouse when our group arrived. Dr. King asked the Registrar, Carl Golson, to explain the situation to him. He was a pot-bellied loud-mouthed man who told Dr. King in a sneering voice to go home to his own backyard, that we had no right to be here at all since we were not residents in the county. I was to see, and not for the last time, an example of the quiet patience of Dr. King. He responded calmly to the bluster, following up one probing question with another. At length he asked the Registrar if he were a Christian.

"Yes, I am. I'm a Methodist, but what has Christianity got to do with voter registration?"

By the time we arrived in Camden, the rain was torrential. A group of black folk clustered together on the steps of a disused, decrepit schoolhouse, where registration was taking place at the rate of five per hour; whites, meanwhile, were registering without delay within the warm shelter of the red brick courthouse. Some fifty state troopers were on hand when we arrived, their blue helmets glistening in the rain, their batons at the ready, looking on in sullen silence, just waiting, in the muddy rain that cascaded down the unpaved street.

Sheltered on the leaking porch of the schoolhouse, I stood beside Dr. King, looking out at the group now grown to a crowd, as news of his presence made the rounds of the houses. I scanned their upturned eager faces shining in the rain, old faces like ancient oaks, young faces smooth and handsome, strong faces lined with toil, like the calloused hands I had shaken.

"Brothers and sisters," Dr. King began, "I am here to announce to you that you are going to get the vote. We are here and we're going to stay here, even if it takes years. You are going to get the vote. We are on the march to the Promised Land through the ballot box, and we are going to reach that Promised Land even if we have to go all the way to Washington to do so. I'm here to lead you all the way, as Moses of old, lead you through this desert of a voteless community to a land of freedom where every man shall sit free under his own fig tree. What do you want?"

"Freedom! Freedom! Freedom!"

"When do you want it?"

"Now! Now! Now!"

"Brothers and sisters, I have a friend with me today who has come all the way from Washington to be with you. He is a Presbyterian preacher, and I am not unmindful that it was his denomination years ago that set up a fine college here in Camden. He preaches in the church where Abraham Lincoln worshiped."

I came forward to cheers and shouts. Above me, I could hear the rain drill on the corrugated roof. I found myself quite speechless. I was glad of the rain at that moment; it washed away the tears streaming down my cheeks. "My dear people, there seems so little I can offer you. But I do offer you our love and such support as we are able to give. My wife and I are here, glad to be here, to show that we are one with you in your cause. We will be returning soon to Washington. I want you to remember that in that big city a minister and his wife are praying for you. One promise I make; it was made once before by a greater than I, Mr. Lincoln himself. He said of slavery, 'I shall hit this thing hard.' I shall preach in season and out to any who will hear me across the land about the injustices you are enduring, and I shall work in whatever way I can to make this land a place of true freedom for all of us."

A grey gloaming was settling in as we drove away through the slanting rain. I tried to keep that promise. I shelved the lectionary sermons I had prepared to preach during that Lenten season when I visited other churches for special services. If spared to see around me my grandchildren, I would be able to tell them that I once stood beside Martin Luther King on the rickety porch of a schoolhouse in Camden, and that Moses before the burning bush was no more certain of the presence of the living God than I was when I looked into the faces of his people there; when I walked in their protest marches, I knew I was marching with the army of the Lord.

During our meeting at Brown's Chapel Thursday night, news reached us that Jimmie Lee Jackson was dead. The following Sunday a memorial service was held at Zion Methodist Church in Wilcox County near Mack's Cafe, where he had been stricken. Jerry and I attended the service. As we walked across the square towards the little building, the paint peeling from its clapboard sides, we became aware of a group of policemen gathered together in conversation. One of them took out a camera and photographed us. Now our faces would be included among the "mugs" of wanted crooks. We were suspects, caught in the act of going to church, by a gestapo police!

The Reverend James Bevel, a slight man with a shaven head like a brown egg, gentle in manner and quiet of speech until he preaches, when there arises within him a controlled passion I have seldom heard from any man, led the service. He chose as his text Acts 12:2−3: "And he [Herod] killed James the brother of John with the sword. And because he saw that it pleased the Jews, he proceeded further to take Peter also."

"I'm not worried about James," Bevel cried out. "I'm worried about Peter. James has found release from the intolerable indignity of being a black. James is no longer to be cowed and coerced and humiliated and beaten. James has broken out of this life of pain to glory everlasting. I'm not worried about James, I'm worried about Peter, who is still being humiliated and cowed and beaten and threatened."

He then turned to his second text, Esther 4:8:

> And [Mordecai] gave to [Hatach] a copy of the writing of the decree that was given at Shushan to destroy the Jews, and to shew it unto Esther, and to declare it unto her, and to charge her to go unto the king, to make supplication unto him, and to make request before him for her people.

"Today it is the black people of Alabama that are being destroyed. And I'll tell you this! The price of Negroes is going up! The last preacher has been hounded out of Wilcox County. The destruction of the black people of Alabama must be challenged. We shall go to the Governor George Wallace in his palace in Montgomery, and we shall make intercession for our cause. We shall not falter, like Esther did. We shall march to Montgomery!"

We came out of church into the peace of a lovely Sabbath. It was difficult to imagine there had been such violence here only a few days before. Police were still watching us warily as we drove off to visit the grieving mother of Jimmie Lee Jackson and her father, Cager. They came out of their house to meet us. The old man was slightly built and shrunken, his lined face like dried leather, his toothless mouth sunken, but his eyes bright. His mouth creased into a radiant smile as we shook hands. Yes, it was true, the police had beaten his head and kicked him in the groin. He spoke to me with a voice that had no trace of bitterness. "I pray for my enemies, as the Lord bids me. I pray that they may behave themselves."

Mrs. Jackson asked us to stay for Sunday dinner. I could see the large purple swelling above her left eye. She led us along a weed-lined pathway to her home, a tarpaper tin-roofed shack with a rickety weather-beaten wooden porch. It was a happy company that sat down to an ample helping of chicken and grits and corn and sweet potatoes. Three or four relatives had joined us to pay respects. I looked through drawn white curtains out onto the Jackson farmstead, no more than a clearing of marginal scrubland over which the old man had moiled twenty years. Several wooden shacks dotted the ground, one balanced precariously on four subsiding brick foundations, that housed about a dozen chickens and two unselfconscious strutting turkeys. Against the rising ground, the red soil showing bare through the scraggy grass, stood a skinny brindled cow (reminding me of William Russell's painting "Last of the 5000") and two calves, one pushing its nose at its mother's shrunken udder. In the Sabbath silence, I felt the Master weeping over this holy poverty.

At Brown's Chapel the following morning it was announced that on Sunday, March 7, there would be a march to Montgomery to lay before Governor George Wallace the grievances of the black community and a demand to end Alabama's invidious unconstitutional system of voter registration. But my visit had to come to an end. I had a congregation to look after in Washington. I flew home on Wednesday morning. That afternoon Jerry traveled in Dr. King's car to the funeral of Jimmie Lee Jackson. A grey day of torrential springtime rains fitted the bleak mood of sorrow. At Marion a funeral service was held at the tragic little Zion Chapel. The minister prayed for the police who would rather see blood in the streets and a man shot down than sit and talk things out. Before a sobbing congregation, Dr. King asked who had killed Jimmie Lee Jackson.

"Jimmie Lee Jackson was the victim of the brutality of sheriffs, the irresponsibility of governors, the timidity of the federal government, and cowardice of every Negro who passively accepts the evils of segregation. Jimmie Lee Jackson's death reminds us again that we must work passionately and unrelentingly to make the American dream a reality. His death must prove that unmerited suffering does not go unredeemed. We must not be bitter and we must not harbor ideas of retaliating with violence. We must not lose faith in our white brothers."

Night was closing in as the line of cars drove through the rain to Heard Cemetery by the side of the highway, no more than a clearing in the pine woods where Jimmie Lee Jackson had eked out a living as a pulpwood cutter. Jerry was the only white woman present. In the darkness, she returned to Selma to spend yet another evening in the warm light of Mrs. Boynton's comfortable home, where they tired the night talking about the tragic events of these days. Next day Jerry returned to her own home.

"This Was Selma" was the title of my sermon on that fateful 7th of March. I felt free as never before to speak. I must have let myself go, for a surge of emotion swept across the congregation as I poured out my pent-up indignation about the plight of the black community. During pauses I could hear some women moan; many were weeping.

"Where is God in all this suffering and injustice? And how long must this kind of injustice be permitted? There will be no second flood as in the days of Noah. Nor will we see in our time the Fire. What I see is the Christ turning on his heel from the white churches, shaking the red dust of Alabama from his shoes, and finding a true home of faith among the minor-chord melodies of the Negro spirituals and the eloquence of their preachers and the music of their prayers. To us whites, he turns for a while and weeps, as he wept over Jerusalem so long ago, crying "Ah! Jerusalem, if only thou hadst known the things that belong to thy peace!"

That evening as we were watching television (I recall it was the movie *Judgment at Nuremburg*) the program was interrupted to announce that violence had broken out in Selma. Marchers on the Edmund Pettus Bridge had been attacked by police. The network's cameras panned a scene of smoking confusion among the steel girders of the bridge. Out of tear gas clouds emerged screaming women clutching their eyes. Horse-borne state troopers were riding into the marchers, mowing down people with long billy clubs. On the sidewalks, white citizens stood cheering as if they were at a ballgame. Along the shoulder of the bridge, black people huddled or struggled on hands and knees to avoid the vicious flailing clubs. To our horror, we saw Emelia Boynton being helped, limp and semi-conscious, along the roadside towards the city. The news broadcast filled in the details with eyewitness accounts of reporters who painted a grisly picture of mayhem. We shut off the television. Fruitlessly, we tried to contact Mrs. Boynton. By midnight the black community responded with a message from Dr. King himself, who had been dissuaded from participating in the march since violence had been anticipated.

"In the vicious maltreatment of defenseless citizens of Selma, where old women and young children were gassed and clubbed at random, we witnessed an eruption of the disease of racism which seeks to destroy all America. No American is without responsibility. The people of Selma will struggle on for the soul of the nation, but it is fitting that all Americans help bear the burden. I call therefore clergy of all faiths . . . to join me for a Ministers' March to Montgomery on Tuesday morning, March 9. . . ."

Ministers, rabbis, and priests across the country responded. Members of my own congregation were eager to participate. Special planes were scheduled. At midnight on Monday, Jerry and I boarded our plane at Dulles accompanied by my associates Jack McClendon and Robert Long.

Tuesday morning Brown's Chapel presented an amazing spectacle. Hundreds of clergy milled around the entrance, crowding the street, like an army of recruits eagerly awaiting battle orders. Some old friends were there. Strangers greeted one another as if they were lifelong friends. Of course Methodist Bishop Townley Lord was there. We had been old campaigners in the cause of civil rights in Washington.

"My dear fellow," I said to this distinguished churchman, "why is it that the only time you and I seem to meet is when we are marching in public, demonstrating against nefarious practices?"

Inside, the church was crowded to the rafters. Everyone was singing or making speeches, none of which I now recall. But I do remember the Reverend Mr. Vivian saying, "On behalf of all of us here in Selma, I welcome you gladly and with heartfelt gratitude. Your presence here is an inspiration to us. But let me issue a warning. After the violence of Sunday, we cannot hope for a peaceful march today, and we can hold out no guarantee for your safety. It is only fair and right, therefore, for me to say that if any of you would wish to withdraw now, you are at liberty to do so."

Not a soul in the hushed gathering stirred.

"Those of you who wish to march with us, please stand."

The congregation rose in a body. There were cheers from the black members.

Mr. Vivian outlined the route of the march. He counseled us on how to react to violence. On the floor of the church, a black lad demonstrated how best to minimize the blows of attackers, assuming a crouching posture, the hands covering the head and other vulnerable parts of the body.

"If attacked by tear gas, it is essential not to panic when it stings the eyes. Don't rub. Keep calm. The effects usually pass off within a few moments. When you see the cloud of gas approach, don't run away from it; walk into it. It means that the wind is carrying it over you."

Then Dr. King, who had been up all night in hourly communication with Washington, gave us his final word: "We have a constitutional right to walk the highways; we have the right to walk to Montgomery, if our feet get us there. I have no alternative but to lead a march from this place to carry our grievances to the seat of government. I have made my choice. I have got to march. I do not know what lies ahead of us there. There may be beatings, jailings, tear gas. But I would rather die on the highways of Alabama than make a butchery of my conscience."

About eight hundred clergy formed a very unmilitary line. I found myself in the front row with Dr. King, Andrew Young, Ralph Abernathy, Mrs. Paul Douglas (wife of the Senator from Illinois), Bishop Lord, and Rabbi Richard Hirsh. I was able to persuade Jerry to stay back in the procession in the safe custody of Jack McClendon.

The great serpentine line of marchers slowly moved off from Sylvan Street, where Brown's Chapel stood, turned right to Water Avenue, and moved towards the Edmund Pettus Bridge singing marching songs, "We Ain't Gonna Be Turned Around" and "We Shall Overcome." Others joined us until it seemed at least three thousand must have been on the move. State troopers were posted at strategic points along sidewalks lined with white spectators who were, in contrast, in a strangely subdued mood from that which Jerry and I had witnessed in other marches to the courthouse. Only here and there did we hear jeering or blasphemies.

At the junction of Broad Street and Water Avenue, where the bridge spans the Alabama River, the march was halted. A U.S. Marshall, H. Stanley Fountain, stepped out and read formally to Dr. King from a document. It was an order from U.S. Judge Frank M. Johnson, a highly respected jurist whose complete objectivity and integrity in all meetings pertaining to civil rights won him high respect in the county. The order stated that the Judge saw no reason why the march could not be delayed until such time as a hearing on the case could be made. There would be no irreparable harm if the plaintiffs would await a judicial determination in the matters involved.

Standing beside Dr. King, I heard his quiet reply: "Since when did I require a judicial ruling from a United States District Court judge to interpret for me the right guaranteed by the Constitution of the United States that people might peaceably assemble and petition the government for redress of grievances?"

Mr. Fountain, stepping back, replied, "I have delivered my order. I shall not interfere with this march, but I do not give you permission to proceed."

The throng continued its slow march up the incline of the bridge. When we reached the top, I looked down at a line of blue-helmeted troopers stretched across the roadway like a Roman phalanx, blocking our way. We marched on steadily without faltering. I was scared. I noted with some relief that the wind was blowing quite strongly at my back; so much for the tear gas at any rate.

When we reached a point about fifty feet from the troopers, Major John McCloud, the officer in charge, walked slowly with deliberate pace towards Dr. King, and raising a bullhorn to his lips announced, "You are ordered to stop and stand where you are. This march will not continue."

We stopped. I could hear protesting voices coming from behind. It seemed to me that we had three choices: to rush the troopers (perish the thought!); to sit down on the bridge and be hailed off to jail; or to return quietly and in order to the church.

"We would like to pray," said Dr. King. Permission was granted. Bishop Lord and Rabbi Hirsh prayed. It was my turn. I found myself looking up to the blue heavens and invoking upon the gathering the Lord's blessing. I was never able to recall that prayer, nor did Jerry. She was only too happy to hear my voice, assuring her that at least I was safe.

The procession ponderously turned around, rather deflated, and made its way back to the church. Some of the younger bloods raised shouts of protest at what seemed to them to be pitiable surrender. They were bent of charging the troopers if necessary, but reason prevailed and we soon found ourselves back on Water Avenue bound for Brown's Chapel.

Later we were to learn that Governor Collins had been flown into town in the wee sma' hours on the President's plane with a personal appeal from the President to Dr. King not to go ahead with the march. None of us were to know the truth about these all-night discussions or whether a compromise had been reached by Dr. King to make only the gesture of a march. It did seem to me that once we were faced with the physical opposition of the state troopers, there was no alternative to retreat, lest blood be spilled on the highways.

That night Jack McClendon and Jerry and I enjoyed the hospitality of a black family — the only safe place for us in town was in the homes of the black community. We talked together around the table about the events that had led up to this day. Our hostess had taken part in the previous Sunday evening march and was able to fill in details of its horror and cruelty. She herself had been chased by a frenzied policeman armed with an electric cattle prod. She was able to scramble over the retaining rail of the bridge and down the steep embankment of the river to escape. She testified that several women had been criminally assaulted in this manner.

At breakfast the radio brought more tragic news. The Reverend James Reeb, a Unitarian minister from Boston, had been attacked outside the Silver Moon Cafe in Franklin Street — the same cafe Jerry and Thelma Odom had visited. Four white men had suddenly rushed three white clergymen as they made their way along Franklin Street, beating them to the ground with flailing blows. Two of the three, the Reverends Miller and Olson, were able to scramble to safety, but Reeb was laid low, and when he finally joined his colleagues, it was obvious from his twitching reflexes and incoherent speech that he had been seriously wounded. At the University hospital it was found that he had received a massive skull fracture with possible brain damage. He died that night.

On our return to Washington, I found on my desk a letter confirming a visit to a town in the South where I had preached every Easter for thirteen years. Year by year I had looked forward to this Lenten experience and had come to know personally many of the church's officers and members. The trip entailed a week of preaching, study group meetings, gatherings in lovely homes to discuss the Bible, and sometimes afternoons of golf. The church was located downtown near a slum through which I used to motor, noting in the yards large iron kettles standing over built-up fireplaces in which water was boiled for the washing, the unpainted decrepit shacks, and crowds of children spilling over into the street at their games. I had felt it was not my place as a visiting preacher to raise the subject of integration in Lenten sermons delivered from their pulpit. Such discussions I took up at the study groups and at the house gatherings, making my position quite clear and often becoming embroiled in argument. I read once more the invitation: "The azaleas are peeking out and the dogwood is in blossom and the jonquils are raising brave heads, and now we know that the time has arrived for the Dochertys' visit."

I replied with a list of my sermon titles, two of which were "This Was Selma" and "The Wind and the Whirlwind," and a note: "I have been to the mountaintop, and I have seen clearly what I had only dimly understood on the plains. Two of my sermons will raise the issue of the plight of the black community. I think it only fair to warn you beforehand in order that you may withdraw the invitation if you feel that these sermons would be too controversial."

Back came a reply assuring me that whatever I preached would be acceptable.

Meanwhile, Washington was simmering over the news of Mr. Reeb's tragic death. One could not but contrast the emotional reaction to the death of a white preacher to that of a Jimmie Lee Jackson. The President had sent flowers to Mrs. Reeb, had spoken to her on the phone, had sent Air Force One to fly her from Boston to Selma.

President Johnson held a special press conference. Gathered around him in his oval office, representatives of the various denominations in the city sat in somber silence. Looking each clergyman in the eye, he said, "Now I want a first-hand report on what is going on. And I want you to be frank about what we ought to do in this matter."

As the long tragic story was unfolded to him, I was told by a minister who was present, the President at one point wheeled around his chair and bowed his head. It seemed to those present that he had been emotionally overcome. He stepped up the process of getting his new Voting Rights Act passed, displaying all his parliamentary skills to woo the verbose Senator Everett Dirksen and dissuade Senator Russell Long of Louisiana from staging a filibuster. Attorney General Katzenbach assured the press that the bill was on its way to being accepted by Congress. The President summoned Governor George Wallace to the White House and in a face-to-face confrontation that lasted for three hours lambasted him, spelling out the implications of the injustices being committed in Alabama. All over the nation, from Boston to St. Augustine, from New York to San Francisco, crowds gathered to pay homage to the martyred clergyman.

On Sunday morning, I preached my second sermon on the situation, "The Wind and the Whirlwind," sharing with my people the events we had experienced the previous week in Selma. "Perhaps no other organization in the land bears such responsibility for these things as the white apartheid churches," I said. "The events in Selma are the whirlwind harvest that was sown by the winds of segregated churches. . . . We are not seeing the emancipation of the Negro; long ago the Christ freed his soul. It is we who are being emancipated—from the fears that prejudice generates and the hardness of the heart that racism breeds. Alabama is not under judgment. Alabama has merely revealed the depth of my guilt. Selma has become the scapegoat for the sins of the apartheid church."

I announced at the service a special meeting of the session for Tuesday; and a special meeting of the congregation on Wednesday.

I shared my concern with Jerry. Had I broken civil law by accompanying Martin Luther King over the Edmund Pettus Bridge in defiance of a court order from Judge Johnson? It is a serious matter for anyone to break the law, but for a clergyman, it is even more reprehensible. Suppose the session voted against me; should I resign? Long ago I had learned: never resign. Let them sack you, throw you out, take whatever action they choose, but never resign—never give up the ship.

The session met in a very serious mood. I outlined the reasons for the meeting. What were they to do with their minister in view of his activities in Selma? One of my dear friends suggested that the matter might best be simply forgotten. I was about to rule him out of order when another member, a judge, broke in. "No! We must come to a decision. It is my belief that the minister, by defying the court order issued at the Edmund Pettus Bridge, is culpable not only before this ecclesiastical body, but before the civil courts. My interpretation of these events is that he broke the law in Selma."

For some three hours the debate went on with not a little distress on both sides. The vote was taken. When the tally turned out to be in my favor by a margin of twenty-four to four, the judge stated that she would submit her resignation from the session forthwith.

The following evening some three hundred members gathered in our large Peter Marshall Hall. Those of us who had traveled to Selma shared with the congregation the startling events we had witnessed. There was an understandable wave of sympathy, but I was somewhat shocked to note that the congregation was not at all surprised that their minister, a Scotsman after all, should be embroiled in such happenings. They were far more amazed to find that Jack McClendon had been involved. The difference in their reactions stemmed from the fact that they knew I had never lived in the South, whereas Jack was a native of Alabama. Jack's witness was far more significant than anything I had done.

Meanwhile, in Selma plans were announced by the black community for yet another attempted march to Montgomery on Sunday, March 21. This time Judge Johnson approved the march: "The right to demonstrate against the enormous wrongs the people had endured should be determined accordingly. The law is clear that the right to petition one's government for the redress of grievances may be exercised by large groups and by marching, even along public highways. The size of the march must, however, be reduced to no more than three hundred persons when it reaches the section of Lowndes County which is only two lanes wide."

When Alabama's Governor Wallace claimed that he could not guarantee the safety of such marchers, President Johnson pointedly reminded him that the entire Alabama National Guard was at his disposal, and stated that if the Governor defaulted in calling up the Guard, he would federalize them.

Governor Wallace did default, and President Johnson federalized the National Guard on Friday, March 19. Thus nineteen hundred men of the Alabama Guard's Dixie Division, two thousand regular army troops, and one hundred F.B.I. agents and U.S. Marshalls were made available to protect the marchers. On that Saturday morning, the inhabitants of Selma were to see the unusual spectacle of camouflaged army jeeps roaring through their streets, dropping off soldiers at strategic points. And included in the equipment of the regular troops were facilities and staff for two large field hospitals.

Millions watched the start of the Montgomery march on television, as Jerry and I did, intently, knowing every street and crossing as the marchers in their hundreds moved toward the bridge, heckled from the sidelines by whites shouting abuse and waving Confederate flags. Between them and the marchers stood the army, at attention, with fixed bayonets, in strict military formation. And as they marched, I could recall once again James Bevel's shrill voice when he had preached at Jimmie Lee Jackson's memorial service: "We shall go to the king, to his palace in Montgomery, and unlike Esther, we shall not hesitate, whatever the cost, to make intercession for our cause."

Where the four-lane highway gave place to two lanes, the marchers were reduced in number to three hundred. Up front walked Dr. King, and by his side was little "Father Abraham" as Bill Coffin loved to call Rabbi Heschel, a Hebrew prophet in a beret. A group of black marshalls made it impossible for even the press to get near.

For four days this small army marched through rain and rested through bitter cold nights, guarded all the way by the watchful eyes of the federalized troops. Overhead, helicopters swooped low over the treacherous and unknown swamplands, and small army target planes seemed at times to buzz the marchers. They camped at the roadside at sundown, resting weary limbs and soothing tired feet in tents that provided little shelter from the cold, sleeping on bivouac beds. Onward they marched, stopping only for snacks at the roadside until they reached a point about seven miles outside Montgomery at a place called the City of St. Jude—an immense church school and medical complex run by the Roman Catholic Church, with red brick church school and medical center. For the last time, after six days of marching, tents were pitched in the vast playing field, arranged in a circle. It was like a big county fair.

It was here on Saturday that Jerry and I and friends from the church met up with the march. If we were not permitted to walk the whole road, we would walk those last ten miles. It was organized chaos. Loudspeakers boomed out. People were now arriving from all over the country by the thousands. The vast area was filling up like a ballgame crowd. We waited in a drizzle for final instructions. Suddenly, I was aware of my name being announced over the loudspeaker. I was requested to come up to the front where the leaders stood ready to march. I tried to persuade Jerry to come with me, but she preferred to stay with the church deputation. The march began. The crowd was in a jubilant mood, singing and chattering as we covered the miles. Not everyone was so happy, though. I noticed a blown-up poster draping an office building wall depicting Dr. King at a study session of a community agrarian group that had been founded by Eleanor Roosevelt and Reinhold Niebuhr to instruct country folk in crafts; under-

neath the poster was printed in large letters "Dr. Martin Luther King —
Communist."

We turned a corner; before us loomed the Wren-like dome of the
statehouse. A lad jubilantly dancing and singing along with us, suddenly
cried out, "Look out, George! You just look out, George! We's acomin',
we's acomin'," and disappeared forever into the crowd.

In front of the statehouse a platform had been erected. It was estimated that twenty-five thousand people were gathered in the square. It
was reported later that the Governor had sat at his desk peeking through
the venetian blinds, greatly impressed.

I recognized among the many speakers little Mama Rosa Parks, who
had started it all back in the fifties in this same city of Montgomery when
she had refused to take the segregated seat at the back of the bus she was
traveling in after a long day's shopping.

During all this time, I seemed to have lost my wife, and found myself
wandering aimlessly through the crowds looking for her, hatless, wearing
my clerical collar, a raincoat over my arm, and growing more miserable
as the day grew damp and chilly. I remember glancing at a guardsman
standing statue-like on duty and finding him staring at me with a rather
disdainful curl on his lip. Finally I espied my wife and our party. The
ceremonies over, we made our way to the airport and were soon back
home, aware once more of the beauty of Washington, remote from the
rage and fears and the courage and joy we had witnessed on that unforgettable day. The Senate was busy jockeying to filibuster the new civil
rights legislation.

After we left Montgomery, four members of the Ku Klux Klan, on
that same Highway 90 where the road narrows to two lanes beside the
swamplands, had buzzed the car of a young married civil rights worker,
Viola Liuzzo, which was being driven by a young Negro. Careening along
the road after the car, they got alongside and shot her dead at point-blank
range, sending her car hurtling over the roadside embankment and seriously injuring the lad.

In Charleston's Magnolia Cemetery, on the graves of the Confederate
dead, are carved these lines:

> There is no holier spot of ground
> Than where defeated valor lies
> By mourning beauty crowned.

A few days later, I received a wire from the church in the South to which
I was due to return for my fourteenth year of Lenten Services telling me
that "because of lack of interest, the mission regretfully has been canceled."
The next day the telephone rang. It was the voice of Larry Crane, Assistant
Minister of the church. He was in Washington. We invited him to spend
the night with us.

I had come to know Larry Crane during previous visits to the church. Slightly built, he was a shy lad, a poet who chose his words carefully. His was a deep faith, "far ben," as we say in Scotland. He lacked the glib effervescence of so many young Protestant ministers. He saw clearly his vocation, working patiently and quietly for the kingdom. It pleased me to think that I earned the friendship of a young man whose moral courage was greatly admired by his congregation.

Larry had really made the journey to Washington specifically to explain that the mission had been canceled for quite different reasons than those stated in the cable. The sight of a hatless preacher seemingly lost in a vast crowd at Montgomery had made a good shot for the television cameras when they had little else of interest to shoot. I had been on camera at intervals all afternoon walking about with an anxious look on my face, viewed by millions across the land — including members of that southern church. A meeting had quickly been called by irate members who wanted nothing to do with a preacher who was prepared to associate himself with such a spectacle as the march on Montgomery. There had been deep feelings expressed on both sides. It seemed best for the peace of the church to cancel my visit. I was never to return.

A few weeks after Easter, the Reverend Larry Crane was interrupted in his study at the church by four red-necks who had forced an entrance. Larry put up a struggle, but was clubbed to the floor, carried out, and thrown into the back of a car. It appeared that they were taking him to the river. The car stopped for gas. Regaining consciousness, Larry was able to struggle away to safety and crawl home. He was dispatched to the hospital immediately, where he was operated on for brain damage. He died on the operating table. One member who attended the funeral service in the church reported that the building was filled to overflowing, garlanded with flowers, just like Easter Day.

The new Voting Rights Act was passed. It abolished the poll tax, the grandfather clause, and the literacy test. Some eleven thousand of Selma's blacks registered to vote. Sometime afterwards we had an overnight visit from a black minister who had been in the forefront of the registration drive.

"Ah, Dr. and Mrs. Docherty, how sad it is! All you have done for us, in vain! Why, those niggers who have the vote are just as corrupt as the whites! They are taking bribes! I'm ashamed, so ashamed! They have let us down!

"My dear brother," I said gently, "life does not progress as quickly as you would wish. But this is progress nonetheless. Before, you did not even have the freedom to cheat. I am certain the black community will learn to use that freedom for good."

In the less than twenty years since the Voting Rights Acts of 1965 was passed, the black community's vote has radically altered the balance of political power in the United States. President Carter owed his election to the solidarity of the black vote in 1976. Sixteen cities boast elected black mayors, including Washington, D.C.; Chicago; Los Angeles; Atlanta; Cleveland; and Philadelphia. As I write, the Reverend Jesse Jackson is posing a fascinating problem to the Democratic Party by publicly seeking the party's nomination for the 1984 presidential race, in hopes of becoming the first black president of the United States.

15

A Violent Society

Poverty can produce a most deadly kind of violence. In this society, violence against the poor people and minority groups is routine. I remind you that starving a child is violence; suppressing a culture is violence; neglecting school children is violence; discriminating against a working man is violence; ghetto housing is violence; contempt for equality is violence; even a lack of will power to help humanity is a sick and sinister form of violence.

—Coretta Scott King,
Solidarity Day speech, Washington, D.C.,
June 10, 1968

THE VOTING RIGHTS ACT of 1965 may have broken open the ballot box to the black community in the South, but it brought little improvement in their living conditions or social status. Inadequate housing, second-class education, and unemployment figures almost three times the national average continued to be the norm. One millionaire Alabama plantation owner with a private airstrip on his forty-thousand-acre property continued to pay cotton laborers at the rate of eighteen cents per hour. Black families continued to live in shacks, some with one lavatory to two houses. Whenever the black community tried to organize itself against such feudal conditions they were promptly threatened with unemployment.

The hot summer of 1967 witnessed ghetto uprisings not only in the South but in the North. Federal troops were sent into the smoking rubble of Detroit. When I preached at the annual Princeton Institute for Ministers I contrasted the vast sums spent on Vietnam with the beggarly budget allocated to carry out the recommendations of the Kerner Commission on Civil Disorders, which had painted a tragic picture of hopeless inner-city neglect and imminent bankruptcy in the great metropolitan areas. Preaching was not enough; we were called as clergy to get out into the streets along with the oppressed, and march with them in protest. "Detroit is only a beginning of the burning," I said. "As James Baldwin prophetically warned us, next time it will not be a flood, but the fire that will destroy." The next morning, newspaper headlines read "Newark in Flames!"

By the summer of 1968, the Southern Christian Leadership Conference began making plans for a dramatic confrontation with the Johnson

Administration in Washington. If the March on Washington in 1963 was Dr. King's *cri de coeur*, his dream of national unity and peace, this new march would come to grips with reality. As he put it in his last fund-raising letter,

> Our national government is playing Russian roulette with riots; it gambles with another summer disaster. Not a single basic social cause of riots has been corrected. Though ample resources are available they are being squandered substantially on war. . . . We have, through this non-violent action, an opportunity to avoid a national disaster and to create a new spirit of harmony.

The plan called for several thousand people — blacks, Mexican Americans, and Native Americans — from all over the land to converge upon Washington. On the grassy glade south of the Reflecting Pool (leased from the National Parks Department) they would construct "Resurrection City," a shantytown made of prefabricated plywood housing units. Six hundred units were immediately ordered, and arrangements were made for first aid and educational facilities. The army of minorities planned to remain permanently if necessary, until their demands for better homes, equality of opportunity, and an end to racial persecution were met. Mass demonstrations were planned for outside the buildings of the Departments of Agriculture and Health, Education, and Welfare. There would be arrest-provoking nonviolent disruption of the city's life. It was hoped there would be simultaneous boycotting of selected businesses in large shopping areas.

Was the Poor People's Campaign a departure from Dr. King's avowed pacifist Gandhian technique? "There is nothing unconstitutional about saving children from starvation!" was James Bevel's reply.

When the advanced guard of the Poor People's Campaign arrived in the city in March 1968, a deputation met with me to request that our church be made the downtown headquarters of the campaign; the executive offices would be located uptown in the black community, in Moore's Motel. Over a cup of tea, I engaged in the following conversation:

"How many rooms would you require in the church?"

"At least one on the floor for the publicity section of the campaign, the speaker's bureau, and a branch for volunteer services. Separate telephone lines and a teletype machine would have to be installed, and we would require space to set up a print plant for publishing our daily newspaper. We would also need a rather large hall for occasional press conferences."

"For how many hours in the day would these rooms be required?"

"Twenty-four."

"How many days of the week?"

"Seven."

227

"For how long would you wish to have these premises?"

"Forever or until Congress bows to our demands."

"You realize that there would be certain overhead costs such as custodial services, especially at night? I am assuming the church would be reimbursed."

"We have no budget at all."

Across the New York Avenue side of our building there was soon displayed a huge banner, "Poor People's Campaign Headquarters." Our kindergarten room was transformed into something like the city room of a newspaper in a forties movie — teletype machine chattering, typewriters pounding, people dashing in and out of the room (which happily had its own street entrance), and a constant commotion of bantering, singing, sometimes shouting folk all apparently carrying out some plan of business that was totally incomprehensible to me. Behind the curtain on the stage in the Radcliffe room, staff were turning out daily newsletters.

It was suggested that the pulpit of New York Avenue should be used by Dr. King to introduce the people of Washington and the press to the plans for the campaign, though these had already been widely publicized by the media. The date would be Passion Sunday, March 31. I was happy to accede and could have made the commitment immediately, since the minister of a Presbyterian church has the final say about who preaches. However, because of the publicity, I made a decision I would later regret: I left the decision in the hands of the session, confident of their backing. To my utter dismay the session ruled against Dr. King preaching. They argued that if he had been coming as supply to preach, they would be honored by his message, but the occasion was to inform Washington about a campaign that very much looked as if it might collapse into civil disobedience and disorder. When my board of deacons protested their decision, the veto held.

On Passion Sunday, Dr. King preached at the invitation of Dean Sayre from the pulpit of the great Washington Episcopal Cathedral. Immediately after the service he flew to Memphis, Tennessee, to inaugurate marches on behalf of the city's sanitation workers, who were already on strike to protest poor conditions and inadequate wages.

On the morning of Thursday, April 4, I flew to Syracuse, New York, for my annual Lenten visit to that city. In the evening at a meeting of Men of the Church, I shared with them the explosive situation among the minorities. "This will be a long, hot summer," I said. "The violence we have already witnessed in the ghettos of the large industrial cities will escalate. Indeed, I fear for the safety of Dr. King as he leads these marches of protest." As I spoke, I became aware of a strange silence. At the conclusion of my speech, one of the men approached and informed me that Dr. King had been assassinated late that afternoon, shot by an unknown assailant on the balcony of his room at the Lorraine Motel in Memphis while he was chatting with colleagues prior to the protest march.

I rushed to phone Jerry. She was sobbing. I left on the late plane back to Washington that evening. As we approached the city, following the gleam of the Potomac, I could see a pall of smoke rising grotesque and yellow against the floodlights of the main buildings, reminiscent of London after an all-night bombing. The late news reported 125 cities in flames and outbreaks of rioting as pent-up frustration and anger exploded across the nation.

On Friday, after I taped my weekly television program (a four-and-a-half-minute meditation with which the station began and ended its daily broadcast), one of the staff sent for me.

"Listen to this, Doctor," he said. "We're going to broadcast this message every hour or so: 'News is reaching this station that downtown Washington is in flames. A curfew has been declared, and federal troops are now occupying the city at strategic points. There are still reports of looting going on, but for the most part the authorities seem to have the situation under control. It is important not to panic. Another bulletin will be broadcast within the hour.' Well, what do you think?"

"My dear fellow," I said as calmly as I could, "I would advise you not to put out these inflammatory broadcasts. I cannot think of anything more likely to lead to panic than going on the air every hour to warn people not to panic. Why don't you put on some classical music — Mozart, shall we say, but not Wagner. Meanwhile, I'm going downtown now to see how my church is surviving."

"That's up to you, Doctor, but I don't think you can count on your clerical collar to keep you out of trouble."

Downtown Washington was like a city of the dead. Its streets were almost totally deserted except for police and some military personnel in trucks awaiting further instructions. Around the church hardly a shop window was intact. Sidewalks were strewn with broken glass. A woman's shoe lay on its side amid the rubble. With Jack McClendon and Paul Watson, my minister of Christian Education, I wandered through the streets, the air filled with the rank smell of smoke and burning cloth. The little tailor's shop at our corner was completely gutted by fire. (He charged exorbitant interest.)

Several miles of Seventh Street were burning, and some families were homeless. We made arrangements to house them overnight, using the sanctuary pew cushions laid out on the floor of the large Peter Marshall Hall above the sanctuary. The manager of the Hollywood Cafeteria next to the church generously offered us as much food as we needed. I experienced a disquieting sense of déjà vu; back came those nights of the Greenock blitz, and the haunting cry of a woman brought into my little Sandyhills Church Hall in Glasgow — "Where's Jimmy? Where's Jimmy?"

Friday evening Jerry, Thelma Odom, and I attended an immense memorial service at Washington Episcopal Cathedral. The sanctuary was crowded with nearly four thousand worshipers, while outside crowds thronged the spacious lawns listening to the service over a public address system. Methodist Bishop John Wesley Lord, Rabbi Martin Halpern, Roman Catholic Bishop John S. Spence, the Reverend Walter E. Founteroy, and Dean Sayre participated in the service. The program contained the immemorial lines of Donne, which Dr. King had himself quoted in his last sermon in this Cathedral,

Any man's death diminishes me, because I am involved in mankind; and therefore never send to know for whom the bell tolls; it tolls for thee.

With Jerry and Thelma, I joined the grieving throng singing:

Precious Lord, take my hand,
Lead me on, help me stand;
I am tired, I am weak, I am worn;
Through the storm, through the night,
Lead me on to the light,
Take my hand, precious Lord, lead me home.

When my way grows drear,
Precious Lord, linger near;
When my life is almost gone,
Hear my cry, hear my call,
Hold my hand lest I fall;
Take my hand, precious Lord, lead me home.

The Poor People's Campaign would proceed. It would have been Dr. King's wish. The burden of leadership now fell upon the broad shoulders of the Reverend Ralph Abernathy.

Dr. King and Dr. Abernathy had shared together in witness to their cause since the mid fifties back in Montgomery, in prison, in protest marches, and in the face of jibes from ignorant red-necks. Ralph, the country preacher, was a natural orator. Dr. King, the Bostonian graduate, no less passionate, brought a deeper theological content to his preaching. Ralph had been often Dr. King's troubleshooter; now he would carry the burden alone.

The Mexican-American and Native American caravans from the West and the black cavaran from the South (via the Edmund Pettus Bridge at Selma) set out on their six-week march upon Washington. Three thousand arrived to find that only half of the six hundred housing units had been erected. Those unable to find shelter were welcomed into many church halls and private homes in the city.

On the 26th of May Dr. Abernathy preached a towering sermon to an overflow congregation in our sanctuary. For the occasion the Shiloh Baptist Church united with us. Joint choirs under the leadership of our Henry Booker were quite magnificent. Wearing the preaching gown of Peter Marshall happily did not inhibit the preacher's rich oratory. Dr. Abernathy thrilled with a thunderous exegesis of 2 Kings 7. Four lepers found themselves caught up in a battle. Before them was the enemy besieging the city of Samaria; behind, the desert to which they had been ostracized by their own people. Deciding to risk death at the hands of the Syrians rather than endure slow starvation in the inhospitable wilderness, they bravely staggered on toward the enemy, come what may. Suddenly, they discovered that the enemy had fled in a panic brought on by the awareness of the presence of a just God. Resurrection City was like these four lepers, trusting in the power of God to put to flight the enemy of injustice and unrighteousness. It was indeed "a day of good tidings" as they had declared.

The campaign rooms in our church, as we had been promised, hummed with noisy activity seven days a week, twenty-four hours a day. But as the days went by, problems arose. Indeed, the logistics of such an unorthodox undertaking, shepherding a pilgrimage of such dimensions across the land and settling in over three thousand people in semi-permanent living quarters, would have taxed the skills of a four-star general. Tactics and strategy also began to wilt. Misunderstandings arose between the minority groups themselves. The Native Americans proved to be very difficult to organize. The vaunted boycotts fizzled out because the Washington community, black and white, did not cooperate. Even the leadership spoke with conflicting voices. Ralph Abernathy was arrested and imprisoned; while it was a brave gesture, it deprived the leadership of a necessary coordination. Meetings planned by James Bevel and Jesse Jackson, fiery orators of the movement, never took place. Andrew Young's calm and balanced appeals fell on deaf ears. Relations between the campaign and the press became very strained. I recall a meeting in our church when the coordinator, the Reverend Bernard Lafayette, planned to meet a large gathering of the nation's press at 1:00 P.M. With that penchant to ignore time so dear to the blacks (and so irritating to us who have worked with them), he was two hours late. To pass the leaden minutes, I suggested it might be time to preach a sermon. The dogged and patient members of the press were not amused.

The day after the official opening of Resurrection City came the rains. Fourteen inches fell during that hot June month. The shacks, constructed on already low-lying ground beside the Potomac, were inundated; floor boards floated out of doorways, pathways became a quagmire. One day, as I was miserably plowing through mud a foot deep, looking on unbelievingly at the plight of those dear extraordinary people, I asked an ageless woman who was bailing out (unsuccessfully) her little shanty house, "How can you go on living in this, my dear?"

"Sir, this is no different from the rainy season in Mississippi. In fact, we got much better houses up here."

June passed; and the rains. An extension of the lease on the park land was granted until July 11 but by now the pilgrims were beginning to make their way back home across the nation, not without a song, though their hearts must have been heavy. Methodically the Parks Department began to remove the huts and were soon, with bulldozers, leveling and landscaping the ground. By autumn the grass was green again. Visitors walked under the cool shade of willows and elms over ground where surely was fought a battle, perhaps an outpost skirmish, in that long war for the victory of human dignity and freedom.

Quiet also descended upon my church, where once ticker tape machines clacked, the busy printery ran off its messages, and the corridors echoed with happy voices, talking and arguing and laughing.

The year 1968 saw another presidential election. On March 31 President Lyndon Johnson had announced dramatically on television, after declaring a bombing pause over the whole of Vietnam, "I shall not seek and I will not accept the nomination of my party as President."

The heir apparent was Vice President Hubert Humphrey, that "happy warrior" whose forthright liberal reforms were repaid by the President's lukewarm support—and even that came too late. Jerry and I, of course, were rooting for Senator Eugene McCarthy, the Irish poet, the Christian philosopher whose quiet voice often articulated paradox beyond the grasp of most of the voters.

Not unexpectedly, Senator Robert Kennedy threw his hat into the ring. By early June he had won four of the five primaries he had entered. Now, flying around California, he knew that this great state's delegates were crucial to the success he desired at the July convention.

It was the 4th of June and past midnight. Jerry and I sat into the wee hours of the morning watching the televised program from the Kennedy headquarters in the Los Angeles Ambassador Hotel. He had won a stunning primary victory. Cameras panned as the jubilant crowd caught sight of him. We recognized the familiar boyish smile, the large natural curl of the shock of hair over his left eyebrow, the clipped Bostonian accent. There was no doubt in anyone's mind we were looking at the next President of the United States.

The security guards at last hustled their protégé, looking now somewhat weary, through the narrow kitchen hallway as a safer route back to his private quarters.

Suddenly above the babble of voices, the distinct though muffled sound of a gunshot! Women screamed; men shouted; pandemonium broke out. No one, not even the TV commentators, seemed able to tell what had happened until in a gap in the crowd the searching eye of the TV camera to our utter horror picked out the figure of Robert Kennedy on his back on the kitchen floor, blood streaming from his head, friends around frantically seeking to elicit some response.

Jerry sobbed. All feeling froze within me. The Senator was dead, shot at point-blank range by a half-crazed Arab immigrant who had no interest whatsoever in the events of that night, Sirhan Bishara Sirhan.

Robert Kennedy was laid to rest in Arlington Cemetery, his grave marked by a simple white wooden cross contrasting with the lush green of the grass beneath the overarching branches of an ancient tulip tree, nearby the vast terraced memorial to his brother John, the everlasting flame flickering in the breeze. As Saul and Jonathan,

> Delightful and dearly loved . . .
> in life, in death, they were not parted.

A few weeks after the interment, the Kennedy family invited Jerry and me to a graveside mass in which I was invited to participate. A modern folk mass it was, with guitars and spiritual songs. Afterward we were guests at the Kennedy home in McLean, Virginia. As we motored up the George Washington Parkway on that cool evening, the thin sickle of new moon was cradling the brightest of evening stars against a cloudless mauve sky.

The home had an eerie ringing silence, as of an absence, behind the animated chatter and tinkle of glasses. Ethel Kennedy was brave and gracious. We were treading into the private life of a very public family. Ted moved about among the guests, now bearing on his shoulders the total responsibility of a family that had suffered as no other family in public life. The furniture was comfortable and unostentatious; a great St. Bernard with sad eyes stretched across the hallway, oblivious of the feet stepping over it; the garden was large and spacious; a basketball hoop hung quiet in the distance. Above the voices, America was intoning,

> Hark, lamentation is heard in Ramah, and bitter weeping,
> Rachel weeping for her sons.

Late in the autumn of 1968 I met with a group of younger ministers of our presbytery. Over breakfast we discussed matters relating to the General Assembly of the United Presbyterian Church (U.S.A.) scheduled to convene the following May. The meeting ended with their suggestion that I consider becoming a candidate for the position of Moderator of the General Assembly. The Moderator does not have any power to speak officially for the church (nor, indeed, does the General Assembly itself), but the position does nevertheless confer some influence, and it does have a good deal of symbolic value as an indication of the tenor of denominational concerns. It was thought that were I to become Moderator, I might be able to lead the church to focus new interest in the great social issues facing us.

It would be coy of me to suggest that I had never aspired to the Moderatorship of the church. Archbishop Temple once said that he had no time for a curate of the Church of England who had no aspiration to become Archbishop of Canterbury someday. Yet formal office lay heavily upon my shoulders. While my loyalty to the Presbyterian Church was deeply ingrained—after all, I was born into it—I had found little time in my busy parish for membership on Assembly committees, though I had enjoyed my work over a period of several years with the Division of Evangelism, on whose behalf I had preached across the nation; in 1962 I had been elected Moderator of the Washington City Presbytery. The presbytery eventually nominated me as a candidate for Moderator of the 1969 General Assembly meeting in San Antonio, Texas.

Unlike their Scottish brethren, the American U. P. Church elects its Moderator by popular vote. In Scotland, a representative committee of all the presbyteries presents its nominee to the Assembly, and he is almost invariably elected by acclamation (only on one occasion do I recall an adverse vote, when a solitary No stalled the proceedings); indeed, the name of the new Moderator is publicized several months before the Assembly meets. The procedure in the United States is not unlike that of a Republican or Democratic Convention nominating its candidate for the presidency.

When the vote was taken, it quickly became clear that the Assembly was reacting to the ominous divisions that had been threatening the church as well as the nation throughout the fractious sixties. On the second ballot I was a poor third behind the candidate of choice, Dr. George Sweezey of the Webster Grove Church of St. Louis, Missouri. George, a good friend for many years, is a gracious colleague whose consummate churchmanship and broad sympathies promised to go a long way toward engendering unity in the church; we would proceed "not by polarization," as he expressed it, "but by inclusiveness."

The matter of the election dealt with, we proceeded to debate what we all expected to be the principal issue facing the Assembly that year: a commission report on the advisability of reorganizing the Synods of the church. As it turned out, however, that issue was overshadowed by another. Few who were present at that Assembly will forget a stunning speech made not by a commissioner, but by a guest. Mr. James Forman, a representative of the National Black Economic Development Conference, had received an invitation from the General Council to lay before the Assembly the claims of the black community on the church and indeed the nation. I was not entirely surprised by his presentation; having met Mr. Forman in Selma back in 1965, I was already aware of his prophetic role among his people. He walked slowly across the platform, a cane assisting his permanent limp (a badge of his protest) and proceeded in simple, unadorned language to outline the history of the black community since the days of slavery, to remind us of the wretched record of the white racist Christian Church. The day of reckoning had at last dawned! He announced in almost matter-of-fact language that members of his black conference were at that moment occupying the eleventh floor of our church headquarters in New York and that it was their intention to remain in the office of Dr. Kenneth Neigh, General Secretary of the Board of National Missions, until the following demands were met:

1. Dr. Neigh was to be dismissed immediately.
2. As a token compensation for the sufferings of the black community since the days of slavery, $80 million was to be turned over for uses outlined in the Conference's Black Manifesto.
3. All of the church's assets in South Africa, including all of its investments (e.g., stocks) in companies doing business there, were to be liquidated immediately.
4. All of the land held by the church in New Mexico, including the 22,000-acre Ghost Ranch, an adult study center located sixty miles northwest of Santa Fe, was to be handed over to poor Mexican-American farmers working in the area.
5. All land owned by the church in the southern states of Alabama, Georgia, South Carolina, and Mississippi was to be turned over to the Black Economic Development Conference.

Mr. Forman was followed to the platform by Eliezer Risco, representing the Spanish-speaking organization La Raza. He made a similar dramatic appeal on behalf of the poor Mexican-Americans. He announced that the previous day in Chicago, fifty Mexican-American families had taken over the newly constructed Administration Building on the campus of McCormick Seminary because demands they had placed before the Trustees of the Seminary had not been met. These demands included payment of $601,000 by the Trustees for the construction around the seminary of low-cost housing to replace the ghetto dwellings they were presently forced to live in, and the immediate removal of insensitive welfare officials from office.

It was an astounding performance. But how does one deal in Christian charity with revolutionaries totally indifferent to *Robert's Rules of Order* and ecclesiastical procedures of the institutional Church? I sat fascinated the next day as the General Council gathered together in a hotel conference room, unusually solemn and slightly apprehensive. At the conclusion of their conference, the Council presented to the General Assembly their decisions in the form of a document:

> In Jesus Christ we have come into confrontation with God, and by His Cross, we are called to respond in faith and love and service. . . . We have listened to them [Forman and Risco] and heard their demands, and we thank them for sharing with us their frustrations and their desires.
>
> We are not negotiating, but we assure them that we will continue to listen and be open to communication and conversation. . . . The General Council reaffirms the importance of the emphasis the General Assembly places on the chicanos and Hispanic Americans as a whole. In our careful consideration of these issues, we respond with concern and respect. . . .

When read out to the commissioners, the statement was met with a growling murmur of dissent as merely one more pious putoff, one more ecclesiastical pronouncement lacking specifics and obfuscating the seriousness of the violence in the depressed communities!

"Moderator! Moderator!" I found myself shouting as I waved my order papers to catch his eye. "Moderator, this is a tired report; it is a timid report. In confronting James Forman and Eliezer Risco, we are not merely confronting passionate leaders of their people, we are confronting the Cross of Christ. We are not dealing merely with the arithmetic of reparations for historical wrongs our church has perpetrated against the black community; we are dealing with the sorry state of our own sinful souls. This is more than a crisis within our society; it is a crisis within the church facing the awfulness of the Cross."

To its everlasting credit, the General Assembly changed course and passed some immediate, specific measures to meet the challenge that had been placed before it. A $50 million campaign was launched and set to be completed before the next General Assembly met in 1970. By June 1, 1969, seed funds of $100,000 from the Board of National Missions would be handed over to Native American groups for use as they saw fit. Additional sums of $50,000 from each of the Boards of National Missions, Ecumenical Missions and Relations, and Christian Education would be given to the National Black Economic Conference.

These were generous responses. The church was finally rousing itself (though not for the first time, of course) to respond to the predicament of the poor in the United States with practical involvement. One saw "Satan himself fall from heaven" and the term *social justice* shaken from the high-sounding rhetoric of academia and incarnated in the marketplace, where the anonymous poor were barely subsisting, taunted daily by Madison Avenue visions of affluent luxuries and self-indulgence.

I was also reminded of the age-old dilemna of the institutional church: How do we deal with prophets when we do not stone them? Was James Forman a latter-day Amos let loose among the gothic arches of mainline Protestantism?

In a service he conducted in a particularly beautiful modernistic $10 million church he had prayed, "O God, forgive us this monstrous sarcophagus of our Christian faith." The week following the General Assembly he was due to arrive in Washington. Not a little apprehensive (I knew he would attend our services), I awaited his visit. He did worship with us, and came back as a regular attender during his stay. We made available to him an office for his work.

Only once before had I been aware of the presence of so overwhelming a personality. His calm quiet voice and serene countenance seemed to shield a soul of iron, a heart as courageous as that of the martyrs, and a radiant awareness of what Augustine calls "the higher freedom." We talked much together.

Even within the councils of the Southern Christian Leadership Conference, James found it difficult to cooperate. Amos was not a committee man. The last I heard of him, he was struggling tirelessly on behalf of the much overlooked Native Americans in the reservations (he is himself twenty-five percent Native American). It was an honor to have handed to him his walking stick.

16

Vietnam

Let every nation know, whether it wishes us well or ill, we shall pay any price, bear any burden, meet any hardship, support any friend, oppose any foe to ensure the survival and success of liberty.

—President John F. Kennedy, Inaugural Address

It is not my duty to make my country the knight errant of the human race.

—John Bright, 1882

War is too serious to be left to the generals.

—Georges Clemenceau, 1917

War is too serious to be left to the politicians.

—Ipse dixit

DURING THE FIFTIES, at the close of a long day of visiting and church meetings, when I knew that Jerry would not appreciate having to endure a restless bedmate, I used to excuse myself to sit back and with a cup of tea enjoy *The Tonight Show* hosted by dimpled-chinned Jack Paar. But by 1962, on Wednesday nights I'd switch over to Channel Five and watch the repeat telecast of President Kennedy's morning press conference. No President and few actors were more photogenic than John Fitzgerald Kennedy.

The TV lens is an X-ray eye, peering into the soul of anyone foolish enough to face up to it. You are told to "be yourself" on TV—as if one could be natural when confronted by this red-eyed Cyclops roaming around a studio, while several shirt-sleeved men wander about, one of them poised behind the camera mumbling into a headset microphone as he steers noiselessly around you, his camera pivoting on a massive metal three-wheeled base, a tiger waiting to spring.

On TV one must ignore the surroundings. The red-eyed monster must be metamorphosed into the "fellow next door," with whom you are having a conversation on his screen porch of a cool summer evening, the air filled with the whir of katydids.

Mr. Nixon was never able to forget he was being watched by millions of potential voters; like a bad golfer, he pressed too much, failing to simulate the ease of the Roosevelt fireside chat. Mr. Eisenhower used to make me uncomfortable with his uncertain choice of words and fumbling memory, especially after his illness. Lyndon Johnson's counterfeit emotion had a hollow ring. TV is always the intimate tête-à-tête.

President Kennedy took to television like the proverbial duck to water. At first his press conferences were held in the Indian Treaty room of the Executive Office Building; later, they were moved to the more showy and larger auditorium of the State Department in Foggy Bottom, with its beige carpeting and orange padded seats. The camera would pan a stage empty save for a single chair and podium emblazoned with a large Presidential seal set before a backdrop of blue curtains that showed up well on color TV and then sweep the faces of a chattering White House press corps. There would be a sudden silence, as if the TV had gone dead; the audience would rise respectfully; the camera would focus on a manly six-foot figure impeccably dressed, shirt cuffs showing slightly as he raised his left hand to pat down the unruly bush of greying brown hair, an immobile face tanned and rugged, giving nothing of his thoughts away, as if he were out for a stroll in the Rose Garden. Behind him amiable Pierre Salinger slowly ambled in.

On reaching the podium, he would look out over his audience. After he had given them a smile and a curt nod, they would resume their seats, while he seemed preoccupied with a shuffle of papers in his hand. Sometimes he would begin by reading a statement. That concluded, he would look up to a flutter of hands darting high all over the auditorium, seeking recognition. "Mr. President!" He would point with his forefinger: "Yes, Mr. Vanocur," or "Mr. Sidney," or perhaps it would be "Mr. Lawrence." As they read out their prepared questions, he would half close his eyes, his head a little to the side as if deep in meditation. Sometimes before the question was completed, a smile would crease his face, as if he were savoring some humorous morsel before sharing it with them, and when he did, they roared with laughter. Sometimes from the back of the auditorium there would unfold a tortuous question that was in fact a prolix statement. The President would listen patiently, and then with exquisite timing answer "No!" They were now in the palm of his hand.

Then it would happen; it always did. He would point to the third front row on his right and in a gentle tone say, "Yes. Miss McClendon."

Sarah McClendon, a buxom matron with a surprisingly harsh voice for a native of Alabama, could be counted on, with aggrieved tone, to elicit a rather penitential response from the President.

"It's about Laos [she pronounced it *louse*], Mr. President. Since your last press conference, when you were good enough, with the assistance of maps, to share with us a rather broad view of the situation in the Far East, and the role of this country, and especially about the advisers we are apparently sending out there. . . ."

It was always a serious President who responded, "You are perfectly correct, Miss McClendon. Laos is a very difficult problem for us. Let me again say what I said last time the subject came up. . . ."

This was my introduction to a subject that was to occupy increasingly his and all subsequent presidential press conferences until Mr. Nixon's second term of office. I had to learn other names being cited — Cambodia and Thailand (Siam) and Vietnam (French Indo-China).

The nation at this time was still rankling from the abortive invasion of the Bay of Pigs by Cuban forces under an umbrella of the United States Air Force. "One lesson I have learned from this terrible experience," said the Commander in Chief; "we must have a political solution in East Asia and not a military solution."

To fill in my own understanding of Far Eastern history, I bought a paperback copy of *The History of Vietnam*, which delineated the political background of the country with emphasis upon those events subsequent to the Geneva Treaty of 1954. I learned that in the Second World War the Japanese had overrun the French Indo-Chinese empire in an amazing advance west. Only the combined forces of the French, British, and Americans had been able to drive them out before the surrender of Japan in 1946. Politics abhors a vacuum as does nature. A young Leninist named Ho Chi Minh, with a small group of zealous nationalists and an unshakable personal drive, nurtured in both Moscow and Paris, led the revolt for independence. After the war, however, the French were determined to maintain their colonial empire, but through overconfidence they badly miscalculated the strength of the Vietnamese desire for self-determination. Vietnamese forces assisted by Chinese equipment totally defeated them despite a courageous Gallic defense mounted at the fateful Dien Bien Phu. When the French General Carpenter saw the impending disaster, he is said to have cried out "It is all my fault" before he fell upon his own hand grenade.

John Foster Dulles refused to sign the Geneva Agreement of 1954, making the United States the only major power at the Geneva Conference to withhold its signature. The Agreement divided the country, as a temporary measure, along the 17th Parallel into the two zones of North and South Vietnam, promising that within two years free elections would be held under the joint chairmanship of Britain and the Soviet Union. Dulles was no doubt right in insisting that free elections would be impossible; but he failed to grasp the subtleties of dealing with Communism. By 1962 I began to see why Miss McClendon was asking so many searching questions concerning the role of Laos in Southeast Asia.

An almost paranoic attitude in the United States toward monolithic Communism, one of the legacies of the witch-hunt days of Senator Joe McCarthy, is still with us. Communism is Communism and democracy is democracy — except, as there are different types of democracy (for example, British democratic socialism), there are, certainly in Europe, various shades of Communism, not all of which are incompatible with the existence or survival of a "free" society.

I remember as a child, in what was known in Britain as the "Red Clyde," watching the Labor May Day parades through the slums of Glasgow. The leading banner of the workers depicted not the face of Marx or Lenin or Stalin, but that of David Livingstone, the Scottish explorer and missionary to Africa in the days of Queen Victoria. I have known of the "kirking of the town council" in a Scottish town where the right wing was the Labor Party, when the procession into church was led by the Communist mayor wearing his gold chain of office and Sunday black clothes and marching to the strains of "Onward Christian Soldiers Marching as to War"!

There are more than nationalistic differences between the Communist parties of France and Italy and Yugoslavia. We have not heard the end of those tragic invasions by Russia of Hungary, Czechoslovakia, and now Afghanistan. Who would dare to guess where Poland is marching, its churches more crowded with young Christians than those of England?

Vietnam to me then, and even more so now, was at heart an endemic nationalist revolution against an outmoded feudal system that had been shakily sustained by a Victorian-era French colonial policy. I was to see occur what was feared most: the war would drive Vietnam back into the arms of China, which had been its hereditary enemy for some eight hundred years.

Once again the personal problem that had dogged me since my student days reared its head: pacifism. We believed that the Great War had been fought to end all war. I was not so sure at the outbreak of the Second World War; my pacifist witness was to leave on my soul a scar that will follow me to the grave. But Vietnam was clearly the wrong war at the wrong time in the wrong place. It was morally and spiritually wrong. Only a blind patriotism could rouse support from the churches. Only death on a gargantuan scale in battle would sustain it. In the name of the Prince of Peace I had no alternative but to protest.

I was remembering my reservations when I had become an American citizen concerning my right as a naturalized citizen to have recourse to conscientious objection.

President Kennedy had set the destiny of the country within the context of world history; he was aware that a new Third World was arising out of the death pangs of the Old. His successor, Lyndon Johnson, however, seemed to have a very limited, domestic *Weltanschauung*. His strength was that of the shrewd parliamentarian who could unravel the tangled skein of congressional debate and who with unhalting energy could draw, at his own price, support for his policies. Mr. Johnson, nurtured in Texas, a state of vast wealth untouched directly by war since the Alamo, pragmatically confident in the omnipotence of economic power, was remote from and unimpressed by the ancient strifes and politics of an aging Europe and the emerging forces in the Far East. His generals naively assured him all that was required to bring this conflict to a successful end — though what that end should be was never coherently spelled out — was an intensification of search-and-destroy missions and the cooperation of ground forces with massive air strikes. The carnage of the artillery bombardments on the Somme in the First World War and the saturation bombing of German cities in the Second World War, which brought only ghastly loss of life without strategic gain, seemed to have been overlooked. Throughout the war, the American military command grossly misjudged the character and will of the people they fought. At the outset they smugly discounted them as primitives. A yellow-skinned race as remote from the modern technological world as the people of Siam portrayed in the musical *The King and I.*

The number of American "advisers" was growing ominously. Suddenly they were being called "troops"; their numbers expanded to thousands, then hundreds of thousands. American families, our own included, began to realize that the draft now meant something more than just two years of service in the armed forces. On our television sets we watched the sights and sounds of the conflict — American boys in camouflaged battle dress trudging through trackless swamps, helicopters swooping down and carrying away to safety the raw-recruit casualties. I was to hear of some of the carnage from my colleague Bill Brooks.

Bill had been a chaplain in the Marine Corps. On his return from two tours of Vietnam, he was posted to a desk at the Pentagon. Wearying to apply himself to his true vocation as a pastor, he had come to me and suggested that he would like to become an honorary assistant. For three years he arrived at his desk in the Pentagon at 5:30 every weekday morning and by early afternoon was down at the church or out in Arlington or Silver Spring visiting our members. No assistant I ever had accomplished so much by sheer discipline of time and abounding energy. A good soldier, he was reticent concerning his combat experiences. Once only did he lift the veil of silence.

"You are posted in a jungle. Above, the moon is shining. You are awaiting the dawn. Orders are no movement, no speaking. That's a dreadful demand to make of these energetic athletic fellows from Kansas who up to now had never seen anything beyond the rolling fields of the farm or a visit to the little local town with its wide streets and the sidewalks crowded on Saturday afternoons with folk come in from the country. One lad I recall, overcome with a nagging desire for a cigarette, whispered to his mate, 'Must have a smoke, dying for a smoke.'

"Hardly breathing, he carefully extracted the pack from his pocket and flicked one into his mouth. Cupping his hands, his helmet sheltering the flickering light, he bent down and puffed — once. A loud crack echoed through the forest. When we looked around to see what had happened, the lad was sprawling grotesquely over a tree root, the half-lit cigarette dangling from his dead lips.

"And there was the fellow, a sucker for dogs, who watched this mangy cur amble arch-backed up the middle of a village street. He went over to pet it. It wagged its tail and came over to him. He bent down and touched it. The booby trap blew them both to kingdom come."

The Advent season of 1966 became increasingly hypocritical. Lyndon Johnson chose that time to return to Texas to attend a ceremony awarding the Medal of Honor to Robert Emmett O'Malley, a twenty-three-year-old marine, for courage beyond the call of duty in Vietnam. "The actions of Sergeant O'Malley," he declared in an emotional speech, "far outweigh the reluctance of men who exercise so well their right to dissent but let others fight to protect them from these very philosophies that do away with their right to dissent."

On Sunday, the 11th of December, 1966, I preached a sermon entitled "Please Listen, Mr. President." It was a reminder that the United States had been born out of revolution, and that the right to dissent, guaranteed by the Constitution, was not to be waived by emotional patriotic speeches, even those given by the President.

"The growing intensity of the conflict and mounting hatred for the enemy are stifling conscience and depersonalizing spiritual values. We are defoliating a fertile land and creating 1,300,000 refugees. To what end?" I asked, "Clearly we are fighting against militant Communism. Can we, however, stop the spread of ideas, good or bad, with bombs? Does not the imposition of democratic self-determination upon any country itself constitute a contradiction?

"The systematic destruction of the land and people of Vietnam has no support by the Christian Church. Pope Paul, speaking to the whole world, pleaded with the nations involved: 'We cry to them, in the name of God, stop.'

"This is my *cri de coeur* at the Advent Season, a time when a preacher would prefer to hold his peace; but this sermon, like the Hosannas at Christ's triumphant entry, must be given expression or the very stones will cry out. How can we share again the ageless tale of shepherds and Wise Men and a star over Bethlehem's stall when we know that the baby Jesus is dying all over again in the villages and rice paddies of Vietnam? We are talking about observing a forty-eight-hour Christmas truce. Why not a forty-eight-day truce? As Zechariah said long ago, 'Not by might, nor by power, but by my Spirit, saith the Lord of hosts.' "

Secretary of Defense Robert McNamara and his wife, Marge, regularly attended our church. I could not but notice that he was taking notes of my sermon. When I returned to the office Tuesday, I was told that Mr. McNamara wished to see me.

Mr. McNarama is a brilliant executive. World War II had seen this young logistics officer achieving a remarkable reputation for himself. A graduate of the University of California at Berkeley and the Harvard Business School, he served under Robert Lovett, the World War I aviator, and played a significant role working out the logistics of the bombing of Europe. He had come to the Pentagon from the Ford Company, where he had been the first chairman of the company not connected with the family. He was also a Presbyterian elder at Ann Arbor, Michigan.

Understandably nervous, I negotiated the vast Pentagon labyrinth to find his office and was finally ushered into a leather armchair beside his large meticulously ordered desk. I had been warned that this efficient Secretary of Defense required even generals to submit a concise summary of all matters they wished to discuss with him, and that he seldom spent more than fifteen minutes on any interview. I noticed on his desk a typed precis of my sermon, made, I presumed, from the notes he had taken during the service.

"It's very good of you to come and see me. I did want to speak to you about last Sunday's sermon. There are two comments I'd like to make. First, you must go on preaching about the war. This is a moral as well as a political conflict, and unless the Church is prepared to speak out, there can be little hope for us laymen who are struggling in our own ways with our consciences. Secondly, your thesis is quite wrong. . . ."

Some fifty-five minutes later, I took my leave more than ever convinced that my understanding of the situation was better than I realized. As I look back, I can see Mr. McNamara really had no answer to my thesis — that the Vietnam War was indeed an internal nationalist revolution; that we were in the eyes of the Vietnamese a second colonial French empire; that the struggle was in fact a war of liberation to bring Vietnam into the twentieth century, to shake off its feudal system and replace it with something better, even though it be a Communist state.

I was convinced I was speaking to a deeply moral man agonizing far more than I ever could over the increasingly disastrous policy we were pursuing, knowing that he could do little about it, who remained in office out of loyalty to the President.

Before I left I did ask Mr. McNamara for permission to be sent to Vietnam to visit the troops, as a gesture of my identification with the men, even if I did not agree with the war.

"It's a touchy question," he responded. "Every day when we travel from the airport to Saigon, the snipers are out for us. I am afraid we could not entirely guarantee your safety. It would simply be an unnecessary risk, and I'm not prepared to sanction it."

Subsequently, I decided I would go to Hanoi. A newspaper journalist

Laying the cornerstone for the new New York Avenue Presbyterian Church
(April 3, 1951)

*George with President Truman, trowel in left hand, setting
the cornerstone in place*

*TO THE GLORY OF GOD
THIS STONE WAS LAID BY
THE PRESIDENT OF THE UNITED STATES
HARRY S. TRUMAN
THE THIRD OF APRIL
NINETEEN HUNDRED FIFTY ONE*

*The fiddling minister at a "Nicht at Hame" Scottish concert in the church hall.
Steve Prussing is accompanying at the piano.*

New York Avenue Presbyterian Church (Photo by Herbert Rucknick)

George with President Eisenhower at the dedication of the Lincoln Document (February 8, 1953)

Karl Barth and George after a morning service at New York Avenue Church (1957)

George with Billy Graham at the Black Mountain Golf Course, Montreat, North Carolina (summer 1954)

The Dochertys —Mairi, Garth, Jerry, George, and David —on vacation in Florida (1964)

George with his brother Jack in the studios of WTTG in Washington, D.C., where George recorded meditations for daily late-night broadcast for six months per year over a period of twenty-two years

George with Lyndon Johnson after the President had attended worship at New York Avenue on the morning of September 13, 1964

The beginning of the Selma March (March 9, 1965). In the front row are (l. to r.) James Farmer, Bishop John Lord, Andrew Young (in the foreground), Dr. Martin Luther King, Jr., and James Forman; George is second from the right in the fourth row, as indicated. (Wide World Photos)

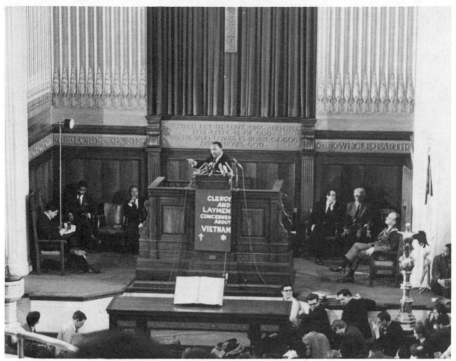

Dr. Martin Luther King, Jr., addressing a meeting of Clergy and Laity Concerned about Vietnam in the sanctuary of New York Avenue Church (February 6, 1968). The platform party includes (r. to l.) George, Rabbi Heschell, Bill Coffin, and Ralph Abernathy. (Photo by John Goodwin)

George with President Nixon — and school teacher Mrs. John Cox, Jr. — on the steps of New York Avenue Church following the service on the morning of February 10, 1974 (United Press International Photo)

George and Sue dressed for the
1974 Tartan Ball of the St. Andrews
Society of Washington

The wee bairns, four-year-old Julie and seven-month-old Bridget (1983)

in Washington who had given me much support in my rather lonely witness said she would personally underwrite the cost of the trip. I was granted an interview at the State Department in Foggy Bottom. My memory may be at fault here, but I seem to recall that the official I spoke to there was a Mr. Cyrus Vance.

"I'm afraid you cannot have permission to go to Hanoi. We're in a state of war with North Vietnam."

"But I am a British subject. I was born in Scotland even though I am a naturalized American citizen. Now, I could get a visa in Britain to take me to Prague; and at Prague I could get a visa to visit Hanoi. What would be your reaction to that?"

"Well, Doctor," he said, "it would be embarrassing all around. When you returned to the U.S.A., you would immediately be arrested for having broken United States law. You are a clergyman, and arresting clergymen is always a predicament in view of public opinion. Nevertheless, I do believe you would have to stand trial and, if convicted, be subject to the penalties for such a crime."

Once more I was walking on the razor edge of decision. Would I be the anarchist? To hell with law and order; let them jail me if they dared; I would walk in the goodly company of the martyrs! Or would I continue within the framework of the Constitution my total opposition to the immoral policy of the government? I realize now that my desire to see Ho Chi Minh savored of the same naiveté I showed when, as Organizing Secretary of the Church of Scotland Peace Society, I believed I could actually avert the coming catastrophe of the Second World War. My wish to see G.I. prisoners of war, however, grew out of genuine compassion and a desire to be with them. Imprisonment was not the real issue. Would such nefarious action hinder my witness against the war? I decided to drop the matter. I now realize I was wrong. I should have accepted the offer and gone to Hanoi.

The terror of the war continued on a scale the average citizen would hardly know. By the end of 1965 the troop concentration in Vietnam had increased to 200,000, and the bombing *for that year alone* exceeded 512,000 tons.

Among friends with whom I had common cause against the war, none was so refreshingly original as Father McSorley of Georgetown University, who had been a tutor to some of Robert Kennedy's children. Our concern was that the United States had the dubious distinction of being the only country in the world manufacturing napalm. Father McSorley suggested that we visit the headquarters of the Dow Chemical Company, the exclusive manufacturers of this deadly material.

Father McSorley has the gentle voice of the second-generation Irish, the music of Erin not quite muted by a harsher Yankee accent. White-haired, lacking every attribute one would ascribe to an athlete, he was possessed of a devastating logic and an indomitable courage.

"You speak first, George," he whispered to me as we waited in the Washington offices of the Dow Chemical Company. After some preliminaries and introductions and a sharing of mutual concerns about the war, I blurted out, "The purpose of this visit is to say that by associating the proud and well-known name of Dow Chemical with the notorious business of manufacturing napalm, you must bring to the goodwill of the company an odor of disgust that does not in any way assist your public image."

"Well," the executive explained, "neither are we happy with this assignment from the government. But if we don't do the job, some other firm will."

"Father McSorley and I would like to suggest that the Dow Chemical Company set up a foundation from all profits accruing from the napalm project to finance the chartering of a hospital ship fully manned with medical staff to sail in Vietnamese waters, succoring victims of this burning cauldron we are upending upon innocent and guilty alike in this war."

He promised to bring the matter before the president of the company. We heard nothing further about the matter.

Edmund Burke once said that the only thing necessary for the triumph of evil is for good men to do nothing. One might amend that to read, "for the Church to do nothing." By Lent 1967, there seemed to be little united witness in the churches condemning the war, especially in my own Presbyterian denomination. My own session, however, had debated the issue. If their views did not agree with those of their minister, it is to be remembered that almost all of them were employed by the government— one was an Assistant Secretary of Defense.

At the presbytery level, no voice was being heard until, with a group of like-minded colleagues, I decided to raise the issue and initiate debate. At the March 1967 meeting of the Presbytery of Washington City, we gave notice of an overture to be discussed at the following month's meeting:

Believing that modern war cannot be equated with the Christian classical definition of a just war;

Believing that the present so-called police action in Vietnam is in danger of escalating into a genocidal war;

Believing that the present conflict in Vietnam is compelling our armed forces to participate in a conflict that does grave harm to the image of respect for persons and international justice which are the core of our foreign policy,

This Presbytery petitions the President of the United States
(a) to bring to halt, immediately, to aerial bombing of North Viet-

nam, and (b) to enter immediately into negotiations with the government of North Vietnam for the withdrawal of armed forces on both sides to a predetermined place as two signals of our desire for participating in a peace conference for the reestablishment of international justice.

There was a crowded house at the Western Presbyterian Church to hear the debate. The main opposition to the overture came from Dr. Edward L. R. Elson, who had been General Eisenhower's Chief of Chaplains in the American Zone in Europe, and later, when Mr. Eisenhower became President, his minister at the National Presbyterian Church. We were treated by him and other opposition speakers to emotional patriotic appeals against which no reasonable overture had any chance of success. We were exhorted to support your boys "out there giving their lives for the preservation of freedom not only in our land, but in the world."

We lost our motion by 86 to 27. The bankruptcy of the church in failing to give any kind of constructive guidance to the nation is reflected in the milquetoast motion that was finally carried, one that I, and everyone else, could do no other than support:

> With every assurance of our prayerful undergirding to the chaplains, to the men and women in Vietnam, to the families who know the pain of separation,
>
> Be it resolved that the Presbytery of Washington City, as a preface to Holy Week, issue a statement to the nation on those things that make for peace, and that the prayers for peace be commended to the clergy and laity and be encouraged as a part of every assembled worship service.

In 1972, five years later—five long, agonizing years that had polarized the nation as nothing else had done since the Civil War split the North from the South, years that brought a stalled Paris Peace Conference and about forty-five thousand dead and over a hundred thousand wounded—the mood of the Church was at last beginning to change. A new President was sitting in the White House. Lyndon Johnson had admitted that he could not contribute a solution to the conflict; Mr. Nixon made enthusiastic claims that he had a plan.

In May, we proposed another overture to the presbytery which included two remarkable statements, the first that

> . . . neither the security nor the national interest of the United States is at stake in this conflict, which is fundamentally an internal civil war within the nation of Vietnam and which can be resolved only by the Vietnamese people . . .

and the second a quotation from the Presbyterian Church's 1967 Confession, that

> the Church, in its own life, is called to practice the forgiveness of enemies and to commend to the nations as practical policies the search for cooperation and peace. This requires the pursuit of fresh and responsible relations across every line of conflict, *even at risk to national security*, to reduce areas of strife and to broaden international understanding.

This quite extraordinary petition was carried by a vote of 121 to 118 — close to be sure, but reflecting a radically different atmosphere toward a war that had itself not changed in its essential nature whatsoever; only the numbers of the wounded, maimed, orphaned, homeless, and dead changed, inching ever upward.

The overture also provided a demonstration of what happens when the Church — in any land, even in the United States with its constitutional separation of Church and State — comes into conflict with Caesar. Immediately a question of "conflict of conscience" arose in the minds of those members of the Presbytery who were also members of the armed services or employed by the government. Their employment in government was conditional on their oath that they would not become "a risk to national security." Now, as loyal Presbyterians, they were being asked to agree with an overture that called upon them in the cause of world peace to be prepared to become such a risk. A minority of the presbytery accordingly appealed to the General Assembly to have our overture turned down. Meanwhile, the Pentagon, which had apparently heard about the debate and vote in the Presbytery, issued a statement that the question of "conflict of conscience" did not arise and assuring all Presbyterians that they could still be loyal citizens and subscribe to our church's creed with a clear conscience! The General Assembly in turn at its May meeting turned down the appeal of the minority on the grounds that the overture was clearly consistent with the church's 1967 Confession. Thus, the patriotically sensitive consciences of the minority were reassured by the state and were overruled by the church met in General Assembly for not upholding the creed!

I recalled the poem "Indifference" by Studdart Kennedy, the Anglican army padre of the First World War:

> When Jesus came to Golgotha, they hanged him on a tree.
> They drove great nails through hands and feet and made a Calvary.
> When Jesus came to Birmingham, they simply passed him by;
> They never hurt a hair of him, they only let him die.
> For men had grown more tender, and they would not give him pain;
> They only just passed down the street and left him in the rain.

In contrast to the embarrassing silence and inaction that seemed to hover over the other congregations in our presbytery, there was evidence of a vital concern in my own church of which I could be proud; it was especially evident in my session, whose members tried to face up to the implications of their Christian faith and the war. No doubt some of those who were invited to serve on the session turned down the invitation because of the antiwar view of the pastor, but on the other hand there always were, as there always ought to be within a session, men and women of Christian charity and conviction who were prepared to debate the matter. It was therefore natural that they should seriously consider the request of a newly formed group, Clergy and Laymen Concerned about Vietnam, to hold their first Washington conference in our church building in February 1968.

This ad hoc group of ministers, priests, and rabbis owed its origin to one man: John Bennett, the distinguished theologian and President of Union Theological Seminary in New York City. John, the most gentle of men in manner and speech, reticent sometimes to the embarrassment of his hearers, was a man of unbounded courage, possessing a brilliance that easily pierced the fog of theological obscurantism.

Dr. Bennett invited a few friends to his apartment, not only to talk about the war but to do something about it. One was Bill Coffin, the Chaplain of Yale University. Bill is a lovable fellow with the smile of a schoolboy who has been caught raiding the biscuit barrel. His style of speech is epigrammatic ("Christ is the answer; the Church is the problem"), and when he speaks in public it seems as if, like Demosthenes of old walking the seashore, he is speaking with pebbles in his mouth. His charismatic presence arouses great enthusiasm. An authentic musician, he had studied piano under Cortot in Paris.

Rabbi Heschel, the Professor of Social Ethics at the Jewish Theological Seminary in New York City, was a small man with a leonine head, a bramble-bush beard, and the face of Moses, as I would imagine him coming down from Mount Sinai, the Tables of the Law in his arms. He always wore a beret. I always associated him with the Gamaliels of Israel; his words were like direct quotes from the Talmud.

There was Rabbi Brickner of the Union of American Hebrew Congregations and Richard Fernandez, who was to become the pragmatic secretary to this nebulous group.

The telephone was their only mode of communication. Across the land, wires hummed, making the case for a nationwide solidarity rally of all religious people in the nation's capital. At this time, a Gallup poll was indicating forty-seven percent of the nation against the war. Would I make available my church for such a gathering?

Decisions concerning the use of the sanctuary were normally left to myself and my colleague Jack McClendon. However, we had been host to so many varied and controversial groups, particularly involving the civil rights movement, that I thought it wise to bring the matter to the attention of the session. A long, deeply felt debate ensued. Could the gathering be categorized as a religious service? Of course, there would be worship services. But wasn't the session involving itself in what seemed to be a covert political action? For three hours the debate continued. The matter was handled in a mature, Christian, statesmanlike manner. Finally it was agreed by a 13-9 vote (three requested that their Nay vote be inscribed in the minutes — just for the record) that "the session, renewing its confidence in the moderator's judgment in opening the church to unrelated groups, . . . welcomes this group to the church for use of the building on 5th and 6th of February, 1968, with such admonition as the moderator deems in order," with the addendum, "the session does not take a position of either supporting or opposing the views of causes espoused."

The news of Clergy and Laymen Concerned about Vietnam coming to Washington was widely publicized in the press. The more conservative members of the congregation were unhappy. One influential member was startled to note the following coming over the news service ticker-tape in his office:

> Two-day demonstration by Clergy and Laymen Concerned about Vietnam to be headquartered at New York Avenue Presbyterian Church . . . Memorial services to be held at Arlington . . . American Council of Christian Churches to hold counterdemonstration concentrating on picketing New York Avenue Presbyterian Church . . .

Uncertain about how many would turn up, we began preparing for over a thousand visitors. Churches in the suburbs and colleagues made available overnight accommodations. An army of volunteers, supplemented by a large group of men and women from our own congregation, arranged for registration, coffee, and snacks. I still recall the amazing spectacle of seven five-gallon metal containers of Coca-Cola syrup on a table in a side room and sandwiches piled up as high as the doorway.

Early in the morning of February 5, the first pilgrims began to arrive — priests, rabbis, clergymen, nuns, students, professional men and women, and craftsmen from almost every state in the union. Some twenty-five hundred were registered and assigned living quarters. Awaiting the opening plenary session, hundreds strolled along the sidewalk on New York Avenue, old friends meeting, new friends getting acquainted. Some overnight travelers slept in the sanctuary on the pews. As I mingled with some old acquaintances, I was aware of a deep sense of committed fellowship everywhere; the cause of peace united us.

By eleven o'clock in the morning, there must have been over two thousand in our sanctuary, which comfortably seats only thirteen hundred.

250

Squatting on the floor around the large communion table were the members of the press, some with pocket tape recorders, restlessly awaiting the beginning of the meeting, gazing up at the large center pulpit decked with a banner announcing "Clergy and Laymen Concerned about Vietnam," bristling with microphones like the missiles of war we were seeking to defuse. Among the foreign correspondents I noticed representatives from London, Paris, Berlin, Tokyo, and — did I really see it, or was it my imagination? — Pravda. Here surely was a gathering that, like the first shot fired at the Bridge of Concord, would be heard around the world.

I entered the pulpit under the blinding arc lamps of television cameras poised on the balcony and looked out at the largest gathering my church had ever known, including Easter Sunday services. A sea of faces stretched everywhere. There was no need to call the meeting to order; I simply raised my two arms and signaled the V of peace. The voices diminuendoed, the gathering arose, hands were raised for one long moment of silence. I invoked the blessing of the God of Abraham and Isaac and Jacob, and the Father of the Prince of Peace. Rabbi Heschel read the prophetic words of faith and hope from Isaiah. "In the days to come, the mountain of the Lord's house shall be set over all other mountains. . . . All the nations shall come streaming to it. . . . They shall beat their swords into mattocks and their spears into pruning knives; nation shall not lift up sword against nation nor ever again be trained for war."

Bill Coffin received a tumultuous reception. Midway through his speech he was shouted down by Dr. Carl McIntyre, the President of the American Council of Churches, who, true to form, had turned out to disrupt the meeting. Bill patiently awaited an opportunity to respond. The audience became restless.

"This is not the religion of St. Paul," McIntyre boomed. "This is politics!"

"If Paul's religion was not political," Bill shouted back, "How come he was so often in the pokey? And by the way, Dr. McIntyre, I think you ought to go outside and speak to those pickets of yours marching round the church. When I asked them what they were picketing, they replied, 'We dunno! All we know is we're getting paid for doing this.' "

I embraced Dr. King once more. He recalled our witness at Selma and reiterated his admiration of Jerry's courage. He received a standing ovation as he entered the pulpit.

"The struggle for peace and the struggle for civil rights are tied together," he said. "Our government spends about five hundred thousand dollars to kill each Vietnamese soldier, but it spends only fifty-three dollars on each person that is characterized as poverty-stricken. The war against poverty is not even a skirmish. We live in a nation that is the greatest purveyor of violence today. It is either nonviolence or nonexistence. The alternative to disarmament will be a civilization plunged into the abyss of

251

annihilation. Our earthly habitat will be transformed into an inferno that the mind of Dante could not envision. Somehow we've got to sing 'I Ain't Gonna Let Nobody Turn Me Around.' We are not going to let those who are trying to identify dissent with disloyalty turn us around."

Senator Gene McCarthy, representing Capitol Hill, spoke quietly and persuasively against the continuation of the conflict in Vietnam. Years later (October 1977), he would report in an interview with Michael Charlton of the BBC that he thought the most significant early protest was one that had been sponsored by clergy and others against the war:

"Senator Morse, Ernest Gruening, and I spoke. I think we were the only three members of the Senate who did. Before that there was nothing really organized, just scattered protests and criticism. We began to build on that, with various letters to the President, protests, and speeches against the policy. The press began to pick it up a little bit more at that point, but there were only three or four papers in the country of any consequence that opposed the war."

After the plenary morning meeting, a march to Arlington Cemetery, two miles from the church, got under way. We had made a request to hold a service of worship at the Tomb of the Unknown Soldier, but when we arrived federal police told us that permission to hold a service had not been granted because our gathering had been classified as a "political rally." Undaunted, we entered the cemetery — no permission required for that — and marched to an area as close as was permissible to the tomb. Jerry and I had marched in the vanguard with Dr. King, who was flanked on one side by Ralph Abernathy, Andrew Young, and a rabbi who carried a Torah, and on the other side by Rabbi Heschel and an Episcopal priest carrying on high an ornate Jerusalem Cross. We paused in a silence broken only by the sound of a plane making its approach to land at the nearby Washington National Airport and offered prayers and a hymn, after which we quietly dispersed.

The afternoon was spent meeting with Congressmen in the church and in their offices on the Hill. I went with a party of seven headed by Bill Coffin, Rabbi Heschel, and Professor John Macafie Brown and talked to Secretary of Defense McNamara at the Pentagon. While we were quietly discussing the issues, Rabbi Heschel spoke up with uncharacteristic passion; the suffering tragedy of the war seemed to stand before him in ghastly shape. All of us, including Mr. McNamara, were moved to silence, catching a rare glimpse of the agony of this deeply religious man.

Through all the various activities I was pleased to note that the groups at the church remained orderly throughout the day (although understandably noisy), though in the Radcliffe Room I noticed an innocent-looking lad with a gentle smile standing at a table eliciting signatures. Tacked on the wall above the table, a large poster enjoined us to "Impeach President Johnson." My head tightened. "I'll give you ten seconds to remove that poster from the wall," I said, trying hard not to blow my top. The lad took down the offending notice with a self-conscious smile. When I returned an hour later, the poster was back on the wall, the lad still smiling innocently beside it. I tore it down myself.

The evening session, a service of worship that filled the sanctuary to overflowing, focused on the nation's need for penitence. Participants included Malcolm Boyd, Rabbi Brickner, Harvey Cox, Channing Philips, Bishop James Shannon, Father Sheerin, and Andrew Young. I led the "Litany of Penitence":

> Who shall ascend the hill of the Lord?
> And who shall stand in his holy place?
> He who has clean hands and a pure heart,
> Who does not lift up his soul to what is false
> And does not speak deceitfully.
> God of our fathers, our hands are unclean, our hearts
> besmirched, our lives have delighted in the false things of the world. . . .

Bill Coffin spent the night with us. We were too tired, too excited to sleep. Bill, a brilliant raconteur, reminisced about his life at Yale, where a splendid administration supported this "turbulent priest's" witness in the civil rights movement. (He was jailed in the South.) He talked of his family life. He had married the daughter of Arthur Rubinstein, who, when he heard that his daughter was going to marry a preacher, had commented somewhat ruefully, "I'm not very happy about having a Billy Graham in the family." To which Bill had responded, "Tell your father, I'm not so hipped about having a Liberace in mine."

Tuesday morning, back at the church, more meetings between delegates and their congressional representatives. It is difficult to assess the value of any conference, yet this assembling of so many citizens from so many diverse backgrounds at least made us aware that we who were resolutely opposed to the war were not alone in our witness. Authority was given to the Executive Committee to bring the convictions we held about the war before the nation and to be the channel for further action.

It was late afternoon on Tuesday when the last delegates bade fond farewells to one another on New York Avenue. Fanning out into the gathering darkness, they left to return home across the nation. I reentered the empty, silent sanctuary, still ablaze with light, and sat down somewhat wearily in a front pew, scarcely believing the events of the past forty-eight hours. Gone were the banner and microphones from the pulpit. The large bronze Celtic Cross, witness of so many events in this unique place, hung majestically against a radiant blue dorsal. At the base of the apse, gold flutings, carved Pentecostal fingers of flame, reached upwards to the royal blue curtain draped like a throne around an empty Cross, for the Christ reigns over all our peace and our war.

In the fresh stillness, like a playback of a videotape, the day flashed before my eyes: faces of businessmen and craftsmen; Yankee accents mingling with the slow music of the South; graying professors and vocal long-haired students in jeans; nuns in black-and-white habits that set off their cherubic smiles; the European press corps in their drab grey clothes wandering around or squatting on the floor during the speeches; the flash bulbs of the ubiquitous photographers and the piercing arc lamps of television cameras poised precariously on the balcony rails; the reverberating voice of Dr. Martin Luther King, Jr.; the white hair and deep blue eyes of Eugene McCarthy looking far beyond the faces of his audience as if to the New Earth he was seeking to bring about; the crowds—clapping, stamping, cheering, laughing, praying, gabbing, embracing, and raising their hands on high silently; the music of Henry Booker at our great organ console; the singing of the African folk song "Kum Ba Ya":

> Bombs are falling, Lord, come by here . . .
>
> A man is tortured, Lord, come by here . . .
>
> People want freedom, Lord, come by here . . .

Lost in thought, I was unaware of Ramon Mason, my beadle, silently watching me. Our eyes met. He smiled and then, with a sparkle in his voice, reached out his hand.

"Doc! How would you like to shake the hand that shook the hand of Dr. Martin Luther King?"

We hugged each other in silence.

The following Sunday, the 11th of February, the day before the celebration of Abraham Lincoln's birthday, was a time when ministers of our church were expected to preach a sermon centered on Lincoln. I decided to draw on what Mr. Lincoln had said in his Second Inaugural Address, delivered in the darkest days of the Civil War, using for my text Matthew 18:7, which President Lincoln had quoted: "Woe unto the world because of offenses! for it must needs be that offenses come; but woe to that man by whom the offenses come!"

"The nation in 1865 was torn as never before in its history by the fury of the War between the States," I said. "As Lincoln was delivering his message to the nation, General Sherman had begun the final push that was to blight the life and culture of the South for two generations. In such an hour, Mr. Lincoln declared, 'Neither of the parties expected for the war the magnitude or the duration which it has already attained.'

"The parallel today is too tragically obvious," I declared. "We threw into South Vietnam 'advisers' until they reached some fifty thousand in order to forestall the infiltration of Communist forces from the north after the signing of the Paris Treaty of 1954. Today there is an army of five hundred thousand troops in Vietnam and an annual budget of twenty-four billion dollars. Back in 1965 the Secretary of Defense had informed us that the troops would be home for Christmas. At this very moment, during the Buddhist religious festival of the Tet, North Vietnamese forces have let loose on the city of Quozan an offensive unprecedented in size and fire power in this war. The Vietcong General Vo Ngyen Giap once defeated the French armies. Are we to see Quozan as our Dien Bien Phu?

"In his Second Inaugural Address, Lincoln also stated, 'Neither anticipated that the cause of the conflict might cease when, or even before the conflict itself should cease.' What is the 'cause' of this Vietnamese conflict that is driving us almost to the limits of our resources in manpower and wealth? Can this nation now withdraw from a conflict with a nonwhite nation of only sixty million without losing face? The dreadful fact is that we have already lost face in the eyes of the world, and even among some of our own allies!

"I see a hardening of the heart and a calcifying of the finer feelings of the soul among us as the intensity of the war deepens and the casualty figures mount. On television we watch with little pain the piles of Vietnamese dead in streets and battlefields. We witnessed the horror of the Police Chief of Saigon, in broad daylight, in the center of the city, become accuser, judge, and jury, as in cold blood he shot a shackled Vietcong prisoner of war through the head with his revolver.

"The other day I was describing something of the horror of this conflict to a little lady. One million babies have been maimed or burned or killed. The countryside has been defoliated to such a degree that it is feared the balance of nature in that land may be permanently upset. We are burning to the ground a whole nation with napalm; we are laying waste nameless villages without the certainty that they really are strongholds of Vietcong guerrillas. And this saintly lady, who probably reads her Bible and says her prayers at night, and who I know attends church, responded without any emotion at all, 'Of course war is terrible — all war is terrible — but we did all that in the Second World War. It's only because we now see it on television that it seems worse.'

"With all my heart I would call upon President Johnson: Mr. President, I do want to support you in all your efforts to bring this war to an end, but I must first know what is its purpose, now that we know there can be no military victory for either side. It is a war in which eight Vietnamese civilians are killed for every Vietnamese soldier, a war that has no sanction within the Christian Church anywhere in the world. You are asking us to support you in a violent conflict against which stands almost half the nation.

"In that Inaugural Address delivered in the midst of battle, the generous heart of Lincoln was laid open to a nation in agony:

With malice toward none, with charity for all. With firmness in the right as God gives us to see the right [Can we really say the right we fight for in Vietnam is the right that God would have us achieve?] let us finish the work we are in, to bind up the nation's wounds . . . to do all which may achieve and cherish a just and lasting peace among ourselves and with all nations.

To that plea we can all say Amen."

On Sunday, March 31, 1968, I was visiting the campus of Macalester College in Minnesota to preach at the dedication of their new chapel-auditorium. Senator Gene McCarthy was also in attendance to address the evening convocation. In the midst of his address, the audience became aware of a disturbance taking place offstage. Finally, during a pause in the Senator's speech, a student dashed onstage and handed him a note. He read it slowly, as if checking twice to be sure of what it said. Then in his quiet voice he announced, "It has just come over the radio that President Johnson will not seek another term as President of the United States."

The audience burst into wild applause. Apparently everyone was thinking, as I was, that Johnson's announcement was tantamount to news that the war had finally ended. I believed the main cause of the interminable on-and-off scheduling of the Paris Peace Conference was largely due to President Johnson's purblind Texas stubbornness, his insistence that he would not be the first American president to lead the nation to defeat, his parochial view of the world, his inexperience in dealing with the subtleties and evasions of the Eastern mind. Now would be the opportunity for Senator McCarthy to grasp the presidency and bring the war to an end. It was Jerry's birthday. What a wonderful present!

Of course the war did not end. Senator McCarthy himself soon withdrew from the presidential race, and Senator Robert Kennedy was plucked tragically from contention. In this atmosphere of gloom, another convocation of Clergy and Laymen Concerned about Vietnam was scheduled to meet in the church with the theme of "A New Mobilization to End the War in Vietnam." An estimated crowd of five hundred thousand arrived in the nation's capital from almost every state in the Union in mid November of 1968.

A "March against Death," a dramatic demonstration of our feelings, was scheduled for the morning of Saturday, November 15. The main participants, leading figures opposed to the war, gathered together in our church. I became aware of an attractive young lady asking me if there was a drum that she might beat. I recognized Shirley MacLaine. I covered one of our metal wastebaskets with red crepe paper. Armed with a ruler, she set off with this "tinkling symbol" in the vanguard of our group towards the Capitol.

There we met representative groups from the states, including families who had been bereaved in the war. The procession was interspersed with a dozen simple unvarnished wooden coffins, borne upon the shoulders of pallbearers. We would walk in long lines, quietly, without fanfare of drums, down Pennsylvania Avenue, the presidential processional route, to the east gate of the White House, where, after a short address, we would deposit the coffins. A multitude of spectators thronged the entire two-mile-long Avenue. It was a somber crowd; the only songs I heard sung were "We Ain't Goin' to Be Turned Around" and "We Shall Overcome." It was the most orderly of processions, a fact confirmed to me personally by a policeman who had stood on duty.

"I never saw anything quite like it," he confessed. "There was no need for us to be called to keep order. We noticed that as soon as any group seemed in any way to get out of line, they were immediately surrounded by other marchers who calmed them down."

I marched with Mr. and Mrs. Olson from Warren, Pennsylvania. Mrs. Olson carried over her left arm the tunic of an army sergeant. She showed me a photograph — a wedding group such as I have looked upon a thousand times: a smiling bride and shy bridegroom poised to cut the three-tier white wedding cake, the happy-sad faces of parents, the cluster of family and children.

"That was on December 23 last year," she said. "My boy was killed in Vietnam on January 10."

We walked on in a ringing silence, a long, long trail indeed away from "the land of their dreams," downhill towards the White House. Overhead, helicopters swooped low over the crowd. A strange pattern, it seemed to me, as if they too were making a noisy but respectful salute to the dead. But later I was informed that they were loaded with canisters of "sick gas" to be unloaded upon us at the first sign of trouble, that behind windows the whole length of Pennsylvania Avenue, soldiers crouching out of sight were poised ready with machine guns; and unseen by us behind the vast circle of sandbags laid out on the White House Lawn, soldiers lay with rifles cocked. Inside the White House sat a bewildered President Nixon. At the east gate we were refused permission to enter. The coffins were laid down quietly and reverently on the sidewalk. We adjourned to the Washington Monument, where a vast throng had gathered to hear speeches and declarations against the war.

Our church was a designated meeting point for buses to pick up the weary travelers and take them back home Saturday night, but so great was the traffic jam of buses on the parking lots around the Reflecting Pool (where Resurrection City had staked out its own brave but futile witness a few months before) that communications broke down completely. I would estimate some four thousand had gathered together within the church awaiting transportation (some twenty-five thousand had passed through our building over the weekend). With nothing to do but wait, they sat around everywhere, in the sanctuary, siderooms, halls, passageways, and some in the Lincoln Chapel. As chilling darkness fell, some of the young-bloods got a bit restless. A few waiting impatiently outside the door up-ended a parked police motorcycle and set fire to some trash cans. A phalanx of police moved quickly in toward the church and fired in tear gas, which was sucked into the church building through the ventilation vents on the sidewalk, contaminating every room inside. Our eyes smarting, stinging tears streaming down our cheeks, we found the first-aid post in the base-ment was quite overwhelmed. I scrambled over legs and bodies of squirm-ing people, telling them not to rub their eyes, just to wait, the pain would go away—a fact I was myself loath to believe, as my own eyes burned.

About one o'clock Sunday morning Jack McClendon counseled me, "Listen, brother, you have to preach tomorrow; go home and get some rest."

When I returned later in the morning, around seven, hundreds were still stranded, some asleep, others propped up on floors, just staring. Our exceedingly well-run Church School was completely disorganized. My teachers were patient. By the end of the first service, at 10:30, almost all our visitors were on their way home. By the end of the second, at noon, only a straggler here and there stood sipping coffee with members. Finally, about two o'clock, the church was cleared. Ramon, my beadle, was able to report that we could now close the doors. Wearily, Jerry and I went to the New York Avenue entrance, where I encountered a stockily built lad with matted hair in jeans and hiking boots with a huge pack on his back.

He looked up at me with tired eyes.

"Well! What do *you* want?" I asked, my patience now at the breaking point.

His look was gentle, his voice soft and polite.

"A glass of water, please, sir."

The quiet words struck like a blow.

"This way, son," I replied, patting his shoulder and leading him to the drinking fountain, where he slaked a long thirst. He hitched his heavy pack over his shoulder and was gone out into the bleak sunshine of that November day, jogging along quite carefree towards the Greyhound Bus Station. And as I watched the receding figure, I looked into Jerry's search-ing eyes. We both knew as surely as the day what the other was thinking.

> I saw a stranger yestreen;
> I put food in the eating place,
> Drink in the drinking place,
> Music in the listening place,
>
> . . . .
> And the lark said in her song,
> Often and often and often
> Goes the Christ in the stranger's guise.

The forbidding specter of the war was now casting its cold shadow over our own family. Garth and David were at college, and on graduation would be eligible for the draft. Garth was a student at Kentucky Wesleyan College in Owensboro, David at George Washington University. On a late spring day when the forsythias and the azaleas in our garden were in full bloom and life seemed very precious, Jerry, the longing, fearful look in her eye that I had noticed so soon as we discussed our boys, suddenly announced, "George, I'm flying down to Kentucky to see Garth."

When she arrived at the airport, a lad, small, somewhat rotund, with horn-rimmed glasses and a mop of black hair, rather breathless, ran up to her.

"Mrs. Docherty?" he panted, "I'm John. Garth asked me to meet you; he's at class. Sorry I'm late. He said I would know you easily —a smashing blonde bombshell! Ha! Ha! Let me carry your bag. The car's outside. I'm afraid it needs a wash. To tell the truth, don't know if it's worth the trouble."

They bounced over the winding rough country roads, the back road to the college, in an ancient jalopy and were soon settling in to the lounge in the fraternity house, so obviously male, a den of undusted chairs and stained carpets that cried out for a thorough spring cleaning.

"Garth says you like your tea strong, with milk and no sugar?" as he poured, apologizing that the cake was a bit hard.

He talked on and on, as students will do when they're away from their pals and have a motherly soul who will listen. He spoke about his family in New Jersey, showing photographs of them. "Taken a few years ago. That's my sister on the right." He confessed he was not a very good student and had to struggle to get his grades. The door flew open suddenly; Garth had arrived.

And that was John . . . of whom, about a year later, Garth was to telephone his mother.

"Mom, you remember John? Well, he did poorly in his grades; only made a C and was drafted. Went down to Fort Bragg for six months' training. He was sent to Vietnam a month ago. We have just learned that he was killed —just two weeks after he arrived at the front. The whole college is terribly upset by the news."

Jerry was weeping when I came home that night.

"This damnable war!" she muttered, her mouth tight and trembling. "What a stupid waste! He was such a dear boy, George, such a dear boy!"

I have sometimes thought if the Johnson and Nixon families had been blessed with sons rather than daughters, they might have had a deeper appreciation of what the war meant to the conscientious student. And I believe if these two presidents had been scholars (like Woodrow Wilson) they might have brought to their decisions a greater historical perspective; certainly they would have known that in Europe revolutions had historically begun on university campuses, that students as well as the hungry mob of the Revolution set up the barricades in Paris streets.

In the 1960s the vigilant F.B.I. had infiltrated the inner councils of a growing Students for a Democratic Society movement, the New Left as they called themselves in their literature. Ever since the civil rights revolution, these students had been in slumbering revolt. In 1965 they were the driving force behind the twenty-thousand-strong student march on Washington protesting the Vietnam War.

Of course they were radicals. They wrote as if American democratic capitalism had failed and they were seeking to establish something more socialistic. Of course there must have been Communists among them, American counterparts of Britain's Maclean-Burgess defectors. Yet the impression given, that the student community in the United States, numbering about six million, was seeking to overthrow the government, was simply fascist paranoia. It was a confusion of dissent with disloyalty.

The vast majority of the students felt it was not only their academic right to freely express their views, however wrong they might be; it was also their constitutional right to dissent as conscience dictated. As the war became more grievous, some became more violent. Under the leadership of such clergymen as the Berrigan brothers, they broke into Selective Service offices and destroyed, burned, and even poured blood on draft card files. The revolts at Stanford and Princeton and Yale and the sit-ins at Columbia were nothing more than expressions of the growing academic indignation at the futility of the war.

Mr. Nixon took pains to catalogue in his memoirs the extent of the riots: "In the academic year 1969–70 there were 1,800 demonstrations, 7,500 arrests, 462 injuries — two-thirds of them were to police — and 247 arsons and 8 deaths [four of them students at Kent State]." These are damning figures taken as statistics. What they do not reveal is a country that was passing through eight years of growing concern about a tragic war, a "silent majority," among them six million students, who did not agree with the war but bridled their tongues and sought how best to live with it. Those who fled the country, finding asylum in Canada or Sweden, did so only as a response to an ultimate provocation, rightly or wrongly. Recent firsthand reports reveal them to be a group of lonely young Americans conscience-stricken over what they did, who will bear for the rest of their lives marks of a deep-seated emotional conflict.

Theological seminaries also became involved. The issue was the exemption for divinity students from serving in the armed services (except as chaplains), a keystone piece of legislation I always felt was designed, both in Britain and the United States, to keep the Church quiescent in time of war. From Princeton and Union and other eastern theological seminaries, four hundred divinity students decided to march on Washington protesting their exemption from the draft. Of course, my church was to be the meeting place for worship and discussion. My session could hardly withhold permission from divinity students using the sanctuary.

Senator Gene McCarthy began the meeting by telling them he was proud to be back in this church where the official opposition of the Senate of the United States to the War was launched. The students decided to stage a sit-down protest on the broad tree-lined sidewalk in front of the White House. The White House police, as always, were calmly balanced and wonderfully controlled. They advised the sprawling students, please, to rise and go away. They could walk if they wished, but they could not lie down or they would be led away to jail. The students, equally solicitous of the police, made it clear there were no hard feelings, but they felt this was something they had to do. Reluctantly and without struggle, about a hundred were hauled off to the fetid vennels of the D. C. jail for the night. It was later revealed that two of the seminarians were homosexually violated there by jail perverts.

Later I read, rather incredulously, the transcript of a commencement address delivered as late as May 28, 1976, by the distinguished Chief Justice of the Supreme Court Warren E. Burger to the University of Pennsylvania. In it he writes "my resentment that young people who were given what seemed the unparalleled opportunity for education, without the barriers of birth or class that exist in other societies, saw fit to tear down, to occupy, to burn, rather than learn . . . has modified . . . now with the tragic episodes resulting from official over-reaction behind us. . . . Perhaps without knowing all the reasons, the peaceful demonstrations were ahead of many of us in seeing something was missing in life. . . ."

Justice Burger obviously failed to grasp or really appreciate the fundamental mood of students in those days; they were deeply concerned about the Vietnam War, whatever action they took. They were not following an aging Wordsworth, retired among the hills of the Lake District, hearing in the quiet of nature "the still sad music of humanity." If they were following Wordsworth, it was the young, dashing poet who in the heady days of the French Revolution with its guillotine-bloodied streets had left the quiet of England to get in on this emancipating event, bringing to birth out the ancien régime, grown corrupt by its own gluttony, a new heaven and a new earth, and who could write "Bliss was it in that dawn to be alive,/But to be young was very Heaven!"

When Justice Burger "occasionally went into the streets, not to talk but to listen" among the milling, hedonistic, discotheque-happy, chanting youth who paraded in mobs along Georgetown's Wisconsin Avenue or in Alexandria of a Saturday night, among "the young men and women with saffron robes and shaved heads singing and praying in public," he was not encountering the serious students of the sixties who found themselves in college knowing that if they did not maintain a C average they would be drafted, and when they graduated they would be drafted anyway, and who, hurting deep down, protested when asked to support a war ten thousand miles away, an irrational genocidal war against an Eastern race gripped in bloody revolution, emerging out of centuries of a mandarin-dominated feudal system.

The tragic climax of student revolt took place on May 4, 1970, at Kent State University in Ohio. Trigger-happy National Guardsmen called out to deal with waves of chanting students milling around the campus opened fire. Four students were shot dead, thirteen injured. The Guardsmen claimed they had fired in self-defense. Bill Dhroeder (19) was standing unarmed 380 feet away from the nearest Guardsman; Sandy Sheuer (19) was 390 feet away; Jeff Miller (20) was closest at 250 feet; and Alison Krause (19) was more than 345 feet away. Bobby Stamps was handing a pretzel to a fellow student when he was shot and maimed. Five years later a former Ohio Guardsmen testified in court that he had lied to a fellow Guardsman about finding a gun on the body of one of the stricken students.

In his memoirs Richard Nixon quotes a statement he had made about this time: "You see these bums, you know, blowing up campuses. Listen, the boys that are on the college campuses today are the luckiest people in the world, going to the great universities, and here they are burning up the books, storming around about this issue. . . . Then out there, we have kids who are just doing their duty. I have seen them. They stand tall, and are proud." He goes on to say, "Those few days after Kent State were among the darkest of my presidency. I felt utterly dejected when I read that the father of one of the dead girls had told a reporter, 'My child was not a bum.' "

Students across the nation rose in protest over the Kent State killings. A march on Washington was arranged. Concern over the prospect of rioting in the city brought a request to me from the office of Senator Edward Kennedy that our church might be made available to hold a memorial service as a symbol of the nation's grief. Once more our faithful went to work to arrange for sleeping accommodations and refreshments for some of the hundred thousand students who would arrive at the capital on Friday, May 8.

When I heard that several Senators had wished to participate in the service, I became sensitive to the possibility that the occasion might be used for covert political purposes. I expressed my fears to Mr. Kennedy's executive, whose assurances to the contrary I accepted.

The sanctuary was filled to overcrowding, as were the church halls; loudspeakers outside in the triangle in front of the church relayed the service to several thousand more.

In the first ten rows of pews sat some of the leading figures in the nation, including Averell Harriman, Robert McNamara, Ethel Kennedy, Benjamin Spock, Earl Warren, and Ramsey Clark. Students from Kent

State University read messages from the bereaved parents. The ecumenical nature of the memorial service was reflected in the participants: Rabbi Sheldon E. Elster, Father Donald Miller of the Newman Center at Kent State, Bill Coffin, Mrs. Coretta Scott King; Judy Collins played her guitar and sang. Scripture was read by Senators Mark Hatfield and Edward Kennedy, the latter reading from St. John 14. I read from Jeremiah 31:

> Hark! lamentation is heard in Ramah, and bitter weeping,
> Rachel weeping for her sons.
> She refuses to be comforted: they are no more. . . .

Many of the students stayed over for the Sunday morning services, finding in the fellowship of the Church some consolation in the bewildering events of their student days. That some of the students viewed the mission of the Church in a new perspective was confirmed by many letters I received. One campus chaplain commented that many of the students had stated that they had not realized the institutional Church was really concerned about what was happening in the real world. This insight opened up new ways of presenting the essential meaning of the gospel. Among some two hundred letters of thanks we received from the students themselves, perhaps the best summing up came in a short note enclosing two dollars and the laconic comment "Thank you for coffee, cookies, and Christianity."

As never before, churches and synagogues were now working as one, protesting the war. I recall one ecumenical service in Lafayette Square, opposite the White House. Rabbis, priests, and Protestant clergy of different denominations participated. I was asked to preach the sermon. When we gathered at St. John's Episcopal Church to make final arrangements at the hour of the open-air service, we were informed that our application to hold the service had been turned down on the grounds that we were holding a political meeting. We decided to defy the order. With $25 in our pockets (to cover bail, none of us wishing to spend even one night in the D. C. slob of a jail) we took our place under the shadow of the rampant equestrian statue of Andrew Jackson, stolidly waving his hat at passersby. The police were present, watching and listening. I preached forthrightly to the unseen President, demanding an immediate cessation of the bombing, which was violating every canon of religion, and a return to the Paris Peace Conference. The benediction was pronounced. None of us was arrested. The wise police no doubt weighed in the balance the ineffectiveness of a few clerics over against the furor that might arise over placing in jail twenty of the leading clergymen and rabbis in the nation's capital.

The fury of the bombing continued. Unknown to the general public, American forces had already invaded the netural country of Cambodia in May of 1970. Daniel Moynihan in his book *A Dangerous Place* unveils the grisly setting of this event: "I sat in the Roosevelt Room in May

1970, while Henry Kissinger briefed the White House staff on the Cambodian Invasion that had been launched a few moments earlier, halfway across the globe. He spoke with sexual excitement. He was going to smash the faces of those sons-of-bitches-no-good-bastards."

To many of us, it seemed that the nadir of national hypocrisy unveiled itself when President Nixon announced that all bombing would cease on Christmas Day, which happened, in 1970, to be a Sunday. Once more the clergy protested. Several hundred Jews and Christians gathered in Lafayette Square on the afternoon of Christmas Day around a row of portable tables on which were placed loaves of bread and bottles of wine. A rabbi officiated, bidding us come forward to share in the bread and wine. "Let each of us according to our faith interpret our own meaning," he said. The service over, we moved across Pennsylvania Avenue to the White House to place before the President our petition of protest. The gates were closed. White House guards explained that it was outside their jurisdiction to bear any message to the President. We pinned a copy of the protest to the gate.

As I turned around, a rather attractive young girl inquired about what we were all doing.

"We are clergymen," I explained. "We are protesting against the motives for the temporary cessation of bombing of Vietnam on Christmas Day. We can understand stopping the bombing because of military strategy, or perhaps because ammunition might be in short supply. But to cease from this fiendish slaughter on Christmas Day on the grounds that it is the birthday of the Prince of Peace is a gesture of monumental national hypocrisy."

It was not until I saw myself on the Walter Cronkite News bulletin that night (coast to coast) that I realized the young lady was a reporter for C.B.S. television.

By 1971, the Paris Peace Talks had stalled; Nixon's vaunted preelection plan seemed so much talk; the bombing of the North was intensified. There were now over five hundred thousand American troops involved in the conflict. Clergy and Laymen Concerned about Vietnam sponsored yet another gathering at our church.

I entered the pulpit holding aloft both arms, my fingers indicating the now traditional V peace sign, and in the strange silence I said, "My dear friends, as the host pastor once more, it is my honor to welcome you back to this beloved church. Yet it grieves me to do so, for it had been the wish of every one of us that these meetings would no longer be necessary and the war would be over. This longest of our wars drags on and there seems no end in sight. For your continuing witness and your faith for peace that bridges the miles that separate us, I thank you and welcome you."

Then Rabbi Brickner did that which both surprised me and, deep down, pleased me: "Friends, this is our third visit to this beloved sanctuary. Dr. Docherty, on behalf of those many friends you have made during these years of war, I thank you. We are proud that this church opened its doors so freely and generously. Please extend to your board our gratitude. This congregation has revived our faith in the institutional Church."

The tragic war dragged on. Not until 1973 were we to see its ending. The conditions of the peace, signed by Nixon's Secretary of State Defense, William Rogers, were similar to the terms that had been offered to Lyndon Johnson in 1968. In that time there had been an additional seventy thousand casualties.

By 1975 the North Vietnamese forces had taken Saigon, meeting only token resistance from the American-supplied army of South Vietnam. The temporary demarcation line of the 1954 Paris Treaty ceased to exist.

By 1979 veterans of the war were beginning to call themselves "the forgotten men." To remind the nation of their courage and sacrifice, President Carter rightly declared a Veterans of Vietnam Week in 1979, lest we forget. Some fifty-one thousand had died for their country — right or wrong. Of the two hundred thousand veterans wounded in Vietnam, twenty-one thousand were permanently disabled and five thousand lost at least one limb. Of the two million who returned, statistics reveal an unusually high rate of suicide, divorce, mental breakdown, and dope addiction. A strain of venereal disease imported from Vietnam, impervious to normal penicillin, was reaching epidemic proportions across the land, a fact that has been strangely pushed under the counter, except for occasional flashes on a public service television commercial. The average veteran has found it difficult to find a new career or job opportunity. One is glad to see that they are beginning to organize and find some recognition, such as the Vietnam memorial finally erected on the mall in Washington.

Where have all the flower children gone, they who once in Shelleyan bucolic dress strolled leisurely through life, smiling sweetly, and talked gently and believed they were indeed disciples of the Galilean, sentimentalizing about love and kindness and forgiveness, innocently unaware of the dimension of evil that anchors the human heart?

But where are the Pied Piper followers of Senators George McGovern and Eugene McCarthy who thought they were being radical when they dressed like tramps and carried posters, cheerleaders in the game of politics? No doubt most of them have trimmed their hair and spend their lives, brief-case and morning paper under their arm, commuting in suburban trains and car pools, returning in the evening to their segregated subdivisions nestled in the lush woodlands of suburbia, hoping to be able to meet the dues for the country club where their indulged children splash in the swimming pool and their pretty wives, whose tomorrows creep in a petty pace from day to day, play bridge, or is it gin-rummy? Overindulging in the wrong food, they have taken up jogging to avoid the Scylla of heart attack, only to land on the Charybdis of slipped disc.

It was said the First World War was the war to end all wars. A poet who never came home from it wrote to his and our own generation,

> To you from failing hands we throw
> The torch; be yours to hold it high.
> If ye break faith with us who die
> We shall not sleep, though poppies grow
> In Flanders fields.

17

Suddenly One Summer

Why did you give no hint that night
That quickly after the morrow's dawn,
And calmly, as if indifferent quite,
You would close your term here, up and be gone
    Where I could not follow
    With wing of swallow
To gain one glimpse of you ever anon!
    Never to bid good-bye,
    Or lip me the softest call,
Or utter a wish for a word, while I
Saw morning harden on the wall. . . .
              —Thomas Hardy, "The Going"

A WOMAN'S VOICE roused me from my dreamless sleep. I blinked up at a tall figure in white, silhouetted against the single bulb hanging from the center of a small ceiling. Gradually consciousness returned. I had been asleep in the guest room of the Forresterhill Hospital in Aberdeen. Jerry was very ill. I had wanted to spend the night at her bedside holding her hand, but the nurses had persuaded me that I needed rest. When I said that I would not sleep anyway, they had given me a sedative, assuring me that everything would be all right until the morning; in the meantime I must have a good night's sleep.

"Dr. Docherty." The voice was gentle. "I'm sorry to tell you that Mrs. Docherty passed away about half an hour ago."

I am still somewhat dumbfounded when I recall my immediate reaction. I simply said "Thank you, nurse," and arose, showered rather leisurely, and climbed the stairs to the elevator which took me to the fifth floor. The corridor along which I had walked over and over again these past eight weeks was dimly lit in the early morning darkness. From the side rooms came the sound of patients' labored breathing. When I reached the Intensive Care Unit at the end of the hall, the nurses were waiting for me. I noticed they no longer offered me the brown paper overshoes or the sterilized green gown that had always been required before. Jerry seemed in a deep sleep, lying on her back and very still. Those thoughtful women had robed her in a night dress with frills around the neck. Gone now the mottled fire from her cheek and the wrinkles from her brow; I looked upon a young face again, such as I had seen on that day long ago when we first met at the counter of a dingy office in the Waterloo Chambers in Glasgow.

A strange sense of relief swept over me as I realized the pain was at last over, replaced by this sweet and gentle sleep — until it dawned upon me like a cold enveloping wave of the sea that this was not sleep. I kissed her cold lips and caressed her soft hand grown heavy and chill. I said no prayer. I wept no tears. I sat oblivious of where I was, not believing what I was experiencing. We were together, Jerry and I; the rest of the world did not exist. The two of us floated together in a timeless, spaceless universe, utterly alone and silent.

"Is there anything you would like us to get you, Doctor?"

The voice was unreal. I had nothing to say to the nurse. We just sat there in the dimness. I had no desire to move and no idea of what the next step ought to be.

We had shared no last words together. Now it was too late. So many things I wanted to say, so much to tell, so often simply to say "I love you" and to talk about the strangely wonderful fun it had all been since we had come together. Jerry was still sleeping. The voice of the nurse interrupted my reverie once more.

"Yes, my dear, you have all been so very wonderful and kind. I cannot find words to thank you. I must phone, please. So many calls to make, to America."

In the office downstairs, I phoned Nuremberg and informed David. And Owensboro, Kentucky, for Garth. And of course I spoke to Jack McClendon in Washington. And the Craigs in Toronto. There would be time for the local calls later.

I ordered a cab, which arrived promptly. I asked the driver to take me to Peterculter, along the North Deeside Road. I got out shortly after we left the city and walked the remaining few miles — it was much too early to disturb Mairi's sleep at the manse of Peterculter where we were staying. The road follows the River Dee, beautifully winding between rows of granite homes. I could hear somewhere in the dark beyond the hawthorn hedge at the roadside the trickle of unseen running water. As the first glimmer of the dawn began to bleach the purple sky, a blackbird broke out in uncertain song. Reaching the village of Peterculter, I turned down the steep brae to the manse, its white walls glimmering in the dawn twilight. During Jerry's illness this had been our welcome home; Tom Howie, the minister, and I had been friends since college days. Sitting on the garden wall overlooking the manse glebe that sweeps down to the placid waters of the River Dee, I awaited full light. Turning quietly the handle of the front door of the manse, I tip-toed upstairs to Mairi's bedroom. I sat down on her bed. She awoke at my presence.

"Mama's passed away, darling."

We hugged each other in a flood of tears.

That summer of 1970 had begun on a joyous note for us. It saw our twentieth anniversary, which the congregation was happy to recognize after the morning service of June 20. The Peter Marshall Hall had been crowded and the speeches were good, some of them very funny. Jerry outdid herself, speaking as she always did from a manuscript meticulously prepared and smoothly delivered. She brought many laughs, chief of which I recall coming in response to her admission that when our call to the church came, she began to wish that Columbus had never discovered America! They presented us with a generous check and an extended three-month vacation.

That evening, we flew to Prestwick from New York's Kennedy Airport. Mairi accompanied us. She was about to begin an art course at Gray's Art School in Aberdeen. Garth remained at Owensboro for summer classes. David was at Bamberg, Germany, with the American army; we were looking forward to seeing him.

At Prestwick we looked in vain for my brother and his faithful Ford Prefect, which had become as much a part of the landscape as Ailsa Craig Rock itself. He had always met us at the airport. I phoned. He had been laid low with emphysema, and the wee car had seen its day. When we visited him and his wife, Lilly, at Giffnock, I was shocked by his appearance. It was as if the aged hand of time had suddenly touched him. He was weak, even his joking painful, making him cough whenever he laughed.

In our rented car, we made for the north. At Aberdeen I performed the marriage service of a lad I had baptized as a child in the North Kirk, the boy Garth had met on his first day at the grammar school, Douglas Farquharson. The service was held in Beechgrove Church, where Dr. Arthur Gossip had preached. I was recalling how it was while he was here that his wife had died. I had no idea that it would be the last service Jerry and I would share together.

In the midst of the toasts at the reception I was summoned to the telephone. It was my nephew George. My brother was in hospital, critically ill. I drove at high speed along the Aberdeen-Glasgow road, whose every turning I know like the palm of my hand. I prayed to the Lord that I might see my brother just once more.

Jack was in a large ward of the Southern General Hospital, propped up in bed, sipping a cup of tea, and looking remarkably well, though weak and pale.

"Jackie, son," I found myself saying, "you do know that I love you dearly?"

"Of course I do, Norton. That's a wee bit strange thing to say, is it not?"

"Well, I just felt I wanted to say it again, even though you know that I have loved you all the time."

Three hours later he died.

I conducted the funeral service at the Western Necropolis Crematorium, where as boys we had walked on Sunday afternoons, the incessant song of lark and thrush filling the sabbath with music.

At the service I wore my clerical robes: Geneva gown, black cassock, preacher's bands, stole, and, not least, the crimson D.D. hood. I had brought them with me across the Atlantic for the first time entirely to please my brother, who had complained that on all my previous visits I had conducted public worship with borrowed robes, often ill-fitting, sometimes tatty, and that I seemed not at all interested in displaying the fact that I was a D.D., D. Litt.

We left Scotland for Germany, to see David at Bamberg. Jerry had complained of stomach pains, but the doctor saw nothing to worry about. We put it down to the annual attack of bile she experienced when tackling the all-too-generous high teas of Scottish hostesses and the fish suppers at Largs prepared by Mr. Nardini. I suggested that we postpone the visit and that she should go to Glasgow's Western Infirmary for X-rays, but Jerry was anxious to see David.

The three-day, six-hundred-mile journey by car to Dover was distressing for Jerry, the Channel crossing to Calais a painful, wearying ordeal, the long overnight train journey to Bamberg a torturous nightmare. On our arrival, David immediately arranged for her to be taken the twenty miles to the American military hospital at Nuremberg, where X-rays revealed a massive distension of the bowel. The next morning she was operated on by two brilliant young American surgeons who had just come back from tending the wounded and dying in Vietnam. During three weeks of Jerry's postoperative convalescence I had opportunity to preach at chapel services and visit some of the American servicemen in their homes.

Further surgery was necessary. The U.S. Army offered to fly us by military plane anywhere in the world. We decided to return to Scotland. I went on ahead to Aberdeen to make preparations. Jerry followed by plane as soon as she was strong enough, accompanied by an army nurse specially assigned for this duty. At Forresterhill Hospital during the course of a six-hour operation, the surgeon, George Smith, uncovered extensive peritonitis. Antibiotics were immediately administered, and we all sat back confident to await a slow recovery.

August passed into September; soon the crisp mornings of autumn gave way to the snell winds of October. All the while I was buoyantly optimistic that all would be well. I planned to return to the church about mid October. Mairi and Jerry would take over an apartment in Aberdeen until such time as Jerry was able to return to Washington. It all seemed to be so straightforward. The doctors were not so sure.

On one occasion Dr. McGregor took me aside and with calm deliberation said, "George, 1 want you to understand that your wife is dangerously ill." But I knew him to be a rather pessimistic sort of fellow. I was much more encouraged by George Smith, who said there was a fifty-fifty chance of recovery.

Jerry's heart stopped. They were able to revive her. I was assured that there was still a ten percent chance. Even then I clung to that ten percent hope confidently. When John Murray arrived at the hospital at midnight, I interpreted his visit as simply another gesture of friendship rather than of his desire to be with me in case the end might come. . . .

The funeral service was held in the North Kirk, Aberdeen. Friends gathered from all over the country. It was a comfort to realize we were still remembered. The Washington City Presbytery sent over Jim MacDonnel, who spoke lovingly and well of the witness Jerry had made to the entire city. From the church itself, George Bergquist, President of the Board of Trustees, came over with Harold Roher, Jack McClendon, and Thelma Odom.

The children agreed that Lossiemouth, where we had all spent so many happy summer holiday hours, should be the place for the new family plot. The cemetery lies about half a mile from the village in a clearing in a thick pine forest within earshot of the surf pounding a sandy shore.

As we returned to Aberdeen, the cold October sun set in a blaze of fire, tinting with saffron the curtains of mist draping the flat fields. Night descended upon our sorrowing hearts and the quiet place we were leaving behind.

Back in Washington a special memorial service was held on the evening of October 25. The church was full; almost half of those in attendance were black. Ernest Somerville of the First Presbyterian Church, Philadelphia, gave the main tribute. In closing we sang the civil rights anthem "We Shall Overcome."

I was grateful for my work, but much more grateful for my congregation. They were now my family; they took me and my bairns lovingly into their homes and their hearts. Strengthened, I got down to my work again. My first sermon when I returned was based on the same text that Dr. Gossip had preached when his wife died, Ezekiel 24:16, 18:

> Man, I am taking from you at one blow
> the dearest thing you have, but you must not
> wail or weep or give way to tears. . . . I
> spoke to the people in the morning; and that very
> evening my wife died.

I have never had the heart either to read the manuscript again or to listen to the tape recording.

But when December came, I was overcome by a great ache to go back to Scotland, a compulsion to spend Hogmanay there. After the Christmas services, I took off for Lossiemouth and spent the remaining days of the year with the Crawfords, whose house I had visited first more than fifty years ago and which had since become our second home. Came the chimes of midnight on Hogmanay, I found myself, coat collar up against the wind from the sea, walking along streets deserted save for a few roistering happy firstfooters making their traditional rounds, along the forest-bound road, picking my way through the dark, starless, moonless night to the cemetery. I stood before the little plot. I found myself whispering "Happy New Year, Darling."

It seems strange to me now that I should have found myself wandering solitary in the moonless dark amidst the silence of a cemetery shortly after midnight on a Hogmanay. At the time it seemed to me to be as natural as a Sunday evening stroll. I had a date with my wife. It was Hogmanay. Had we not celebrated at least thirty-two Hogmanays together?

Around me in the darkness loomed the shadows of the stolid little tombstones with their carvings of loving memories. But this earth at my feet did not belong to the dead. It was sacramental of life, not death; of a presence, not an absence; of a precious present shared together, not a memory of the bewildering past. This clean sandy earth, which the tides of the Moray Firth had inundated and washed pure over a thousand years ago, would be home for me also. Together, bone of bone, flesh of flesh, we would sleep together.

The eerie pantheism of Rupert Brooke's poem "Dust" suddenly came alive for me:

> When the white flame in us is gone
> And we that lost the world's delight
> Stiffen in darkness, left alone
> To crumble in our separate night . . .
> We'll ride the air, and shine and flit,
> Around the places where we died,
> And dance as dust before the sun
> And light of foot and unconfined . . .
> And every mote, on earth or air,
> Will speed and gleam, down later days,
> And like a secret pilgrim fare
> By eager and invisible ways,
> Nor ever rest, nor ever lie,
> Till beyond thinking, out of view,
> One mote of all that's dust that's I
> Will meet one atom that was you.

No longer for me St. John the Seer's vision of the dead — mute, immobile, at rest in death until that Day when the grave would release its imprisoned, who would then enter into eternal glory. For me the distinctions between flesh and spirit, life and death, here and there, then and now, seemed abolished. Death had been lifted into a new omnipresence where abides him who assures us "I am with you always, to the end of time."

Not a shadowy dark valley but a veil thin as gossamer separated us. I would turn on my heel and leave this silent place, soon to be on my way across the Atlantic. And forever afterward at every service of worship I conducted, I would include above every other prayer thanksgiving for the Communion of Saints — thanksgiving for victory over the grave and thanksgiving for their abiding presence with us now.

At no time did I have any doubts about the existence of God; for me that would have been like denying the sunset or the moonrise. I did, however, begin to question the wisdom of his Providence. God surely had made a mistake! I was the one ready to go. I had more or less lived my life and, wonderful as it had been, there seemed little more for me to do or say. But Jerry had attained that wonderful time of life that perhaps only women fully appreciate. Her family was now grown and would soon be married with homes of their own and children. I am sure she must have dreamed of that day when she would take her grandchildren in her arms and, cooing them to sleep, see once more reflected in the sleeping faces the very image of her own. My wise son Garth was aware of this. When he saw his mother asleep in death, his first words were "Mama, you will not now see your own grandchildren."

My guilt became almost unbearable. The things I had foolishly said and done. My quick temper. I could have been kinder. Did I really need to be out of our home so much? I remembered when Jerry was abed six months after Garth's birth how my work took me out of the house six nights a week and often during the day; she had uttered not one word of complaint, made not one show of self-pity, had never complained that she was missing so much that was fun in my work. Those endless committee meetings — were they so very important? A married priesthood presents its own conflicts of interest, between the Bride of Christ which is the Church and the bride of our human love.

Back home again in Washington, I found my work time-consuming and fulfilling; it left me little room to sit and brood in self-pity. There was the weekly discipline of sermon preparation, visiting the congregation (especially the sick in hospitals far flung across the city), dialogue about the mission of the church with men and women who made time for it in their busy lives because they loved not only the Lord but his Church also. My staff were brothers and sisters to me. Work in the presbytery became more engrossing, and I valued the deepening friendships with my fellow clergy.

In the long view, my life became quite clear. I would retire in about five years, go back to Scotland, and buy a house in Lossiemouth. Indeed, I had my eye on the perfect location, an elegant stone villa overlooking the eighteenth green and the first tee of the Moray Golf course with the Moray Firth reaching to the far distance of the mainland, where the Paps of Caithness were clearly visible. We had planned this already, Jerry and I. There would be tea in the long forenight at the bay window lost in the glories of unrivaled sunsets casting a tremulous lane of gold over the glistering sea. I would climb the hill road near the little Normanesque red-tile-roofed church of St. Gerardine and view the harbor, its majestic break-water breasting the heavy surf; and the ancient sea town of Lossiemouth and the east sands; and in the distance the dark green line of Lossie Forest embracing a hallowed place that would be my daily walk.

I would pattern my life along the contours said to have been observed by St. Columba himself in an article written by Dr. George F. MacLeod I remembered appearing in *The Coracle*, the newsletter of the Iona Community:

> In the tradition of Columba's time, there were three stages which every man had to achieve if his development was to be complete — the quest of youth, the mission of maturity, and the free pilgrimage of age: the first, the training and conquest of self; the second, service to others; and finally, the achievement of that inner freedom that releases him from all earthly ties, so that he is really motivated as a pilgrim, knowing this world's system is alien, his home already in Heaven.

Surely I had achieved the second stage, if not the first? In New York Avenue Church, I had sought sincerely to serve others. Now life had no longer a perceptible horizon, no longer any mountains beckoning to be conquered, no deserts to be explored. Life had suddenly shrunk, had become a very short story, and I was nearing the last paragraph. I would retire to this lovely fishing village and grow old in fulfilled contentment, a pilgrim in an alien world, my home already in heaven, surrounded by good people who spoke my mother's tongue. In the meantime I must get to my feet again, back to my work at the church.

18

A Second Springtime

It's in a lonesome place you do have to be talking to someone, and looking for someone, in the evening of the day.

—J. M. Synge, *In the Shadow of the Glen*

ALMOST EVERY YEAR since that memorable visit to the States in 1949, I have been one of the speakers on the faculty at the August Bible Conference at Massanetta Springs, nestling among the lovely low-lying hills of the Shenandoah Valley of Virginia. Bible conferences do not make the impact on the life of the Church that once they did, but Massanetta has survived because it has adapted itself to the changing emphases of the faith in a questioning age. I have seen it transformed from a segregated faculty of prima donna preachers to a center of open discussion with the laity on the vital questions of faith and life.

I missed the Conference in that black summer of 1970. When I returned in 1971, I received a heartwarming welcome from the many friends I had come to know there. Jerry was sorely missed, especially by the younger preachers and their wives. I recall those happy discussions into the wee sma' hours after the meetings in our little wooden cottage among the trees; the whole gamut of the Church's mission was analyzed, the most important topic being the impact of the gospel on the problems of racial integration among the white churches. The authentic martyrs of those days of the black revolt were not the big-name preachers secure in the success of their famous pulpits, but such young couples of the manse as we were meeting. Gallantly they tolerated abuse that shames the Christian Church. Their children on the way to school were hooted as "nigger lovers." Manse telephones were tapped. In the middle of the night messages of obscenity or silence came over the phone. Some of the young preachers were confronted by their boards and simply told to get out. One, I recall, was told that if he did not clear out by afternoon he would be shot. These young wives had found in Jerry not merely a motherly figure, but an experienced colleague in the subtle art of being the minister's wife.

Jerry was a figure in her own right in the church. It was incumbent upon me for that reason alone to pay tribute at a service of worship. For

275

forty-five minutes I shared a little of our life in the Church and my own experience of grief and its bedfellows, guilt and regret. I spoke of the cosmic loneliness I was experiencing. "What do we do when the prayer we seek an answer to is not answered and our loved one dies?"

After the service a friend informed me that a young widow in the congregation who had been helped wished to see me. I was tired. I would see her in the morning, after breakfast.

In the cool of the following morning as I sat on a seat under the great trees on the lawn in front of the main building, I was approached by a tall young woman with fine features and dark blue-grey eyes, a brunette who spoke in a gentle voice. She was impeccably dressed. Sue Hollingshead shared her story with me. She had married Larry, an athletic, six-foot-three basketball coach and reading specialist at the Milton Hershey School in Hershey, Pennsylvania. Within eight months he was dead of a rare disease. Why Larry? Why did this fine Christian lad, this dedicated teacher, have to be taken just as they were beginning their life together so happily? After four years of marriage? Jerry and I had known so many more years of happiness than Sue and Larry.

"Actually, Sue, our circumstances, while similar, are really fundamentally different," I told her. "I shall never marry again: I'm in the autumn of my years; but you are young, too young to carry around this albatross of grief all your days. You must marry again. One day this suggestion will not sound so terrible as it does now. If indeed our loved ones are spectators to the travail of this world, would they not rejoice in a new start for you, even the rekindling of love, facing with courage whatever lies before you, rather than have you go through life with this burden of unredeemed grief?"

Early October, among the cards I received from friends who had attended Massanetta arrived a letter from Sue Hollingshead. She would be visiting Washington and wanted to know whether I would be in my own pulpit the first Sunday in November.

After the service on that day, the young lady who had spoken to me about her bereavement at Massanetta Springs shook my hand. In my office later, I asked my question: "Are you married yet? Any developments? No? Well, my advice is still the same. Get married as soon as possible!"

A week later when I received a note of thanks, I felt I wanted to see this young woman again. I telephoned Hershey.

"Sue? This is George Docherty. Could I have dinner with you on Friday night? Shall we say five-thirty? I am sure you will know a convenient restaurant in Hershey. I'll call for you at your apartment."

Friday afternoon I set off in my wee Renault on the 150-mile journey north, taking Route 15, which carves its way through the Battlefield of Gettysburg, past the memorials and cannon by the roadside, on through Maryland to Pennsylvania. I arrived in good time for my appointment, but to my dismay found that I had forgotten Sue's last name and address! I had left without the little chit on which my secretary, Henry Booker, always typed out details of my visits. I consulted a large telephone book. I knew the name began with *H* — Holdsworth? Harmsworth? There were literally scores of pages of names beginning with *H*: Hahn, Hein, Himmel, Hoch, Hochen, Hochensburger. . . . All of them German, too. In despair I gave up. I started to look for a high-rise apartment along the ten miles of Chocolate Avenue running through the town but saw nothing save white painted wooden or shingle-tile homes. It was now seven o'clock. Suddenly, I remembered Friday was choir practice night, and that Henry, who was also our organist, would be in the Church office.

"Henry, I'm lost," I shouted over the telephone.

"I'm not surprised at that. You left your chit behind. The name is Sue Hollingshead and the telephone number is 533-3258."

I phoned very penitently. Sue pointed out that I had been consulting the large Harrisburg telephone directory; the Hershey listings were in a small section at the back of the book!

Over dinner, we spoke of many things — of the Church and Peter and Catherine Marshall, of Sue's teaching at Hershey School and the serendipitous tale of Milton Hershey the chocolate king. We spoke of Scotland and of Sue's family and, of course, of Larry and Jerry. It seemed so spontaneous and natural, as if we had known one another for years. I felt an upsurge of joy that I had not known for many a long day. Finally I dared to express the thought that had been in my mind since I had first telephoned her for our dinner date.

"Sue, my dear, I want you to consider what's on my mind. . . . I want to marry you. . . . I'm falling in love with you. . . . Please think seriously about it. . . . For I am deadly serious. I do so very much want us to meet again."

We had coffee at her little apartment. At the door I presumed to kiss her lips before I went out into the dark chill of the night and took off in a hurry on my three-hour trip to Washington, negotiating icy roads through the windswept farmlands of Maryland. About three in the morning, from the comfort of my bed back in Washington, I telephoned to thank her for a memorable evening together. There was no sleep for me. The possibility of an entirely new life seemed to be opening up for me. I put away the thought. It was presumptuous and even unfair to expect a lass like Sue to consider marrying a man double her age. And what of the future? If I were spared my allotted span, she would be left a widow again. Yet, had not both of us discovered through grief and pain that life seldom matched our dreams? Sue seemed to fill the echoing loneliness in my life by her presence, the sound of her voice, her laugh.

It was not a question of my being alone in the sense that I could not make do at home. I had maid help and believed I was as expert in domestic chores as any other male. The church was too fulfilling to allow time to feel lonely, Washington was an exciting city to live in, and friends I had in abundance, especially my fellow clergymen. In their own subtle yet loving way they were trying to help. At parties I would find myself seated at table with the only unattached lady in the company. One preacher came to the point: "Now, George, you are not going to like what I am about to say to you, but some of us have decided that the sooner you get married the better. You don't realize it, but you are going around the odd man out. Now, there's a widow in my congregation. . . ."

They did not realize that mine was not that kind of loneliness. It was not simply the need for companionship; it was an inner sense of being alone in a great cold universe, once more little Georgie shut out of my home when the rest of the world was singing. At night after a long day at the church, as I turned the key in the lock with the familiarity of the years, in the hallway I would call out happily as I had ever done, "Jerry dear, I'm home," my voice echoing in the empty house. Gigi, our wise little poodle, would jump up and bark and then dart past me to meet that someone who always followed in my footsteps up the garden path. I found myself in the mornings setting out breakfast for two.

After our Christmas services at the church were over, I flew back to Prestwick, Scotland, and motored north through the Grampions to Lossiemouth to keep yet another Hogmanay vigil. I had commissioned a stone to be erected on the grave, and nearby a garden bench. To this spot I journeyed every day to sit brooding about my life under leaden skies, with high sea winds and at times the splash of rain on my face that seemed to echo the cold melancholy of my heart. Day by day I sat there completely alone except for the gravedigger whom I would catch out of the corner of my eye raking dead branches and leaves. Gradually I realized that there was something wrong, something emotionally cloying bordering almost on the morbid with this pattern of living, something totally alien to everything I was sure Jerry would wish for me. I was clinging not to the memory of a beloved spouse, but selfishly to my own grief, subconsciously deriving from these moods a strange perverted peace. (O *Grief*, that will not let me go.) I decided that for my own spiritual life I would have to let go of this devouring grief, I would have to relinquish the past. Life could never again be the same. I remembered King David, who when his love-child was ill had dressed in sackcloth and ashes, but when the child died had risen and dressed once more like a king. "I shall go to him; he will not come back to me."

Life is in large measure the process of letting go of something. We let go of youth that we might not look foolish. We let go of our children when they become adults that they may become truly mature. One day we must let go of life itself. And now it was time for me to let go of Jerry.

Back in Washington ten days later, I resumed my work. One night

I attended a concert with one of my church members, Harold Roher, who had traveled across the Atlantic to be with me when Jerry died. Eugene Ormandy was conducting the Philadelphia Symphony Orchestra in the Kennedy Center. The main work was Brahms's Fourth Symphony. The majestic music must have touched a deep and sensitive chord; I found myself when I returned to the empty house writing my last love letter to Jerry, letting her go. It was a poem, and it came as spontaneously as a written note. The first and last stanzas read,

> Sleep on sweet one, sleep, sleep, sleep.
> Sleep that stills the pulse and pain,
> Becalms the panting, parting breath
> On a sea of soundless sleep,
> Untroubled sleep,
> Sweet sleep. . . .
>
> Yet I still breast the tides of life,
> Carrying in my heart
> That quiet where my loved one sleeps,
> Until the morn of my own mute moment's dawning.
> There will be light and song
> In the stillness of your sleep,
> My sweet one.

I had already told my children about Sue. I reached out to my little brood — I, who had always been there when they had reached out to me. They were grown to maturity themselves now: Garth, with his business degree, worked at a Holiday Inn in downtown Washington; David, back from the army in Germany, was resuming his studies at George Washington University; Mairi, forsaking art when she saw the wonderful ministry of healing that had surrounded her mother in Aberdeen, was now training to be a nurse at the Washington Hospital Center. They all approved of my hopes, not least Mairi. I introduced Sue to them in Washington; she seemed then, and now is, like an older sister to Mairi.

I decided to consult the chairman of my Board of Trustees, George Bergquist, an Assistant Secretary of Defense. He has an alert face crowned with brindle hair and a twinkle in his eye, and is hard-headed like most Swedes — and Scots.

"George, what would you say if I told you that your minister was seriously thinking of getting married again?"

"I'd say this," he replied with surprising alacrity: "it would be one of the best pieces of news I'd heard in a long time. And let me add that I know it is the kind of news that many members of the congregation could welcome."

"Well, that surprises me."

279

"Don't you realize that we have all been worried about you? You look pale and drawn. The zing seems to have gone out of your preaching. Some of the women have gone so far as to say that it's time the minister got married again; he needs a wife."

Sue and I were married on June 3, 1972.

We had planned a quiet wedding — just a few friends outside the family circles. But how does one choose from fifteen hundred members of a church of whom so many had become lifelong friends? We ended by sending out fifteen hundred invitations! About a thousand attended the service in the church sanctuary, which was conducted by Ernest Sommerville of Philadelphia First Presbyterian Church and my beloved colleague Jack McClendon. Afterward, over seven hundred gathered in the Peter Marshall Hall for the reception. It was a gala day in the church that brought a new light to those dark days of Vietnam. No couple ever embarked on their honeymoon with so many heartfelt prayers and good wishes. We honeymooned in Europe. In Scotland Sue received an affectionate welcome from all my friends.

On our return, the impact of Sue upon the life of the church was immediate and splendid. She was soon getting to know the younger couples and their growing children. The manse was thrown open once more for entertainment. At Christmastide, we entertained the boards of the church on a Saturday afternoon, some 130 guests mingling happily, drinking punch in almost every room in the house and out on the lawn. Together we visited the older members of the church, who were excited to meet the minister's young wife, of whom they had been hearing so much. With Thelma Odom, Sue became enthusiastically involved in our inner-city work. The women's organizations welcomed her happily. Her almost perfect memory astounded everyone, as it still amazes me. She knew the first name of almost every member of our large choir. Even yet when we greet the congregation after services, no name ever escapes her as she smilingly offers warm handshakes.

After our honeymoon, I was back with a new-found driving enthusiasm at my desk, pecking out my weekly 3,500-word sermons. There did not seem to be enough Sundays in the year to meet the flood of new ideas. Looking back, I believe these four years between the time of my marriage to Sue and my retirement in 1976 to be among the most productive of my ministry. Was not I the lucky man indeed? Who was ever given such a second chance as Providence had unfolded for me? A second springtime had arrived in the autumn of my days. And it's no longer a lonesome place; I now have someone to be talking to and to be looking for in the evening of the day.

19

Pandora's Box

If Congress accepts my six proposals, the Ninety-Second Congress at the end of its term will be able to look back on a record more splendid than any in our history. . . . This Congress can be remembered for its opening the way to a new American Revolution — a peaceful revolution in which power was turned back to the people — in which government at all levels, was refreshed and renewed and made truly responsive. . . . Five years from now America will enter its third century as a young nation new in spirit, with all the vigor and freshness with which it began its first century.

—President Richard Milhous Nixon,
1971 State of the Union Address

DURING OUR HONEYMOON in Europe, Sue and I read an item in the *Herald Tribune*, that remarkable daily that encapsulates for Americans abroad the best of all the news that's fit to print from the *New York Times* and the *Washington Post*. It was scarcely headline news. A burglary had been committed in Washington, D.C. At 2:30 A.M. on June 17, 1972, five men had been arrested for unauthorized entry into the headquarters of the Democratic National Committee located in the Watergate office-apartment-hotel complex where Rock Creek Park merges with Virginia Avenue on the banks of the Potomac, where I had on occasion enjoyed Sunday brunch in the dim irreligious light of its restaurant located on the ground floor.

The details of the burglary sounded bizarre. The culprits were by no means typical crooks. They were dressed in smart business suits, were wearing surgical gloves and carrying a walkie-talkie, forty rolls of unexposed film, two 35mm cameras, lock picks, pen-sized tear gas guns, and bugging devices apparently capable of picking up both telephone and room conversations.

By the time Sue and I had reached Florence American papers were starting to make a great deal of the story. There were even ludicrous allegations that the Republican Committee for the Re-election of the President was behind the break-in, that the purpose was apparently to lay hands on documentary evidence that would link presidential candidate George McGovern to Communist interests, especially out of Cuba. It was alleged that one of the culprits, James McCord, a former C.I.A. agent, had been paid by C.R.E.E.P. to carry out this nefarious business.

All of this was of course indignantly denied by John Mitchell, the former United States Attorney General and now the Nixon Campaign Manager: "The person involved [McCord] is the proprietor of a private security agency who was employed by our committee months ago to assist with the installation of our security system. . . . We want to emphasize that this man and the other people involved were not operating on either our behalf or with our consent. There is no place in our campaign or in the electoral process for this type of activity, and we will not permit or condone it."

But Lawrence O'Brien, the Democratic Chairman, was not at all satisfied; he told reporters that the break-in "raised the ugliest question about the integrity of the political process that I have encountered in a quarter-century of political activity. No mere statement of innocence by Mr. Nixon's Campaign Manager, John Mitchell, will dispel these questions."

From the White House at Key Biscayne, Presidential Press Secretary Ron Ziegler, speaking for the President, said, "Certain elements may try to stretch this beyond what it is." He described the incident as a "third-rate burglary attempt not worthy of further White House comment." The President himself announced publicly on June 22 that "The White House has had no involvement whatever in this particular incident."

Meanwhile Sue and I had been happily strolling among the glories of the Italian Renaissance in Rome, admiring the cypress groves and the lovely terraced vineyard countryside as we motored north. We crossed the border into Yugoslavia, turned westwards along the German autobahns toward Switzerland and, leaving the best wine to the end, completed our vacation in Scotland, whence we flew back at the end of August to Dulles Airport in Washington, to discover that public opinion polls were rating Mr. Nixon nineteen points ahead of Senator George McGovern, a fact that depressed me, devoted admirer that I was of the all-too-naive honesty of the Senator. This poll surely gave the lie to the involvement of the Republicans in the break-in. Why a James Bond stunt by the Republicans when it seemed a foregone conclusion already that their man would be elected for a second term in the White House?

The daily reporting by two busy press beavers of the *Washington Post*, Bob Woodward and Carl Bernstein, of further "revelations" took a secondary place in the new life upon which I was now embarking with my new bride. We visited assiduously, especially the older members of the congregation and those in hospitals and nursing homes. We dined out almost every night of the week. The congregation was receiving Sue with open arms, and I blessed their generous hearts.

Looking back in my files, I notice that I preached on my return sermons entitled "Amazing Grace" and "Christian Marriage — Ordained of God," which a happy Christian minister might readily preach. On the Sunday of Labor Day weekend, I punned in a sermon title, "The Cost of

Living." For some reason I cannot now understand, I preached, about that time, on the unlikely but perennial subject of "Divorce." On Reformation Sunday at the end of October, on the eve of the presidential election, I was back on the theme of Vietnam, presenting a plea for a new approach for a withdrawal from Vietnam. Mr. Nixon had claimed to have a new peace plan. On television, with Billy Graham in the studio audience, he actually reached into his inside coat pocket, as if the plan were there, already written out. I was hoping that it was not another laundry list such as Senator Joseph McCarthy in the fifties had held up in front of television cameras, leading us to believe he possessed proof of 201 Communists employed by the government.

It must have been about this time that Bernard Norlinger, President of the Bar Association of the District of Columbia, phoned me requesting that his Association be permitted to use our sanctuary for an ad hoc lunchtime meeting on "a matter of pressing urgency to all lawyers." I welcomed them — some four hundred lawyers. We were always glad to make available our sanctuary, so conveniently located downtown, for such meetings. Only then did I begin to realize the legal and constitutional implications of the Watergate break-in. These trained and responsible lawyers were asking some fundamental questions. If Watergate were indeed known to the President, if this had been a plot by his reelection committee, the country was facing something more than an unsuccessful break-in. Maybe Messrs. Woodward and Bernstein had got on to something big after all. Were we seeing an overspill of the cynicism that Vietnam had spawned? Was the war's wanton meaninglessness beginning to corrupt the inner circles of the nation's political power?

Came the November election. George McGovern was swamped; Nixon carried every state in the Union except Massachusetts and the District of Columbia. With an unbelievable resilience, Mr. Nixon had rebounded once more into the center of national life. It seemed only yesterday when we had witnessed his sad exit from the California gubernatorial election of 1962 as he stood before a forest of cameras conceding defeat and snarling that the press wouldn't have Dick Nixon to kick around any more. No political prediction has ever been quite so wrong!

It was a memorable inaugural parade in the fitful January sunshine. Facing Lafayette Square in front of the White House, a bulletproof glassed-in pavilion had been erected for the President to watch the procession of representatives of the fifty states with banners, bunting, and brass bands. A special cheer for the Whittier High School Band brought the President to his feet with his well-known wide grin; to all appearances, no man could be happier.

By February, Watergate was no longer a mere witch-hunt by reporters of the *New York Times* and the *Washington Post*. A special Senate Watergate Committee was set up under the chairmanship of Senator Sam

Ervin of North Carolina. By May, when the proceedings of this committee were nationally televised, the nation was party to a spectacle even more memorable than the forty-six-day coverage of the Army-McCarthy hearings in the fifties, as a long list of White House staff members was subpoenaed, solemnly sworn in, and closely questioned. Day by day, week by week, month by month, the televised proceedings came into almost every home in the nation. The whole structure of White House politics was ruthlessly revealed; it was not a pretty picture.

One remembers the expansive bulk of Sam Ervin in the Chair, bushy eyebrows, heavy jowls, his small eyes peering out of his large moon face, doodling with his horn-rimmed spectacles, his words coming slowly with the music of North Carolina in them, his mind like most southerners I have met — razor-edged, acute, working in inverse ratio to the flow of his words. This could have been Abe Lincoln himself presiding over a circuit court hearing, probing gently with slow and infinitely patient questioning. He seemed to be thinking as he spoke, though I am sure he had already rehearsed it all in his mind. His comments and observations were those of a preacher whose thinking is molded by the idiom of the King James Bible. From his lips flowed pontifically a legal gobbledygook. He shared with us anecdotes from his years of court experience and was not averse to quoting Old Testament Scripture. This astute, benign nonhero statesman was becoming the unlikely star of the television screen. For me *The Tonight Show* lost out as I watched reruns of the committee proceedings at the end of the day.

When Senator Ervin read out to the Committee the contents of certain documents that Counsel to the President John W. Dean III had held for safekeeping in his office and referred to their contents as indicative of the "Gestapo mentality" of the Nixon administration, I was both shocked and rather fearful. As a preacher who ought in some measure to be speaking out on the morality of the situation, I wondered what specifically I ought to be doing. I was embarrassed when James "Scotty" Reston of the *New York Times* commented on the silence of institutional Christianity. Despite the accumulating evidence of witnesses, innuendo, and second guessing, there seemed a lack of hard legal evidence against the President himself. I watched his face on television and carefully studied his circumlocutions as he wriggled out of compromising situations, always with an air of hurt innocence, laying the blame upon the shoulders of his staff, claiming a dubious ignorance of what was really happening. I became convinced that he was in fact hiding some dark secrets.

Opportunity to speak out came when I was invited to preach at the fine Liberal Arts Presbyterian Church of Wooster in Ohio at their commencement on June 17, 1973. Commencement addresses normally exhort graduates to be loyal to the high principles their college has inculcated, to make the world a better place to live in than they had found it (I had been so enjoined). But the hour seemed too grave for such platitudes.

I reminded the students that they were graduating at a significant hour in the nation's history: there was the cancerous growth of Vietnam abroad and now the tragedy of Watergate at home. For such a time Rupert Brooke had cried out,

> Now, God be thanked, Who has matched us with His hour,
> And caught our youth, and wakened us from sleeping.

We had not heeded the voice of Reinhold Niebuhr warning for thirty years against presumptuous human pretension in the face of tragedy. The chirpy optimism of the nineteenth century, born out of the Darwinian belief that every day in every way we were getting better and better as a society was no longer supportable. Even Walter Lippmann, dean of the American press corps, whom I had admired since my student days when I had read his *Preface to Morals*, was now writing, "The malaise of our day is the belief in the Jacobean and Rousseauan view of the perfectibility of man both as an individual and certainly in his corporate life. There seems to be in man what the theologians called 'original sin.'"

Behind Watergate lay the greed for power. Vietnam had rendered us insensitive to human values. Watergate was the fruit of the war's moral anarchy. Always there had been political corruption, but in the past it had been a matter of lust for money. Revealed before our eyes in Washington was the lust for power for its own sake. "Power tends to corrupt; absolute power corrupts absolutely" wrote Lord Acton long ago. To grasp the power of the presidency, there was little that this Washington clique would not do — bug telephones, muzzle the F.B.I., use the C.I.A. in the name of national security to withhold legal inquiry. Nor were these perpetrators gangsters like Hitler's Göring or Goebbels or Stalin's atheistic partymen; that would at least have been understandable. Instead we were seeing attractive young Ivy League graduates, most of them members of some branch of the Christian Church — indeed, of fundamentalist churches, which stress personal morality and spiritual self-discipline.

"Few words were more poignant," I said to the graduates, "than those of Mr. Jeb Magruder (who happens to be a Presbyterian) in response to a question by Sam Ervin, who seemed to set aside his role as lawyer and become a friend, an elderly but sincere friend. 'What advice would you give to young people coming out of college?' he asked. 'Whatever they do, it must not be government service,' was his reply. When asked why he did what he did, Magruder responded, 'It is a time when everyone is flouting law and order. Even my old teacher and friend Bill Coffin, Chaplain at Yale, has been arrested!'

"There was, however, a qualitative moral difference between what

Coffin did and what Magruder and the others had tried to pull off," I continued. "Coffin did it in the name of conscience, a good conscience, a Christian conscience that may defy even the law. When the powers that be fail to see that justice is done, when the protectors of the law become themselves lawless, there is a place in Christian commitment for conscientious objection, for defiance of the law and the courage to accept the consequences. But Magruder and his ilk had concealed what they were doing. Only when they were found out did they confess. Their conduct had no support in the Christian faith. These men were the products of civil religion — whatever the denomination may be — bellhops of the power structure and lackeys of the status quo."

I'm an old hand at commencement addresses. This one was received with the strange silence one might find in a funeral parlor, though some of the students came up and shook my hand. By the look in their eyes, I did feel that perhaps something of what I was trying to convey had in fact pierced the haze of their understandable preoccupation with their own future. I preached the same sermon the following Sunday to my own congregation. It received a cool reception from our Republican members.

My concern as a clergyman lay with the moral implications as well as the legality of Watergate. A close friend in these days was Arnold Keller, the distinguished minister of the Lutheran Church of the Reformation, which stands on Capitol Hill facing the Capitol with the Supreme Court Building on one side and the Library of Congress on the other and the Folger Shakespeare Library across the street. George Bernard Shaw might have described Arnold as he described the Rev. James Morell in his drama *Candida*: a "first-rate clergyman, able to say what he likes to whom he likes, to lecture people without setting himself up against them." No quietist Lutheran this man! He was smitten by the fond ambition that one day he would, like myself, break eighty on the Brettan Woods Golf Course where we all too infrequently played together. When I play golf, I become a Thoreau strolling around a Walden pond, forsaking the world and by the world hopefully forsaken for a brief hour or two. But the subject of Watergate intruded even into our golf.

"I want you to have breakfast with me tomorrow morning," Arnold announced to me on Monday as we ate our hamburgers in the clubhouse after a game. "I'm due to meet Father John McLaughlin, the resident priest in the White House. He wants to see me for some reason. I suspect it's because I am chairman of the Council of Churches in Washington."

Father McLaughlin, who ironically lived in the Watergate complex, was a shrewd but gracious middle-aged Jesuit. Over breakfast he sounded us out on what our churches were thinking about the Watergate affair. We told him that we were not alone in believing Watergate to be a moral problem almost demonic in nature. We promised to meet again. We never did. This Vicar of Bray was to be loyal to his President until the end. He did not see what Arnold and I tried to show him — that the path the President was taking would lead to impeachment.

Actually, I was not myself sure of the possibility of impeachment until I met for breakfast with a group of clergymen on Capitol Hill as a guest of Republican Congressman Paul N. McCloskey, Jr., of California. We had been talking around the matter when suddenly I blurted out, rather rudely I fear, "Congressman, if you will permit me to say this: I do not believe the House will move for an impeachment trial of the President. You are too much of a trade union up here on Capitol Hill. If you merely censured Senator Joseph McCarthy, is it likely that you will take the unprecedented step of impeaching the President of the United States?"

"You're wrong, Doctor, quite wrong," he responded. "Already there are several counts, any one of which might lead to impeachment of the President. Mr. Nixon approved the Huston Plan, which expanded covert domestic intelligence activities such as tampering with the mail, wiretapping, and breaking and entering into private premises such as the offices of Dr. Fielding, Daniel Ellsberg's psychiatrist. There was the creation of the Plumbers Unit to investigate leaks of information. There were seventeen wiretaps placed on reporters' phones by orders of the C.I.A. There was the order given to the C.I.A. to limit the F.B.I.'s initial investigation into the burglary at Watergate. And there have been alleged payments to the burglars in return for their silence about persons behind the break-in."

The nation at this time was further shocked by a Baltimore inquiry into the affairs of Vice President Spiro Agnew when he had been Governor of Maryland. This was the man who had in June denounced the "swelling of prejudiced publicity" and the "Perry Mason impact of the televised hearings," declaring that "they can hardly hope to find the truth and can hardly fail to muddy the waters of justice beyond repair." This was the man who had thundered that theirs would be an administration based upon law and order. Now he was charged by Baltimore federal prosecutors who had gathered enough evidence to indict him for having accepted illegal cash payoffs for years. Elliot Richardson, the Attorney General, set up plea-bargaining procedures in October. Vice President Agnew pleaded "no contest" before the courts. And resigned.

Worse was to erupt upon our already bewildered heads. Back in April 1973, Professor Archibald Cox of Harvard, who had been appointed special prosecutor to handle Watergate by his friend Elliot Richardson (who had himself only just been appointed Attorney General), probed into the possible existence of tapes that Mr. Nixon had made and collected over the years that might provide a fertile source for evidence pertinent to the case. When Professor Cox requested the relevant tapes, the President forwarded some, but refused to surrender others, claiming executive privilege. Cox subpoenaed the tapes. The President refused to hand them over. The Special Prosecutor broke the stalemate by announcing he would hold a press conference on national television. All of us expected he would state his case and resign forthwith. He declared he had no intention of resigning. He cited the case of a former President of the United States, Andrew Jackson, who had demanded deposits from the Bank of the United States. His Secretary of the Treasury refused to comply with this presidential order; President Jackson fired him and appointed another Secretary of the Treasury. On refusing to hand over the funds, this second Secretary was fired too. President Jackson finally got a third nominee who would do as he wished. "That's one way of proceeding," Cox said.

General Haig, acting for the President, asked Richardson to fire Cox. Richardson, to his eternal credit, refused and resigned. When his deputy William D. Ruckelshaus, acting as Attorney General, was asked to fire Cox, he also resigned. Haig is reported to have said, "Well, you know what it means when an order comes down from the Commander in Chief and a member of his team cannot execute it." It was now left to Solicitor General Robert H. Bork to fire Cox. He signed a two-paragraph letter written by White House aides accomplishing just that. "The office of the Watergate Special Prosecutor has been abolished as of approximately 8:00 P.M. today, 26 October 1973" was the stunning news that came over television at ten o'clock. It became known as "the Saturday Night Massacre."

A tidal wave of protests from all over the country seemed to inundate the White House. Sam Ervin was right: this was gestapo politics. Long ago Plato had warned us that a corrupt democracy is replaced by oligarchy; that, in our day, means fascism. In my own lifetime, I had watched it consume Germany, climaxing in the Reichstag fire.

Ten o'clock Saturday night is too late an hour to prepare a sermon free from anger. On November 4, however, it was ready — "The Writing on the Wall." The book of Daniel contains an account of how "Belshazzar the king made a great feast to a thousand of his lords, and drank wine before the thousand." The drunken king demands that his wine be served in the sacred golden and silver goblets he has plundered from the Temple of Jerusalem, thereby defiling their sanctity. The king beholds a hand, writing upon the wall *mene mene tekel u-pharsin*. Called in to interpret the strange language, the eighty-three-year-old Daniel could easily have placated the king with such a gloss as "You have been weighed and there is none like you, not even the Persians." He would have earned both favor and gifts. But this was a Daniel come to pronounce the judgment of Yahweh upon a wicked, corrupt regime: "Here is the interpretation: *mene*: God has numbered the days of your kingdom and brought it to an end; *tekel*: you have been weighed in the balance and found wanting; *u-pharsin*: and your kingdom has been divided and given to the Medes and Persians."

Even as they feasted, Darius king of Persia and his triumphant army were storming the doors of the sleeping city. The sin of Belshazzar was the desecration of the holy, the blasphemy of defiling that which belongs to God alone. Truth also is holy. He who would desecrate the holy vessels of truth will suffer God's judgment.

"What we have seen in the Saturday Night Massacre," I said, "is the attempt to corrupt the vessels of integrity and justice and truth. In a world of situation ethics, when everyone believes that whatever is done in the name of expediency is right, let us be reminded that we live in a moral universe.

"The voice of God will not be silenced, nor those who speak for his truth. Neither king nor president can claim to be above the moral law without incurring the consequences that befall all who would dare to ignore it. The office of the Special Prosecutor represented integrity and the search for justice. No man can withstand the tide of truth, any more than King Canute could, by dint of will, restrain the incoming tide."

"Watergate has become our Pandora's box, letting loose the evils of our age. This nation is in greater jeopardy today than it would be from a threat of invasion from all the armies of the world. The Constitution and all it stands for is at stake. Watergate is doing what Hitler failed to do: undermining the very foundations of the moral order upon which the founding fathers built when first they dreamed of a state in which the people could enjoy a life of liberty and the pursuit of happiness. Our only assurance lies in Hope, still hidden in Pandora's box. So long as the people preserve Hope, there will be the chance of new beginnings. The writing is on the wall for the nation. Let him who has ears and eyes look and listen. . . ."

I was encouraged by the reaction of my people. Adverse criticism came from those who insisted on confusing party politics with real politics, which is not simply "the art of the possible," as Lyndon Johnson claimed, but the science of statecraft. I was accused of being a Democrat (which I am) and of gunning for Mr. Nixon's blood (which I was not); or they accused me of being a foreigner (which I am not) who did not understand the American way of life. I believed I was speaking out on behalf of concerned Americans. As Hugh Sidey put it during a television panel broadcast, "What is the conservative view of burglary, and what is the liberal attitude towards larceny?"

Mr. Nixon held Sunday morning worship services in the White House when he was in town. These family services, as might be expected, grew in size until the East Room was crowded with distinguished citizens from all walks of life. Church choirs were also invited to sing and lead the praise (my own church choir, under Steve Prussing, participated twice). There were those who objected to such services, citing the principle of the separation of Church and State: the White House is a federal building, they said, and if prayer is prohibited in public schools, why should it be permitted in the White House? I did not think this argument had much validity. The President of the United States ought to have the freedom to hold private family services in his own residence, and it was to be expected that such gatherings of colleagues and friends would be large.

In the course of a conversation I asked Arnold Keller what he would preach if he were invited to one of these White House services.

"I'd refuse to go," was his prompt reply. "You can't just go into a man's home and in the presence of leading figures in the land start to preach about Watergate and political corruption."

"The prophet Nathan accused King David of infidelity in his own palace."

"I'm no Nathan, George."

As it happened neither of us was given opportunity to become the nation's Nathan: we were never invited to the White House services — which may well have been a kind of Irish compliment. A book of White House sermons made both Arnold and me blush at its homiletical pabulum and civil religion theology. And when I inquired why the choir of New York Avenue Presbyterian Church should be invited twice to these services but not the minister of the church, I was informed that different White House committees were in charge of choirs and preachers! There was one unique achievement of these White House Services, however: they broke up traditional Sunday morning golf foursomes at the Burning Tree Club. Knowing some of the distinguished members of that club, I can testify that to sunder such a Burning Tree tradition could only have been accomplished by presidential order!

Further shocks rocked the nation. John Dean was sacked; John Ehrlichman and H. R. Haldeman resigned. In announcing over television the departure of these loyal assistants, the President told the nation he had been misled by his subordinates into believing that no one in his administration or in his campaign committee was implicated and that for the first time in his political career he had left the management of his campaign to others.

It was apparent that John Dean was not going to take such an ignominious end to his career passively. Sitting before the committee, he read out his statement — 245 pages of it — as if he were reading a railroad timetable or a report of stock exchange prices, in a voice devoid of emotion. Not far away sat his lovely blonde wife, who was to be at his side throughout the proceedings. He confirmed that the phones of individuals the White House considered to be opposed to its policies were routinely tapped; that the office of Dr. Fielding (the psychiatrist of Daniel Ellsberg, who had released copies he had made of some of the relevant papers concerning the Vietnam War) had been burglarized by the White House "plumbers unit"; that secret funds had been held in cash in a White House safe for distribution to unknown persons; that great quantities of money had been laundered through Mexican banks; that an "enemies list" had been compiled (which included Dr. Eugene Carson Blake, who was then the Executive Secretary of the World Council of Churches). Not all of his evidence was documented, and there seemed nothing that directly implicated the President. However, despite the fact that the evidence was legally inconclusive, the picture it painted of the way Mr. Nixon ran his White House was profoundly shocking to the average citizen.

In January of 1973, the men indicted for the Watergate burglary stood trial. All of the seven pled guilty except G. Gordon Liddy and James McCord, and they were both convicted by the jury. New names began appearing in the press. Judge John J. Sirica was proving to be immovable by anything but the Constitution of the United States, a man of fearless integrity. When over a year later he was stricken by a heart attack, Sue and I delivered the church flowers from the Sunday service to George Washington University Hospital. He was too ill to receive visitors outside his family circle. I said a prayer with the family, representing in a small way the many who could not otherwise express their admiration for his courage.

On Friday morning, the 8th of February 1974, my telephone at the church rang and a friendly voice said, "Doctor, this is the White House. Col. S — — speaking. The President has asked me to say that he and Mrs. Nixon and Mrs. Eisenhower would like very much to attend services at your church on Sunday first."

"Why of course," I stuttered in disbelief. "It would indeed be an honor."

"Fine, Doctor. Well, we will be sending around some of our men on Saturday morning to get to know the procedures for the Presidential party's entrance to the sanctuary and so on; I'm sure you're acquainted with this sort of thing."

"Of course."

"Shall we say ten o'clock on Saturday morning?"

Then as if recalling something, his voice changed, becoming very casual.

"Oh, by the way, Doctor, there's just one other matter. I do hope you won't preach a political sermon."

In all my years of trying hard to be a diplomat, I have never learned that there are some questions you do not try to answer; you must throw them back at the questioner and let him explain what he means. I didn't!

"If you mean about Watergate, I have preached at least twice on the subject already. In fact my sermon for Sunday is already prepared, and the order of service is printed."

"Well, that's just fine, Doctor; I knew you'd understand."

There was a click and silence. I slowly hung up the receiver and found myself beating my closed fist on my desk. I had been struck out by a curve ball! Too late now to phone back and try to explain that he had asked a question no one has any right to ask of any preacher, especially a Presbyterian preacher whose covenanting ancestors' blood had stained with a deeper hue the purple heather moors of Scotland, martyred in the cause of freedom to proclaim the gospel as conscience dictates.

The next morning a group of Secret Service men and an adjutant arrived. Young he was, with the dry-look hairdo, gallant in his naval uniform, friendly and solicitous. When he had finished the business of entrances and exits, I told him about the telephone conversation I had had with Col. S——.

"I'm afraid his question embarrassed me," I said quietly. Pointing to my large center pulpit, I continued, "That's my pulpit. I preach from it almost every Sunday and have done so for coming on a quarter of a century. I like to think of it as one place in the land where uninhibited freedom of speech is still recognized."

"I'm glad you mentioned the matter, Doctor. I shall convey your message to Col. S——."

"Well, George," I found myself saying, "what about the prophet Nathan and King David now? 'Thou art the man! Wherefore hast thou despised the commandment of the Lord to do evil in his sight?' "

Any preacher who takes his calling seriously knows that Nathan haunts him night and day with his finger-pointing challenge. Martin Luther in his day had declared before the Diet of Worms, "Here stand I! I can do no other." I tried to analyze my own conscience. Deep down I knew I was rationalizing. I tried to excuse myself. Nathan had been engaged in a private conversation with King David in his palace, whereas I was to be preaching at public worship, with the President facing me seated in the Lincoln pew. Suppose I did preach on the subject of Watergate? It would be to reiterate only what a hundred newspapers across the land were clambering for—resignation or impeachment. Might it not be that the President, bearing an intolerable burden, required not so much censure as consolation? It would be the Sunday nearest to Lincoln's birthday, and my prepared sermon had been built around Lincoln. Might not Mr. Nixon catch again a glimpse of Lincoln's towering courage and dedication that would both shame his own deviousness and uplift him, challenging him to follow in the footsteps of such a president? I decided to ignore the fact that among the congregation that morning would be the First Family; I would preach the sermon I had already prepared.

Came Sunday morning. Between the two morning services about twenty Secret Service men literally searched every square inch of every pew cushion in our sanctuary, which seats about fourteen hundred. The young attaché delivered to me personally a verbal apology from Col.

S — —, who had admitted that he did not realize the implications of his question about preaching a political sermon.

At precisely 11:10 there was a knock on my study door. I looked up from my desk. Ramon, my beadle, stood smiling at me as he had done those many years. Today, however, there was a humorous twinkle in his eye.

"He's here, all right, Doctor! Saw the big black limousine draw up at the New York Avenue entrance."

Robed, I gathered up my manuscript and prayer book, and with my associate Jack McClendon made my way the short distance to the small anteroom that leads into the apse of the sanctuary.

"Are you nervous, brother?" Jack asked, in his husky Alabaman accent.

We bowed while Ramon offered up his prayer for blessing upon the service. There was the perennial pause as each Sunday we awaited the tolling of the bells in the church tower signifying the commencement of the service. CLANG-KING-CLANG-BOOM! . . . Ramon opened the door and preceded us to the lectern, where he opened the pulpit Bible and arranged the book markers—white for the Epiphany season, symbolizing Christ's presence. Jack walked to his stall. I mounted the five steps of the large central pulpit. The sound of the bells died away as the congregation, still standing, sang the Doxology. I looked out over the sea of faces before me like a skipper on his bridge scanning white-crested waves. With a nonchalant air, I glanced towards the third pew on my left on the central aisle, the darker one, the original pew used by Mr. Lincoln in our old church. The First Family, already seated there, included Julie Nixon and her husband David Eisenhower and Mrs. Mamie Eisenhower, who looked rather frail, although the radiance the nation had known still lingered over her features. In the same pew stood a smartly dressed young man, his head tilted a little to the side like that of an inquisitive bird, no doubt receiving radio instructions from the other Secret Service agents who were assigned to their various positions in both area and gallery.

Under the gallery to my right, beside the stained-glass window of the Last Supper, which depicts Judas who betrayed our Lord refusing the proffered bread, sat Mr. Leon Jaworski and his wife in the pew they had been occupying regularly since he had been appointed Watergate Special Prosecutor some three months before. He had brightly alert eyes and a pleasing mouth, a round face crowned with receding white hair. His having made time to attend church in these hectic days was testimony to his upbringing in a Baptist manse.

The unfolding drama of Watergate was suddenly brought before my very eyes, its two principal figures under the same roof for the first time — in my kirk! Mr. Jaworski had resolutely refused to meet with the President in a face-to-face encounter; now they were together, worshiping, praying for light and guidance from the same God upon the tangled moral skein that was Watergate.

Came the time for the sermon, I announced the title as I always did: "What Has Happened to Courage?" (Later I would reflect on this Freudian slip!) The thesis: moral courage stems from situations of defeat; the courageous man is often he who has lost the battle but fights on. But our society recognizes only winners. Who remembers the man who came in second? The pursuit of success in every walk of life has become the end of all our strivings. In order to succeed, there is nothing we will not do; if necessary, we will be devious, cheat, lie when the opportunity comes. Our culture has an almost paranoic fear of failure.

Nevertheless, life is not to be measured by success, but how we acquit ourselves. Of this history speaks eloquently. Lincoln in his day counted himself a failure; reviled by sadistic enemies, lampooned in the press, he was forced to preside over a terrible fratricidal civil war. In retrospect, we know this was courage.

"In 1968 there was the Poor People's Campaign, symbol of the black community's idealism and courage, setting off on an ox-cart-drawn eight-hundred-mile trek from Selma, Alabama, to the nation's capital to lay directly their grievances before Congress. Our church was their head-quarters. They built their shantytown — Resurrection City, they called it — near the Reflecting Pool in front of the Lincoln Memorial during May and June, when fourteen inches of rain fell, inundating them and their dreams. Two months later they turned back to their homes in the South, beaten, their demands unmet. In that glorious failure they displayed courage of the highest order.

"During the Vietnam War hundreds of our citizens gathered outside this church and took to the streets to protest the political bankruptcy and inhuman destruction of the war. They failed to stop its tragic conflict, but their effort took great courage.

"Paul himself knew what it was to fail, but found strength in the presence of his Lord and in the fellowship of his friends that gave him courage. To learn to live with failure: that's where moral courage lies. . . ."

After the benediction, I went down to the Lincoln pew and introduced Sue and Mairi to our distinguished visitors. I then escorted the President down the center aisle while Sue accompanied Mrs. Nixon and Mrs. Eisenhower. Our Mairi held the President's left arm. He gripped my left hand. He smiled from pew to pew. At the entrance to the church, under the great Georgian Colonial portico, we paused at the top of the steps and looked out at the large gathering of people who had assembled to see the President.

"An eloquent sermon," Mr. Nixon said to me.

We descended the steps into a barrage of press photographers thronging the sidewalk of New York Avenue. Reporters were crying out, "Mr.

President!" A little lady darted out and energetically shook his hand. "Let's have a photograph of this," he cried, grinning, and the next day the front page of the *Washington Post* carried a photograph of Mrs. John Cox, Jr., a black schoolteacher from Tennessee, shaking the smiling President's hand. We talked again briefly about the game of golf we had never been able to play at the Burning Tree Club (and now, alas, never will). When the gregarious photographers had been satisfied, he went into his car. I stood watching as the black limousine moved off slowly towards the Treasury Building, where, through the bare sepia trees, was visible the outline of the White House, three blocks away.

One of my ushers told me that the Jaworskis had quietly made their exit down the opposite stairway to H Street almost unrecognized, back to the hotel where they were staying at this time. Later I was to read in John Dean's book *Blind Ambition* what Mr. Jaworski had told him about his own impressions of the service:

> "Last Sunday I went to the Presbyterian Church up on New York Avenue. It's convenient to where I stay in Washington. As I went into the service, I stopped to say hello to the deacon, who was greeting people at the front door. The deacon stopped me and said, 'Mr. Jaworski, President Nixon is coming this morning.' I told the deacon that was fine and went along to my seat. I opened my program and saw that the sermon was on 'Moral Courage,' which made me chuckle to myself. . . . When the minister began his sermon he was very nervous, and he had a rough time getting it together for about ten minutes. But once he got going it was a good sermon. I guess he was worried about what he had to say with the President there. Anyway, I kept thinking if the President only had the moral courage to admit his wrongs, this wouldn't have gone as far as it has."

Back in my study at the church, Sue and Mairi were awaiting me. We picked up our car in the car park and made our way home along Pennsylvania Avenue past the White House and on towards Rock Creek Park, where we passed the Watergate Complex, a ten-story modernistic concrete structure of curving buildings. Pointing toward the river like the prow of a vast Spanish galleon, its balustrades looked like a monster shark's teeth. Opposite stands the less pretentious Howard Johnson Hotel. We sped along that well-known and indeed beloved tree-lined parkway whose leaves I have watched changing with the seasons year after year, until at last I was home — a tired preacher. Once home, I collapsed in front of the television set to watch *Meet the Press* while I ate a snack lunch. I know of no better way to uncoil than to sit and drowse before a television set. Today there was to be little peace of mind, and no sleep. Perhaps I should have preached more directly instead of by inference? I probably succeeded in doing the opposite of what I tried to do — it often happens with a sermon. Mr. Nixon sitting in the Lincoln pew would see himself as a latter-day Lincoln, misunderstood by his contemporaries, his work for world peace and the ending of the Vietnam War forgotten in an incident called "Watergate." I snapped out of my self-recriminations.

On July 27, 1974, the House Judiciary Committee passed the first article of impeachment by a vote of 27 to 11, charging the President of the United States with having obstructed justice in an attempt to cover up the crimes committed at Watergate. On August 8, the President spoke to the nation on television, announcing that he had decided to resign. The next day, Vice President Gerald R. Ford took the oath to become the 38th President of the United States.

The nation's most gripping television drama suddenly took on the character of a Greek tragedy. I was not aware of any elation among my friends who had bitterly opposed the President from the beginning. Each morning when I arose, I was aware of a strange ache in my heart, like a grief that would not go away.

Mr. Nixon's problem, I believe, was that dichotomy in the soul that confronts all politicians — the hunger to inhabit both a fantasy world of power and personal gratification and the less dramatic but much more real world of their domestic and personal life. The two worlds stood in especially sharp contrast for the young lad from Whittier, California, winner of the elocution prize at college, the hard-working young lawyer who became a friend of the rich and the politically powerful, finally seated at the most famous and powerful desk in the world, of which the wise Harry Truman had said, "The buck stops here!"

To some degree, all of us have fantasies of power or success or riches. When they remain merely dreams, the fantasy can spur us on to high achievement. But when fantasy becomes an end in itself and we are then forced to return to the world, the real world of love and fear and death, our will power is enervated and our judgment is colored. Mr. Nixon began his political life with singleness of heart, purpose, and dedication that deservedly brought success in the sphere of public service, but the fantasy gradually took over his life, became a "habit structure." His memoirs eloquently attest that after all he endured he is still prisoner in the fantasy of his own world of power politics. "The hands are the hands of Esau; but the voice is the voice of Jacob."

There were times when I caught, momentarily, rare glimpses of what I would like to believe was the real man, the authentic Richard Milhous Nixon. On the morning of August 9, 1974, he left the White House, bidding farewell to members of his staff and cabinet, "We can be proud of it — five and a half years." Then, departing from notes, and it seemed to me without any forethought, his eyes glistening in the light of the television lights, he was looking beyond us all, across the wide prairies westward, beholding again a little boy in the humble surroundings he once knew as home:

> "Nobody will ever write a book, probably, about my mother. My mother was a saint. And I think of her, two boys dying of tuberculosis, nursing four others in order that she could take care of my older brother for three years in Arizona, and seeing each of them die, and when they died, it was like one of her own. Yes, she will have no books written about her. But she was a saint."

Utterly alone, the focal point of hundreds of millions of people, he was reaching out to her from the lonely cloud-covered mountain where presidents dwell for the only hand that could comfort, to feel it again as he had known her in his childhood, now lost in the swirling winds of history. I have often wondered whether he was not longing for that same touch of comfort when he held my hand as we walked together out of my church.

A friend of mind, a Washington minister, once told me of an encounter he had with then Vice President Nixon back in the fifties. My friend had been asked to deliver the prayer that would open that day's proceedings in the United States Senate. As Vice President, Mr. Nixon was President of the Senate, and it was the custom for the preacher to visit with the President of the Senate for the few minutes before the twelve o'clock bell rings.

"Tell me about your family," Mr. Nixon said.

"We have a daughter, nine years old."

"Fine! Our Tricia is nine years old."

"Our daughter is in the hospital."

"Oh! I hope it isn't serious."

"Leukemia."

Mr. Nixon paled, and with genuine concern asked if there were anything at all he could do to help. Couldn't he at least visit her in the hospital? My friend, an old hand on the Washington scene who knew the phony emotions that politicians can conjure up to get themselves more votes, did not wish his daughter to be subjected to the publicity of a visit from the Vice President — her photograph in the newspapers, and perhaps on television. He declined to accept the offer. But Mr. Nixon insisted.

"Please, I would like to visit her."

And he did. At the Georgetown Hospital that afternoon, two large black limousines drew up to the back door. Two Secret Service agents ran round and opened the door as Mr. Nixon alighted, holding in his arms two enormous dolls, one thoughtfully brought along for the other little girl sharing the room with the minister's daughter. He sat down on the bedside of the child he had come to see.

"Now, I have a little girl, and she is very pretty, just like you. And

297

she is also nine. And she has a doll like this. And I thought you would like to have a doll like my Tricia's. Now, this is the way Tricia undresses her doll."

Mr. Nixon proceeded to undress the doll — the ruffle-necked dress and the little undergarments and the frilled panties and the socks and shoes, all the while the eyes of the doll opening and closing, as if falling to sleep. The child's eyes were shining like the morning star.

"Now you will have to help me to dress her."

Two stalwart Secret Service agents at the doorway stood beside two nurses and an internist, all of them hushed in silence. Mr. Nixon arose. Silently he shook the hand of the minister and hurried out of the room, back to the debate and battle on the floor of the United States Senate. The incident never reached the media. I suppose, after all these years, Mr. Nixon and I might be the only people who know of it. The minister and his wife — and the child — are dead.

After the publication of the memoirs in 1978, I was willing to bend over backward to give Mr. Nixon the benefit of the doubt, remembering the accomplishments of his administration such as his foreign policy triumphs and the unorthodox but very effective visits he had paid as late as the summer of the resignation to Peking and Moscow. But, unhappily for all of us, fantasy took over once more when Mr. Nixon was induced to take part in a series of television interviews with the Englishman David Frost.

Mr. Frost, who had been a clever host on the BBC television series *That Was the Week That Was,* naively believed that after some of the finest legal and political minds in the land had failed to get to the truth that was Watergate, as a latter-day David he would face up to Goliath himself in his spacious San Clemente home. The original boy David, son of Jesse, came armed with only a sling and some small pebbles he gathered up from the burn in the glen. David Frost came with a half-million-dollar contract in his pocket and the concentrated study of a journalist's facile overnight homework to face his adversary. His anglicized, clipped pebblestone words stotted off the sad-thoughtful-grinning brow of this Goliath. As they say in sports, "It was no contest." In the end, I found myself turning off a program embarrassingly incredulous. The fantasy had deepened from a "habit structure" to a "pattern of character" — which the grace of God alone can heal.

Watergate ended, as the world of all "Hollow Men" will end, in T. S. Eliot's words, "Not with a bang, but a whimper."

20

The Autumn of My Days

What's a man's age? He must hurry more, that's all;
Cram in a day what his youth took a year to hold;
When we mind labour, then only we're too old. . . .
— Robert Browning, "The Flight of the Duchess"

IN THE FALL of 1976 I retired as pastor of the New York Avenue Presbyterian Church, although I could have remained another five years until I was seventy. Long ago I dispensed with the vanity of believing that the ushering in of the Kingdom of God lay exclusively as my responsibility or that I was indispensable to the work and witness of my congregation. Besides, it was a new day, and a new voice was required to continue what I had begun and what I had inherited from my predecessors. Civil rights were being fought for on another battlefield, the movement's generals drawn from the black community itself; the tragedy of Vietnam had become history; the mission of the church, so splendidly activistic and sociopolitical in the late sixties and seventies, seemed to be returning yet again to a phase more personalistic and liturgical. More positively I wanted to write, to leave behind in print, other than in cassettes or tapes, some of the things I had noticed and believed in about the task of the ministry, the glory of preaching; and since there is in every one of us a novel clamoring to be born, I believed that even I might be able to try my hand at one, concerning the only subject I could claim to have any authority about — a preacher.

Sue and I would have liked so very much to retire to Washington, a city I had come to love second only to my beloved Glasgow. Washington is an exciting place to live in, a window looking out upon the world. In contrast to London, where one can be lost in its sheer vastness and submerged in its class-structured society, in Washington one feels always on the edge of things political. Personally it would have suited us. Our boys, Garth and David (the former a tax accountant with the District government and the latter a real estate broker), had made their homes in the metropolitan area. Sue's family were only some 150 miles north among the Pennsylvania mountains. Lifelong friends resided there. And there was the Burning Tree Golf Club, and the Kennedy Center, and the art galleries,

299

and not least the Library of Congress. I was even prepared to endure its torrid summers, through which for over a quarter of a century I had whimpered like a lost puppy.

Professionally, it would have been impossible to remain in Washington. I would have interfered however unwittingly with the ministry of my successor. One cannot turn aside a request to visit a hospital where a friend of over twenty years lies gravely ill with the response "I'm sorry, my dear, I am no longer your minister." I was being requested to marry young people I had baptized as children. This spring, because the church was once more vacant, I acceded to the request to baptize a child whose father I had baptized and whose grandparents I had married.

We would retire to a university town, either Chapel Hill, North Carolina, or St. Andrews in Scotland. So it was St. Andrews, a strange choice, for I had known the ancient medieval city only from a vacation during the war. However, too many ghosts walked the streets of Glasgow and Aberdeen, and Edinburgh, the only other medieval university town, however historic and classical in architecture, was never a place where I would have felt permanently at home. St. Andrews boasts the oldest university in the land (est. 1412 A.D.). Here I could continue with my studies and writing — though my friends would hear nothing of this palpable rationalization; "The Old Course will be your field of study," they claimed.

Once more it is autumn in this waning year of 1983; the first blush of crimson creeps over the gallant prunus tree at the bottom of our spacious classical garden. (We purchased the bottom flat of a Victorian villa built in 1872). It is the sort of garden my dear father would have exulted in — and is it not his voice I hear when I delve the vegetable patch or prune the apple trees or spray the abundant roses which bloom gallantly even in December? It will be winter soon. In a month or so the night air will be filled with the honking of Brent geese, flying in V formation in instinctive perennial pilgrimage to warmer climes.

I am rocking peacefully in the garden swing seat, watching our Julie, who is now four, playing in her Wendy house, serving afternoon tea to an array of dolls with Bungles, her teddy bear, in the principal seat. Sue has come out into the garden carrying Bridget, who is now seven months, requesting that I keep my eye on her as she explores the shrubbery. In the seventy-third year of my life, I sit back and ponder with all the time in the world — at least what's left to me.

Few men have been so blessed as I have in my life. Out of our common sorrow together, Sue and I found love again, a joyous fulfillment in one another and not least the blessings of our bairns, Julie and Bridget. And fun has returned, and the beckoning adventures of new beginnings and renewed experiences as we travel back across the Atlantic every year. To date, in her four years of life, our Julie has flown fifty thousand miles.

The Autumn of My Days

I had neither longed to retire nor desired to leave my church; retirement was to be still another stage in the business of living. Yet in so many ways retirement turned out to be so different from what I had envisaged. Sometimes in sentimental moods in the midst of a busy time at the church, I would daydream about retirement and how, when I had the time, I would visit the manses of my many friends across Scotland and spend the time with them that it seemed the locusts had eaten. Alas, like myself, they have all retired. Our meeting again when I visited the General Assembly of the Kirk in Edinburgh, the first time in twenty-five years, was a melancholy experience. I reintroduced myself to a group of aged divines with the stoop of a scholar, all grey, some bald, all of them sadly touched with time. Were these the boisterous, carefree lads with whom I used to cut classes to play chess or table tennis at Trinity College? But the real shock came when meeting a well-kent face, I did *not* introduce myself, but asked him to guess who I was. After four fatuous attempts he still did not recognize me! My white thatch of thinning hair and the lineaments of an old man apparently threw him!

Yet the dear dead days were recalled when I met these old friends over coffee in a tearoom in Princes Street. As I sat back and looked at them again, I closed my eyes. The voices had not changed; the nuances of accent the same; the way they told stories had remained unaltered through the years. Indeed I found that Tom, who used to interrupt Professor Fulton in the midst of a seminar on Spinoza's philosophy with some story about his aunt who, as Dylan Thomas would say, "is no longer whinnying with us," was now holding forth about the precocity of his *wunderkind* grandchild. And there were faces I would no longer look upon.

Thoughts of death intrude more often, and we face up to the ultimate mystery, the "ultimate enemy" as Paul describes death. Though, truth to tell, I can say that certainly for the past forty years thoughts of death and dying have been a daily staple. I have sat beside too many deathbeds, have gazed into too many cold dark open graves not to be reminded for myself, *memento mori*. Indeed, I can say "as sure as death," as the Scots have it; I know that one day in some unknown household at breakfast time, as the husband looks over his morning paper and his wife is bent over the kitchen stove cooking his bacon and eggs, he will suddenly look up and call out, "Oh, I say, Jean; I see George Docherty is dead. Heard him preach once. . . . Come on, dear, do hurry up with my breakfast or I'll miss my train. . . ."

I suppose we all ought to be like Socrates. When asked in those ultimate moments of life before he was to drink the hemlock whether he was afraid to die, Socrates replied, as we have it in the *Phaedo*, "The philosopher has every reason to be of good cheer when he is about to die. He is ever pursuing death and dying. And if this is true, why, having had

301

the desire for death all of his life long, should he repine at the arrival of that which he has always been pursuing and seeking?"

But surely it is not merely life after death, "the undiscover'd country from whose bourne / No traveller returns," that concerns us. We are concerned about the future of those who come after us; for me, what will happen to my two babies? What would I not give to be witness to their growing maturity; might I even dare to hope to be there to officiate in their marriage?

As it is, I feel no urge to make my own quietus without deep regret. Life is and has been too exciting easily to part with it. Time has never bored me. Time has been the always-too-swift athlete I have tried to race. Like Rupert Brooke, I too have been the Great Lover, feeling stirrings within my breast at the intimation that spring is on the wing after the dark bleakness of winter, at daffodil trumpets couched in dew, the incoming tide booming white over brown sands, a solitary gull perched on the edge of a sea-smoothed rock, the bustle of city streets, the unmistakable quiet of Sunday afternoons, the satisfaction of seeing my golf ball fly straight as an arrow in defiance of the truant crosswind, and the arts — books and music, the violin, my first love (Kreisler playing Beethoven), and the piano, my second (Horowitz playing the slow movement of the *Moonlight Sonata*).

> Not all my passion, all my prayers, have power
> To hold them with me through the gate of death.

Must all these things I too have loved be halted at the gate of death? To speculate about life after death from our human experience usually results in a gross spiritualization of that life and a basic misunderstanding of what the New Testament tells us about resurrection. Resurrection is not the rejuvenation of these frail bodies of ours into a far better life lived anew in terms of earthly existence in which everything that is unjust will be justified and the good and the true and the beautiful will abide forever. Resurrection is the abolition of both death and life as we humans understand it in the "here and now." Life beyond the grave is a "wholly other" dimension beyond the profoundest metaphysical speculation of the theologians.

I have found this homely analogy not unhelpful. Suppose I were walking on the bank of a brown burn watching a trout dart among the brown rocks and flowing reeds. Suppose I were able to ask the trout about its views of a fish's heaven. No doubt the trout would think of heaven in terms of its own existence — the freshest and coldest of trout streams, breathing cool oxygen through gills, and gliding idly, three-dimensionally, the long day amidst the lushest of weeds. But from my standpoint, existing at the bottom of an ocean of air, such a view of life is quite different. So must the angels "look down" upon us, smiling at our credulous imprisoning incarnationality, as we seek to speculate about God's heaven.

This we do know: we shall behold Jesus not as through a dim bronze mirror, but face to face; and the loves of this earth will no longer be severed by death, but made perfect and fulfilled.

I have never been afraid of a fiery brimstone hell, though final judgment there must be. I was reared in a home where the horrors of hell were not a subject of discussion, and so I was saved by my parents from a neurotic juridical view of religion, though often there were thoughts of heaven in our home. Nor do I fear an ultimate judgment that will cast me off forever from the presence of all the living, a nonexistence, banished even from the presence of God himself. If the Judge of all the earth is my Savior, there is hope for even such a one as I.

Then there is not merely death, but the dying. Ah! there's the rub. This past summer I bade farewell on earth to a dear colleague. He knew he was dying. I knew he was dying. He knew I knew he was dying; and though we did not discuss the matter directly, we did share the fact in our prayers together. "I would hope," was his simple comment — and he was the gentlest of men — "that it will not be too painful a waiting until I reach out for the arms of my savior! . . ."

"Daddy! Daddy!" Julie comes running toward me. She stops breathlessly and looks up at me with her great round brown eyes. "Daddy! Who painted the sky blue?"

"God painted the sky blue, my dear."

"Oh," and she is off once more to serve a second cup of tea to her guests in the Wendy house.

As I watch her run back, I realize that she and our Bridget and all the other children of the earth are my greatest concern when I think of my own death. What is their future? What kind of world will the children of this generation reach in their maturity? Our Julie will be twenty-one in the 2000th year of this age. Will she be able to enjoy the birthright of every child, to know love and perhaps heartbreak, her own home and children, the joyous adventure of this world, rich in so many values, a living faith in God?

Yet these children will grow up in a period in history when there is a threat to the existence of the entire human race. Less than a thousand miles from this peaceful garden in this medieval city, near the eastern border of West Germany, two vast modern armies vie with each other — the NATO forces of the West and the Warsaw Pact forces of the Eastern bloc nations. It is a matter of record that, should the numerically superior armies of the east attack and drive the NATO forces into a militarily untenable position, NATO commanders are prepared to wage what they call "limited nuclear war" using tactical nuclear weapons (mini-bombs in shells and rockets). Surely this would only draw an immediate response in kind from the opposing forces. How long can any nuclear war remain limited?

I have been reading in the press and watching the more graphic reports on television of the new master plan of the United States to push nuclear defense into space in the form of satellites armed with lasers and particle beam weapons that are supposed to be able to detect and destroy any attacking warheads in the few minutes between the time they are launched and the time they would explode. While such devices are still in the experimental stage, the "enemy" is already devising ways of getting past them. Supercomputers are being built to run all these lethal machines without any human intervention; their inventors claim these computers think!

There is no sane strategy for fighting a nuclear war. There is no workable defence against a nuclear attack. The very term *war* loses all meaning in such a context. Even up to the end of the Second World War we could find meaning in the term: we could point to one side as victorious and the other as defeated. But a nuclear war means holocaust, genocide, race suicide; it makes all previous wars look like medieval jousting.

The consequences of such a holocaust are almost impossible to contemplate. Modern warheads can be delivered over two thousand miles with awesome accuracy (one launched from the Sears Tower in Chicago could be aimed at New York City with enough accuracy to ensure its hitting home plate in Yankee Stadium). A nuclear reaction releases most of its energy in less than a ten-millionth of a second, creating temperatures hotter than those of the surface of the sun.

A single one-megaton bomb (a typical size, having the explosive force of one million tons of TNT), if exploded on the ground, would rip a crater out of the earth three city blocks in diameter and two hundred feet deep, and create a fireball almost two miles across, throwing up tons of deadly radioactive fallout and leveling all structures within four miles of the burst. Buildings out to eight miles would be severely damaged. Glass buildings would be instantly converted into a storm of shards traveling at a thousand miles per hour.

Having converted hundreds of square miles of city to rubble, the explosion would simultaneously ignite everything combustible — gasoline in cars and underground tanks, natural gas in city mains, wood, paper, fabric, human beings would all burst into flame, creating a firestorm stoked by winds reaching hundreds of miles per hour that would consume all oxygen for miles around in addition to producing toxic gases. Those who might have survived the blast in shelters would soon be asphyxiated and incinerated if they remained in them. The heat of the firestorm would be enough to melt glass and metal.

The aftermath of the blast would be horrible for the survivors as well.

People dozens of miles away would have been blinded and burned by the flash and injured by collapsing buildings, flying debris, and other effects of the shock wave. Radioactivity from the initial explosion and subsequent fallout would kill many outright and lead to radiation sickness and later cancers for many others. Since exposure to radiation reduces the body's ability to fight off disease, a host of new plagues would doubtless ravage the survivors. There would be little medical help left to treat the over-whelming number of casualties.

At present it is estimated that the United States has twenty-six thou-sand nuclear warheads and the Soviet Union twenty thousand — enough nuclear power to destroy thirty-five times over every Russian and Amer-ican city with a population of more than a hundred thousand. There are enough nuclear weapons in existence to explode a Hiroshima-size atom bomb every minute around the clock for the next two years and two months.

The Poseidon-class nuclear submarine of the United States fleet carries sixteen missiles, each equipped with fourteen independently targetable warheads — enough to destroy all the major cities of the Soviet Union. A single Poseidon-class submarine can deploy megatons of firepower equal to three times the tonnage of conventional explosives used in every theater of the Second World War. The United States at the moment has thirty-one Poseidon submarines. The new Triton nuclear submarine, now in production, carries weapons with twenty-four megatons of firepower, enough to destroy every city in the Northern Hemisphere, the equivalent of eight times the amount of conventional explosives used in World War II.

Long ago I renounced doctrinaire pacifism, if by pacifism one means complete nonparticipation in any form of war. Even in the Second World War the civilian population found itself in the front trenches of the conflict. Sadly, the world has not reached that stage of brotherhood or respect for human rights where we can dispense with *conventional* weap-ons. But I am a pacifist when it means condemning nuclear warfare in any form and demanding the complete destruction of all present stocks of atomic weapons possessed by both the United States and the Soviet Union. Let the future lie in the hands of these two giants not in armed confron-tation, but united to preserve world peace and to censor any nation that would dare to seek to manufacture nuclear warheads.

What has been the response of the Christian Church to the nuclear arms race and its race-suicide threat? Roman Catholic bishops have already given notice to the United States in a brave pastoral letter where that Church stands. In England a group of young bishops (who will soon be the mouthpiece of the Church of England) have in their pamphlet "The Bomb" spelled out the threat to humankind in the present nuclear arms race. One is encouraged by groups of Christians across the world taking a definite stand against any form of nuclear armaments.

On the other hand, there have been too many well-meaning but innocuous resolutions passed by church assemblies in what has been called the cause of peace. Across the United States, Presbyterian congregations are solemnly engaged Sunday by Sunday in classes studying "Peacemaking." Such laudable but theoretical discussions tend to remind me of the proceedings of the Eastern Orthodox Church engaged in solemn convocation including on its agenda the problem of how many tassles a bishop ought to wear on the hem of his cassock, while outside their windows in Moscow, Vladimir Ilyich Ulyanov (Lenin) was proclaiming the end of the Tsarist regime and the birth of the New Socialism.

The Church must get outside its protective walls and protest in cities and towns and villages. The women who have spent two years outside Greenham Common protesting the installation in Britain of Cruise Missiles are the Joan of Arcs of our day. And millions of women in Europe and America are pointing the way with self-sacrificing peaceful demonstration.

It is a day for the barricades with the strength not of stones but the Spirit, not of fire but the burning conviction of the gospel, not in disorder but constitutional protest. Only then will the media, especially television, realize that the Church's one foundation is Jesus Christ Her Lord.

In my garden a child's voice is calling to me. "Please come and have tea with Bungles in my Wendy house!"

I rise. On my way I pass our baby Bridget asleep in her pram. This child's voice is the voice of the future beckoning me, but not to the never-never land of make-believe, of dolls and Bungles; her wonderful, beautiful innocency is warning me that too soon she will be a woman bearing the responsibilities of the mothers of every race.

Retire at such time as this? Let me get back to my desk, let me get into a pulpit, let me return to the streets once more to witness as I knew it so long ago. This spring I did return to the streets, one of three thousand, bearing placards — "No M.X. Missile" — and with police protection we paraded before the Capitol of the United States of America.

May the good Lord grant such time and strength that I may not be too unfaithful to the call that came to the young twenty-year-old customs clerk that I once was one spring evening, on my way home from the shipping office where I worked, under the *grand horloge* at Charing Cross, Glasgow — a call no less from God than that received by John Knox, "to the dignitie of a preachour."

Glossary of
Scottish Words and Phrases

SCOTTISH DIALECTS, like demons, are legion. The words in this glossary were part of the Glaswegian tapestry of the author's youth. Had they been anglicized, something vital would surely have been lost in the translation.

AIRTS. Points of the compass, as in Burns's "Of a' the airts the wind can blaw, / I dearly like the west."

ASHLAR. Masonry of squared stones laid in regular rows. Glasgow's tenements were mostly built of soft grey sandstone, which was easily corroded and blackened by its smog.

BACKLAND. A building located in an area behind street buildings.

BAD YIN. Literally "bad one"; a mild epithet usually used without connotations of wickedness, and sometimes affectionately.

BED RECESS. A rectangular wall recess containing a built-in, or "bun-in," bed. When the bed was not in use, curtains would be drawn across its open front. The author saw the first light of day in such a bed.

BEN. *See* FAR BEN.

BOSEY. Affectionate term for a woman's bosom.

BURN. A small stream or creek.

BUT AND BEN. A two-room cottage with a parlor and a kitchen-dining-sitting room, each having a *bed recess* (q.v.).

CAUSEY STONES; CAUSIES. Cobblestones, three by eight by five inches in size, laid across the street so as to allow the hook in a horse's shoe to get a grip.

CLOAKING HEN. A hen expressing in loud and triumphal song its satisfaction at having just laid an egg.

CLOSE. Originally the enclosed courtyard behind a tenement; later, a narrow lane between *backlands* (q.v.) or the common passage leading from the street to the courtyard and thence to the stairwell. The CLOSE MOUTH was a favorite gathering place for gossip.

CLOSET. A small cubicle with water closet or toilet either in a room-and-kitchen flat or on the stairhead; often shared by three or more families.

CORNCRAKE. A lark-like bird now sadly an endangered species (because it nests vulnerably on the ground); its cry, especially at night, is a grating metallic screech.

307

CUPPA. A cup of hot tea.

DREICH. Dull, as of weather or a sermon.

FANKLE. A bothersome knot, especially in a bootlace.

FAR BEN. Literally "far through"; also used metaphorically to describe one whose thoughts are deep or whose spiritual life is profound.

FLIT. To move a household.

GRANNY. A metal hood over the chimney that turned with the wind to prevent smoke from being blown back down the flue.

GREET. To weep, with connotations of petulance. "You're aye greeting" means, roughly, "You're always complaining."

HAUFF. A congenial public eating place.

HODDEN GREY. Lifeless drab grey clothing made from a coarse undyed woolen cloth; usually worn by workmen.

HOT WATER PIG. A stone bottle which, when filled with hot water, made an excellent footwarmer in bed—and a mighty thump when it fell out.

KEELIE. One born in the tenements of Glasgow; no native of Kelvinside would ever confess to being a Glasgow Keelie.

LEAL. Loyal. The "land of the leal" is heaven.

LINKS. A stretch of undulating sand downs along the seashore, formerly covered by the sea, but now covered with grass. Some of the world's great golf courses (e.g., St. Andrews) have evolved out of them.

ONDING. A downpour; usually used of rain, but also metaphorically of words, especially in an argument.

OXTERS. Underarms.

PAN DROPS. An oval-shaped minty confection, a favorite in church, sometimes used to measure the length of the sermon: "two pan drops—and nae crunching."

PEND. A wide *close* (q.v.), broad enough to allow vehicular traffic access to a back courtyard.

PRESS. A shallow cupboard.

REDD. To tidy up the house, as of dishes after a meal.

RHONE PIPES. Downspouts.

RUSTICATED MASONRY. Masonry hewn with grooves between the courses to accentuate the joints; the effect is outstanding.

SNELL. Icy cold, cutting, as of a wintry wind.

STOTTING. Bouncing, as a ball; often used to describe raindrops in a heavy downpour.

TACKETY BOOT. Hobnail boot worn mostly by workmen and boys because of its ability to hold up well under hard wear.

TERRACE. A row of houses, the midpoint in the great hierarchy of class consciousness that spans *Street, Road, Terrace, Crescent,* and (the crown of all) *Quadrant.*

TURNPIKE STAIR. A spiral staircase in a tenement, an architectural remnant of the days of castle towers.